Baseball Managers

Stats, Stories,
and Strategies

Bob Bloss

 Temple University Press

Philadelphia

Dedication

This book is dedicated to the memories of my parents, Ellen and Bernard Bloss, and to my late cousins and uncles Z. Wayne Adams, Kenneth C. Benson, Lawrence Blazejewski Jr., Fred W. Henck, Paul L. Himmelman, and Bronislaw S. Kosicki. They gladly pointed a young boy in the direction of classrooms and opportunities . . . and ballparks, and, with warmth and care and by example, toward the values of sportsmanship and fellowship.

Temple University Press, Philadelphia 19122
Copyright © 1999 by Temple University
All rights reserved
Published 1999
Printed in the United States of America

♾ The paper used in this publication meets the requirements of the American National Standard for Information Sciences—Permanence of Paper for Printed Library Materials, ANSI Z39.48-1984

Text design by Gary Gore

Library of Congress Cataloging-in-Publication Data
Bloss, Bob
    Baseball managers : stats, stories, and strategies / Bob Bloss.
       p. cm. — (Baseball in America)
    Includes index.
    ISBN 1-56639-661-1 (hardcover : alk. paper)
    1. Baseball managers—United States—Biography. 2. Baseball managers—United States—Statistics. 3. Baseball managers—Rating of—United States. 4. Baseball records—United States. I. Title. II. Series.
GV865.A1B588 1999
796.357′ 092′ 273—dc21
    [B]   98-25276

Contents

Photos appear on pages 117–124 and 195–206

Acknowledgments

A humble tip of the hat here and a nod of thanks are offered to the following people, for these published pages would not have been completed without them. Each, in his or her own way, contributed significantly as an interviewee, a technical advisor, a research expert, or a good friend with encouraging words.

From baseball's official family of managers, players, executives, umpires, scouts, and Hall of Famers . . . Felipe and Moises Alou, Rich Ashburn, Dusty Baker, Don Baylor, Terry Bevington, Bob Boone, Lou Boudreau, Al Clark, Jerry Coleman, Pat Corrales, Bobby Cox, Jim Fregosi, Cito Gaston, Bill Giles, Monte Irvin, Tom Kelly, Kevin Kennedy, Don Kessinger, Chuck Knoblauch, Ed Liberatore, Al Lopez, Frank Malzone, Brian and Hal McRae, Johnny Pesky, Bill Ripken, Mike Scioscia, Bobby Shantz, Bobby Valentine, John Vukovich, Earl Weaver, Bobby Wine.

And from the corps of publicists, researchers, editorial consultants, technical aides and men-and-women-Friday . . . Chuck Adams, Michael Ames, Rob Antony, Dick Bresciani, George Brightbill, Rick Cerrone, Paul Cunningham, Gene Dias, Joe Dittmar, Elias Sports Bureau (Steve Hirdt, Seymour Siwoff), Katy Feeney, Bruce Garner, Sean Harlin, Kathy Hennigan, Angela and Jim Hopes, Bob Ibach, Knollmede Horseshoes Assn., Leonard Koppett, Allen Lewis, Peter Loyello, Jim Luker, Marie MacMurray, Elaine and Nick Manno, John Maroon, Phyllis Merhige, Jim Moorehead, Barry Morrill, the National Baseball Hall of Fame and Museum (Bill Guilfoile, Darci Harrington, Jeff Idelson, John Ralph), Billy O'Sullivan, Sharon Pannozzo, Nancy and Neal Perrine, Rich Pilling, Mike Ringering, Mary Jane Ryan, Russell Schneider, Jim Schultz, Betty and Tom Sementelli, Kevin Shea, Larry Shenk, Brad Smith, Howard Starkman, Leigh Tobin, Jim Trdinich, Dolores Ziff, and Rich Westcott, a baseball author/journalist extraordinaire, who saw merit in exploring baseball managers' history, and who knew what publishing office doors to knock on.

I gratefully applaud David E. Wilson, too. An award-winning television producer, director, and programmer and a one-time stylish first baseman for Sigma Phi Epsilon (Orel Hershiser's college fraternity), Dave would often forgo his own Mill Valley, California, agenda to help organize my subject matter into logical sequence, to escort me through what seemed a morass of uncharted computerese and cyberspace, and to offer cheerful encouragement. I value his decades of friendship.

Finally, but in fact foremost . . . to Floriana, Connie, and Linda and Rich . . . thank you for your unwavering enthusiasm for this book and your caring support of its author.

Mr. Mack and Mr. Mauch

Bobby Shantz, a small, left-handed pitcher from Pottstown, Pennsylvania, advanced quickly through the Philadelphia Athletics farm system and, at age 23, was elevated to the major leagues. In only his third full season at Philadelphia, Shantz distinguished himself by winning the 1952 American League Most Valuable Player Award in recognition of his league-leading 24 victories, which had vaulted the A's, who often finished deep in the second division, to fourth place.

The agile southpaw was also highly regarded for his defensive ability and was an eight-time Gold Glove winner. Before his 16-year career ended, "Shantzie" would appear in the 1957 and 1960 World Series for Casey Stengel's New York Yankees and would pitch for seven big league teams under 10 managers.

When Shantz joined the Athletics, the legendary Connie Mack was his manager. By 1964, when he retired in the same home ballpark where it all began, his skipper was the Philadelphia Phillies' Gene Mauch. Mauch was still directing big-league teams in 1987—precisely 125 years after Shantz's first manager, Connie Mack, was born.

Mack and Mauch. One was an infant during the Civil War. The other was a teenage rookie infielder with Brooklyn during World War II. They are separated by less than a page in the *Baseball Encyclopedia's* alphabetical listing of managers, but their baseball experiences—and their managing styles—were as different as their personalities.

And that sets one to wondering. For among those of us who have watched baseball for a lifetime—from a cramped general admission seat in right field or maybe from close-up in a sandlot dugout next to an inept coach—one of the most puzzling questions revolves around how much field managers have to do with the success or failure of our teams. It's a knotty query, because of the myriad variables that ultimately influence won-lost records. Quality of players, strength of bench, canny (or overmatched) front offices, and leadership ability—or the lack of it— are just a few of the factors.

In *Baseball Managers: Stats, Stories, and Strategies,* we take a crack at this question. But the task is still daunting, and conclusions will be highly subjective, because 421 men have spent widely varying amounts of time in charge of major league dugouts this century with varying degrees of won-lost success. Clearly they're a mixed bag, as most any group of nearly a half thousand people would be. Included among them are father figures, babysitters, brawlers, autocrats, charlatans, puppets, an illiterate or two, and—within the context of their game—a few geniuses. I spotlight these geniuses, regardless of their records, but I also look at the lesser lights among managers—including the 25 or so who filled in for just a game or two as interim pilots.

In this book we visit each Hall of Fame skipper and some men likely to be Hall of Famers soon (Sparky Anderson, Jim Leyland, Tony LaRussa, Bobby Cox, perhaps others). In outlining the accomplishments of the great managers, on the theory that "the whole is greater than the sum of the parts" we study performances of some men who consistently fielded respectable teams whose parts really didn't add up to all that much. Among them would be Leyland, Felipe Alou, and even Connie Mack, whose skimpy pocketbooks necessitated turning in their best players for newer, less expensive models. Conversely, of course, the extremely successful Joe McCarthy, Walter Alston, John McGraw, and others like them enjoyed long careers, and numerous postseason engagements, in environments in which cost was less significant.

It's generally accepted that over the 162 games that make up a major league season, even the worst teams will muddle their way to about 60 victories, and the best will usually lose more than one out of three. It's those other 55 or so games where the cream rises to the top. History suggests that the best managers, through strategy, motivation, instinct, or guile, will influence more of these contested games positively than will less talented skippers. This book, by examining the records of everyone who's managed since 1901, uncovers those men who made the most of the hands they were dealt, and who were constantly looking for the innovative edge to win those 55 games that make a difference.

The following pages will carry you along the gamut of managers. Skippers who persuaded successfully with kindness (McKechnie, O'Neill) and those for whom intimidation worked (McGraw, Martin, Durocher). A mild-mannered gentleman such as Connie Mack and the acerbic, aggressive McGraw both achieve solid success during the same era. A gregarious "night owl," Stengel, wins nearly every American League pennant in the 1950s, while another Midwest native, Walter Alston, perceived as dull and withdrawn, wins and contends in the National League year after year in roughly the same time period. It is hard to imagine two more divergent personalities than Bill McKechnie and Dick Williams, yet they are the only two managers to have led three different franchises to the World Series.

We'll also see oddities and anomalies, such as the short-lived Cubs committee of coaches; fathers managing sons; best records winding up as mere also-rans in the age of division races; one man's recollection of controversial managerial decisions; even a collection of unusual, often goofy nicknames given managers. Baseball is the only team sport whose field leaders wear the uniform of their teams' players, so we look into the background of that practice.

In baseball managing through the ages it's partly true, as Bobby Cox tells us in Chapter 1, that the more things change the more they stay the same. On the other side of the coin, we examine the vast changes relative to the responsibilities and even the intellect required of managers during the profession's evolution from Harry Wright's Cincinnati Red Stockings to the media grilling of managers in today's cyberspace age of instant information.

Many of baseball's young pioneer managers of the late 1800s became legends of the modern era that began in 1900, when the National League realigned as an eight-team league. Typically, especially in this century's first decade and in the teens, team owners frequently engaged youthful, aggressive player-managers as their field directors. Some of them, including John McGraw, Hughie Jennings, Fred Clarke, and Frank Chance, are baseball immortals. Now we rarely see a player-manager. Pete Rose, in the late 1980s, was the most recent.

Baseball, the *game* between the white lines, has changed little over the years. The complexities of managing a baseball *team,* however, are far different now than they were decades or even just a generation ago. Still, old adages live on: "A manager's hired to be fired!" "It's easier to sack the manager than to fire 25 players!" "No manager can win without good players!" Conversely, "Anybody could manage *that* bunch of all-stars to the pennant!"

Playing for 10 managers from 1949 through 1964, Bobby Shantz remembers some of their different styles and characteristics.

"Mr. Mack was truly a nice man, no question about it. A real gentleman. But when I came up to the majors he was very old and had slowed down quite a bit. He'd give signs to his son, Earle, one of the coaches on our bench, who would relay signals to the first-base coach. Trouble was, by the time all those relays were completed the pitch was on its way.

"When I was in New York, Casey Stengel was ending his Yankee years. Yes, sometimes he'd nod off right there on the bench. But he had a great knack of knowing who to play when and where. I remember several times he'd have Enos Slaughter, a left-handed batter, pinch-hit against a southpaw pitcher. And he'd come through with a hit. Taking nothing away from Stengel, but a lot of credit for the team's success goes to some of the good coaches he hired—Jim Turner, Frank Crosetti, Ralph Houk, and some of the others.

"The manager who made the best impression on me was Jimmie Dykes, who replaced Mr. Mack with the A's. He was another very nice man—didn't platoon much, just let the players play.

"And finally there was Gene Mauch. One of my better managers, although I was with him for only a month or so at the end of '64. He had a reputation for having a bad temper, but I didn't witness much of that. In fact, during that 10-game losing streak when the Phillies lost their big lead in September, I can truthfully say that I never saw him get all riled up or lose his cool on the bench or in the clubhouse. In retrospect, though, he shouldn't have kept starting [Chris] Short and [Jim] Bunning with just two days' rest."

Perhaps, also in retrospect, the veteran Shantz might have stopped the skid had he been given a starting assignment.

"Maybe," he muses. "But Gene wanted me in the bull pen, which seemed like good strategy at the time."

Criticizing managers has always been a popular pastime, especially for fans. In fact, baseball's dugout directors believe that no other profession is second-guessed to the extent theirs is. More than a century's worth of evidence supports their position. However, not any of them—from McGraw to Bucky Harris to the Deacon McKechnie to feisty Billy Martin and on to today's Dusty Baker, Tom Kelly, and Bobby Cox (or even to Tom Hanks in *A League of Their Own*) would forgo the opportunity to manage a baseball team.

It is a unique craft, managing a big-league ball club. Yet the job description from team to team and city to city is pretty standard. Know the game; develop long-range plans but be prepared to make strategic revisions instantly; be fully aware of your players' and your opponents' strengths and weaknesses; maintain discipline while building morale; have complete command of the team but be sensitive to individual players' concerns and problems; be a diplomat, a public relations expert, and a marketing specialist. A thick skin, a good rapport with the general manager, and a lengthy attention span when the owner speaks are other assets of value to a baseball manager.

Because those are the "simple" criteria, one might conclude that managers can be created from the same cookie cutter or graduate with equal standing from the same baseball clinic classroom. No notion could be more erroneous, as evidenced by the varied backgrounds, characteristics, and techniques of the 421 men who have managed during these 98 summers. Nearly two dozen of them—11 active managers (at the time of our interviews) and 10 former big-league pilots—graciously shared their thoughts and their time to provide material for this book. I am grateful to them, and to other Hall of Fame members, too, whose comments and recollections are of great value.

For a certainty, this book will assist you in any backyard or barroom argument about who managed whom when, and how well or poorly his teams performed. It categorizes the names and records of every manager of every team in this century. On the other hand, it dispels many widely held notions (the managers' "musical chairs" theory, for instance, is largely a myth).

The book reviews this century's managers and their managing. It traces the evolution of their craft and describes humorous encounters as well as poignant incidents (several managers have died in office). I examine the special abilities and careers of managers honored at Cooperstown and wonder why certain other successful skippers have been overlooked. From the pioneer pathfinders in the 1800s, to the young men who will still be managing well into the 21st century, the book chronicles their performances as leaders and strategists. I hope that, after reading this book and referencing its listings sections, you will have a better understanding of the effect a manager can have on the fate of your favorite game's favorite teams. And of the multitude of duties and enormous responsibilities shouldered by those select 2 ½ dozen men who fill out the lineup cards in a typical 1990s summer.

What follows, then, is a complete coverage of major league managers from 1901 through 1998—every one of them, from the one-game interim fill-ins to the prominent veterans such as Connie Mack and Casey Stengel and Gene Mauch who crossed Bobby Shantz's path.

Managing: Its Evolution

In baseball's pioneering days a man named Fred Dunlap managed 1880s major league teams known as the Cleveland Blues, St. Louis Maroons, and Pittsburgh Alleghenys. His four-season record was 145 victories, 102 losses, five ties, one league pennant, and three second-division finishes.

Fred Dunlap could not read or write, according to old reports. He was illiterate.

During the 100-plus years since Dunlap last managed, baseball's dugout directors have often been described as far worse than "illiterate." Aware of Dunlap, some critics question the degree of intellect required of a manager. If Dunlap, with his acknowledged deficiencies, could win a pennant, must be an easy job, eh?

Mountains of evidence repudiate such a suggestion. Hundreds of firing notices, and dozens of managerial resignations citing various pressures, testify to the difficulties surrounding what has become an extremely high-visibility occupation. On the other hand, when analyzing only the wins-losses aspect of a manager's job, even the most successful of modern-day pilots will tell you that the manager's in-game decisions have but minimal connections with his team's final standing. Said Johnny Keane, a 1964 World Series victor at St. Louis, "If he's [a manager] really great he might be the difference in six to 10 games. If he's lousy, of course, he could lose a lot. But for most of us, once the game starts it's really the players that have to do it for us." Whitey Herzog, a Cardinals' multiple pennant winner: "There are 50 games you're going to lose no matter what. You'll win 50 no matter what. Those other 50 are the one- or two-run games that can go either way. And of those, maybe a dozen or so can be directly decided by a manager's strategy." Casey Stengel, probably the most frequently quoted of managers, was an egoist of large proportion. But when he focused purely on the business of baseball, which was most of the time, he admitted after his Yankees came from a 3–1 deficit to win the 1958 World Series over Milwaukee, "I couldn't have done it without the players."

While managerial strategy during most games is arguably overemphasized by second-guessers, the importance of a man's leadership abilities in both the dugout and the clubhouse cannot be over estimated. The converse of Stengel's "I couldn't have done it without the players" quote is the occasional player's debatable opinion that "we *could* have done it without *that* manager."

The 1940 "mutiny on Lake Erie" comes to mind. Oscar Vitt, a hardboiled infielder in his Detroit playing days under Old Oriole Hughie Jennings, was Cleveland's skipper for three seaons—1938 through '40. His team ranked a competitive third in his first two seasons, then challenged for the 1940 pennant. The Indians lineup featured several All-Stars, including Lou Boudreau, Jeff Heath, Mel Harder, Ken Keltner, Bob Feller, and Hal Trosky. At midseason Harder, later an interim pilot at Cleveland, was the chief spokesman when a majority of players signed a petition calling for Vitt's ouster. Newspapers and opponents referred to the incident as "the Crybaby Rebellion." Harder presented the plea to owner Alva Bradley, who promised to investigate the complaints. Whatever his findings, he chose to keep Vitt (who was eventually dismissed after the season ended). Cleveland finished just one game behind flag winner Detroit, and many of the players believed a change in managership at midyear would have made a difference. Players weren't comfortable with Vitt, feeling that he was overly critical of mistakes. Boudreau, later a successful player-manager at Cleveland, remembers the situation this way: "Vitt was a good baseball man, but a two-timer. He'd tell you one thing, applaud your good efforts, but then criticize you behind your back. He was forever giving players hell on the bench in front of teammates."

A rarity—sacking a first-place pilot—occurred 43 years later. This time the owner acted long before the season was over. Manager Pat Corrales had the 1983 Phillies in first place in early July when owner Bill Giles abruptly fired him. Why? "It seemed to me that he disliked the players," Giles recalls. "He'd be in my office every other day saying so-and-so is no good, somebody else is an s.o.b., and so forth. I knew we had a chance to win the pennant [they did] and I didn't want the manager to mess up our chances. There was simply too much pressure in the clubhouse." General manager Paul Owens was sent "downstairs" as manager. He had players' respect, and the also had a close-up view for long-range personnel planning. Bench coach Bobby Wine, who later managed Atlanta briefly, was Owens's chief strategist.

More than a decade later Corrales reminisced about the 1983 circumstances: "I was shocked, sure. We were in first place at the time. But, hey, Bill was the boss. It was his team, and he can make those kinds of decisions. When I left I wished him and the organization success, and thanked him for the opportunity to manage. [Two weeks later Corrales was named as successor to manager Mike Ferraro at Cleveland.] The thing that disappointed me more than anything was that Bill didn't speak to me for 10 years, but during the 1993 National League Championship Series (NLCS) [Corrales was then a coach at Atlanta, which met Philadelphia in the playoffs], we had a nice little talk."

An earlier Phillies team, back in 1898, was more successful in ousting its manager than was Cleveland 42 years later. George Stallings, who would later manage the "Miracle" Boston Braves of 1914 to a World Series sweep of Connie Mack's Athletics, was in his second year at Philadelphia when players threatened to strike unless he was removed. The manager, throughout his 13-year piloting career, was tyrannical and abusive, according to the vast majority of men who played for him. A native of Georgia, Stallings was reputed to be a dignified southern gentleman at home in the off-season. But according to Hank Gowdy, one of his Braves catchers, once the season began, "tongue-lashing was an art with him."

Stallings was one of the few pilots of his day who were not player-managers. He normally eschewed wearing a uniform, managing instead in street clothes. Connie Mack also wore civilian apparel to the dugout. Burt Shotton at Brooklyn managed in street clothes, too, but when he and Mack retired following the 1950 season a regulation was instituted compelling managers to wear their team's uniform during games. Baseball is the only major sport with such a requirement. Connie Mack was also the last club owner who legally operated as field manager. A rule prohibiting that dual-capacity role was adopted after the Cardinals traded player-manager Rogers Hornsby to the New York Giants for Frankie Frisch after St. Louis won the 1926 World Championship. Hornsby, a stockholder in the Cardinals at the time, refused to sell his financial interest unless he received an exhorbitant buyout. Agreement was eventually reached, but the new regulation was soon put on the books. Mack was "grandfathered" in and allowed to own and manage at the same time.

Ted Turner, chief executive of the Atlanta Braves, was evidently unaware of the owner-manager prohibition. His 1977 troops had lost 16 straight when he chose to replace manager Dave Bristol with—himself. Turner "directed" the Braves to their 17th loss in a row, a 2–1 defeat at Pittsburgh. (Actually, Vern Benson and other coaches ran the ball game, but Turner, offering advice occasionally, was officially charged with the loss.) The next day Commissioner Bowie Kuhn notified Turner that his action was "not in the best interests of baseball" and ordered him to relinquish his managership. He did, returning Bristol to the post.

Turner was philosophical in commenting on his one game as skipper. "This losing streak is bad for the fans, no doubt, but look at it this way: We're making a lot of people happy in other cities!"

The team was Bristol's again for the rest of that season. Then he was gone, to resurface two years later in San Francisco. It begs that shopworn question, If a manager is fired for incompetency, then why do others hire him? Answers vary from owner to owner and sometimes involve box office attraction or, simply, impulse. The most logical conclusion relates to ability. Perhaps the situation was different in the early days of this century when the recycled men— most of them having been player-managers—were considered inspirational field "captains" whose all-star-caliber playing careers insured instant recognition by the ticket-buying public. Today, the question of Why him, again? can usually be answered more rationally: Recent history confirms that nearly all of the men who've managed three or more teams have been successful in their initial assignments. Perhaps not in terms of multiple championships, but in regard to their qualifications as thoughtful strategists and leaders.

Billy Martin, in addition to his five terms as Yankees leader, managed Minnesota, Detroit, Texas, and Oakland. Invariably, the team he took over rapidly improved its standings position. Tony LaRussa is handling his third big-league assignment at St. Louis now. He was successful at both Chicago and Oakland. Joe Torre, at Yankee Stadium, is engaged in his fourth managing job. He brought along solid credentials. Dick Williams, in spite of his ornery disposition, was hired by six major league owners because his previous managing was continually productive. The less-qualified managers do not get recycled. Thus, the "good ol' boy network" theory is largely a myth.

Jimmie Dykes was an exception. He was head man of six teams—White Sox, Athletics, Orioles, Reds, Tigers, Indians—during 21 seasons. Only Williams and John McNamara piloted as many different clubs (although Hornsby also is officially credited with six when his interim assignment with the Giants during John McGraw's 33-game absence in 1927 is included). Dykes never won a pennant but was considered a top-drawer inspirational leader.

Dykes forged this long-term formula for evaluating managers: "Managers are usually hired to restore a team's health. Their first year should be devoted to a study of the team's weaknesses and needs. New players should carefully be fitted into the pattern in the second season. By the third year the manager should be able to improve the team's standing. Only then can his talents be fairly judged." At his final four posts Dykes did not get three years to accomplish his task. Toward the end of his single season at Baltimore, when he correctly assumed his contract would not be renewed, Edgar Munzel of the *Chicago Sun Times* dropped by the Orioles' clubhouse and casually inquired, "What goes around here?" "Dykes," answered Dykes.

Managers' musical chairs were little more than a memory by the 1990s. Entering the 1998 season, 15—precisely half—of the major leagues' 30 skippers were in their first managing assignments. Ten others—Gene Lamont, Jim Leyland, Ray Miller, Bobby Valentine, Jimy Williams, Jim Riggleman, Buck Showalter, Art Howe, Johnny Oates, and Terry Collins—were then in only their second terms. It's true that a record number of manager firings occurred in 1991. However, with few exceptions, rookie managers took over.

Figures confirm that most managers, despite notions otherwise, do not automatically enter a recycle bin when their dugout time runs out. Of the 421 pilots since 1901, 256 of them—61 percent—managed only one team. Just one. Another 99 men were hired by two teams, but no more. Only 66 of the 421 big league managers signed on with three or more different clubs. We know that managers don't get the luxury of a second guess. They seldom get a second chance, either.

What aspects of the game, and the managing of it, have changed since John McGraw, Connie Mack, Clark Griffith, and their pioneering colleagues stamped their leadership imprints on it when the 20th century was new? On a continually growing list, over which managers have minimal influence, would be artificial turf, double-knit uniforms (much more comfortable than the baggy flannel of generations past), radio and television's pervasiveness, free agency's replacement of the old reserve clause, multimillion attendance figures instead of a few hundred thousand fans, standing room only at many spring training games, salaries (players' and managers'), and roster size.

Back in 1901 the new American League's managers rarely had tough lineup decisions to make. Only 18 players per team were permitted, and by May that was reduced to 14. Seventeen men on a team was standard in 1908, and in 1912, for the first time, rosters expanded to 25 from May 15 through August 20. Generally low attendance, World War I, and encroachment by the Federal League dictated the reducing of rosters to 21 in 1915, but since 1919 most teams most years have operated with 25 players. A typical roster breakdown from 1906 would look something like this: seven pitchers (up from four or five just a year or two earlier), four infielders, three outfielders, and three catchers. Spare pitchers and reserve catchers would fill in as fielders if necessary. And typically, as we've seen, one of the players was also the manager.

Managers didn't have scouting reports back in the old days. They pretty much relied on their own observation of the opposition, and on appraisals offered by confidants. When there was scouting, it usually involved the evaluation of amateur youngsters rather than assessing the big-league opposition. One exception was Connie Mack's assigning pitcher Howard Ehmke to scout the Chicago Cubs, Philadelphia's forthcoming opponent in the 1929 World Series. Ehmke earned an A for espionage. On the mound for the Series opener, he struck out 13 Cubs, a World Series record that stood for 24 years. Today each big-league club has at least one advance scout on its payroll, in addition to scouts who scour the majors for players that might be targets for trades.

Ed Liberatore, a scouting official with the Reds, Dodgers, and Orioles for many years, confirms that scouts keep an eye on managers as well as on the players. "We try to focus on tendencies—does he often hit-and-run in particular situations, will he usually pitch out on the same count with a runner on first, is the guy a hothead whose team gets a little out of control when the manager's excited, does he always play the infield in with a runner on third and less than two out— things like that. And you notice if he might have a tendency to overmanage by using most of his bench early in a game or running out of righty or lefty pitchers. That kind of information is useful to the team you're working for."

Former Red Sox All-Star third baseman Frank Malzone has been scouting at the major league level for Boston for many years. He agrees with Liberatore. When scouting opposing managers, he focuses on areas of repitition. "For instance, I write down the count on the batter. You might discover that the manager always tries the hit-and-run on the same count." Malzone also talks about his daily responsibility to the Boston manager. "It's important to get your scouting report to your manager so that he and his coaches can evaluate the team's next opponent quickly and pass on their observations to the players. With modern technology—voice mail, e-mail, and so forth—there's no excuse for being late with a report. Right now I'm more involved with watching players in both leagues. Maybe we'll find somebody that might become available who's doing a better job than the guy we have at his position now. When I was doing advance scouting, Ralph Houk was a Red Sox manager for four years. He was always patient with us scouts and suggested you take a couple of days off once in a while to avoid getting stale. He'd call you for your ideas, and to let you know he appreciated your efforts. Eddie Kasko did that a lot, too."

Baltimore manager Earl Weaver was often called a "printout pilot" for his alleged reliance on detailed statistics when making up his lineup card. But as he says in this book's section on Hall of Fame managers, he used the computerized information selectively, as a guideline rather than as a dictator. High-tech conditioning equipment in every clubhouse and video cameras for recording a player's every movement at bat, on the mound, or in the field are other useful 1990s evaluation tools for the manager and his coaches.

The expanded size of a team's coaching staff is another of baseball's significant evolutionary developments. Hall of Famer Al Lopez notes that most teams into the 1930s had no more than two coaches, and sometimes just one man. He would handle one of the coaching boxes; the manager or a utility player would be stationed in the other one. Now managers are assisted by at least a half dozen coaches, each of whom has a specialized assignment or a combination of them—outfield and defense, baseline coaching, pitching and hitting instructors, a bull-pen coach who might also be the catchers' tutor, and the bench coach, who's sometimes known as the dugout assistant. In football he would be titled assistant head coach.

There's no disagreement among today's managers about the necessity for the enlarged coaching staff. Two major factors dictate it. First, young players are advanced to the major leagues far more quickly than in earlier years, and with less training and experience. The instruction that coaches give them is vital. And second, managers now are required to spend much more time before and after games with reporters, and in representing the club with corporate marketers and civic groups at luncheons, dinners, and other special appearances. When Lou Piniella was managing Cincinnati in the early 1990s, a clubhouse visitor one evening was an old friend from his New York days, football coach Bill Parcells. After listening in on Lou's formal and informal question-and-answer forum for about a half hour, Parcells asked Piniella, "Why do you do this? Why do you let the reporters take up so much of your time before the game? We don't permit that in football."

"That's just the way it is in baseball," Lou replied. "It's something you get used to, though, and most of the time it's not a big bother. Of course the league requires writers to clear the clubhouse 45 minutes before game time, so we do have time together with just the team."

One baseball change with a positive effect for managers is expansion. It means more job openings. Until 1961 only 16 teams existed this century—eight in each league. As of the 1998 season the number has nearly doubled. We now have 30 major league teams. Not only more managing opportunities are available, but improved chances to finish first. With three division winners from the National League, three from the American, plus wild-card postseason entries, more managers are still working in October than ever did before.

While expansion has created more managing positions, it has invariably assured those new pilots failure in the standings for awhile. New teams have approached managing hirings differently, but whoever the new man was, he experienced tough sledding. The American League was the first to grow to 10 teams. The Angels (then known as the Los Angeles Angels) employed Bill Rigney as manager. He had been popular with San Francisco fans when the Giants, whom he had skippered in New York, moved to California. He was also considered a good judge of young talent and an able mixer of veterans and youth in his lineups. Washington (the second-edition Senators after their forerunners had transferred to Minnesota) was the league's other new team. The approach was different there, for Washington already had a base of big-league baseball fans. One of the legitimate stars of the old Senators was two-time batting champion Mickey Vernon. Vernon had no prior managing experience at any level; he was hired mainly for his gate appeal as a local hero.

National League expansion came the next year. Again, two philosophies ruled. Houston hired Harry Craft as manager. Craft was popular in Ohio two decades earlier as a solid outfielder on Bill McKechnie's champion Reds, was considered a good instructor in his minor league managing days, yet was virtually unknown to Houston fans. But in New York, where the Mets were born in 1962, Casey Stengel was a natural choice as pilot. His previous success with the Yankees had earned him national recognition and local popularity, and management believed that Stengel's name alone would be a major asset in netting hefty turnstile figures, despite a ragtag team on the field. They were right.

Another National League expansion year was 1993, when the Florida Marlins and Colorado Rockies came on board. Don Baylor, the Rockies' initial manager, would lead them to unprecedented baseball honors—a wild-card berth in the 1995 National League Championship Series—in only their third year of existence. He well remembers some of the stumbling blocks encountered by the new kids in town. "We had to do so many things from scratch. If a manager's hired to take over an established team he has the advantage of being able to pick up some of the pieces. With most expansion teams, though, the manager just has to babysit until the team's ready to win. We were fortunate here in Colorado. The organization agreed to spend money to build quickly, and that enabled us get quality players like Larry Walker, Bill Swift, Charlie Hayes, and Walt Weiss, who normally wouldn't come to an expansion team. I had just come from being the hitting coach at St. Louis, where Joe Torre [then the Cardinals' skipper] gave me a lot of leeway in doing my job, and here we had less than three weeks to analyze the list of available eligible players. Florida was in the same situation. Somebody asked me afterward if there'd be a natural rivalry between us expansion teams. I figured that instead of us against Florida it would be the Rockies against the rest of the National League.

"It all worked out pretty well, even though I hadn't managed before. I knew the league, from coaching in St. Louis, and I learned a lot about motivation from Earl Weaver when I played for him in Baltimore. You heard about some griping there, but I can tell you that most of his players really appreciated him after they left. If you pay attention, a guy can learn a lot about managing from the men you play for. Under Jim Fregosi at California, for example, I was real impressed when he had the entire team on the top step of the dugout for the national anthem every night. That's class. And over the years I learned a lot about mutual respect between players and their manager. That's probably the number one thing. A clubhouse will get out of hand when they lose respect for you. And you can't get it back."

Casey Stengel figured that every team had a few players that lacked respect for him; nevertheless, he had a philosophy for holding the team together. "The secret to managing is to keep the five guys who hate you away from the guys who are undecided."

Billy Martin put it another way (although he might have been quoting Stengel, his mentor). "Out of 25 guys there should be 15 who would run through a wall for you, two or three who don't like you at all, five who are indifferent, and maybe three undecided. My job is to keep the last two groups from going the wrong way."

Manager Eddie Sawyer had no trouble in his relationships with the team during his second term as Phillies manager, but he foresaw nothing but trouble from the rest of the National League as his lackluster squad broke from spring training in 1960. He managed the season's opening game, then quit. Naturally, reporters wondered why. "I'm 49 years old," he barked, "and I want to live to be 50." In retrospect his family was delighted with his decision, for Sawyer survived well into his 80s, continuing to reminisce about his Phillies, nicknamed the Whiz Kids, who won the 1950 National League championship.

If candid, every baseball manager would admit to frustrations during his career. Not many take the route of abrupt departure Sawyer did, but many simply pack it in before complete burnout brings them down. We'll see that later in this book with the underrated Billy Southworth. Billy Martin's first New York term ended when he resigned to avoid a nervous breakdown. Clark Griffith probably would have given Walter Johnson a second tenure at Washington, but after surviving strife as Cleveland's pilot, Johnson had had enough of managing. The remarkably successful Joe McCarthy signed out for the last time after managing the Red Sox into the 1950 season. Some years earlier, while directing Yankee pennant winners nearly every season, he was overcome with frustration one summer. "Sometimes I think I'm in the greatest business in the world. Then I lose four straight and I want to change places with a farmer."

Managers' job frustration doesn't end with turmoil in the clubhouse, peeves with the front office, or a disappointing ranking in the standings. Manager-umpire relationships have also elevated blood to the boiling point—on both sides. "It's a matter of respect," says veteran American League arbiter Al Clark. "Umpires respect the job that managers have to do, and we hope they have respect for ours. I know a lot of managers have tried to intimidate rookie umpires. I never worked in the National League, but I've heard a lot of stories about Leo Durocher's yapping all through the game about missed calls, half swings, and so forth. Nowadays managers like Tony LaRussa, Tom Kelly, Mike Hargrove, and Johnny Oates leave you alone until they have a serious beef about something. I've been asked about certain no-no's—words that automatically get somebody ejected. There are no words—plural. Only one word. That word is 'you.' We'll put up with a certain amount of profane grumbling, but when a manager [player or coach, too] looks you in the eye and says, 'You (fill in the blank),' he's gone.

"Most of the time, umpires and managers get along pretty well. In fact, a lot of humorous incidents happen. I remember when Jim Fregosi managed the Angels back in '79. He'd been in the job just a short time, and they had a big crowd—maybe 40,000—at Anaheim Stadium one night. I'm working third base, there's a close play, and the Angels runner is out. Clearly out. No question. No beef by the third-base coach or the runner. All of a sudden here comes Fregosi from the dugout, screaming, waving his arms, bobbing his head. He's still going through all those motions when he says, 'Al, you've been out here six innings now and haven't had the courtesy to introduce yourself to Preston Gomez [the Angels' new third-base coach]. I'm not leaving 'til you say hello.' I'm grinning, and simply turned and said, 'Nice to meet you, Preston, I'm Al Clark.' Fregosi says, 'That's all I wanted. Thanks.' He goes back to the dugout to the cheers of 40,000 fans who think he ripped me pretty good. No harm done, so we overlook the interruption in a case like that. As a matter of fact, sometimes managers tell you in advance that they might come out sometime that night and appear to give you grief just to stir up their team. They respect you enough to warn you."

Cardinals, Pirates, and Cubs manager Frankie Frisch was an umpire baiter in the Jimmie Dykes mold. Both enjoyed badgering the officials, but usually with tongue-in-cheek. Many umpires admitted they enjoyed these sparring matches, which produced no long-term enmity. Oldtime National League umpire Beans Reardon often told this story involving Frisch: "He was a good friend, but he'd annoy you with his loud remarks. One day he shouted something, so I whipped off my mask and headed toward the Pittsburgh dugout. 'What was that you hollered, Frisch?' 'You've been guessing all day,' he yells, 'now guess what I said.' 'I can't guess,' I hollered back, 'but I can imagine what it was. You're out of the game!' "

"Respect" was the word most often repeated by the umpires, players, managers, coaches, and owners who offered comments for this book. On the subject of hiring a manager, Phillies principal owner Bill Giles said, "Respect is the most important element in successful managing. Players and the manager don't necessarily have to like each other a lot, but there must be mutual respect. Before hiring a manager you should get a scouting report from men who've managed or played with or against him. In addition to his baseball smarts, is he respected? Most baseball men have high integrity; they'll give you an honest opinion. Along those lines a manager should have some significant baseball success in his background either as player or manager or both. It's hard for players to respect a manager who was not successful in some way."

By any measure, Sparky Anderson has been a successful manager. Collaborating with Dan Ewald, the Tigers' senior vice president of public relations for the book *Sparky!*, he wrote, "A manager must not expect respect, but he must know how to earn it. If a manager acts like a jerk, players will, too. But if he conducts himself with dignity, as Tony LaRussa does, players will likely do the same."

Anderson, an odds-on cinch to enter the Hall of Fame's managers' wing someday, has five pennants to his credit (four at Cincinnati, the other with Detroit) and is one of only five men to have won championships in each league—Joe McCarthy, Yogi Berra, Alvin Dark, and Dick Williams are the others. For three decades his counterparts have welcomed his sage advice, such as this: "Preparation is the single most important duty of any manager, and his single most important responsibility is to have his team play as hard as it can every single day. Once the manager makes his decision, he must turn his team loose. And when the game's over, he needs to prepare them for the next day. Good managers don't get taken by surprise; they anticipate situations before they happen. I learned from Al Lopez to watch every single pitch; nothing's more important. I've often told young managers not to blame the front office for their problems. Work out your problems with the players they've given you. If you show the front office you're worried enough they'll soon give you something to worry about. Play the hand you're given.

"Sometimes the best managers—and Gene Mauch is a good example—wind up fourth or fifth. Mauch was the opposing manager for my first game with the Reds. He came over with this advice: 'Enjoy the moment, because you'll never pass this way again.' He told me something else when we were talking about how much more media coverage there is now than years ago—probably tripled since I went to Cincinnati in 1970. Gene said he managed 486 games a year. The 162 on the schedule, 162 in his mind preparing for each one, and 162 replayed for the media!"

That second set of games Mauch refers to, "preparation," is most likely where he spent most of his time—planning, strategizing, and scheming to land that extra edge. Here's a good example from his early years in Philadelphia at his first big-league managing assignment.

The Phillies, playing in Connie Mack Stadium then, sat in the third-base dugout. A high wall stretched from the right-field foul line to dead center field, a configuration similar to Washington's Griffith Stadium or Ebbets Field in Brooklyn, or a barrier akin to Fenway Park's "green monster." As was customary, the Phils' bull pen was down the left-field line, just a few sections beyond their dugout. Visitors, assigned to the first-base dugout, used the right-field bull pen. Perfectly within legal bounds, Mauch one day reversed the bull pen locations. Thereafter the Phillies' reserve pitchers and catchers went to the right-field pen.

Mauch's reasoning? When his team was at bat with runners on base, and a long, high drive was hit toward that outfield wall, his Phillies in the bull pen would wave a towel to signify that the batted ball would reach the wall rather than be caught by the opposing right fielder. Of course, by not signaling, they warned runners that the ball was likely to be snared. The relocated bull-pen caper of Mauch's enabled his club to score countless runs over the years when runners, seeing that wagging white towel, left base at the crack of the bat rather than waiting to see whether or not the ball would be caught.

Apart from Mauch, another opponent whom Anderson has long admired is Tom Lasorda. "One aspect of Tommy's success was his relationship with the players. He has a feeling for all of the team—from the cleanup hitter to the bull-pen catcher." Retired from the dugout now after leading the Dodgers to four World Series and seven NL West division titles, Lasorda continues to promote baseball. "It's the greatest game in the world," he reminds everyone, from the banquet hall audience to the taxi driver. "During the labor disputes in recent years two words were always missing from the negotiations. 'Fan.' And 'compromise.' Without compromise we lose the fans. And then what's to become of our game?" Because of Lasorda's national celebrity status, his Hollywood connections, and his popularity as a raconteur, his unique ability to lead a team and maintain high morale has often been overlooked. As Sparky Anderson said, "He has a feeling for all the team." And long ago he mastered the skill of persuasiveness.

Mike Scioscia was the Dodgers' catcher for a dozen seasons into the 1990s. Upon his retirement he decided to train to be a manager. Many, in fact, expected him to replace Lasorda eventually, but that job went to longtime coach Bill Russell in 1996. That spring Scioscia told me about his planning. "Managing's a long-term goal, but I'm not ready yet. A lot of groundwork is needed, and what I'm doing now—coaching catchers in the Dodgers' minor league system—is part of that groundwork. I'm observing more now from the dugout. When you're a catcher, as I was, you see the game from only one perspective. It's interesting now. I watch managers' moves, and I learned a long time ago—first from Tommy [Lasorda]—that handling people is the most important part of the job. I learned about strategy when I caught; thinking a few batters ahead, always aware of the count and of runners on base. But there's much more to managing than strategy. Sure, big-league managing is a dream of mine, but just a fuzzy goal now. There'll be a lot of detours from point A to point Z."

A year later, when Russell began his first full season as skipper, Scioscia was elevated to the position of Dodgers bench coach.

With few exceptions, his contemporaries who have preceded Scioscia to that point Z know the pitfalls he refers to. Invariably, still more stumbling blocks faced them when they reached major league managing. Cito Gaston, a gentle man with Alston-like stoicism, did a masterful job in leading the Blue Jays. Toronto won two consecutive World Series under Gaston's command in 1992 and 1993. Then free agency enabled many of the Jays' top players to seek better contracts elsewhere. Gaston's lineup was weakened considerably for a few years, before some of its younger players matured and the front office made some useful trades. "It was tough, of course, not to be able to make long-range plans because of the way free agency works. But a manager just has to understand the way the circumstances are, and adjust. You still are involved with teaching, with strategic planning, and with trying to maintain a professional and comfortable clubhouse. I was blessed with excellent coaches at Toronto; they helped in so many ways to make the job comfortable. I feel sorry for Jim Leyland. [Leyland was then beginning his final Pittsburgh season, prior to joining the Marlins.] But despite so many of his top players going elsewhere in recent years, he still keeps his head high and manages as smart as ever. The way he handles all of that is a model for all of us other managers."

Gaston, back then, could not foresee Leyland's roller-coaster ride. In 1997

Florida Marlins owner Wayne Huizenga enticed Leyland to manage the costly free agents that Huizenga's bountiful billfold attracted. Finally, Leyland earned a long-coveted World Series Championship ring. But before a fortnight passed, the owner peddled away most of his stars—and their big contracts. For Jim Leyland it was Pittsburgh all over again—a paucity of top-shelf talent and the virtual assurance of a disappointing NL East standing, the price of major rebuilding.

Kevin Kennedy, managing Boston at the time, echoed most of his contemporaries in connection with free agency. "It's the biggest change in baseball since I've been around," he observed. Kennedy had spent 16 years in the Orioles and Dodgers organizations as minor league player and manager before he piloted Texas, and then led Boston to the 1995 American League East title. "Knowing that your lineup is not likely to be set for long range, it's more important than ever to communicate with your players. Get to know them, and vice versa. I make it a point to sit down and talk with my players, discuss their problems. Jose Canseco, when we've been together at both Texas and here with the Red Sox, is at ease with me—and I with him—when discussing anything about baseball or personal matters. I'm pleased when players have the confidence in me to talk about anything. That attitude, working both ways, helps establish team rapport. It's simply a matter of mutual respect." (There's that emphasis on two-way respect again.)

Kennedy offered this observation, ironical in hindsight. "In a manager's relationship with his team, the biggest thing is when you have the general manager's backing. Then you have no lingering discipline problems." Boston got off to a rocky start that 1996 season, then turned things around to finish over .500 and become a long-shot contender for a play-off berth by September. But the Sox couldn't quite make up the ground they'd lost in April and May, and Kennedy was dismissed at season's end. One of the reasons, as reported by the Boston press: general manager Dan Duquette's opinion that Kennedy was too close to his players.

Bill Rigney, the Giants' last New York manager and their first in San Francisco, took over the Polo Grounds dugout in 1956 and finished his piloting 20 seasons later after assignments with the Angels and Twins and a final year back with the Giants. Players usually found Rig approachable. He was considered a good instructor, and his clubhouse was always upbeat. His rapport with players was excellent. Some of his thoughts on changes in managing: "Young people today are always looking for a reason and excuses for the things they do. They'll corner the manager with 'Why can't I have a better hotel room? How come we don't fly on better planes? Why shouldn't I be hitting second?' Those kinds of things were never a point years ago." Indeed they weren't, agreed Leo Durocher, Rigney's immediate predecessor with the New York Giants. In 1973 when he left Houston, his last job, Leo had this to say: "It's a different breed, and they're going to keep right on doing it their way. Well, I'm a guy who has to do it my way." And he was gone.

Bobby Cox, the most successful of National League pilots in the 1990s, isn't convinced that baseball is much different now than before. "I honestly don't know that it's changed much at all," he reflects. "I guess players have changed some, but not much really. I was reading a paper the other day that talked about players holding out, insisting on more money, better clubhouse conditions, and so forth. Then I looked at the date. It was a 1917 newspaper. We hear about this kind of squabbling now. It was the same way back then."

Most current managers are in their forties and fifties, so they've been around baseball for two or three decades. To a man, they mention the evolution of mass media's involvement—from a couple of regular writers and the game announcers covering the team to today's typical postgame interview room peopled by a few dozen daily paper reporters, broadcasters, and feature story writers.

Cox remarks on radio call-in programs: "Managing's sure changed in regard to those kinds of shows," he says. "The radio guys and the callers are tough on managers. They make it sound like managers don't know anything, and we get blamed for everything. Whether your team is successful or not, they rip the manager. It's gotten way out of control. We like to think that whenever we go on the ball field that we have a chance to win the game. But those people expect you to win every night. That'd be nice, but in baseball it just doesn't work that way. If you listen to these programs, they'll drive a manager nuts. And it's that way in every city in baseball.

"Don't get me wrong. I'm talking about just one aspect of how things have changed. It's not just those radio shows that put pressure on you; it's the nature of the job that does that. It always has. The conscientious managers put pressure on themselves to excel. Even when you sign a long-term contract, the pressure doesn't go away. It only gets worse for some people. After the success we've been able to achieve these last few years in Atlanta, there's a different kind of pressure on the players, the coaches, and the manager, too. Fans' expectations are unbelievable—you're expected to keep winning forever. Fortunately, ours is a good organization. The farm system has developed some outstanding talent year after year, and the front office has made some good deals that have benefited us. And my coaches are just outstanding. I go for coaches who can do a good job, and our guys have been just great. Most of our coaches have been with me quite awhile, fellas like Pat Corrales; Jim Beauchamp; Leo Mazzone, our pitching coach; Clarence Jones; Ned Yost. Jimy Williams was with me for many years before he got the Red Sox managing job. They get their jobs done without me even asking most of the time. Williams and Corrales had been big-league managers, you know, and somebody asked me if I felt my job is threatened by having them around. The fact is, it's just the opposite. I'm delighted to be surrounded by good baseball men."

Cox is often asked if he patterned his successful style after any particular manager. "I only played in the majors briefly, and that was for Ralph Houk on the Yankees. I guess I try to treat the players the way Ralph did. He treated the guys like human beings. He was communicating with players back then like many of us try to do now. Like Houk, I try to be honest and up-front with them. And when there is a problem, the best thing to do is take care of it right away. Clear the air.

"Even though I was talking about pressure a minute ago, I go back to thinking that baseball really hasn't changed all that much. Players need some discipline now, but they always did. Managers need to build their style of play around the talents of their players, but the good ones have always done that, too. The job can be frustrating sometimes, but that's nothing new either."

At that point, buttoning his uniform shirt in preparation for that evening's game, Bobby Cox—winner of as many Braves pennants in the 1990s as the franchise had collected during the entire first nine decades of the century—sat back, relaxed for a moment, and reflected. "You know, all in all managing's a lot of fun. It was in the old days, and it is these days. I know I've had a lot of fun with it."

Pathfinders

Imagine Billy Martin, Tom Lasorda, or for that matter any of their contemporaries trying to manage a baseball game from the grandstand, in street clothes, far from his team's dugout. Such a circumstance, of course, is incomprehensible today. But when the new National League officially started out in 1876, that's precisely what the regulations required. "Non-playing managers are not allowed near the bench during games."

In those pathfinding days most teams' field managers were uniformed player-managers, so they were legitimately admitted to the playing area. It was bench managers, as we now call them, who were barred. The reason: Many of them had been found guilty of boisterous conduct, loud profanity, rough criticism of umpires, and various other ungentlemanly behaviors that too frequently disrupted the normal flow of games. (Imagine that, Leo Durocher. Or Earl Weaver.) The rule was rescinded after a year or so, but, reading between the lines of journalistic reports of that time, it's a good bet that today's bench jockeys are mild mannered in comparison.

Notable Managers before 1900

This book focuses on the 20th-century managers and their exploits. However, this brief section reviews some of the notable managing pioneers of the late 1800s, and their influences that carried into the modern era. Eight of the men who are cited with plaques in the managers' or executives' wings of the National Baseball Hall of Fame played, managed, or did both for late 19th-century major league teams—Charlie Comiskey, Ned Hanlon, Clark Griffith, Connie Mack, John McGraw, Wilbert Robinson, George Wright, and Harry Wright. In total, 14 men managed on both sides of the turn of the 20th century—Frank Bancroft, Al Buckenberger, Fred Clarke, George Davis, Patsy Donovan, Horace Fogel, Hanlon, Tom Loftus, Mack, McGraw, Deacon McGuire, Frank Selee, Bill Shettsline, and George Stallings.

Harry Wright and Albert Goodwill (A. G., or Al) Spalding were two of early baseball's most farsighted figures. The budding enterprise they helped develop, the National League, would blossom more fruitfully than even they might have predicted.

Wright, an English-born cricket aficionado who eventually excelled in baseball, was largely reponsible for founding America's first professional baseball (two words then: "base ball") team, the 1869 Cincinnati Red Stockings, who toured nationally, taking on challenges from local all-star teams. With Wright managing, at one stretch Cincinnati was undefeated in 90 consecutive matches. "Manager," rather than a term such as head coach, was a good title for Wright, because he was a combination business manager, sales promoter, traveling secretary, and, by the way, field captain. The term "manager" has survived, even though other executives are now responsible for administrative functions. Most baseball skippers admit to being proud of their title of manager. It helps set baseball apart from our other team sports.

Young men's interest in baseball back then had been stoked during the Civil War. At seemingly any opportunity during lulls in combat or at protected barracks sites, soldiers would round up comrades to play baseball on makeshift open fields. After the war thousands of former militiamen, North and South alike, maintained their interest in the game, and town teams proliferated rapidly. Not only was baseball the nation's leading organized form of athletics, it was also a swiftly accelerating spectator sport. Soon after Wright's Cincinnati club captured public attention, the loosely constructed National Association, the first league with standings and an attempt at formal scheduling, operated from 1871 through 1875. Twenty-four different teams played in the National Association at one time or another, some for less than a full season. All were East Coast and Midwest entries. Only three—the New York Mutuals, Philadelphia Athletics, and Boston Red Stockings—remained in business for each of the association's five years. Most—the Elizabeth Resolutes, Middletown Mansfields, and Keokuk Westerns, for example—came and went in just one season, or less.

Wright and Spalding had known each other from an earlier season when

Spalding led his Rockford, Illinois, locals to a rare victory over Wright's Red Stockings. When the National Association formed, Wright was tapped to pilot Boston, and he signed Spalding to his roster. In those days teams seldom carried more than a dozen players and usually used the same pitcher in almost every game. Schedules then were shorter, and games were rarely played on back-to-back days. Both men were ambitious, had entreprenurial talents, and shared a dream of a more formally constructed professional league. Wright and Spalding were gentlemanly and dignified, and they believed that, to attract solid citizens to its box offices, baseball must clean up its act. They knew that an overabundance of rowdy characters populated most of the rosters back then. Their design for a new league included signing only "clean-living gentlemen" (who, of course, happened to possess excellent athletic skills). As you might expect, though, an occasional playboy or two slipped in anyway! In concert with Chicago businessman William Hulbert, who would become the circuit's second president, Wright and Spalding were largely responsible for creating the National League. Its initial season was 1876. Wright was Boston's first NL manager; Spalding was assigned to manage the league's Chicago club. The National League has been open for business ever since.

Spalding was a pitcher and Wright an outfielder, but by 1876 their playing careers were nearly over. They had been player-managers before that, a typical circumstance then and on into the 1900s. More about that in our Player-Manager chapter. While Wright played in only two games in the NL's first two seasons, Spalding was the ace of Chicago's 1876 staff. He pitched in 61 of his team's 66 games that year, winning 47 of them. All right, teams played an average of only once every three days back then. Still, compared to today's five-man starting rotations and the rarity of pitching complete games, those men of a hundred and more years ago put on quite a display of strength and durability. By the way, Spalding's ERA in 1876 was 1.75. And he batted .312.

After 1877 he retired from the dugout but then spent nearly 20 years as president of the White Stockings (forerunners of the team we now know as the Cubs). And he continued to be a major figure in official National League matters. Spalding attempted to suppress a revolt that resulted in players' mass exodus to the Brotherhood, or Players, League in 1890, but he failed in that effort. Even though the Players League lasted for just one season, it was considered to have been a major league. (The pre-1901 managers list that follows includes men who piloted Brotherhood teams.)

Spalding's and Wright's 1876 clubs are the only two National League entries still surviving from that inaugural season. The Cubs, of course, remain in Chicago; the Boston franchise has since moved to Milwaukee, then to Atlanta.

While Spalding gave up field managing to handle administrative matters, and to join his brother, Walter, in starting the ultrasuccessful sporting goods business that still bears the Spalding name, Harry Wright continued to build his solid reputation as a manager. He was one of the game's first proponents of instruction, detailed preparation, and defense as vital ingredients of winning baseball. Wright's Boston club won two National League pennants and finished second another time during his six seasons in Massachusetts. Later, managing through 1893 (two years at Providence and 10 with the Phillies), he never won another pennant but consistently directed his teams to first-division finishes. His overall record, beginning in 1876, was 1,000–825, an excellent .548 winning percentage. Gene Mauch, with a 1,331 figure, holds the Phillies' franchise record for most games managed; Wright's 1,227 games (636 of them victories) rank second. During the 1890 season at Philadelphia, Wright was afflicted with blindness. It turned out to be temporary, but it forced him to miss 65 midseason games. In first place when he was sidelined, the team had dropped from the league lead by the time he returned.

Wright managed for three more years, then was dismissed when the Phillies' ownership grew weary of the team's failure to win the pennant despite its nearly annual contention. A year later he died and was buried near Philadelphia, where his tombstone bears the inscription "The Father of Baseball."

Out in Chicago, when Spalding relinquished his managership, he was replaced for one year by a man with baseball's most unusual nickname, Bob "Death to Flying Things" Ferguson. Then along came Adrian Anson, another Hall of Fame member, who guided Chicago to five pennants and five runner-up finishes during his 19 years as skipper, the fourth-longest managing stretch with one team in National League history—behind only John McGraw, Walter Alston, and Tom Lasorda.

Cap, the nickname forever associated with Anson, is short for "captain." Anson was a standout first baseman who batted .329 lifetime and played in more than 2,000 of the games he managed. As player-manager he led by example, as a captain should. Not only managers came and went during Anson's tenure (the National League listed 112 managers in the century's last quarter); so did three entire leagues. We've already noted the one year (1890) of the Players League existence, with such teams as the Brooklyn Wonders and Pittsburgh Burghers. Before that the Union Association, in 1884, billed its 13 teams as a major league. But the most formidable major opposition to the National League was the American Association, operating from 1882 through 1891, and coexisting relatively peacefully with the National League. The two circuits worked together on what became known as the National Agreement, in a successful effort to put the short-lived Union Association out of business. They agreed on the reserve-clause structure (players remained under contract indefinitely) to curtail league jumping, and they staged postseason series between their champions in something of a lukewarm prelude to what we know as the World Series.

Many of the prominent managers between 1876 and 1900 piloted teams in more than one of that era's four major leagues. Charlie Comiskey is a good example. Remembered mainly as an American League founder and longtime chief executive of the White Sox (two Chicago ballparks have been named for him), Comiskey twice managed St. Louis of the American Association, the Players League's 1890 Chicago entry, and Cincinnati in the National League for three years. His St. Louis Browns won four straight AA pennants, helping to propel Comiskey's lifetime winning percentage to .608.

A fellow named Bill Barnie managed for 14 years before 1900, mainly with the American Association's Baltimore club. Following the AA's disbanding after 1891, Barnie skippered three teams in the National League.

Ned Hanlon, a 1996 Hall of Fame inductee and once a Players League manager, earned notoriety for developing the National League's Baltimore Orioles into what was considered by many as baseball's best team prior to the 20th century. Hanlon had a modest playing career, 13 seasons, mostly as an outfielder. As an instructor and motivator, however, he excelled. His planning and strategy focused on "inside baseball"—hit-and-run, stolen bases, tight defense centered on infield teamwork, strong pitching, and, to the disgust of opponents, badgering and taunting. Hanlon's leadership led to success in the standings and served as a fundamental foundation for the managing techniques of several Old Orioles players who would become prominent managers themselves, men such as McGraw, Hughie Jennings, Wilbert Robinson, and Joe Kelley.

However, lengthy managing careers with only one team were rare in those days. The relatively stable employment of Anson, Harry Wright, Hanlon, Barnie, Comiskey, and Boston's John Morrill and Frank Selee was unusual. More typical were other pilots of the time, men such as "Death to Flying Things" Ferguson, 11 years, six teams in two leagues; Frank Bancroft, eight years, six teams; the long-forgotten John Clapp, five National League teams in five seasons; Gus Schmelz, five teams and two leagues in 11 seasons; Bill Watkins, 12 years, five clubs from two leagues; and Ted Sullivan, a native of Ireland, who managed four teams, in three different leagues, in only three years. From 1876 through 1900 an astounding total of 171 different men managed major league teams. Many of them piloted several clubs, as we've seen, and nearly 30 worked in two leagues or more.

Only one man in history—pre-1901 and then later—managed in as many as four major leagues. He was Tom Loftus, and this is his resumé: Union Association—1884 Milwaukee; American Association—1888 Cleveland; National League—1889 Cleveland, 1890–91 Cincinnati, 1900–1901 Chicago; American League—Washington 1901–3. One season over .500. Two first-division finishes. Winning percentage of .439. (The recycling of managers today is minuscule compared with that of a century ago, in spite of notions to the contrary.)

Most of the managers in those late-1800s seasons were discarded as soon as an owner saw his team slip in the standings, experienced even a slight decrease in box office business, or simply decided that one of his team's members would be a more dynamic leader as player-manager than his current player-manager. Whims and personality quirks often dictated such ownership decisions.

Conversely, a few managers of modest achievement were forever eager to jump to another team for a better paycheck. Arthur Irwin was notorious for that. Over a span of only eight seasons he signed managing contracts a half dozen times—three with Washington, alone, then of the National League. He also led the Phillies and Giants and earned his only claim to success by managing Boston to the 1891 American Association championship.

Irwin not only jumped teams with regularity. He also, it is assumed, jumped ship. Literally, and under mysterious and unconfirmed circumstances. At age 63, 22 years after he had last managed, Irwin's body was found in the Atlantic Ocean soon after he booked passage on a steamship from New York to Boston. After the apparent suicide was reported, it was alleged that Mr. Irwin had been leading a double life with wives and families in both New York and Boston. On the ball field too many double plays against you can drive a manager to distraction, maybe even get him fired. But a double life, as we see with Arthur Irwin, can be an even bigger problem.

The Federal League

Like a boxer's TKO victim, the Federal League staggered helplessly at the end. It was less than two years old. The names of its major components are long forgotten, along with its achievements. It had grand intentions, but it was ambushed by some schizophrenic economics and a briskly brewing world war.

Although this book is designed to focus on the exploits of every man who managed in the American and National leagues since 1901, it is important, from a historical perspective, to acknowledge the 20th century's major league

Text continues on page 34

The National League, formed in 1876 = NL; American Association, 1882–91 = AA; Players League, 1890 = P; Union Association, 1884 = U.

Manager	Years	Team	League
Bob Addy	1877	Cincinnati	NL
Bob Allen	1890	Philadelphia	NL
	1900	Cincinnati	NL
Cap Anson	1879–97	Chicago	NL
	1898	New York	NL
Frank Bancroft	1880	Worcester	NL
	1881–82	Detroit	NL
	1883	Cleveland	NL
	1884–85	Providence	NL
	1887	Philadelphia	AA
	1889	Indianapolis	NL
	(also see listing after 1900)		
Sam Barkley	1888	Kansas City	AA
Billy Barnie	1883–91	Baltimore	AA
	1892	Washington	NL
	1893–94	Louisville	NL
	1897–98	Brooklyn	NL
Joe Battin	1883–84	Pittsburgh	AA
	1884	Pittsburgh	U
Bickerson	1884	Washington	AA
(first name unknown)			
Tommy Bond	1882	Worcester	NL:
Freeman Brown	1882	Worcester	NL
Tom Brown	1897–98	Washington	NL
Al Buckenberger	1888–90	Columbus	AA
	1892–94	Pittsburgh	NL
	1895	St. Louis	NL
	(also see listing after 1900)		
Charlie Buffington	1890	Philadelphia	P
Jack Burdock	1883	Boston	NL
Watch Burnham	1887	Indianapolis	NL
Tom Burns	1892	Pittsburgh	NL
	1898–99	Chicago	NL
Ormand Butler	1883	Pittsburgh	AA
Charlie Byrne	1885–87	Brooklyn	AA
Bill Cammeyer	1876	New York	NL
Count Campau	1890	St. Louis	AA
Bob Caruthers	1892	St. Louis	NL
Ollie Caylor	1885–86	Cincinnati	AA
	1887	New York	AA

Continued

Manager	Years	Team	League
Jack Chapman	1876–77, '92	Louisville	NL
	1878	Milwaukee	NL
	1882	Worcester	NL
	1883–84	Detroit	NL
	1885	Buffalo	NL
	1889–91	Louisville	AA
John Clapp	1878	Indianapolis	NL
	1879	Buffalo	NL
	1880	Cincinnati	NL
	1881	Cleveland	NL
	1883	New York	NL
Fred Clarke	1897–99	Louisville	NL
	1900	Pittsburgh	NL
	(also see listing after 1900)		
Jack Clements	1890	Philadelphia	NL
Charles Comiskey	1883–89, '91	St. Louis	AA
	1890	Chicago	P
	1892–94	Cincinnati	NL
Roger Connor	1896	St. Louis	NL
Sam Crane	1880	Buffalo	NL
	1884	Cincinnati	U
George Creamer	1884	Pittsburgh	AA
Jack Crooks	1892	St. Louis	NL
Lave Cross	1899	Cleveland	NL
Ed Curtis	1884	Altoona	U
Charlie Cushman	1881	Milwaukee	AA
Ned Cuthbert	1882	St. Louis	AA
Mordecai Davidson	1888	Louisville	AA
George Davis	1895, 1900	New York	NL
	(also see listing after 1900)		
John Day	1899	New York	NL
Harry Diddlebock	1896	St. Louis	NL
Patsy Donovan	1897, '99	Pittsburgh	NL
	(also see listing after 1900)		
Mike Dorgan	1879	Syracuse	NL
	1880	Providence	NL
	1881	Worcester	NL
Tommy Dowd	1896–97	St. Louis	NL
Jack Doyle	1895	New York	NL
	1898	Washington	NL
Fred Dunlap	1882	Cleveland	NL
	1884	St. Louis	U

Continued

29

Manager	Years	Team	League
Fred Dunlap	1885	St. Louis	NL
	1889	Pittsburgh	NL
Charlie Ebbetts	1898	Brooklyn	NL
Joe Ellick	1884	Pittsburgh	U
Dude Esterbrook	1889	Louisville	AA
Buck Ewing	1890	New York	P
	1895–99	Cincinnati	NL
	1900	New York	NL
Jay Faatz	1890	Buffalo	P
Jack Farrell	1881	Providence	NL
Bob Ferguson	1876–77	Hartford	NL
	1878	Chicago	NL
	1879–82	Troy	NL
	1883	Philadelphia	NL
	1884	Pittsburgh	AA
	1886–87	New York	AA
Wally Fessenden	1890	Syracuse	AA
Silver Flint	1879	Chicago	NL
Jim Fogarty	1890	Philadelphia	P
Horace Fogel	1887	Indianapolis	NL
	(also see listing after 1900)		
Dave Foutz	1893–96	Brooklyn	NL
George Frazer	1890	Syracuse	AA
John Gaffney	1886–87	Washington	NL
Pud Galvin	1885	Buffalo	NL
Joe Gerhardt	1883	Louisville	AA
	1890	St. Louis	AA
Jim Gifford	1884	Indianapolis	AA
	1885–86	New York	AA
Jack Glasscock	1889	Indianapolis	NL
	1892	St. Louis	NL
George Gore	1892	St. Louis	NL
Charlie Gould	1876	Cincinnati	NL
Mase Graffen	1876	St. Louis	NL
Mike Griffin	1898	Brooklyn	NL
Sandy Griffin	1891	Washington	AA
Charlie Hackett	1884	Cleveland	NL
	1885	Brooklyn	AA
Bill Hallman	1897	St. Louis	NL
Ned Hanlon	1889, '91	Pittsburgh	NL
	1890	Pittsburgh	P
	1892–98	Baltimore	NL

Continued

Manager	Years	Team	League
Ned Hanlon	1899–1900	Brooklyn	NL
	(also see listing after 1900)		
Jim Hart	1885–86	Louisville	AA
	1889	Boston	NL
Guy Hecker	1890	Pittsburgh	NL
Louie Heilbroner	1900	St. Louis	NL
Bill Henderson	1884	Baltimore	U
Ed Hengle	1884	Chicago	U
Walter Hewett	1888	Washington	NL
Fred Hoey	1899	New York	NL
Bill Holbert	1879	Syracuse	NL
Holly Hollingshead	1884	Washington	AA
Tim Hurst	1898	St. Louis	NL
Arthur Irwin	1889, '92, '98–'99	Washington	NL
	1891	Boston	AA
	1894–95	Philadelphia	NL
	1896	New York	NL
Bill Joyce	1896–98	New York	NL
John Kelly	1887–88	Louisville	AA
King Kelly	1887	Boston	NL
	1890	Boston	P
	1891	Cincinnati	AA
Jim Kennedy	1890	Brooklyn	AA
John Kerins	1888	Louisville	AA
	1890	St. Louis	AA
Lon Knight	1883–84	Philadelphia	AA
Henry Larkin	1890	Cleveland	P
Arlie Latham	1896	St. Louis	NL
Juice Latham	1882	Philadelphia	AA
Bob Leadley	1888	Detroit	NL
	1890–91	Cleveland	NL
Tom Loftus	1884	Milwaukee	U
	1888	Cleveland	AA
	1889	Cleveland	NL
	1890–91	Cincinnati	NL
	1900	Chicago	NL
	(also see listing after 1900)		
Connie Mack	1894–96	Pittsburgh	NL
	(also see listing after 1900)		
Denny Mack	1882	Louisville	AA
Jimmy Macullar	1879	Syracuse	NL
Fergy Malone	1884	Philadelphia	U

Continued

Manager	Years	Team	League
Jack Manning	1877	Cincinnati	NL
Charlie Mason	1887	Philadelphia	AA
Tommy McCarthy	1890	St. Louis	AA
Jim McCormick	1879–80, '82	Cleveland	NL
Mike McGeary	1880	Providence	NL
	1881	Cleveland	NL
John McGraw	1899	Baltimore	NL
	(also see listing after 1900)		
Deacon McGuire	1898	Washington	NL
	(also see listing after 1900)		
Bill McGunnigle	1888–89	Brooklyn	AA
	1890	Brooklyn	NL
	1891	Pittsburgh	NL
	1896	Louisville	NL
Alex McKinnon	1885	St. Louis	NL
Denny McKnight	1884	Pittsburgh	AA
George McManus	1876–77	St. Louis	NL
Cal McVey	1878–79	Cincinnati	NL
Doggie Miller	1894	St. Louis	NL
John Morrill	1882–88	Boston	NL
	1889	Washington	NL
Charlie Morton	1884, '90	Toledo	AA
	1885	Detroit	NL
Felix Moses	1884	Richmond	AA
Jim Mutrie	1883–84	New York	AA
	1885–91	New York	NL
Henry Myers	1882	Baltimore	AA
Billy Nash	1896	Philadelphia	NL
Hugh Nicol	1897	St. Louis	NL
Dan O'Leary	1884	Cincinnati	U
Jim O'Rourke	1881–84	Buffalo	NL
	1893	Washington	NL
Dave Orr	1887	New York	AA
Fred Pfeffer	1892	Louisville	NL
Lew Phelan	1895	St. Louis	NL
Horace Phillips	1879	Troy	NL
	1883	Columbus	AA
	1884–86	Pittsburgh	AA
	1887–89	Pittsburgh	NL
Lip Pike	1877	Cincinnati	NL
Matt Porter	1884	Kansas City	U

Continued

Manager	Years	Team	League
Pat Powers	1890	Rochester	AA
	1892	New York	NL
Al Pratt	1882–83	Pittsburgh	AA
Jim Price	1884	New York	NL
Blondie Purcell	1883	Philadelphia	NL
Joe Quinn	1895	St. Louis	NL
	1899	Cleveland	NL
Al Reach	1890	Philadelphia	NL
Jim Rogers	1897	Louisville	NL
Chief Roseman	1890	St. Louis	AA
Dave Rowe	1886	Kansas City	NL
	1888	Kansas City	AA
Jack Rowe	1890	Buffalo	P
Mike Scanlon	1884	Washington	U
	1886	Washington	NL
Gus Schmelz	1884, '90–'91	Columbus	AA
	1886	St. Louis	NL
	1887–89	Cincinnati	AA
	1890	Cleveland	NL
	1894–97	Washington	NL
Frank Selee	1890–1900	Boston	NL
	(also see listing after 1900)		
Dan Shannon	1889	Louisville	AA
	1891	Washington	AA
Bill Sharsig	1886, '88–'91	Philadelphia	AA
Bill Shettsline	1898–1900	Philadelphia	NL
	(also see listing after 1900)		
Joe Simmons	1884	Wilmington	U
Lew Simmons	1886	Philadelphia	AA
Pop Snyder	1882–84	Cincinnati	AA
	1891	Washington	AA
Al Spalding	1876–77	Chicago	NL
Harry Spence	1888	Indianapolis	NL
George Stallings	1897–98	Philadelphia	NL
	(also see listing after 1900)		
Harry Stovey	1881	Worcester	NL
	1885	Philadelphia	AA
Cub Stricker	1892	St. Louis	NL
Pat Sullivan	1890	Columbus	AA
Ted Sullivan	1883	St. Louis	AA
	1884	St. Louis	U
	1884	Kansas City	U
	1888	Washington	NL

Continued

MAJOR LEAGUE MANAGERS, 1876–1900 (continued)

Manager	Years	Team	League
George Taylor	1884	Brooklyn	AA
Patsy Tebeau	1890	Cleveland	P
	1891–98	Cleveland	NL
	1899–1900	St. Louis	NL
Fred Thomas	1887	Indianapolis	NL
Andrew Thompson	1884	St. Paul	U
Sam Trott	1891	Washington	AA
George Van Haltren	1892	Baltimore	NL
Chris Von Der Ahe	· 1895–97	St. Louis	NL
Mike Walsh	1884	Louisville	AA
John Waltz	1892	Baltimore	NL
Monte Ward	1880	Providence	NL
	1884, '93–'94	New York	NL
	1890	Brooklyn	P
	1891–92	Brooklyn	NL
Bill Watkins	1884	Indianapolis	AA
	1885–88	Detroit	NL
	1888–89	Kansas City	AA
	1893	St. Louis	NL
	1898–99	Pittsburgh	NL
Harvey Watkins	1895	New York	NL
Harry Wheeler	1884	Kansas City	U
Deacon White	1879	Cincinnati	NL
Will White	1884	Cincinnati	AA
Jimmy Williams	1884	St. Louis	AA
	1987–88	Cleveland	AA
Chicken Wolf	1889	Louisville	AA
George Wood	1891	Philadelphia	AA
Al Wright	1876	Philadelphia	NL
George Wright	1879	Providence	NL
Harry Wright	1876–81	Boston	NL
	1882–83	Providence	NL
	1884–93	Philadelphia	NL
Tom York	1878, '81	Providence	NL

"pretender," the Federal League, established in eight cities in 1914. Its operators believed that growing fan enthusiasm for baseball could support their new venture. They also were aware that many players had complained of greediness on the part of certain penurious owners, and they vowed to deliver bigger paychecks to those who would agree to bolt the American and National leagues to sign on with the Feds. But relatively few prime stars defected, and after two seasons the Federal League was out of business.

Baltimore, Indianapolis, Kansas City, and Buffalo were the localities in which the Federal League restored "major league" baseball for the first time in more than a decade. The other four clubs in the eight- team circuit went head to head with the established majors in Chicago, Brooklyn, St. Louis, and Pittsburgh. One reflection of the new league's shaky footing was the franchise shift of its pennant winner after that first season, 1914. Indianapolis moved to New Jersey to become the Newark Peppers, or, as they were commonly called, the Peps. If that was something of a wacky nickname, how about the Chicago Chi-Feds who were saddled in their second season with the glamorless moniker of Whales, the Buffalo Buffeds, or the Brooklyn Tip-Tops?

Most of the Federal franchises were financially troubled throughout those two seasons. Teams in Chicago, Brooklyn, Pittsburgh, and St. Louis failed to elicit significant defections in fan loyalty from their American and National League competition, although the Federal League did, indeed, upset major

FEDERAL LEAGUE MANGERS

Manager	Years	Team
Otto Knabe	1914–15	BALTIMORE Terrapins
Bill Bradley	1914	BROOKLYN Tip-Tops
Lee Magee	1915	
John Ganzel	1915	
Harry Schlafly	1914	BUFFALO Buffeds
Harry Schlafly	1915	Blues
Walter Blair		
Harry Lord		
Joe Tinker	1914	CHICAGO Chi-Feds
Joe Tinker*	1915	Whales
Bill Phillips†	1914	INDIANAPOLIS Hoosiers
		franchise transferred to
Bill Phillips	1915	NEWARK Peppers
Bill McKechnie	1915	
George Stovall	1914–15	KANSAS CITY Packers
Doc Gessler	1914	PITTSBURGH Rebels
Rebel Oakes	1914	
Rebel Oakes	1915	
Three Finger Brown	1914	ST. LOUIS Terriers
Fielder Jones	1914	
Fielder Jones	1915	

†1914 pennant winner
*1915 pennant winner

league owners whenever an occasional headliner jumped to the upstart circuit. As we have seen throughout baseball history, and particularly during the past quarter century of labor-management disputes, economics rule baseball decision making and policies. After the Federal's 1915 season ended, an agreement was reached whereby the American and National Leagues would provide each Federal League team with a buy-out package if the Feds would terminate their operation. Having found that their enterprise was not especially profitable, Federal officials closed their ballparks—some of them spartan and makeshift—for good. One exception was Chicago's Weeghman Field, the Windy City's Federal League home. With the team's departure, the Chicago Cubs took over the ballpark. That storied arena, still in business, is "beautiful" Wrigley Field.

Fifteen different managers led the eight Federal franchises during their brief two-year existence. Some of them—Bill Bradley, Joe Tinker, Bill McKechnie, George Stovall, John Ganzel, and Fielder Jones—managed previously or later in the American or National leagues. Jones, in 1906, had directed the White Sox to their first World Series championship. The legendary McKechnie was one of only two men to guide three different teams to the World Series. He is enshrined in the managers' section of baseball's Hall of Fame. His first skippering assignment? The 1915 Newark Peps of the Federal League.

A pilot of minimal distinction headed the Pittsburgh club for awhile. He is remembered in Federal League archives not so much for his performance as for his name: Rebel Oakes . . . of the Pittsburgh Rebels . . . of a long-ago rebel baseball league.

All the Teams' Men

April 1901 at first glance was pretty much like any other April before or since—time for "Play ball!" in the big leagues.

That 1901 springtime was a little different, though, because for the first time the well-established National League was getting some major competition. The upstart American League opened its doors for the first time as a self-proclaimed major league. New job opportunities were suddenly available, among them, more field manager posts.

Ninety-eight years later the American and National Leagues are still in business (increasingly more "business," in fact, than sport). Those 16 managerships have multiplied to more than 400 big-league pilots during major league baseball's evolution from a pair of eight-team circuits in 1901 to nearly double that number of teams today, with each league divided into quasiregional divisions and the experimentation with interleague play come to fruition.

Over the course of nearly a hundred years the original 16 franchises are still active, although seven have been involved in geographic transfers—the National League's Braves, Dodgers, and Giants; and in the American, the Athletics twice, the original Senators, the Browns (nee first-edition Brewers), and the Yankees, who first saw light of day as the 1901–02 Baltimore Orioles. So have some of the additions, notably the short-lived Seattle Pilots of 1969 to Milwaukee a year later, and the expansion Washington club to Dallas–Ft. Worth as the Texas Rangers. We've even seen a franchise transfer between leagues recently when the Brewers went from American to National.

The Dodgers, in both Brooklyn and Los Angeles, have provided their managers with significantly greater stability than their brethren among the original 16 and the expansionists. Only 18 men (about half the average of the other teams since 1901) have been assigned manager jobs by the Dodgers. Two of them, Walter Alston and Tom Lasorda, were in harness more than 20 years each; Wilbert Robinson directed the Brooklyn dugout for nearly two decades. The New York Yankees, prior to the ownership era of George Steinbrenner, also retained their pilots for relatively long periods of time. Of course, the renewed contracts continually extended to pilots such as Miller Huggins, Joe McCarthy, and Casey Stengel reflected the success of those teams and their leaders. Other teams—the Phillies, Indians, Cubs, and White Sox come to mind—have rarely achieved consistent on-field brilliance, so it is not surprising that the accompanying lists show those clubs with a relatively frequent succession of managers. (The old adage, remember? It's easier to dispose of the manager than it is to fire your 25 players!)

An examination of the year-by-year managing charts of all 30 franchises this century, along with a study of the managers listed alphabetically elsewhere in this book, refutes the "musical chairs" belief that a small group of men—once admitted to the fraternity of managers—are simply recycled from one town to another after they've worn out their owners' welcomes. Just a handful fuels that erroneous perception—Dick Williams, Jimmie Dykes, and John McNamara as leaders of six different teams; Billy Martin employed by five clubs, including the Yankees on five separate occasions; and a dozen or so men with as many as four different clubs. The continual hiring of veteran skippers is infrequent, but whenever it occurs it is probably because of their abilities and the generally high esteem in which they are held rather than the good ol' boys' network in action. Far more prevalent have been the one-term managers with just one or two managerships during their careers. Of this century's 400-plus major league skippers, only about one-fourth have piloted more than two teams—most, in fact, managed only a single club. Sometimes, as was Billy Martin in New York, organization favorites are persuaded to return to the scene of earlier and popular successes. Red Schoendienst, who held the Cardinals' managing post longer than any other man in the team's history, twice returned as an interim pilot. Earl Weaver, in Baltimore, is another instance of a returning hero's "reupping," as is Danny Murtaugh at Pittsburgh. All three never managed elsewhere.

Rogers Hornsby, who was a pennant winner with the Cardinals in his first managing job—but never finished in first place again as a manager—technically joins Williams, Dykes, and McNamara with six different clubs to his skippering credit. He started with the Redbirds, then managed the Boston Braves, the Chicago Cubs, the St. Louis Browns twice, and Cincinnati (where general manager Warren Giles would confide later that the hiring of Hornsby as manager was his biggest mistake). After winning the Cardinals' first of 15 National League championships in 1926, player-manager Hornsby was traded to the Giants for second baseman Frankie Frisch (who would eventually manage three clubs, including the pennant-winning Cardinals of 1934). During Hornsby's only season in New York (1927), veteran manager John McGraw took ill after 122 games and named Hornsby to succeed him. McGraw's health and his enthusiasm for managing were soon renewed, and he returned for the 1928 season after trading Hornsby to the Boston Braves. History considers Hornsby's leadership of the Giants an interim assignment, so New York goes on his official record as one of six teams managed.

The team charts that follow offer some suprises, and they suggest a century's worth of patterns. Among the trends is this one: Teams that replace managers seldom advance or decline much in the standings immediately. The team's roster has not been altered appreciably, and tones and attitudes are already established. New directions, with few exceptions, are gradual if perceptible at all. In short, the team still plays about the same as it did when its previous boss commanded the dugout. One exception is, again, Billy Martin. Another was Steve O'Neill, a prominent figure in this book's spotlight on overlooked or underrated managers. Martin invariably turned his new clubs into dramatically improved combines. In his first managership, with the 1969 Twins, he took his team to the American League West title after it had ranked seventh the year before with essentially the same players. Then, as the Detroit chart shows, Martin, in his second big-league piloting job, advanced the Tigers rapidly to a division title. His next assignment, Texas, did not result in a championship, but the team showed marked improvement during Martin's first full season there. His 84–76 record in 1974 brought the Rangers home second, the highest finish, to that point, in the franchise's 14-year history. Martin's first of five tenures at Yankee Stadium was relatively serene (in comparison with his four return engagements) and featured his only pennant-winning achievements. He led the Yankees into the 1976 and 1977 World Series. The first of those represented the team's first American League championship in 12 years—its longest pennant drought since 1901 through 1920. Between his second and third Yankee stints, Martin led the Oakland Athletics to the 1981 West

Division crown after having directed his first A's team, the 1980 squad, to a significant 29-game improvement over the 1979 Athletics' record.

Those Athletics were formed in Philadelphia when the American League got underway as a major league in 1901. Connie Mack, their manager during 50 seasons (1901–50), and the chief executive for most of those years, is generally thought to have led the A's without interruption for that half century. Technically, that is not so. In both 1937 and 1939 Connie Mack developed serious illnesses that forced him into lengthy recuperations before his return to the dugout. In each of those seasons he assigned his son Earle, who also served as a Philadelphia coach at the time, to be the team's interim manager. When Connie's health returned each time, so did he. But let the record show that his unprecedented and never-to-be equaled 50-year American League managing was not without interruption.

Mack's contemporary, John McGraw, also took leaves of absence, with Hornsby as his fill-in in 1927 and with his Old Oriole pal Hughie Jennings taking over in 1924 for awhile. Jennings and McGraw had met as players under Baltimore manager Ned Hanlon in the 1890s, when the scrappy Orioles were part of the 12-team National League. This pair of tough Irishmen quickly learned and favored the "inside baseball" taught by Hanlon. Later, during early springs, they co-coached the St. Bonaventure College baseball team. Eventually they achieved national fame as major league managers. Jennings, who was Ty Cobb's first manager, led Detroit to its first American League pennants in the consecutive seasons of 1907, 1908, and 1909. He piloted the Tigers through 1920, when he was replaced by Cobb. McGraw, widely known for his frequent outbursts of unsportsmanlike conduct and his aggressive behavior on the field as player and then as manager, was a decidedly different man away from the diamond when baseball matters were not involved. There he was often a welcomed and popular social companion, especially in mixed company, and was considered something of a soft touch with a sensitivity for old friends, and new too, who had fallen into medical or financial misfortune. One of them was long time compatriot Jennings. In failing health (recent years of hard drinking had been a key contributor), Jennings resigned in 1920 after 14 years as manager at Detroit. Soon after, McGraw signed him to a Giants coach's contract. Then, in 1924, when a serious leg injury sidelined McGraw with more than half of the season remaining, he assigned the team to Jennings—more healthy and enthusiastic than he had been in 1920—for what became 44 games during the boss's absence. That interim post was Jennings's final managing job, and he successfully posted a 32–12 record and elevated the Giants to first place, where they would remain under McGraw for the rest of the year. Jennings died with tuberculosis in 1928.

The following rosters of teams' managers will list Jennings and all other interim pilots, because during their brief assignments they were fully and officially in charge. Some interim skippers served for as little as a single game, some for upwards of a half season. Not included are those men who have been designated "acting" managers, but not interim managers. Typical among them are men who took the controls briefly when the full-time pilot had been ejected from a game, was ill for a short time, or asked for time off to attend to pressing personal matters.

Every team's records that follow include the primary statistics of each manager who has directed their dugouts this century. If there is a single repetitive theme, it is this: Big-league baseball managing is but a very brief interlude in a man's life. More than 400 men have managed, for an average of less than six years per career. And that includes the men who've directed more than one team, and the Macks, McGraws, Alstons, Lasordas, Bucky Harrises, and others with well more than a decade of service. In analyzing every team's pattern of hiring and terminating managers, you find that the average length of each tenure—per man, per team—is a mere 3.15 years.

As the 1998 season began, the manager with the most consecutive seasons directing the same club was Minnesota's Tom Kelly, a 12-year veteran with two World Championship rings to his credit. Next was Atlanta's Bobby Cox, eight successive seasons as Braves pilot. At the other end of the longevity scale we find solid evidence that the "musical chairs/old boys' club" notion is imaginary because 15 men—Tim Johnson, Mike Hargrove, Buddy Bell, Kelly, Jerry Manuel, Tony Muser, Phil Garner, Felipe Alou, Terry Francona, Larry Dierker, Bill Russell, Dusty Baker, Larry Rothschild, Don Baylor, and Bruce Bochy—were in their first terms with their very first big-league managing assignments.

Note: If a team had more than one manager in a particular season, the figure in parentheses (x) after a man's name denotes the team's standing following the last game he managed. End-of-season standings positions and games-behind statistics are listed after the name of the man who was the team's official manager at season's end.

National League Teams and Managers

Year	Manager	W	L	NL West	Games Behind
1998	Buck Showalter	65	97	5th	33

ATLANTA Braves 1966–98
MILWAUKEE Braves 1953–65
BOSTON Braves 1901–52

(Also known as Boston Beaneaters to 1906; Doves, 1907–10; Rustlers, 1911; Bees 1936–40.)

Year	Manager	W	L	NL Rank	Games Behind
BOSTON					
1901	Frank Selee	69	69	5th	20.5
02	Al Buckenberger	73	64	3rd	29
03	Al Buckenberger	58	80	6th	32
04	Al Buckenberger	55	98	7th	51
05	Fred Tenney	51	103	7th	54.5
06	Fred Tenney	49	102	8th	66.5
07	Fred Tenney	58	90	7th	47
08	Joe Kelley	63	91	6th	36
09	Harry Smith	23	54	(8th)	
	Frank Bowerman	22	54	8th	65.5
1910	Fred Lake	53	100	8th	50.5
11	Fred Tenney	44	107	8th	54
12	Johnny Kling	52	101	8th	52
13	George Stallings	69	82	5th	31.5
14	George Stallings	94	59	1st	—[a]
15	George Stallings	83	69	2nd	7
16	George Stallings	89	63	3rd	4
17	George Stallings	72	81	6th	25.5
18	George Stallings	53	71	7th	28.5
19	George Stallings	57	82	6th	38.5
1920	George Stallings	62	90	7th	30
21	Fred Mitchell	79	74	4th	15
22	Fred Mitchell	53	100	8th	39.5
23	Fred Mitchell	54	100	7th	41.5
24	Dave Bancroft	27	3	(6th)	
	Dick Rudolph	11	27	(8th)	
	Dave Bancroft	15	35	8th	40

Continued

Year	Manager	W	L	NL Rank	Games Behind
25	Dave Bancroft	70	83	5th	25
26	Dave Bancroft	66	86	7th	22
27	Dave Bancroft	60	94	7th	34
28	Jack Slattery	11	20	(7th)	
	Rogers Hornsby	39	83	7th	44.5
29	Judge Fuchs	56	98	8th	43
1930	Bill McKechnie	70	84	6th	22
31	Bill McKechnie	64	90	7th	37
32	Bill McKechnie	77	77	5th	13
33	Bill McKechnie	83	71	4th	9
34	Bill McKechnie	78	73	4th	16
35	Bill McKechnie	38	115	8th	61.5
36	Bill McKechnie	71	83	6th	21
37	Bill McKechnie	79	73	5th	16
38	Casey Stengel	77	75	5th	12
39	Casey Stengel	63	88	7th	32.5
1940	Casey Stengel	65	87	7th	34.5
41	Casey Stengel	62	92	7th	38
42	Casey Stengel	59	89	7th	44
43	Bob Coleman	21	25	(6th)	
	Casey Stengel	47	60	6th	36.5
44	Bob Coleman	65	89	6th	40
45	Bob Coleman	42	51	(7th)	
	Del Bissonette	25	34	6th	30
46	Billy Southworth	81	72	4th	15.5
47	Billy Southworth	86	68	3rd	8
48	Billy Southworth	91	62	1st	—b
49	Billy Southworth	55	54	(4th)	
	Johnny Cooney	20	25	4th	22
1950	Billy Southworth	83	71	4th	8
51	Billy Southworth	28	31	(5th)	
	Tommy Holmes	48	47	4th	20.5
52	Tommy Holmes	13	22	(6th)	
	Charlie Grimm	51	67	7th	32
MILWAUKEE					
1953	Charlie Grimm	92	62	2nd	13
54	Charlie Grimm	89	65	3rd	8
55	Charlie Grimm	85	69	2nd	13.5
56	Charlie Grimm	24	22	(5th)	
	Fred Haney	68	40	2nd	1
57	Fred Haney	95	59	1st	—c
58	Fred Haney	92	62	1st	—d

Continued

Year	Manager	W	L	NL Rank	Games Behind
59	Fred Haney	86	70	2nd	2[e]
1960	Chuck Dressen	88	66	2nd	7
61	Chuck Dressen	71	58	(3rd)	
	Birdie Tebbetts	12	13	4th	10
62	Birdie Tebbetts	86	76	5th	15.5
63	Bobby Bragan	84	78	6th	15
64	Bobby Bragan	88	74	5th	5
65	Bobby Bragan	86	76	5th	11
ATLANTA					
1966	Bobby Bragan	52	59	(5th)	
	Billy Hitchcock	33	18	5th	10
67	Billy Hitchcock	77	82	(7th)	
	Ken Silvestri	0	3	7th	24.5
68	Lum Harris	81	81	5th	16
	NL West				
69	Lum Harris	93	69	1st	—[f]
1970	Lum Harris	76	86	5th	26
71	Lum Harris	82	80	3rd	8
72	Lum Harris	47	57	(5th)	
	Eddie Mathews	23	27	4th	25
73	Eddie Mathews	76	85	5th	22.5
74	Eddie Mathews	50	49	(4th)	
	Clyde King	38	25	3rd	14
75	Clyde King	58	76	(5th)	
	Connie Ryan	9	18	5th	40.5
76	Dave Bristol	70	92	6th	32
77	Dave Bristol	8	21	(6th)	
	Ted Turner	0	1	(6th)	
	Vern Benson	1	0	(6th)	
	Dave Bristol	52	79	6th	37
78	Bobby Cox	69	93	6th	26
79	Bobby Cox	66	94	6th	23.5
1980	Bobby Cox	81	80	4th	11
81	Bobby Cox	50	56	5th	15
82	Joe Torre	89	73	1st	—[g]
83	Joe Torre	88	74	2nd	3
84	Joe Torre	80	82	2nd T	12
85	Eddie Haas	50	71	(5th)	
	Bobby Wine	16	25	5th	29
86	Chuck Tanner	72	89	6th	23.5
87	Chuck Tanner	69	92	5th	20.5
88	Chuck Tanner	12	27	(6th)	

Continued

Year	Manager	W	L	NL West	Games Behind
	Russ Nixon	42	79	6th	39.5
89	Russ Nixon	63	97	6th	28
1990	Russ Nixon	25	40	(6th)	
	Bobby Cox	40	57	6th	26
91	Bobby Cox	94	68	1st	—h
92	Bobby Cox	98	64	1st	—i
93	Bobby Cox	104	51	1st	—j
				NL East	
94	Bobby Cox	68	46	Season not completed	
95	Bobby Cox	90	54	1st	—k
96	Bobby Cox	96	66	1st	—l
97	Bobby Cox	101	61	1st	—m
98	Bobby Cox	106	56	1st	—n

[a]Defeated Philadelphia in World Series

[b]Lost to Cleveland in World Series

[c]Defeated New York in World Series

[d]Lost to New York in World Series

[e]Lost to Los Angeles in best-of-three playoff for NL title

[f]Lost to New York in NLCS

[g]Lost to St. Louis in NLCS

[h]Defeated Pittsburgh in NLCS; lost to Minnesota in World Series

[i]Defeated Pittsburgh in NLCS; lost to Toronto in World Series

[j]Lost to Philadelphia in NLCS

[k]Defeated Colorado in NLC first round; defeated Cincinnati in NLCS; defeated Cleveland in World Series

[l]Defeated Los Angeles in NLC first round; defeated St. Louis in NLCS; lost to New York in World Series

[m]Defeated Houston in NLC first round; lost to Florida in NLCS

[n]Defeated Chicago in NLC first round; lost to San Diego in NLCS

Manager Summary

Most seasons—Cox 13

Most games—Cox 1,910

Most wins—Cox 1,063

Most losses—Cox 846

NL pennants—Cox 4, Haney 2, Southworth 1, Stallings 1

Division titles—Cox 7, Harris 1, Torre 1

Multiple terms as manager—Bancroft 2, Bristol 2, Coleman 2, Cox 2, Southworth 2, Stengel 2, Tenney 2

Fewest games managed—Benson 1, Turner 1

Number of different managers—42

(Also known as Chicago Orphans, 1901.)

Year	Manager	W	L	NL Rank	Games Behind
1901	Tom Loftus	53	86	6th	37
02	Frank Selee	68	69	5th	34
03	Frank Selee	82	56	3rd	8
04	Frank Selee	93	60	2nd	13
05	Frank Selee	37	28	(4th)	
	Frank Chance	55	33	3rd	13
06	Frank Chance	116	36	1st	—a
07	Frank Chance	107	45	1st	—b
08	Frank Chance	99	55	1st	—c
09	Frank Chance	104	49	2nd	6.5
1910	Frank Chance	104	50	1st	—d
11	Frank Chance	92	62	2nd	7.5
12	Frank Chance	91	59	3rd	11.5
13	Johnny Evers	88	65	3rd	13.5
14	Hank O'Day	78	76	4th	16.5
15	Roger Bresnahan	73	80	4th	17.5
16	Joe Tinker	67	86	5th	26.5
17	Fred Mitchell	74	80	5th	24
18	Fred Mitchell	84	45	1st	—e
19	Fred Mitchell	75	65	3rd	21
1920	Fred Mitchell	75	79	5th T	18
21	Johnny Evers	41	55	(6th)	
	Bill Killefer	23	34	7th	30
22	Bill Killefer	80	74	5th	13
23	Bill Killefer	83	71	4th	12.5
24	Bill Killefer	81	72	5th	12
25	Bill Killefer	33	42	(7th)	
	Rabbit Maranville	23	30	(8th)	
	George Gibson	12	14	8th	27.5
26	Joe McCarthy	82	72	4th	7
27	Joe McCarthy	85	68	4th	8.5
28	Joe McCarthy	91	63	3rd	4
29	Joe McCarthy	98	54	1st	—f
1930	Joe McCarthy	86	64	(2nd)	
	Rogers Hornsby	4	0	2nd	2
31	Rogers Hornsby	84	70	3rd	17
32	Rogers Hornsby	53	46	(2nd)	
	Charlie Grimm	37	18	1st	—g
33	Charlie Grimm	86	68	3rd	6
34	Charlie Grimm	86	65	3rd	8
35	Charlie Grimm	100	54	1st	—h

Continued

Year	Manager	W	L	NL Rank	Games Behind
36	Charlie Grimm	87	67	2nd T	5
37	Charlie Grimm	93	61	2nd	3
38	Charlie Grimm	45	36	(3rd)	
	Gabby Hartnett	44	27	1st	⌐
39	Gabby Hartnett	84	70	4th	13
1940	Gabby Hartnett	75	79	5th	25.5
41	Jimmie Wilson	70	84	6th	30
42	Jimmie Wilson	68	86	6th	38
43	Jimmie Wilson	74	79	5th	30.5
44	Jimmie Wilson	1	9	(8th)	
	Roy Johnson	0	1	(8th)	
	Charlie Grimm	74	69	4th	30
45	Charlie Grimm	98	56	1st	⌐
46	Charlie Grimm	82	71	3rd	14.5
47	Charlie Grimm	69	85	6th	25
48	Charlie Grimm	64	90	8th	27.5
49	Charlie Grimm	19	31	(8th)	
	Frank Frisch	42	62	8th	36
1950	Frank Frisch	64	89	7th	26.5
51	Frank Frisch	35	45	(7th)	
	Phil Cavaretta	27	47	8th	34.5
52	Phil Cavaretta	77	77	5th	19.5
53	Phil Cavaretta	65	89	7th	40
54	Stan Hack	64	90	7th	33
55	Stan Hack	72	81	6th	26
56	Stan Hack	60	94	8th	33
57	Bob Scheffing	62	92	7th T	33
58	Bob Scheffing	72	82	5th T	20
59	Bob Scheffing	74	80	5th T	13
1960	Charlie Grimm	6	11	(8th)	
	Lou Boudreau	54	83	7th	35
61	HEAD COACHES: Harry Craft 7–9, Vedie Himsl 10–21, Lou Klein 5–6, El Tappe 42–54	64	90	7th	29
62	HEAD COACHES: Lou Klein 12–18, Charlie Metro 43–69, El Tappe 4–16	59	103	9th	42.5
63	HEAD COACH: Bob Kennedy	82	80	7th	17

Continued

Year	Manager	W	L	NL Rank	Games Behind
64	HEAD COACH:				
	Bob Kennedy	76	86	8th	17
65	HEAD COACH:				
	Bob Kennedy	24	22	(9th)	
	HEAD COACH: Lou Klein	48	58	8th	25
66	Leo Durocher	59	103'	9th	42.5
67	Leo Durocher	87	74	3rd	14
68	Leo Durocher	84	78	3rd	13
				NL East	
69	Leo Durocher	92	70	2nd	8
1970	Leo Durocher	84	78	2nd	5
71	Leo Durocher	83	79	3rd T	14
72	Leo Durocher	46	44	(4th)	
	Whitey Lockman	39	26	2nd	11
73	Whitey Lockman	77	84	5th	5
74	Whitey Lockman	41	52	(5th)	
	Jim Marshall	25	44	6th	22
75	Jim Marshall	75	87	5th T	17.5
76	Jim Marshall	75	87	4th	26
77	Herman Franks	81	81	4th	20
78	Herman Franks	79	83	3rd	11
79	Herman Franks	78	77	(5th)	
	Joey Amalfitano	2	5	5th	18
1980	Preston Gomez	38	52	(6th)	
	Joey Amalfitano	26	46	6th	27
81	Joey Amalfitano	38	65	6th	21.5
82	Lee Elia	73	89	5th	19
83	Lee Elia	54	69	(5th)	
	Charlie Fox	17	22	5th	19
84	Jim Frey	96	65	1st	—k
85	Jim Frey	77	84	4th	23.5
86	Jim Frey	23	33	(5th)	
	John Vukovich	1	1	(5th)	
	Gene Michael	46	56	5th	37
87	Gene Michael	68	68	(5th)	
	Frank Lucchesi	8	17	6th	18.5
88	Don Zimmer	77	85	4th	24
89	Don Zimmer	93	69	1st	—ˡ
1990	Don Zimmer	77	85	4th T	18
91	Don Zimmer	18	19	(4th)	
	Joe Altobelli	0	1	(5th)	
	Jim Essian	59	63	3rd T	20

Continued

Year	Manager	W	L	NL East	Games Behind
92	Jim Lefebvre	78	84	4th	18
93	Jim Lefebvre	84	78	4th	13
				NL Central	
94	Tom Trebelhorn	49	64	Season not completed	
95	Jim Riggleman	73	71	3rd	12
96	Jim Riggleman	76	86	4th	12
97	Jim Riggleman	68	94	5th	16
98	Jim Riggleman	90	73	2nd	125[m]

[a]Lost to Chicago in World Series
[b]Defeated Detroit in World Series
[c]Defeated Detroit in World Series
[d]Lost to Philadelphia in World Series
[e]Lost to Boston in World Series
[f]Lost to Philadelphia in World Series
[g]Lost to New York in World Series
[h]Lost to Detroit in World Series
[i]Lost to New York in World Series
[j]Lost to Detroit in World Series
[k]Lost to San Diego in NLCS
[l]Lost to San Francisco in NLCS
[m](NL Wild Card) Lost to Atlanta in NLC first round after defeating San Francisco in one-game wild-card playoff

Manager Summary

Most seasons–Grimm 14
Most games–Grimm 1,737
Most wins–Grimm 946
Most losses–Grimm 782
NL pennants–Chance 4, Grimm 3, Hartnett 1, McCarthy 1, Mitchell 1
Division titles–Frey 1, Zimmer 1
Multiple terms as manager–Grimm 3, Amalfitano 2, Evers 2,
Fewest games managed–Altobelli 1, Johnson 1
Number of different managers–46

CINCINNATI Reds 1901–98

(Known as Cincinnati Redlegs, 1953–58)

Year	Manager	W	L	NL Rank	Games Behind
1901	Bid McPhee	52	87	8th	38
02	Bid McPhee	27	37	(7th)	
	Frank Bancroft	9	7	(5th)	
	Joe Kelley	34	26	4th	33.5

Continued

Year	Manager	W	L	NL Rank	Games Behind
03	Joe Kelley	74	65	4th	16.5
04	Joe Kelley	88	65	3rd	18
05	Joe Kelley	79	74	5th	26
06	Ned Hanlon	64	87	6th	51.5
07	Ned Hanlon	66	87	6th	41.5
08	John Ganzel	73	81	5th	26
09	Clark Griffith	77	76	4th	33.5
1910	Clark Griffith	75	79	5th	29
11	Clark Griffith	70	83	6th	29
12	Hank O'Day	75	78	4th	29
13	Joe Tinker	64	89	7th	37.5
14	Buck Herzog	60	94	8th	34.5
15	Buck Herzog	71	83	7th	20
16	Buck Herzog	34	49	(8th)	
	Ivy Wingo	1	1	(8th)	
	Christy Mathewson	25	43	7th T	33.5
17	Christy Mathewson	78	76	4th	20
18	Christy Mathewson	61	57	(4th)	
	Heinie Groh	7	3	3rd	15.5
19	Pat Moran	96	44	1st	—a
1920	Pat Moran	82	71	3rd	10.5
21	Pat Moran	70	83	6th	24
22	Pat Moran	86	68	2nd	7
23	Pat Moran	91	63	2nd	4.5
24	Jack Hendricks	83	70	4th	10
25	Jack Hendricks	80	73	3rd	15
26	Jack Hendricks	87	67	2nd	2
27	Jack Hendricks	75	78	5th	18.5
28	Jack Hendricks	78	74	5th	16
29	Jack Hendricks	66	88	7th	33
1930	Dan Howley	59	95	7th	33
31	Dan Howley	58	96	8th	43
32	Dan Howley	60	94	8th	30
33	Donie Bush	58	94	8th	33
34	Bob O'Farrell	30	60	(8th)	
	Burt Shotton	1	0	(8th)	
	Chuck Dressen	21	39	8th	42
35	Chuck Dressen	68	85	6th	31.5
36	Chuck Dressen	74	80	5th	18
37	Chuck Dressen	51	78	(8th)	
	Bobby Wallace	5	20	8th	40
38	Bill McKechnie	82	68	4th	6

Continued

Year	Manager	W	L	NL Rank	Games Behind
39	Bill McKechnie	97	57	1st	—[b]
1940	Bill McKechnie	100	53	1st	—[c]
41	Bill McKechnie	88	66	3rd	12
42	Bill McKechnie	76	76	4th	29
43	Bill McKechnie	87	67	2nd	18
44	Bill McKechnie	89	65	3rd	16
45	Bill McKechnie	61	93	7th	37
46	Bill McKechnie	64	86	(6th)	
	Hank Gowdy	3	1	6th	30
47	Johnny Neun	73	81	5th	21
48	Johnny Neun	64	89	(7th)	
	Bucky Walters	20	33	7th	27
49	Bucky Walters	61	90	(7th)	
	Luke Sewell	1	2	7th	35
1950	Luke Sewell	66	87	6th	24.5
51	Luke Sewell	68	86	6th	28.5
52	Luke Sewell	39	59	(7th)	
	Earle Brucker	3	2	(7th)	
	Rogers Hornsby	27	24	6th	27.5
53	Rogers Hornsby	64	82	(6th)	
	Buster Mills	4	4	6th	37
54	Birdie Tebbetts	74	80	5th	23
55	Birdie Tebbetts	75	79	5th	23.5
56	Birdie Tebbetts	91	63	3rd	2
57	Birdie Tebbetts	80	74	4th	15
58	Birdie Tebbetts	52	61	(7th)	
	Jimmie Dykes	24	17	4th	16
59	Mayo Smith	35	45	(7th)	
	Fred Hutchinson	39	35	5th T	13
1960	Fred Hutchinson	67	87	6th	28
61	Fred Hutchinson	93	61	1st	—[d]
62	Fred Hutchinson	98	64	3rd	3.5
63	Fred Hutchinson	86	76	5th	13
64	Fred Hutchinson	54	45	(3rd)	
	Dick Sisler	3	3	(4th)	
	Fred Hutchinson	6	4	(3rd)	
	Dick Sisler	29	18	2nd T	1
65	Dick Sisler	89	73	4th	8
66	Don Heffner	37	46	(8th)	
	Dave Bristol	39	38	7th	18
67	Dave Bristol	87	75	4th	14.5
68	Dave Bristol	83	79	4th	14

Continued

CINCINNATI (continued)

Year	Manager	W	L	NL Rank	Games Behind
				NL West	
69	Dave Bristol	89	73	3rd	4
1970	Sparky Anderson	102	60	1st	_e
71	Sparky Anderson	79	83	4th T	11
72	Sparky Anderson	95	59	1st	_f
73	Sparky Anderson	99	63	1st	_g
74	Sparky Anderson	98	64	2nd	4
75	Sparky Anderson	108	54	1st	_h
76	Sparky Anderson	102	60	1st	_i
77	Sparky Anderson	88	74	2nd	10
78	Sparky Anderson	92	69	2nd	2.5
79	John McNamara	90	71	1st	_j
1980	John McNamara	89	73	3rd	3.5
81	John McNamara	66	42	1st	*
82	John McNamara	34	58	(6th)	
	Russ Nixon	27	43	6th	28
83	Russ Nixon	74	88	6th	17
84	Vern Rapp	51	70	(5th)	
	Pete Rose	19	22	5th	22
85	Pete Rose	89	72	2nd	5.5
86	Pete Rose	86	76	2nd	10
87	Pete Rose	84	78	2nd	6
88	Pete Rose	11	12	(4th)	
	Tommy Helms	12	15	(4th)	
	Pete Rose	64	47	2nd	7
89	Pete Rose	59	66	(4th)	
	Tommy Helms	16	21	5th	17
1990	Lou Piniella	91	71	1st	_k
91	Lou Piniella	74	88	5th	20
92	Lou Piniella	90	72	2nd	8
93	Tony Perez	20	24	(	
	Davey Johnson	53	65	5th	31
				NL Central	
94	Davey Johnson	66	48	Season not completed	
95	Davey Johnson	85	59	1st	_l
96	Ray Knight	81	81	3rd	7
97	Ray Knight	43	56	(4th)	
	Jack McKeon	33	30	3rd	8
98	Jack McKeon	77	85	4th	25

[a]Defeated Chicago in World Series
[b]Lost to New York in World Series

Continued

cDefeated Detroit in World Series

dLost to New York in World Series

eDefeated Pittsburgh in NLCS; lost to Baltimore in World Series

fDefeated Pittsburgh in NLCS; lost to Oakland in World Series

gLost to New York in NLCS

hDefeated Pittsburgh in NLCS; defeated Boston in World Series

iDefeated Philadelphia in NLCS; defeated New York in World Series

jLost to Pittsburgh in NLCS

kDefeated Pittsburgh in NLCS; defeated Oakland in World Series

lDefeated Los Angeles in NLC first round; lost to Atlanta in NLCS

* Posted best overall record in NL West in split season, but failed to win either half

Manager Summary

Most seasons—Anderson 9, McKechnie 9

Most games—Anderson 1,450

Most wins—Anderson 863

Most losses—McKechnie 631

NL pennants—Anderson 4, McKechnie 2, Hutchinson 1, Moran 1, Piniella 1

Division titles—Anderson 5, Johnson 1, Piniella 1

Multiple terms as manager—Helms 2, Hutchinson 2, Rose 2, Sisler 2

Fewest games managed—Wingo 2

Number of different managers—46

COLORADO Rockies 1993–98

Year	Manager	W	L	NL West	Games Behind
1993	Don Baylor	67	95	6th	37
94	Don Baylor	53	64	Season not completed	
95	Don Baylor	77	67	2nd	1a
96	Don Baylor	83	79	3rd	7.5
97	Don Baylor	83	79	3rd	7
98	Don Baylor	77	85	4th	21

a(NL Wild Card) Lost to Atlanta in NLC first round.

Manager Summary

All of the Rockies' managing records through 1998 were held by Don Baylor.

FLORIDA Marlins 1993–98

Year	Manager	W	L	NL East	Games Behind
1993	Rene Lachemann	64	98	6th	33
94	Rene Lachemann	51	64	Season not completed	

Continued

FLORIDA (continued)

Year	Manager	W	L	NL East	Games Behind
95	Rene Lachemann	67	76	4th	22.5
96	Rene Lachemann	39	47	(4th)	
	Cookie Rojas	1	0	(4th)	
	John Boles	40	35	3rd	16
97	Jim Leyland	92	70	2nd	9[a]
98	Jim Leyland	54	108	5th	52

[a](NL Wild Card) Defeated San Francisco in NLC first round; defeated Atlanta in NLCS; defeated Cleveland in World Series.

Manager Summary

Most seasons–Lachemann 4

Most games–Lachemann 506

Most wins–Lachemann 221

Most losses–Lachemann 285

NL pennants–Leyland 1

Division titles–none

Multiple terms as manager–none

Fewest games managed–Rojas 1

Number of different managers–4

HOUSTON Astros 1962–98

(Also known as Houston Colt .45s, 1962–64.)

Year	Manager	W	L	NL Rank	Games Behind
1962	Harry Craft	64	96	8th	36.5
63	Harry Craft	66	96	9th	33
64	Harry Craft	61	88	(9th)	
	Lum Harris	5	8	9th	27
65	Lum Harris	65	97	9th	32
66	Grady Hatton	72	90	8th	23
67	Grady Hatton	69	93	9th	32.5
68	Grady Hatton	23	38	(10th)	
	Harry Walker	49	52	10th	25
				NL West	
69	Harry Walker	81	81	5th	12
1970	Harry Walker	79	83	4th	23
71	Harry Walker	79	83	4th T	11
72	Harry Walker	67	54	(3rd)	
	Salty Parker	1	0	(2nd)	
	Leo Durocher	16	15	2nd	10.5

Continued

Year	Manager	W	L	NL West	Games Behind
73	Leo Durocher	82	80	4th	17
74	Preston Gomez	81	81	4th	21
75	Preston Gomez	47	80	(6th)	
	Bill Virdon	17	17	6th	43.5
76	Bill Virdon	80	82	3rd	22
77	Bill Virdon	81	81	3rd	17
78	Bill Virdon	74	88	5th	21
79	Bill Virdon	89	73	2nd	1.5
1980	Bill Virdon	93	70	1st	—[a]
81	Bill Virdon	61	49	3rd	6[b]
82	Bill Virdon	77	85	(5th)	
	Bob Lillis	28	23	5th	12
83	Bob Lillis	85	77	3rd	6
84	Bob Lillis	80	82	2nd T	12
85	Bob Lillis	83	79	3rd T	12
86	Hal Lanier	96	66	1st	—[c]
87	Hal Lanier	76	86	3rd	14
88	Hal Lanier	82	80	5th	12.5
89	Art Howe	86	76	3rd	6
1990	Art Howe	75	87	4th T	16
91	Art Howe	65	97	6th	29
92	Art Howe	81	81	4th	17
93	Art Howe	85	77	3rd	19
				NL Central	
94	Terry Collins	66	49	Season not completed	
95	Terry Collins	76	68	2nd	9
96	Terry Collins	82	80	2nd	6
97	Larry Dierker	84	78	1st	—[d]
98	Larry Dierker	102	60	1st	—[e]

[a]Defeated Los Angeles in one-game playoff for NL West title; lost to Philadelphia in NLCS
[b]Lost to Los Angeles in one-game playoff for NL West second-half, split-season title
[c]Lost to New York in NLCS
[d]Lost to Atlanta in NLC first round
[e]Lost to San Diego in NLC first round

Manager Summary:
Most seasons—Virdon 8
Most games—Virdon 1,117
Most wins—Virdon 572
Most losses—Virdon 545
NL pennants—none
Division titles—Dierker 2, Lanier 1, Virdon 1
Fewest games managed—Parker 1
Multiple terms as manager—none
Number of different managers—13

Continued

(Also known as Brooklyn Superbas to 1910, Robins, 1914–31.)

Year	Manager	W	L	NL Rank	Games Behind
BROOKLYN					
1901	Ned Hanlon	79	57	3rd	9.5
02	Ned Hanlon	75	63	2nd	27.5
03	Ned Hanlon	70	66	5th	19
04	Ned Hanlon	56	97	6th	50
05	Ned Hanlon	48	104	8th	56.5
06	Patsy Donovan	64	87	5th	50
07	Patsy Donovan	65	83	5th	40
08	Patsy Donovan	53	101	7th	46
09	Harry Lumley	55	98	6th	55.5
1910	Bill Dahlen	64	90	6th	40
11	Bill Dahlen	64	86	7th	33.5
12	Bill Dahlen	58	95	7th	46
13	Bill Dahlen	65	84	6th	34.5
14	Wilbert Robinson	75	79	5th	19.5
15	Wilbert Robinson	80	72	3rd	10
16	Wilbert Robinson	94	60	1st	—[a]
17	Wilbert Robinson	70	81	7th	26.5
18	Wilbert Robinson	57	69	5th	25.5
19	Wilbert Robinson	69	71	5th	27
1920	Wilbert Robinson	93	61	1st	—[b]
21	Wilbert Robinson	77	75	5th	16.5
22	Wilbert Robinson	76	78	6th	17
23	Wilbert Robinson	76	78	6th	19.5
24	Wilbert Robinson	92	62	2nd	1.5
25	Wilbert Robinson	68	85	6th T	27
26	Wilbert Robinson	71	82	6th	17.5
27	Wilbert Robinson	65	88	6th	28.5
28	Wilbert Robinson	77	76	6th	17.5
29	Wilbert Robinson	70	83	6th	28.5
1930	Wilbert Robinson	86	68	4th	6
31	Wilbert Robinson	79	73	4th	21
32	Max Carey	81	73	3rd	9
33	Max Carey	65	88	6th	26.5
34	Casey Stengel	71	81	6th	23.5
35	Casey Stengel	70	83	5th	29.5
36	Casey Stengel	67	87	7th	25
37	Burleigh Grimes	62	91	6th	33.5
38	Burleigh Grimes	69	80	7th	18.5
39	Leo Durocher	84	69	3rd	12.5

Continued

Year	Manager	W	L	NL Rank	Games Behind
1940	Leo Durocher	88	65	2nd	12
41	Leo Durocher	100	54	1st	_c
42	Leo Durocher	104	50	2nd	2
43	Leo Durocher	81	72	3rd	23.5
44	Leo Durocher	63	91	7th	42
45	Leo Durocher	87	67	3rd	11
46	Leo Durocher	96	60	2nd	2*
47	Clyde Sukeforth	2	0	(1st)	
	Burt Shotton	92	60	1st	_d
48	Leo Durocher	35	37	(5th)	
	Ray Blades	1	0	(5th)	
	Burt Shotton	48	33	3rd	7.5
49	Burt Shotton	97	57	1st	_e
1950	Burt Shotton	89	65	2nd	1
51	Chuck Dressen	97	60	2nd	1†
52	Chuck Dressen	96	57	1st	_f
53	Chuck Dressen	105	49	1st	_g
54	Walter Alston	92	62	2nd	5
55	Walter Alston	98	55	1st	_h
56	Walter Alston	93	61	1st	_i
57	Walter Alston	84	70	3rd	11
LOS ANGELES					
1958	Walter Alston	71	83	7th	21
59	Walter Alston	88	68	1st	_†j
1960	Walter Alston	82	72	4th	13
61	Walter Alston	89	65	2nd	4
62	Walter Alston	102	63	2nd	1§
63	Walter Alston	99	63	1st	_k
64	Walter Alston	80	82	6th	13
65	Walter Alston	97	65	1st	_l
66	Walter Alston	95	67	1st	_m
67	Walter Alston	73	89	8th	28.5
68	Walter Alston	76	86	7th T	21
NL West					
69	Walter Alston	85	77	4th	8
1970	Walter Alston	87	74	2nd	14.5
71	Walter Alston	89	73	2nd	1
72	Walter Alston	85	70	3rd	10.5
73	Walter Alston	95	66	2nd	3.5
74	Walter Alston	102	60	1st	_n
75	Walter Alston	88	74	2nd	20
76	Walter Alston	90	68	(2nd)	

Continued

Year	Manager	W	L	NL West	Games Behind
	Tom Lasorda	2	2	2nd	10
77	Tom Lasorda	98	64	1st	—o
78	Tom Lasorda	95	67	1st	—p
79	Tom Lasorda	79	83	3rd	11.5
1980	Tom Lasorda	92	71	2nd	1‖
81	Tom Lasorda	63	47	1st	—q
82	Tom Lasorda	88	74	2nd	1
83	Tom Lasorda	91	71	1st	—r
84	Tom Lasorda	79	83	4th	13
85	Tom Lasorda	95	67	1st	—s
86	Tom Lasorda	73	89	5th	23
87	Tom Lasorda	73	89	4th	17
88	Tom Lasorda	94	67	1st	—t
89	Tom Lasorda	77	83	4th	14
1990	Tom Lasorda	86	76	2nd	5
91	Tom Lasorda	93	69	2nd	1
92	Tom Lasorda	63	99	6th	35
93	Tom Lasorda	81	81	4th	23
94	Tom Lasorda	58	56	Season not completed	
95	Tom Lasorda	78	66	1st	—u
96	Tom Lasorda	41	35	(1st)	
	Bill Russell	49	37	2nd	1v
97	Bill Russell	88	74	2nd	2
98	Bill Russell	36	38	(3rd)	
	Glenn Hoffman	47	41	3rd	16

[a]Lost to Boston in World Series
[b]Lost to Cleveland in World Series
[c]Lost to New York in World Series
[d]Lost to New York in World Series
[e]Lost to New York in World Series
[f]Lost to New York in World Series
[g]Lost to New York in World Series
[h]Defeated New York in World Series
[i]Lost to New York in World Series
[j]Defeated Chicago in World Series
[k]Defeated New York in World Series
[l]Defeated Minnesota in World Series
[m]Lost to Baltimore in World Series
[n]Defeated Pittsburgh in NLCS; lost to Oakland in World Series
[o]Defeated Philadelphia in NLCS; lost to New York in World Series
[p]Defeated Philadelphia in NLCS; lost to New York in World Series
[q]Defeated Houston in NL West split-season playoff; defeated Montreal in NLCS; defeated New York in World Series

Continued

ʳLost to Philadelphia in NLCS
ˢLost to St. Louis in NLCS
ᵗDefeated New York in NLCS; defeated Oakland in World Series
ᵘLost to Cincinnati in NLC first round
ᵛ(NL Wild Card) Lost to Atlanta in NLC first round
*Lost best-of-three NL Playoff to St. Louis
†Lost best-of-three NL Playoff to New York
‡Defeated Milwaukee in best-of-three NL Playoff
§Lost best-of-three NL Playoff to San Francisco
‖Lost one-game NL West Playoff to Houston

Manager Summary

Most seasons—Alston 23
Most games—Alston 3,658
Most wins—Alston 2,040
Most losses—Alston 1,613
NL pennants—Alston 7, Lasorda 4, Dressen 2, Robinson 2, Shotton 2, Durocher 1
Division titles—Lasorda 7, Alston 1
Multiple terms as manager—Durocher 2, Shotton 2
Fewest games managed—Blades 1
Number of different managers—17

MILWAUKEE Brewers 1970–98
SEATTLE Pilots 1969

Note: Following the 1997 season the Milwaukee Brewers were transferred to the National League. It marks the only time in the 20th century that a franchise was moved from one major league to the other. However, the team was accustomed to moving. Founded as the Seattle Pilots in 1969, this American League West club was transferred to Milwaukee after just one season. It was bounced into the East division two years later, then became an AL Central entry in 1994.

Year	Manager	W	L	AL West	Games Behind
SEATTLE					
1969	Joe Schultz	64	98	6th	33
MILWAUKEE					
1970	Dave Bristol	65	97	5th	33
71	Dave Bristol	69	92	5th	32
				AL East	
72	Dave Bristol	10	20	(6th)	
	Roy McMillan	1	1	(6th)	
	Del Crandall	54	70	6th	21

Continued

59

Year	Manager	W	L	AL East	Games Behind
73	Del Crandall	74	88	5th	23
74	Del Crandall	76	86	5th	15
75	Del Crandall	67	94	(5th)	
	Harvey Kuenn	1	0	5th	28
76	Alex Grammas	66	95	6th	32
77	Alex Grammas	67	95	6th	33
78	George Bamberger	93	69	3rd	
79	George Bamberger	95	66	2nd	8
1980	Buck Rodgers	26	21	(2nd)	
	George Bamberger	47	45	(3rd)	
	Buck Rodgers	13	10	3rd	
81	Buck Rodgers	62	47	1st	—a
82	Buck Rodgers	23	24	(5th)	
	Harvey Kuenn	72	43	1st	—b
83	Harvey Kuenn	87	75	5th	11
84	Rene Lachemann	67	94	7th	36.5
85	George Bamberger	71	90	6th	28
86	George Bamberger	71	81	(6th)	
	Tom Treblehorn	6	3	6th	18
87	Tom Treblehorn	91	71	3rd	
88	Tom Treblehorn	87	75	3rd T	2
89	Tom Treblehorn	81	81	4th	8
1990	Tom Treblehorn	74	88	6th	14
91	Tom Treblehorn	83	79	4th	8
92	Phil Garner	92	70	2nd	4
93	Phil Garner	69	93	7th	26
				AL Central	
94	Phil Garner	53	62	Season not completed	
95	Phil Garner	65	79	5th	35
96	Phil Garner	80	82	3rd	19.5
97	Phil Garner	78	83	3rd	8
				NL Central	
98	Phil Garner	74	88	5th	28

aLost to New York in AL East split-season playoffs
bDefeated California in ALCS; lost to St. Louis in World Series

Manager Summary

Most seasons—Garner 7
Most games—Garner 1,068
Most wins—Garner 511
Most losses—Garner 557
AL pennants—Kuenn 1
Division titles—Kuenn 1
Multiple terms as manager—Bamberger 3, Kuenn 2, Rodgers 2

Continued

Fewest games managed–McMillan 2

Number of different managers–11

MONTREAL EXPOS 1969–98

Year	Manager	W	L	NL East	Games Behind
1969	Gene Mauch	52	110	6th	48
1970	Gene Mauch	73	89	6th	16
71	Gene Mauch	71	90	5th	25.5
72	Gene Mauch	70	86	5th	26.5
73	Gene Mauch	79	83	4th	3.5
74	Gene Mauch	79	82	4th	8.5
75	Gene Mauch	75	87	5th T	17.5
76	Karl Kuehl	43	85	(6th)	
	Charlie Fox	12	22	6th	46
77	Dick Williams	76	87	5th	26
78	Dick Williams	76	86	4th	14
79	Dick Williams	95	65	2nd	2
1980	Dick Williams	90	72	2nd	1
81	Dick Williams	60	48	(6th)	
	Jim Fanning	16	11	2nd	2[a]
82	Jim Fanning	86	76	3rd	6
83	Bill Virdon	82	80	3rd	8
84	Bill Virdon	64	67	(5th)	
	Jim Fanning	14	16	5th	18
85	Buck Rodgers	84	77	3rd	16.5
86	Buck Rodgers	78	83	4th	29.5
87	Buck Rodgers	91	71	3rd	4
88	Buck Rodgers	81	81	3rd	20
89	Buck Rodgers	81	81	4th	12
1990	Buck Rodgers	85	77	3rd	10
91	Buck Rodgers	20	29	(6th)	
	Tom Runnells	51	61	6th	26.5
92	Tom Runnells	17	20	(4th)	
	Felipe Alou	70	55	2nd	9
93	Felipe Alou	94	68	2nd	3
94	Felipe Alou	74	40	Season not completed	
95	Felipe Alou	66	78	5th	24
96	Felipe Alou	88	74	2nd	8
97	Felipe Alou	78	84	4th	23
98	Felipe Alou	65	97	4th	41

[a]Defeated Philadelphia in NL East split-season playoff; lost to Los Angeles in NLCS

Manager Summary

Most seasons–Alou 7, Mauch 7, Rodgers 7

Most games–Mauch 1,128

Continued

Most wins–Alou, 535

Most losses–Mauch 627

NL pennants–none

Division titles–Fanning 1

Multiple terms as manager–Fanning 2

Fewest games managed–Fox 34

Number of different managers–9

NEW YORK Mets 1962–98

Year	Manager	W	L	NL Rank	Games Behind
1962	Casey Stengel	40	120	10th	60.5
63	Casey Stengel	51	111	10th	48
64	Casey Stengel	53	109	10th	40
65	Casey Stengel	31	64	(10th)	
	Wes Westrum	19	48	10th	47
66	Wes Westrum	66	95	9th	28.5
67	Wes Westrum	57	94	(10th)	
	Salty Parker	4	7	10th	40.5
68	Gil Hodges	73	89	9th	24
				NL East	
69	Gil Hodges	100	62	1st	—[a]
1970	Gil Hodges	83	79	3rd	6
71	Gil Hodges	83	79	3rd T	14
72	Yogi Berra	83	73	3rd	13.5
73	Yogi Berra	82	79	1st	—[b]
74	Yogi Berra	71	91	5th	17
75	Yogi Berra	56	63	(3rd)	
	Roy McMillan	26	27	3rd T	10.5
76	Joe Frazier	86	76	3rd	15
77	Joe Frazier	15	30	(6th)	
	Joe Torre	49	68	6th	37
78	Joe Torre	66	96	6th	24
79	Joe Torre	63	99	6th	35
1980	Joe Torre	67	95	5th	24
81	Joe Torre	41	62	5th	18.5
82	George Bamberger	65	97	6th	27
83	George Bamberger	16	30	(6th)	

Continued

Year	Manager	W	L	NL East	Games Behind
	Frank Howard	52	64	6th	22
84	Davey Johnson	90	72	2nd	6.5
85	Davey Johnson	98	64	2nd	3
86	Davey Johnson	108	54	1st	—c
87	Davey Johnson	92	70	2nd	3
88	Davey Johnson	100	60	1st	—d
89	Davey Johnson	87	75	2nd	6
1990	Davey Johnson	20	22	(4th)	
	Bud Harrelson	71	49	2nd	4
91	Bud Harrelson	74	80	(3rd)	
	Mike Cubbage	3	4	5th	20.5
92	Jeff Torborg	72	90	5th	24
93	Jeff Torborg	13	25	(7th)	
	Dallas Green	48	78	7th	38
94	Dallas Green	55	58	Season not completed	
95	Dallas Green	69	75	2nd T	21
96	Dallas Green	59	72	(4th)	
	Bobby Valentine	12	19	4th	25
97	Bobby Valentine	88	74	3rd	13
98	Bobby Valentine	88	74	2nd	18

[a]Defeated Atlanta in NLCS; defeated Baltimore in World Series
[b]Defeated Cincinnati in NLCS; lost to Oakland in World Series
[c]Defeated Houston in NLCS; defeated Boston in World Series
[d]Lost to Los Angeles in NLCS

Manager Summary:

Most seasons—Johnson 7
Most games—Johnson 1,012
Most wins—Johnson 595
Most losses—Torre 420
NL pennants—Berra 1, Hodges 1, Johnson 1
Division titles—Johnson 2, Berra 1, Hodges 1
Multiple terms as manager—none
Fewest games managed—Cubbage 7
Number of different managers—16

(Also known unofficially as Philadelphia Blue Jays, 1944-45.)

Year	Manager	W	L	NL Rank	Games Behind
1901	Bill Shettsline	83	57	2nd	7.5
02	Bill Shettsline	56	81	7th	46
03	Chief Zimmer	49	86	7th	39.5
04	Hugh Duffy	52	100	8th	53.5
05	Hugh Duffy	83	69	4th	21.5
06	Hugh Duffy	71	82	4th	42.5
07	Billy Murray	83	64	3rd	21.5
08	Billy Murray	83	71	4th	16
09	Billy Murray	74	79	5th	36.5
1910	Red Dooin	78	75	4th	25.5
11	Red Dooin	79	73	4th	19.5
12	Red Dooin	73	79	5th	30.5
13	Red Dooin	88	63	2nd	12.5
14	Red Dooin	74	80	6th	20.5
15	Pat Moran	90	62	1st	—a
16	Pat Moran	91	62	2nd	2.5
17	Pat Moran	87	65	2nd	10
18	Pat Moran	55	68	6th	26
19	Jack Coombs	18	46	(8th)	
	Gavvy Cravath	29	46	8th	47.5
1920	Gavvy Cravath	62	91	8th	30.5
21	Bill Donovan	25	62	(8th)	
	Kaiser Wilhelm	26	41	8th	43.5
22	Kaiser Wilhelm	57	96	7th	35.5
23	Art Fletcher	50	104	8th	45.5
24	Art Fletcher	55	96	7th	37
25	Art Fletcher	68	85	6th T	27
26	Art Fletcher	58	93	8th	29.5
27	Stuffy McInnis	51	103	8th	43
28	Burt Shotton	43	109	8th	51
29	Burt Shotton	71	82	5th	27.5
1930	Burt Shotton	52	102	8th	40
31	Burt Shotton	66	88	6th	35
32	Burt Shotton	78	76	4th	12
33	Burt Shotton	60	92	7th	31
34	Jimmie Wilson	56	93	7th	37
35	Jimmie Wilson	64	89	7th	35.5
36	Jimmie Wilson	54	100	8th	38
37	Jimmie Wilson	61	92	7th	34.5
38	Jimmie Wilson	45	103	(8th)	

Continued

Year	Manager	W	L	NL Rank	Games Behind
	Hans Lobert	0	2	8th	43
39	Doc Prothro	45	106	8th	50.5
1940	Doc Prothro	50	103	8th	50
41	Doc Prothro	43	111	8th	57
42	Hans Lobert	42	109	8th	62.5
43	Bucky Harris	38	52	(5th)	
	Freddy Fitzsimmons	26	38	7th	41
44	Freddy Fitzsimmons	61	92	8th	43.5
45	Freddy Fitzsimmons	18	51	(8th)	
	Ben Chapman	28	57	8th	52
46	Ben Chapman	69	85	5th	28
47	Ben Chapman	62	92	7th T	32
48	Ben Chapman	37	42	(7th)	
	Dusty Cooke	6	6	(6th)	
	Eddie Sawyer	23	40	6th	25.5
49	Eddie Sawyer	81	73	3rd	16
1950	Eddie Sawyer	91	63	1st	_b
51	Eddie Sawyer	73	81	5th	23.5
52	Eddie Sawyer	28	35	(6th)	
	Steve O'Neill	59	32	4th	9.5
53	Steve O'Neill	83	71	3rd T	22
54	Steve O'Neill	40	37	(3rd)	
	Terry Moore	35	42	4th	22
55	Mayo Smith	77	77	4th	21.5
56	Mayo Smith	71	83	5th	22
57	Mayo Smith	77	77	5th	18
58	Mayo Smith	39	45	(7th)	
	Eddie Sawyer	30	40	8th	23
59	Eddie Sawyer	64	90	8th	23
1960	Eddie Sawyer	0	1	(8th)	
	Andy Cohen	1	0	(4th)	
	Gene Mauch	58	94	8th	36
61	Gene Mauch	47	107	8th	46
62	Gene Mauch	81	80	7th	20
63	Gene Mauch	87	75	4th	12
64	Gene Mauch	92	70	2nd T	1
65	Gene Mauch	85	76	6th	11.5
66	Gene Mauch	87	75	4th	8
67	Gene Mauch	82	80	5th	19.5
68	Gene Mauch	27	27	(6th)	
	George Myatt	1	0	(5th)	
	Bob Skinner	48	59	7th T	21

Continued

Year	Manager	W	L	NL Rank	Games Behind
				NL East	
69	Bob Skinner	44	64	(5th)	
	George Myatt	19	35	5th	37
1970	Frank Lucchesi	73	88	5th	15.5
71	Frank Lucchesi	67	95	6th	30
72	Frank Lucchesi	26	50	(6th)	
	Paul Owens	33	47	6th	37.5
73	Danny Ozark	71	91	6th	11.5
74	Danny Ozark	80	80	3rd	8
75	Danny Ozark	86	76	2nd	6.5
76	Danny Ozark	101	61	1st	—c
77	Danny Ozark	101	61	1st	—d
78	Danny Ozark	90	72	1st	—e
79	Danny Ozark	65	67	(5th)	
	Dallas Green	19	11	4th	14
1980	Dallas Green	91	71	1st	—f
81	Dallas Green	59	48	3rd	2.5g
82	Pat Corrales	89	73	2nd	3
83	Pat Corrales	43	42	(1st)	
	Paul Owens	47	30	1st	—h
84	Paul Owens	81	81	4th	15.5
85	John Felske	75	87	5th	26
86	John Felske	86	75	2nd	21.5
87	John Felske	29	32	(5th)	
	Lee Elia	51	50	4th T	15
88	Lee Elia	60	92	(6th)	
	John Vukovich	5	4	6th	35.5
89	Nick Leyva	67	95	6th	26
1990	Nick Leyva	77	85	4th T	18
91	Nick Leyva	4	9	(6th)	
	Jim Fregosi	74	75	3rd T	20
92	Jim Fregosi	70	92	6th	26
93	Jim Fregosi	97	65	1st	—i
94	Jim Fregosi	54	61	Season not completed	
95	Jim Fregosi	69	75	2nd T	21
96	Jim Fregosi	67	95	5th	29
97	Terry Francona	68	94	5th	33
98	Terry Francona	75	87	3rd	31

aLost to Boston in World Series
bLost to New York in World Series
cLost to Cincinnati in NLCS
dLost to Los Angeles in NLCS
eLost to Los Angeles in NLCS

Continued

[f]Defeated Houston in NLCS; defeated Kansas City in World Series

[g]Lost to Montreal in NL East split-season playoff

[h]Defeated Los Angeles in NLCS; lost to Baltimore in World Series

[i]Defeated Atlanta in NLCS; lost to Toronto in World Series

Manager Summary:

Most seasons—Mauch 9

Most games—Mauch 1,331

Most wins—Mauch 645

Most losses—Mauch 684

NL pennants—Fregosi 1, Green 1, Moran 1, Owens 1, Sawyer 1

Division titles—Ozark 3, Fregosi 1, Green 1, Owens 1

Multiple terms as manager—Lobert 2, Myatt 2, Owens 2, Sawyer 2

Fewest games managed—Cohen 1

Number of different managers—39

PITTSBURGH Pirates 1901–98

Year	Manager	W	L	NL Rank	Games Behind
1901	Fred Clarke	90	49	1st	—
02	Fred Clarke	103	36	1st	—
03	Fred Clarke	91	49	1st	—[a]
04	Fred Clarke	87	66	4th	19
05	Fred Clarke	96	57	2nd	9
06	Fred Clarke	93	60	3rd	23.5
07	Fred Clarke	91	63	2nd	17
08	Fred Clarke	98	56	2nd T	1
09	Fred Clarke	110	42	1st	—[b]
1910	Fred Clarke	86	67	3rd	17.5
11	Fred Clarke	85	69	3rd	14.5
12	Fred Clarke	93	58	2nd	10
13	Fred Clarke	78	71	4th	21.5
14	Fred Clarke	69	85	7th	25.5
15	Fred Clarke	73	81	5th	18
16	Nixey Callahan	65	89	6th	29
17	Nixey Callahan	20	40	(8th)	
	Honus Wagner	1	4	(8th)	
	Hugo Bezdek	30	59	8th	47
18	Hugo Bezdek	65	60	4th	17
19	Hugo Bezdek	71	68	4th	24.5
1920	George Gibson	79	75	4th	14

Continued

Year	Manager	W	L	NL Rank	Games Behind
21	George Gibson	90	63	2nd	4
22	George Gibson	32	33	(5th)	
	Bill McKechnie	53	36	3rd T	8
23	Bill McKechnie	87	67	3rd	8.5
24	Bill McKechnie	90	63	2nd	4
25	Bill McKechnie	95	58	1st	—c
26	Bill McKechnie	84	69	3rd	4.5
27	Donie Bush	94	60	1st	—d
28	Donie Bush	85	67	4th	9
29	Donie Bush	67	51	(2nd)	
	Jewel Ens	21	14	2nd	10.5
1930	Jewel Ens	80	74	5th	12
31	Jewel Ens	75	79	5th	26
32	George Gibson	86	68	2nd	4
33	George Gibson	87	67	2nd	5
34	George Gibson	27	24	(4th)	
	Pie Traynor	47	52	5th	19.5
35	Pie Traynor	86	67	4th	13.5
36	Pie Traynor	84	70	4th	8
37	Pie Traynor	86	68	3rd	10
38	Pie Traynor	86	64	2nd	2
39	Pie Traynor	68	85	6th	28.5
1940	Frank Frisch	78	76	4th	22.5
41	Frank Frisch	81	73	4th	19
42	Frank Frisch	66	81	5th	36.5
43	Frank Frisch	80	74	4th	25
44	Frank Frisch	90	63	2nd	14.5
45	Frank Frisch	82	72	4th	16
46	Frank Frisch	62	89	(7th)	
	Spud Davis	1	2	7th	34
47	Billy Herman	61	92	(8th)	
	Bill Burwell	1	0	7th T	32
48	Billy Meyer	83	71	4th	8.5
49	Billy Meyer	71	83	6th	26
1950	Billy Meyer	57	96	8th	33.5
51	Billy Meyer	64	90	7th	32.5
52	Billy Meyer	42	112	8th	54.5
53	Fred Haney	50	104	8th	55
54	Fred Haney	53	101	8th	44
55	Fred Haney	60	94	8th	38.5
56	Bobby Bragan	66	88	7th	27
57	Bobby Bragan	36	67	(8th)	
	Danny Murtaugh	26	25	7th T	33

Continued

Year	Manager	W	L	NL Rank	Games Behind
58	Danny Murtaugh	84	70	2nd	8
59	Danny Murtaugh	78	76	4th	9
1960	Danny Murtaugh	95	59	1st	—e
61	Danny Murtaugh	75	79	6th	18
62	Danny Murtaugh	93	68	4th	8
63	Danny Murtaugh	74	88	8th	25
64	Danny Murtaugh	80	82	6th T	13
65	Harry Walker	90	72	3rd	7
66	Harry Walker	92	70	3rd	3
67	Harry Walker	42	42	(6th)	
	Danny Murtaugh	39	39	6th	20.5
68	Larry Shepard	80	82	6th	17
	NL East				
69	Larry Shepard	84	73	(3rd)	
	Alex Grammas	4	1	3rd	12
1970	Danny Murtaugh	89	73	1st	—f
71	Danny Murtaugh	97	65	1st	—g
72	Bill Virdon	96	59	1st	—h
73	Bill Virdon	67	69	(2nd)	
	Danny Murtaugh	13	13	3rd	2.5
74	Danny Murtaugh	88	74	1st	—i
75	Danny Murtaugh	92	69	1st	—j
76	Danny Murtaugh	92	70	2nd	9
77	Chuck Tanner	96	66	2nd	5
78	Chuck Tanner	88	73	2nd	1.5
79	Chuck Tanner	98	64	1st	—k
1980	Chuck Tanner	83	79	3rd	8
81	Chuck Tanner	46	56	4th	
82	Chuck Tanner	84	78	4th	8
83	Chuck Tanner	84	78	2nd	6
85	Chuck Tanner	57	104	6th	43.5
86	Jim Leyland	64	98	6th	44
87	Jim Leyland	80	82	4th T	15
88	Jim Leyland	85	75	2nd	15
89	Jim Leyland	74	88	5th	19
1990	Jim Leyland	95	67	1st	—l
91	Jim Leyland	98	64	1st	—m
92	Jim Leyland	96	66	1st	—n
93	Jim Leyland	75	87	5th	22
	NL Central				
94	Jim Leyland	53	61	Season not completed	
95	Jim Leyland	58	86	5th	27
96	Jim Leyland	73	89	5th	15

Continued

PITTSBURGH (continued)

Year	Manager	W	L	NL Central	Games Behind
97	Gene Lamont	79	83	2nd	5
98	Gene Lamont	69	93	6th	33

[a]Lost to Boston in World Series
[b]Defeated Detroit in World Series
[c]Defeated Washington in World Series
[d]Lost to New York in World Series
[e]Defeated New York in World Series
[f]Lost to Cincinnati in NLCS
[g]Defeated San Francisco in NLCS; defeated Baltimore in World Series
[h]Lost to Cincinnati in NLCS
[i]Lost to Los Angeles in NLCS
[j]Lost to Cincinnati in NLCS
[k]Defeated Cincinnati in NLCS; defeated Baltimore in World Series
[l]Lost to Cincinnati in NLCS
[m]Lost to Atlanta in NLCS
[n]Lost to Atlanta in NL

Manager Summary

Most seasons—Clarke 15,* Murtaugh 15
Most games—Clarke 2,287
Most wins—Clarke 1,343
Most losses—Murtaugh 950
NL pennants—Clarke 4, Murtaugh 2, Bush 1, McKechnie 1, Tanner 1
Division titles—Murtaugh 4, Leyland 3, Tanner 1, Virdon 1
Multiple terms—Murtaugh 4, Gibson 2
Fewest games managed—Burwell 1
Number of different managers—24
* Clarke also managed Pirates for 140 games prior to 1901.

ST. LOUIS Cardinals 1901–98

Year	Manager	W	L	NL Rank	Games Behind
1901	Patsy Donovan	76	64	4th	14.5
02	Patsy Donovan	56	78	6th	44.5
03	Patsy Donovan	43	94	8th	46.5
04	Kid Nichols	75	79	5th	3.5
05	Kid Nichols	5	9	(7th)	
	Jimmy Burke	34	56	(6th)	
	Matt Robison	19	31	6th	47.5
06	John McCloskey	52	98	7th	63
07	John McCloskey	52	101	8th	55.5

Continued

70

Year	Manager	W	L	NL Rank	Games Behind
08	John McCloskey	49	105	8th	50
09	Roger Bresnahan	54	98	7th	56
1910	Roger Bresnahan	63	90	7th	40.5
11	Roger Bresnahan	75	74	5th	22
12	Roger Bresnahan	63	90	6th	41
13	Miller Huggins	51	99	8th	49
14	Miller Huggins	81	72	3rd	13
15	Miller Huggins	72	81	6th	18.5
16	Miller Huggins	60	93	7th T	33.5
17	Miller Huggins	82	70	3rd	15
18	Jack Hendricks	51	78	8th	33
19	Branch Rickey	54	83	7th	40.5
1920	Branch Rickey	75	79	5th T	18
21	Branch Rickey	87	66	3rd	7
22	Branch Rickey	85	69	3rd T	8
23	Branch Rickey	79	74	5th	16
24	Branch Rickey	65	89	6th	28.5
25	Branch Rickey	13	25	(8th)	
	Rogers Hornsby	64	51	4th	18
26	Rogers Hornsby	89	65	1st	—[a]
27	Bob O'Farrell	92	61	2nd	1.5
28	Bill McKechnie	95	59	1st	—[b]
29	Billy Southworth	43	45	(4th)	
	Gabby Street	1	0	(4th)	
	Bill McKechnie	34	29	4th	20
1930	Gabby Street	92	62	1st	—[c]
31	Gabby Street	101	53	1st	—[d]
32	Gabby Street	72	82	6th T	18
33	Gabby Street	46	45	(5th)	
	Frankie Frisch	36	26	5th	9.5
34	Frankie Frisch	95	58	1st	—[e]
35	Frankie Frisch	96	58	2nd	4
36	Frankie Frisch	87	67	2nd T	5
37	Frankie Frisch	81	73	4th	15
38	Frankie Frisch	63	72	(6th)	
	Mike Gonzalez	8	8	6th	17.5
39	Ray Blades	92	61	2nd	4.5
1940	Ray Blades	14	24	(6th)	
	Mike Gonzalez	1	5	(7th)	
	Billy Southworth	69	40	3rd	16
41	Billy Southworth	97	56	2nd	2.5
42	Billy Southworth	106	48	1st	—[f]

Continued

Year	Manager	W	L	NL Rank	Games Behind
43	Billy Southworth	105	49	1st	—g
44	Billy Southworth	105	49	1st	—h
45	Billy Southworth	95	59	2nd	3
46	Eddie Dyer	98	58	1st	—i
47	Eddie Dyer	89	65	2nd	5
48	Eddie Dyer	85	69	2nd	6.5
49	Eddie Dyer	96	58	2nd	1
1950	Eddie Dyer	78	75	5th	12.5
51	Marty Marion	81	73	3rd	15.5
52	Eddie Stanky	88	66	3rd	8.5
53	Eddie Stanky	83	71	3rd T	22
54	Eddie Stanky	72	82	6th	25
55	Eddie Stanky	17	19	(5th)	
	Harry Walker	51	67	7th	30.5
56	Fred Hutchinson	76	78	4th	17
57	Fred Hutchinson	87	67	2nd	8
58	Fred Hutchinson	69	75	(5th)	
	Stan Hack	3	7	5th T	20
59	Solly Hemus	71	83	7th	16
1960	Solly Hemus	86	68	3rd	9
61	Solly Hemus	33	41	(6th)	
	Johnny Keane	47	33	5th	13
62	Johnny Keane	84	78	6th	17.5
63	Johnny Keane	93	69	2nd	6
64	Johnny Keane	93	69	1st	—j
65	Red Schoendienst	80	81	7th	16.5
66	Red Schoendienst	83	79	6th	12
67	Red Schoendienst	101	60	1st	—k
68	Red Schoendienst	97	65	1st	—l
				NL East	
69	Red Schoendienst	87	75	4th	13
1970	Red Schoendienst	76	86	4th	13
71	Red Schoendienst	90	72	2nd	7
72	Red Schoendienst	75	81	4th	21.5
73	Red Schoendienst	81	81	2nd	1.5
74	Red Schoendienst	86	75	2nd	1.5
75	Red Schoendienst	82	80	3rd T	10.5
76	Red Schoendienst	72	90	5th	29
77	Vern Rapp	83	79	3rd	18
78	Vern Rapp	6	11	(6th)	
	Jack Krol	1	1	(6th)	
	Ken Boyer	62	81	5th	21

Continued

Year	Manager	W	L	NL East	Games Behind
79	Ken Boyer	86	76	3rd	12
1980	Ken Boyer	18	33	(6th)	
	Jack Krol	0	1	(6th)	
	Whitey Herzog	38	35	(5th)	
	Red Schoendienst	18	19	4th	17
81	Whitey Herzog	59	43	1st	_m
82	Whitey Herzog	92	70	1st	_n
83	Whitey Herzog	79	83	4th	11
84	Whitey Herzog	84	78	3rd	12.5
85	Whitey Herzog	101	61	1st	_o
86	Whitey Herzog	79	82	3rd	28.5
87	Whitey Herzog	95	67	1st	_p
88	Whitey Herzog	76	86	5th	25
89	Whitey Herzog	86	76	3rd	7
1990	Whitey Herzog	33	47	(6th)	
	Red Schoendienst	13	11	(6th)	
	Joe Torre	24	34	6th	25
91	Joe Torre	84	78	2nd	14
92	Joe Torre	83	79	3rd	13
93	Joe Torre	87	75	3rd	10
				NL Central	
94	Joe Torre	53	61	Season not completed	
95	Joe Torre	20	27		
	Mike Jorgensen	42	54	(4th)	
96	Tony LaRussa	88	74	1st	_q
97	Tony LaRussa	73	89	4th	11
98	Tony LaRussa	83	79	3rd	19

[a]Defeated New York in World Series

[b]Lost to New York in World Series

[c]Lost to Philadelphia in World Series

[d]Defeated Philadelphia in World Series

[e]Defeated Detroit in World Series

[f]Defeated New York in World Series

[g]Lost to New York in World Series

[h]Defeated St. Louis in World Series

[i]Defeated Brooklyn in best-of-three playoff for NL title; defeated Boston in World Series

[j]Defeated New York in World Series

[k]Defeated Boston in World Series

[l]Lost to Detroit in World Series

[m]Posted best overall record in NL East in split season, but failed to win either half.

[n]Defeated Atlanta in NLCS; defeated Milwaukee in World Series

[o]Defeated Los Angeles in NLCS; lost to Kansas City in World Series

Continued

PDefeated San Francisco in NLCS; lost to Minnesota in World Series
QDefeated San Diego in NLC first round; lost to Atlanta in NLCS

Manager Summary

Most seasons—Schoendienst 14

Most games—Schoendienst 1,999

Most wins—Schoendienst 1,041

Most losses—Schoendienst 955

NL pennants—Herzog 3, Southworth 3, Schoendienst 2, Street 2, Dyer 1, Frisch 1, Hornsby 1, Keane 1, McKechnie 1

Division titles—Herzog 3, LaRussa 1

Multiple terms as Manager—Schoendienst 3, Gonzalez 2, Herzog 2, Krol 2, McKechnie 2, Southworth 2, Street 2

Fewest games managed—Krol 3

Number of different managers—33

SAN DIEGO Padres 1969–98

Year	Manager	W	L	NL West	Games Behind
1969	Preston Gomez	52	110	6th	41
1970	Preston Gomez	63	99	6th	39
71	Preston Gomez	61	100	6th	28.5
72	Preston Gomez	4	7	(4th)	
	Don Zimmer	54	88	6th	36.5
73	Don Zimmer	60	102	6th	42
74	John McNamara	60	102	6th	42
75	John McNamara	71	91	4th	37
76	John McNamara	73	89	5th	29
77	John McNamara	20	28	(5th)	
	Bob Skinner	1	0	(5th)	
	Alvin Dark	48	65	5th	29
78	Roger Craig	84	78	4th	11
79	Roger Craig	68	93	5th	22
1980	Jerry Coleman	73	89	6th	19.5
81	Frank Howard	41	69	6th	26
82	Dick Williams	81	81	4th	8
83	Dick Williams	81	81	4th	10
84	Dick Williams	92	70	1st	—a
85	Dick Williams	83	79	3rd T	12
86	Steve Boros	74	88	4th	22
87	Larry Bowa	65	97	6th	25
88	Larry Bowa	16	30	(5th)	
	Jack McKeon	67	48	3rd	11
89	Jack McKeon	89	73	2nd	3

Continued

Year	Manager	W	L	NL West	Games Behind
1990	Jack McKeon	37	43	(4th)	
	Greg Riddoch	38	44	4th T	16
91	Greg Riddoch	84	78	3rd	10
92	Greg Riddoch	78	72	(3rd)	
	Jim Riggleman	4	8	3rd	16
93	Jim Riggleman	61	101	7th	43
94	Jim Riggleman	47	70	Season not completed	
95	Bruce Bochy	70	74	3rd	8
96	Bruce Bochy	91	71	1st	_b
97	Bruce Bochy	76	86	4th	14
98	Bruce Bochy	98	64	1st	_c

[a]Defeated Chicago in NLCS; lost to Detroit in World Series
[b]Lost to St. Louis in NLC first round
[c]Defeated Houston in NLC first round; defeated Atlanta in NLCS; lost to New York in World Series

Manager Summary
Most seasons—Bochy 4, Gomez 4, McNamara 4, Williams 4
Most games—Williams 648
Most wins—Williams 337
Most losses—Gomez 316
NL pennants—Bochy 1, Williams 1
Division titles—Bochy 2, Williams 1
Multiple terms as manager—none
Fewest games managed—Skinner 1
Number of different managers—15

Year	Manager	W	L	NL Rank	Games Behind
NEW YORK					
1901	George Davis	52	85	7th	37
02	Horace Fogel	18	23	(4th)	
	Heinie Smith	5	27	(8th)	
	John McGraw	25	38	8th	53.5
03	John McGraw	84	55	2nd	6.5
04	John McGraw	106	47	1st	_*
05	John McGraw	105	48	1st	_a
06	John McGraw	96	56	2nd	20
07	John McGraw	82	71	4th	25.5

Continued

Year	Manager	W	L	NL Rank	Games Behind
08	John McGraw	98	56	2nd T	1
09	John McGraw	92	61	3rd	18.5
1910	John McGraw	91	63	2nd	13
11	John McGraw	99	54	1st	_b
12	John McGraw	103	48	1st	_c
13	John McGraw	101	51	1st	_d
14	John McGraw	84	70	2nd	10.5
15	John McGraw	69	83	8th	21
16	John McGraw	86	66	4th	7
17	John McGraw	98	56	1st	_e
18	John McGraw	71	53	2nd	10.5
19	John McGraw	87	53	2nd	9
1920	John McGraw	86	68	2nd	7
21	John McGraw	94	59	1st	_f
22	John McGraw	93	61	1st	_g
23	John McGraw	95	58	1st	_h
24	John McGraw	16	13	(3rd)	
	Hughie Jennings	32	12	(1st)	
	John McGraw	45	35	1st	_i
25	John McGraw	86	66	2nd	8.5
26	John McGraw	74	77	5th	13.5
27	John McGraw	70	52	(4th)	
	Rogers Hornsby	22	10	3rd	2
28	John McGraw	93	61	2nd	2
29	John McGraw	84	67	3rd	13.5
1930	John McGraw	87	67	3rd	5
31	John McGraw	87	65	2nd	13
32	John McGraw	17	23	(8th)	
	Bill Terry	55	59	6th T	18
33	Bill Terry	91	61	1st	_j
34	Bill Terry	93	60	2nd	2
35	Bill Terry	91	62	3rd	8.5
36	Bill Terry	92	62	1st	_k
37	Bill Terry	95	57	1st	_l
38	Bill Terry	83	67	3rd	5
39	Bill Terry	77	74	5th	18.5
1940	Bill Terry	72	80	6th	27.5
41	Bill Terry	74	79	5th	25.5
42	Mel Ott	85	67	3rd	20
43	Mel Ott	55	98	8th	49.5
44	Mel Ott	67	87	5th	38
45	Mel Ott	78	74	5th	19

Continued

Year	Manager	W	L	NL Rank	Games Behind
46	Mel Ott	61	93	8th	36
47	Mel Ott	81	73	4th	13
48	Mel Ott	37	38	(4th)	
	Leo Durocher	41	38	5th	13.5
49	Leo Durocher	73	81	5th	24
1950	Leo Durocher	86	68	3rd	5
51	Leo Durocher	98	59	1st	—m
52	Leo Durocher	92	62	2nd	4.5
53	Leo Durocher	70	84	5th	35
54	Leo Durocher	97	57	1st	—n
55	Leo Durocher	80	74	3rd	18.5
56	Bill Rigney	67	87	6th	26
57	Bill Rigney	69	85	6th	26
SAN FRANCISCO					
1958	Bill Rigney	80	74	3rd	12
59	Bill Rigney	83	71	3rd	4
1960	Bill Rigney	33	25	(2nd)	
	Tom Sheehan	46	50	5th	16
61	Alvin Dark	85	69	3rd	8
62	Alvin Dark	103	62	1st	—o
63	Alvin Dark	88	74	3rd	11
64	Alvin Dark	90	72	4th	3
65	Herman Franks	95	67	2nd	2
66	Herman Franks	93	68	2nd	1.5
67	Herman Franks	91	71	2nd	10.5
68	Herman Franks	88	74	2nd	9
	NL West				
69	Clyde King	90	72	2nd	3
1970	Clyde King	19	23	(4th)	
	Charlie Fox	67	53	3rd	16
71	Charlie Fox	90	72	1st	—p
72	Charlie Fox	69	86	5th	26.5
73	Charlie Fox	88	74	3rd	11
74	Charlie Fox	34	42	(5th)	
	Wes Westrum	38	48	5th	30
75	Wes Westrum	80	81	3rd	27.5
76	Bill Rigney	74	88	4th	28
77	Joe Altobelli	75	87	4th	23
78	Joe Altobelli	89	73	3rd	6
79	Joe Altobelli	61	79	(4th)	
	Dave Bristol	10	12	4th	19.5
1980	Dave Bristol	75	86	5th	17

Continued

Year	Manager	W	L	NL West	Games Behind
81	Frank Robinson	56	55	4th	11.5
82	Frank Robinson	87	75	3rd	2
83	Frank Robinson	79	83	5th	12
84	Frank Robinson	42	64	(6th)	
	Danny Ozark	24	32	6th	26
85	Jim Davenport	56	88	(6th)	
	Roger Craig	6	12	6th	33
86	Roger Craig	83	79	3rd	13
87	Roger Craig	90	72	1st	—q
88	Roger Craig	83	79	4th	11.5
89	Roger Craig	92	70	1st	—r
1990	Roger Craig	85	77	3rd	6
91	Roger Craig	75	87	4th	19
92	Roger Craig	72	90	5th	26
93	Dusty Baker	103	59	2nd	1
94	Dusty Baker	55	60	season not completed	
95	Dusty Baker	67	77	4th	11
96	Dusty Baker	68	94	4th	22.5
97	Dusty Baker	90	72	1st	—s
98	Dusty Baker	89	74	2nd	9.5†

[a]Defeated Philadelphia in World Series
[b]Lost to Philadelphia in World Series
[c]Lost to Boston in World Series
[d]Lost to Philadelphia in World Series
[e]Lost to Chicago in World Series
[f]Defeated New York in World Series
[g]Defeated New York in World Series
[h]Lost to New York in World Series
[i]Lost to Washington in World Series
[j]Defeated Washington in World Series
[k]Lost to New York in World Series
[l]Lost to New York in World Series
[m]Defeated Brooklyn in best-of-three playoff for NL pennant; lost to New York in World Series
[n]Defeated Cleveland in World Series
[o]Defeated Los Angeles in best-of-three playoff for NL pennant; lost to New York in World Series
[p]Lost to Pittsburgh in NLCS
[q]Lost to St. Louis in NLCS
[r]Defeated Chicago in NLCS; lost to Oakland in World Series
[s]Lost to Florida in NLC first round
*No World Series conducted in 1904
†Lost one-game playoff to Chicago for NL Wild Card

Continued

Manager Summary

Most seasons–McGraw 31

Most games–McGraw 4,604

Most wins–McGraw 2,690

Most losses–McGraw 1,863

NL pennants–McGraw 10, Terry 3, Durocher 2, Craig 1, Dark 1

Division titles–Craig 2, Baker 1, Fox 1

Multiple terms as manager–McGraw 3, Rigney 2

Fewest games managed–Smith 32

Number of different managers–23

American League Teams

(Also known as Los Angeles Angels, 1961–64; California Angels, 1965–96.)

Year	Manager	W	L	AL Rank	Games Behind
1961	Bill Rigney	70	91	8th	38.5
62	Bill Rigney	86	76	3rd	10
63	Bill Rigney	70	91	9th	34
64	Bill Rigney	82	80	5th	17
65	Bill Rigney	75	87	7th	27
66	Bill Rigney	88	82	6th	18
67	Bill Rigney	84	77	5th	7.5
68	Bill Rigney	67	95	8th T	36
				AL West	
69	Bill Rigney	11	28	(6th)	
	Lefty Phillips	60	63	3rd	26
1970	Lefty Phillips	86	76	3rd	12
71	Lefty Phillips	76	86	4th	25.5
72	Del Rice	75	80	5th	18
73	Bobby Winkles	79	83	4th	15
74	Bobby Winkles	30	44	(6th)	
	Whitey Herzog	2	2	(6th)	
	Dick Williams	36	48	6th	22
75	Dick Williams	72	89	6th	25.5
76	Dick Williams	39	57	(4th)	
	Norm Sherry	37	29	4th T	14
77	Norm Sherry	39	42	(5th)	
	Dave Garcia	36	46	5th	28
78	Dave Garcia	25	20	(3rd)	
	Jim Fregosi	62	55	2nd T	5
79	Jim Fregosi	88	74	1st	—a
1980	Jim Fregosi	65	95	6th	31
81	Jim Fregosi	22	25	(4th)	
	Gene Mauch	29	34	5th	13.5
82	Gene Mauch	93	69	1st	—b
83	John McNamara	70	92	5th T	29
84	John McNamara	81	81	2nd T	3
85	Gene Mauch	90	72	2nd	1
86	Gene Mauch	92	70	1st	—c
87	Gene Mauch	75	87	6th T	10
88	Cookie Rojas	75	79	(4th)	
	Larry Stubing	0	8	4th	29
89	Doug Rader	91	71	3rd	8

Continued

Year	Manager	W	L	AL West	Games Behind
1990	Doug Rader	80	82	4th	23
91	Doug Rader	61	63	(7th)	
	Buck Rodgers	20	18	7th	14
92	Buck Rodgers	19	20	(5th)	
	John Wathan	39	50	(5th)	
	Buck Rodgers	14	20	5th T	24
93	Buck Rodgers	71	91	5th T	23
94	Buck Rodgers	16	23	(4th)	
	Bobby Knoop	1	1	(4th)	
	Marcel Lachemann	30	44	Season not completed	
95	Marcel Lachemann	78	67	2nd	1[d]
96	Marcel Lachemann	52	59	(4th)	
	John McNamara	18	32	4th	19.5
97	Terry Collins	84	78	2nd	6
98	Terry Collins	85	77	2nd	3

[a]Lost to Baltimore in ALCS
[b]Lost to Milwaukee in ALCS
[c]Lost to Boston in ALCS
[d]Lost one-game playoff to Seattle for AL West title

Manager Summary

Most seasons—Rigney 9
Most games—Rigney 1,350
Most wins—Rigney 633
Most losses—Rigney 717
AL pennants—none
Division titles—Mauch 2, Fregosi 1
Multiple terms as manager—Mauch 2, McNamara 2, Rodgers 2
Fewest games managed—Knoop 2
Number of different managers—18

Year	Manager	W	L	AL Rank	Games Behind
MILWAUKEE					
1901	Hugh Duffy	48	89	8th	35.5
ST. LOUIS					
1902	Jimmy McAleer	78	58	2nd	5

Continued

Year	Manager	W	L	AL Rank	Games Behind
03	Jimmy McAleer	65	74	6th	26.5
04	Jimmy McAleer	65	87	6th	29
05	Jimmy McAleer	54	99	8th	40.5
06	Jimmy McAleer	76	73	5th	16
07	Jimmy McAleer	69	83	6th	24
08	Jimmy McAleer	83	69	4th	6.5
09	Jimmy McAleer	61	89	7th	36
1910	Jack O'Connor	47	107	8th	57
11	Bobby Wallace	45	107	8th	56.5
12	Bobby Wallace	12	27	(8th)	
	George Stovall	41	74	7th	53
13	George Stovall	50	84	(7th)	
	Jimmy Austin	2	6	(8th)	
	Branch Rickey	5	6	8th	39
14	Branch Rickey	71	82	5th	28.5
15	Branch Rickey	63	91	6th	39.5
16	Fielder Jones	79	75	5th	12
17	Fielder Jones	57	97	7th	43
18	Fielder Jones	22	24	(5th)	
	Jimmy Austin	7	9	(6th)	
	Jimmy Burke	29	31	5th	15
19	Jimmy Burke	67	72	5th T	20.5
1920	Jimmy Burke	76	77	4th	21.5
21	Lee Fohl	81	73	3rd	17.5
22	Lee Fohl	93	61	2nd	1
23	Lee Fohl	52	49	(3rd)	
	Jimmy Austin	22	29	5th	24
24	George Sisler	74	78	4th	17
25	George Sisler	82	71	3rd	16.5
26	George Sisler	62	92	7th	29
27	Dan Howley	59	94	7th	50.5
28	Dan Howley	82	72	3rd	19
29	Dan Howley	79	73	4th	26
1930	Bill Killefer	64	90	6th	38
31	Bill Killefer	63	91	5th	45
32	Bill Killefer	63	91	6th	44
33	Bill Killefer	34	67	(8th)	
	Allen Sothoron	2	6	(8th)	
	Rogers Hornsby	19	33	8th	43.5
34	Rogers Hornsby	67	85	6th	33
35	Rogers Hornsby	65	87	7th	28.5
36	Rogers Hornsby	57	95	7th	44.5

Continued

BALTIMORE (continued)

Year	Manager	W	L	AL Rank	Games Behind
37	Rogers Hornsby	25	52	(7th)	
	Jim Bottomley	21	56	8th	56
38	Gabby Street	53	90	(7th)	
	Oscar Melillo	2	7	7th	44
39	Fred Haney	43	117	8th	64.5
1940	Fred Haney	67	87	6th	23
41	Fred Haney	15	29	(7th)	
	Luke Sewell	55	55	6th T	31
42	Luke Sewell	82	69	3rd	19.5
43	Luke Sewell	72	80	6th	25
44	Luke Sewell	89	65	1st	—a
45	Luke Sewell	81	70	3rd	6
46	Luke Sewell	53	71	(7th)	
	Zack Taylor	13	17	7th	38
47	Muddy Ruel	59	95	8th	38
48	Zack Taylor	59	94	6th	37
49	Zack Taylor	53	101	7th	44
1950	Zack Taylor	58	96	7th	40
51	Zack Taylor	52	102	8th	46
52	Rogers Hornsby	22	29	(8th)	
	Marty Marion	42	61	7th	31
53	Marty Marion	54	100	7th	31
BALTIMORE					
1954	Jimmie Dykes	54	100	7th	57
55	Paul Richards	57	97	7th	39
56	Paul Richards	69	85	6th	28
57	Paul Richards	76	76	5th	21
58	Paul Richards	74	79	6th	17.5
59	Paul Richards	74	80	6th	20
1960	Paul Richards	89	65	2nd	8
61	Paul Richards	78	57	(3rd)	
	Lum Harris	17	10	3rd	14
62	Billy Hitchcock	77	85	7th T	19
63	Billy Hitchcock	86	76	4th	18.5
64	Hank Bauer	97	65	3rd	2
65	Hank Bauer	94	68	3rd	8
66	Hank Bauer	97	63	1st	—b
67	Hank Bauer	76	85	6th T	15.5
68	Hank Bauer	43	37	(3rd)	
	Earl Weaver	48	34	2nd	12
	AL East				
69	Earl Weaver	109	53	1st	—c
1970	Earl Weaver	108	54	1st	—d

Continued

Year	Manager	W	L	AL East	Games Behind
71	Earl Weaver	101	57	1st	—e
72	Earl Weaver	80	74	3rd	5
73	Earl Weaver	97	65	1st	—f
74	Earl Weaver	91	71	1st	—g
75	Earl Weaver	90	69	2nd	4.5
76	Earl Weaver	88	74	2nd	10.5
77	Earl Weaver	97	64	2nd T	2.5
78	Earl Weaver	90	71	4th	9
79	Earl Weaver	102	57	1st	—h
1980	Earl Weaver	100	62	2nd	3
81	Earl Weaver	59	46	2nd	1
82	Earl Weaver	94	68	2nd	1
83	Joe Altobelli	98	64	1st	—i
84	Joe Altobelli	85	77	5th	19
85	Joe Altobelli	29	26	(4th)	
	Cal Ripken, Sr.	1	0	(4th)	
	Earl Weaver	53	52	4th	16
86	Earl Weaver	73	89	7th	22.5
87	Cal Ripken, Sr.	67	95	6th	31
88	Cal Ripken, Sr.	0	6	(6th)	
	Frank Robinson	54	101	7th	34.5
89	Frank Robinson	87	75	2nd	2
1990	Frank Robinson	76	85	5th	11.5
91	Frank Robinson	13	24	(7th)	
	Johnny Oates	54	71	6th	24
92	Johnny Oates	89	73	3rd	7
93	Johnny Oates	85	77	3rd T	10
94	Johnny Oates	63	49	Season not completed	
95	Phil Regan	71	73	3rd	15
96	Davey Johnson	88	74	2nd	4j
97	Davey Johnson	98	64	1st	—k
98	Ray Miller	79	83	4th	35

aLost to St. Louis in World Series

bDefeated Los Angeles in World Series

cDefeated Minnesota in ALCS; lost to New York in World Series

dDefeated Minnesota in ALCS; defeated Cincinnati in World Series

eDefeated Oakland in ALCS; lost to Pittsburgh in World Series

fLost to Oakland in ALCS

gLost to Oakland in ALCS

hDefeated California in ALCS; lost to Pittsburgh in World Series

iDefeated Chicago in ALCS; defeated Philadelphia in World Series

Continued

ʲ(AL Wild Card) Defeated Cleveland in ALC first round; lost to New York in ALCS
ᵏDefeated Seattle in ALC first round; lost to Cleveland in ALCS

Manager Summary
Most seasons—Weaver 17
Most games—Weaver 2,541
Most wins—Weaver 1,480
Most losses—Weaver 1,060
AL pennants—Weaver 4, Altobelli 1, Bauer 1, Sewell 1
Division titles—Weaver 6, Altobelli 1, Johnson 1
Multiple terms as manager—Austin 3, Hornsby 2, Ripken 2, Taylor 2, Weaver 2
Fewest games managed—Melillo 8, Sothoron 8
Number of different managers—35

BOSTON Red Sox 1901–98

(Also known as Boston Americans or Pilgrims, Puritans, Plymouth Rocks, and Somersets, 1901–7.)

Year	Manager	W	L	AL Rank	Games Behind
1901	Jimmy Collins	79	57	2nd	4
02	Jimmy Collins	77	60	3rd	6.5
03	Jimmy Collins	91	47	1st	—a
04	Jimmy Collins	95	59	1st	—b
05	Jimmy Collins	78	74	4th	16
06	Jimmy Collins	35	79	(8th)	
	Chick Stahl	14	26	8th	45.5
07	Cy Young	3	3	(4th)	
	George Huff	2	6	(6th)	
	Bob Unglaub	9	20	(8th)	
	Deacon McGuire	45	61	7th	32.5
08	Deacon McGuire	53	62	(6th)	
	Fred Lake	22	17	5th	15.5
09	Fred Lake	88	63	3rd	9.5
1910	Patsy Donovan	81	72	4th	22.5
11	Patsy Donovan	78	75	4th T	24
12	Jake Stahl	105	47	1st	—c
13	Jake Stahl	39	41	(5th)	
	Bill Carrigan	40	30	4th	15.5
14	Bill Carrigan	91	62	2nd	8.5
15	Bill Carrigan	101	50	1st	—d
16	Bill Carrigan	91	63	1st	—e
17	Jack Barry	90	62	2nd	9
18	Ed Barrow	75	51	1st	—f

Continued

Year	Manager	W	L	AL Rank	Games Behind
19	Ed Barrow	66	71	5th T	20.5
1920	Ed Barrow	72	81	5th	25.5
21	Hugh Duffy	75	79	5th	23.5
22	Hugh Duffy	61	93	8th	33
23	Frank Chance	61	91	8th	37
24	Lee Fohl	67	87	7th	25
25	Lee Fohl	47	105	8th	49.5
26	Lee Fohl	46	107	8th	44.5
27	Bill Carrigan	51	103	8th	59
28	Bill Carrigan	57	96	8th	43.5
29	Bill Carrigan	58	96	8th	48
1930	Heinie Wagner	52	192	8th	50
31	Shano Collins	62	90	6th	45
32	Shano Collins	11	44	(8th)	
	Marty McManus	32	67	8th	64
33	Marty McManus	63	86	7th	34.5
34	Bucky Harris	76	76	4th	24
35	Joe Cronin	78	75	4th	16
36	Joe Cronin	74	80	6th	28.5
37	Joe Cronin	80	72	5th	21
38	Joe Cronin	81	61	2nd	9.5
39	Joe Cronin	89	62	2nd	17
1940	Joe Cronin	82	72	4th T	8
41	Joe Cronin	84	70	2nd	17
42	Joe Cronin	93	59	2nd	9
43	Joe Cronin	68	84	7th	29
44	Joe Cronin	77	77	4th	12
45	Joe Cronin	71	83	7th	17.5
46	Joe Cronin	104	50	1st	—[g]
47	Joe Cronin	83	71	3rd	14
48	Joe McCarthy	96	59	2nd	1[h]
49	Joe McCarthy	96	58	2nd	1
1950	Joe McCarthy	31	28	(4th)	
	Steve O'Neill	63	32	3rd	4
51	Steve O'Neill	87	67	3rd	11
52	Lou Boudreau	76	78	6th	19
53	Lou Boudreau	84	69	4th	16
54	Lou Boudreau	69	85	4th	42
55	Mike Higgins	84	70	4th	12
56	Mike Higgins	84	70	4th	13
57	Mike Higgins	82	72	3rd	16
58	Mike Higgins	79	75	3rd	13

Continued

Year	Manager	W	L	AL Rank	Games Behind
59	Mike Higgins	31	42	(8th)	
	Rudy York	0	1	(8th)	
	Billy Jurges	44	36	5th	19
1960	Billy Jurges	15	27	(8th)	
	Del Baker	2	5	(8th)	
	Mike Higgins	48	57	7th	32
61	Mike Higgins	76	86	6th	33
62	Mike Higgins	76	84	7thT	19
63	Johnny Pesky	76	85	7th	28
64	Johnny Pesky	70	90	(8th)	
	Billy Herman	2	0	8th	27
65	Billy Herman	62	100	9th	40
66	Billy Herman	64	82	(10th)	
	Pete Runnels	8	8	9th	26
67	Dick Williams	92	70	1st	—ʲ
68	Dick Williams	86	76	4th	17
				AL East	
69	Dick Williams	82	71	(3rd)	
	Eddie Popowski	5	4	3rd	22
1970	Eddie Kasko	87	75	3rd	21
71	Eddie Kasko	85	77	3rd	18
72	Eddie Kasko	85	70	2nd	0.5
73	Eddie Kasko	88	73	(2nd)	
	Eddie Popowski	1	0	2nd	8
74	Darrell Johnson	84	78	3rd	7
75	Darrell Johnson	95	65	1st	—ʲ
76	Darrell Johnson	41	45	(3rd)	
	Don Zimmer	42	34	3rd	15.5
77	Don Zimmer	97	64	2nd T	2.5
78	Don Zimmer	99	64	2nd	1ᵏ
79	Don Zimmer	91	69	3rd	11.5
1980	Don Zimmer	82	73	(4th)	
	Johnny Pesky	1	4	4th T	19
81	Ralph Houk	59	49	5th	2.5
82	Ralph Houk	89	73	3rd	6
83	Ralph Houk	78	84	6th	20
84	Ralph Houk	86	76	4th	18
85	John McNamara	81	81	5th	18.5
86	John McNamara	95	66	1st	—ʲ
87	John McNamara	78	84	5th	20
88	John McNamara	43	42	(4th)	
	Joe Morgan	46	31	1st	—ᵐ

Continued

Year	Manager	W	L	AL East	Games Behind
89	Joe Morgan	83	79	3rd	6
1990	Joe Morgan	88	74	1st	—[n]
91	Joe Morgan	84	78	2nd T	7
92	Butch Hobson	73	89	7th	23
93	Butch Hobson	80	82	5th	15
94	Butch Hobson	54	61	Season not completed	
95	Kevin Kennedy	86	58	1st	—[o]
96	Kevin Kennedy	85	77	3rd	7
97	Jimy Williams	78	84	4th	20
98	Jimy Williams	90	72	2nd	22[p]

[a]Defeated Pittsburgh in World Series
[b]No World Series conducted in 1904
[c]Defeated New York in World Series
[d]Defeated Philadelphia in World Series
[e]Defeated Brooklyn in World Series
[f]Defeated Chicago in World Series
[g]Lost to St. Louis in World Series
[h]Lost to Cleveland in one-game playoff for AL title
[i]Lost to St. Louis in World Series
[j]Defeated Oakland in ALCS; lost to Cincinnati in World Series
[k]Lost to New York in one-game playoff for AL East title
[l]Defeated California in ALCS; lost to New York in World Series
[m]Lost to Oakland in ALCS
[n]Lost to Oakland in ALCS
[o]Lost to Cleveland in ALC first round
[p](AL Wild Card) Lost to Cleveland in ALC first round

Manager Summary

Most seasons—Cronin 13
Most games—Cronin 1,996
Most wins—Cronin 1,064
Most losses—Cronin 912
AL Pennants—J. Collins 2, Corrigan 2, Barrow 1, Cronin 1, Johnson 1, McNamara 1, J. Stahl 1, Williams 1
Division titles—Morgan 2, Johnson 1, Kennedy 1, McNamara 1
Multiple terms as manager—Carrigan 2, Higgins 2, Pesky 2, Popowski 2
Fewest games managed—York 1
Number of different managers—41

Continued

(Also known as Chicago White Stockings, 1901–3.)

Year	Manager	W	L	AL Rank	Games Behind
1901	Clark Griffith	83	53	1st	–
02	Clark Griffith	74	60	4th	8
03	Nixey Callahan	60	77	7th	30.5
04	Nixey Callahan	23	18	(4th)	
	Fielder Jones	66	47	3rd	6
05	Fielder Jones	92	60	2nd	2
06	Fielder Jones	93	58	1st	–a
07	Fielder Jones	87	64	3rd	5.5
08	Fielder Jones	88	64	3rd	1.5
09	Billy Sullivan	78	74	4th	20
1910	Hugh Duffy	68	85	6th	35.5
11	Hugh Duffy	77	74	4th T	24
12	Nixey Callahan	78	76	4th	28
13	Nixey Callahan	78	74	5th	17.5
14	Nixey Callahan	70	84	6th T	30
15	Pants Rowland	93	61	3rd	9.5
16	Pants Rowland	89	65	2nd	2
17	Pants Rowland	100	54	1st	–b
18	Pants Rowland	57	67	6th	17
19	Kid Gleason	88	52	1st	–c
1920	Kid Gleason	96	58	2nd	2
21	Kid Gleason	62	92	7th	36.5
22	Kid Gleason	77	77	5th	17
23	Kid Gleason	69	85	7th	30
24	Johnny Evers	10	11	(6th)	
	Ed Walsh	1	2	(6th)	
	Eddie Collins	14	13	(6th)	
	Johnny Evers	41	61	8th	
25	Eddie Collins	79	75	5th	18.5
26	Eddie Collins	81	72	5th	9.5
27	Ray Schalk	70	83	5th	39.5
28	Ray Schalk	32	42	(6th)	
	Lena Blackburne	40	40	5th	29
29	Lena Blackburne	59	93	7th	46
1930	Donie Bush	62	92	7th	40
31	Donie Bush	56	97	8th	51.5
32	Lew Fonseca	49	102	7th	56.5
33	Lew Fonseca	67	83	6th	31
34	Lew Fonseca	4	11	(8th)	
	Jimmie Dykes	49	88	8th	47
35	Jimmie Dykes	74	78	5th	19.5

Continued

Year	Manager	W	L	AL Rank	Games Behind
36	Jimmie Dykes	81	70	3rd T	20
37	Jimmie Dykes	88	68	3rd	16
38	Jimmie Dykes	65	83	6th	32
39	Jimmie Dykes	85	69	4th	22.5
1940	Jimmie Dykes	82	72	4th T	8
41	Jimmie Dykes	77	77	3rd	24
42	Jimmie Dykes	66	82	6th	34
43	Jimmie Dykes	82	72	4th	16
44	Jimmie Dykes	71	83	7th	18
45	Jimmie Dykes	71	78	6th	15
46	Jimmie Dykes	10	20	(7th)	
	Ted Lyons	64	60	5th	30
47	Ted Lyons	70	84	6th	27
48	Ted Lyons	51	101	8th	44.5
49	Jack Onslow	63	91	6th	34
1950	Jack Onslow	8	22	(8th)	
	Red Corriden	52	72	6th	38
51	Paul Richards	81	73	4th	17
52	Paul Richards	81	73	3rd	14
53	Paul Richards	89	65	3rd	11.5
54	Paul Richards	91	54	(3rd)	
	Marty Marion	3	6	3rd	17
55	Marty Marion	91	63	3rd	5
56	Marty Marion	85	69	3rd	12
57	Al Lopez	90	64	2nd	8
58	Al Lopez	82	72	2nd	10
59	Al Lopez	94	60	1st	—d
1960	Al Lopez	87	67	3rd	10
61	Al Lopez	86	76	4th	23
62	Al Lopez	85	77	5th	11
63	Al Lopez	94	68	2nd	10.5
64	Al Lopez	98	64	2nd	1
65	Al Lopez	95	67	2nd	7
66	Eddie Stanky	83	79	4th	15
67	Eddie Stanky	89	73	4th	3
68	Eddie Stanky	34	45	(9th)	
	Les Moss	0	2	(9th)	
	Al Lopez	6	5	(9th)	
	Les Moss	12	22	(9th)	
	Al Lopez	15	21	8th T	36
	AL West				
69	Al Lopez	8	9	(4th)	
	Don Gutteridge	60	85	5th	29

Continued

Year	Manager	W	L	AL West	Games Behind
1970	Don Gutteridge	49	87	(6th)	
	Bill Adair	4	6	(6th)	
	Chuck Tanner	3	13	6th	42
71	Chuck Tanner	79	83	3rd	22.5
72	Chuck Tanner	87	67	2nd	5.5
73	Chuck Tanner	77	85	5th	17
74	Chuck Tanner	80	80	4th	9
75	Chuck Tanner	75	86	5th	22.5
76	Paul Richards	64	97	6th	25.5
77	Bob Lemon	90	72	3rd	12
78	Bob Lemon	34	40	(5th)	
	Larry Doby	37	50	5th	20.5
79	Don Kessinger	46	60	(5th)	
	Tony LaRussa	27	27	5th	14
1980	Tony LaRussa	70	90	5th	26
81	Tony LaRussa	54	52	3rd	8.5
82	Tony LaRussa	87	75	3rd	6
83	Tony LaRussa	99	63	1st	—[e]
84	Tony LaRussa	74	88	5th T	10
85	Tony LaRussa	85	77	3rd	6
86	Tony LaRussa	26	38	(6th)	
	Doug Rader	1	1	(5th)	
	Jim Fregosi	45	51	5th	20
87	Jim Fregosi	77	85	5th	8
88	Jim Fregosi	71	90	5th	32.5
89	Jeff Torborg	69	92	7th	29.5
1990	Jeff Torborg	94	68	2nd	9
91	Jeff Torborg	87	75	2nd	8
92	Gene Lamont	86	76	3rd	10
93	Gene Lamont	94	68	1st	—[f]
				AL Central	
94	Gene Lamont	64	46	Season not completed	
95	Gene Lamont	11	20	(4th)	
	Terry Bevington	57	56	3rd	32
96	Terry Bevington	85	77	2nd	14.5
97	Terry Bevington	80	81	2nd	6
98	Jerry Manuel	80	82	2nd	9

[a]Defeated Chicago in World Series
[b]Defeated New York in World Series
[c]Lost to Cincinnati in World Series
[d]Lost to Los Angeles in World Series
[e]Lost to Baltimore in ALCS
[f]Lost to Toronto in ALCS

Continued

Manager Summary

Most seasons–Dykes 13

Most games–Dykes 1,852

Most wins–Dykes 901

Most losses–Dykes 940

AL pennants–Gleason 1, Griffith 1, Jones 1, Lopez 1, Rowland 1

Division titles–Lamont 1, LaRussa 1

Multiple terms as manager–Lopez 3, Callahan 2, Collins 2, Evers 2, Moss 2, Richards 2

Fewest games managed–Rader 2

Number of different managers–36

CLEVELAND Indians 1901–98

(Also known as Cleveland Blues, 1901; Bronchos, 1902–4; Naps, 1905–14.)

Year	Manager	W	L	AL Rank	Games Behind
1901	Jimmy McAleer	55	82	7th	28.5
02	Bill Armour	69	67	5th	14
03	Bill Armour	77	63	3rd	15
04	Bill Armour	86	65	4th	7.5
05	Nap Lajoie	37	21	(1st)	
	Bill Bradley	20	21	(2nd)	
	Nap Lajoie	19	36	5th	19
06	Nap Lajoie	89	64	3rd	5
07	Nap Lajoie	85	67	4th	8
08	Nap Lajoie	90	64	2nd	0.5
09	Nap Lajoie	57	57	(6th)	
	Deacon McGuire	14	25	6th	27.5
1910	Deacon McGuire	71	81	5th	32
11	Deacon McGuire	6	11	(7th)	
	George Stovall	74	62	3rd	22
12	Harry Davis	54	71	(6th)	
	Joe Birmingham	21	7	5th	30.5
13	Joe Birmingham	86	66	3rd	9.5
14	Joe Birmingham	51	102	8th	48.5
15	Joe Birmingham	12	16	(6th)	
	Lee Fohl	45	79	7th	44.5
16	Lee Fohl	77	77	6th	14
17	Lee Fohl	88	66	3rd	12
18	Lee Fohl	73	54	2nd	2.5
19	Lee Fohl	44	34	(3rd)	
	Tris Speaker	40	21	2nd	3.5
1920	Tris Speaker	98	56	1st	—a

Continued

Year	Manager	W	L	AL Rank	Games Behind
21	Tris Speaker	94	60	2nd	4.5
22	Tris Speaker	78	76	4th	16
23	Tris Speaker	82	71	3rd	16.5
24	Tris Speaker	67	86	6th	24.5
25	Tris Speaker	70	84	6th	27.5
26	Tris Speaker	88	66	2nd	3
27	Jack McCallister	66	87	6th	43.5
28	Roger Peckinpaugh	62	92	7th	39
29	Roger Peckinpaugh	81	71	3rd	24
1930	Roger Peckinpaugh	81	73	4th	21
31	Roger Peckinpaugh	78	76	4th	30
32	Roger Peckinpaugh	87	65	4th	19
33	Roger Peckinpaugh	26	25	(5th)	
	Bibb Falk	1	0	(5th)	
	Walter Johnson	48	51	4th	23.5
34	Walter Johnson	85	69	3rd	16
35	Walter Johnson	46	48	(5th)	
	Steve O'Neill	36	23	3rd	12
36	Steve O'Neill	80	74	5th	22.5
37	Steve O'Neill	83	71	4th	19
38	Oscar Vitt	86	66	3rd	13
39	Oscar Vitt	87	67	3rd	20.5
1940	Oscar Vitt	89	65	2nd	1
41	Roger Peckinpaugh	75	79	4th T	26
42	Lou Boudreau	75	79	4th	28
43	Lou Boudreau	82	71	3rd	15.5
44	Lou Boudreau	72	82	5th T	17
45	Lou Boudreau	73	72	5th	11
46	Lou Boudreau	68	86	6th	36
47	Lou Boudreau	80	74	4th	17
48	Lou Boudreau	97	58	1st	—b
49	Lou Boudreau	89	65	3rd	8
1950	Lou Boudreau	92	62	4th	6
51	Al Lopez	93	61	2nd	5
52	Al Lopez	93	61	2nd	2
53	Al Lopez	92	62	2nd	8.5
54	Al Lopez	111	43	1st	—c
55	Al Lopez	93	61	2nd	3
56	Al Lopez	88	66	2nd	9
57	Kerby Farrell	76	77	6th	21.5
58	Bobby Bragan	31	36	(5th)	
	Joe Gordon	46	40	4th	14.5

Continued

93

Year	Manager	W	L	AL Rank	Games Behind
59	Joe Gordon	89	65	2nd	5
1960	Joe Gordon	49	46	(4th)	
	Jo-Jo White	1	0	(4th)	
	Jimmie Dykes	26	32	4th	21
61	Jimmie Dykes	77	83	(5th)	
	Mel Harder	1	0	5th	30.5
62	Mel McGaha	78	82	(6th)	
	Mel Harder	2	0	6th	16
63	Birdie Tebbetts	79	83	5th T	25.5
64	George Strickland	33	39	(8th)	
	Birdie Tebbetts	46	44	6th T	20
65	Birdie Tebbetts	87	75	5th	15
66	Birdie Tebbetts	66	57	(5th)	
	George Strickland	15	24	5th	17
67	Joe Adcock	75	87	8th	17
68	Alvin Dark	86	75	3rd	16.5
	AL East				
69	Alvin Dark	62	99	6th	46.5
1970	Alvin Dark	76	86	5th	32
71	Alvin Dark	42	61	(6th)	
	Johnny Lipon	18	41	6th	43
72	Ken Aspromonte	72	84	5th	14
73	Ken Aspromonte	71	91	6th	26
74	Ken Aspromonte	77	85	4th	14
75	Frank Robinson	79	80	4th	15.5
76	Frank Robinson	81	78	4th	16
77	Frank Robinson	26	31	(6th)	
	Jeff Torborg	45	59	5th	28.5
78	Jeff Torborg	69	90	6th	29
79	Jeff Torborg	43	52	(6th)	
	Dave Garcia	38	28	6th	22
1980	Dave Garcia	79	81	6th	23
81	Dave Garcia	52	51	6th	7
82	Dave Garcia	78	84	6th T	17
83	Mike Ferraro	40	60	(7th)	
	Pat Corrales	30	32	7th	28
84	Pat Corrales	75	87	6th	29
85	Pat Corrales	60	102	7th	39.5
86	Pat Corrales	84	78	5th	11.5
87	Pat Corrales	31	56	(7th)	
	Doc Edwards	30	45	7th	37
88	Doc Edwards	78	84	6th	11
89	Doc Edwards	65	78	(6th)	

Continued

CLEVELAND (continued)

Year	Manager	W	L	AL East	Games Behind
	John Hart	8	11	6th	16
1990	John McNamara	77	85	4th	11
91	John McNamara	25	52	(7th)	
	Mike Hargrove	32	53	7th	34
92	Mike Hargrove	76	86	4th T	20
93	Mike Hargrove	76	86	6th	19
				AL Central	
94	Mike Hargrove	66	47	Season not completed	
95	Mike Hargrove	100	44	1st	_d
96	Mike Hargrove	99	62	1st	_e
97	Mike Hargrove	86	75	1st	_f
98	Mike Hargrove	89	73	1st	_g

aDefeated Brooklyn in World Series

bDefeated Boston in one-game playoff for AL title; defeated Boston in World Series

cLost to New York in World Series

dDefeated Boston in ALC first round; defeated Seattle in ALCS; lost to Atlanta in World Series

eLost to Baltimore in ALC first round

fDefeated New York in ALC first round; defeated Baltimore in ALCS; lost to Florida in World Series

gDefeated Boston in ALC first round; lost to New York in ALCS

Manager Summary

Most seasons—Boudreau 9

Most games—Boudreau 1,389

Most wins—Boudreau 728

Most losses—Boudreau 649

AL pennants—Hargrove 2, Boudreau 1, Lopez 1, Speaker 1

Division titles—Hargrove 4

Multiple terms as manager—Harder 2, Lajoie 2, Peckinpaugh 2, Strickland 2, Tebbetts 2

Fewest games managed—Falk 1, White 1

Number of different managers—40

DETROIT Tigers 1901–98

Year	Manager	W	L	AL Rank	Games Behind
1901	George Stallings	74	62	3rd	8.5
02	Fred Dwyer	52	83	7th	30.5
03	Ed Barrow	65	71	5th	25
04	Ed Barrow	32	46	(7th)	
	Bobby Lowe	30	44	7th	32
05	Bill Armour	79	74	3rd	15.5
06	Bill Armour	71	78	6th	21

Continued

Year	Manager	W	L	AL Rank	Games Behind
07	Hughie Jennings	92	58	1st	_a
08	Hughie Jennings	90	63	1st	_b
09	Hughie Jennings	98	54	1st	_c
1910	Hughie Jennings	86	68	3rd	18
11	Hughie Jennings	89	65	2nd	13.5
12	Hughie Jennings	69	84	6th	36.5
13	Hughie Jennings	66	87	6th	30
14	Hughie Jennings	80	73	4th	19.5
15	Hughie Jennings	100	54	2nd	2.5
16	Hughie Jennings	87	67	3rd	4
17	Hughie Jennings	78	75	4th	21.5
18	Hughie Jennings	55	71	7th	20
19	Hughie Jennings	80	60	4th	8
1920	Hughie Jennings	61	93	7th	37
21	Ty Cobb	71	82	6th	27
22	Ty Cobb	79	75	3rd	15
23	Ty Cobb	83	71	2nd	16
24	Ty Cobb	86	68	3rd	6
25	Ty Cobb	81	73	4th	16.5
26	Ty Cobb	79	75	6th	12
27	George Moriarty	82	71	4th	27.5
28	George Moriarty	68	86	6th	33
29	Bucky Harris	70	84	6th	36
1930	Bucky Harris	75	79	5th	27
31	Bucky Harris	61	93	7th	47
32	Bucky Harris	76	75	5th	29.5
33	Bucky Harris	73	79	(5th)	
	Del Baker	2	0	5th	25
34	Mickey Cochrane	101	53	1st	_d
35	Mickey Cochrane	93	58	1st	_e
36	Mickey Cochrane	29	24	(3rd)	
	Del Baker	18	16	(4th)	
	Mickey Cochrane	36	31	2nd	19.5
37	Mickey Cochrane	16	13	(3rd)	
	Del Baker	34	20	(3rd)	
	Mickey Cochrane	39	32	2nd	13
38	Mickey Cochrane	47	51	(5th)	
	Del Baker	37	19	4th	16
39	Del Baker	81	73	5th	26.5
1940	Del Baker	90	64	1st	_f
41	Del Baker	75	79	4th T	26
42	Del Baker	73	81	5th	30

Continued

Year	Manager	W	L	AL Rank	Games Behind
43	Steve O'Neill	78	76	5th	20
44	Steve O'Neill	88	66	2nd	1
45	Steve O'Neill	88	65	1st	—g
46	Steve O'Neill	92	62	2nd	12
47	Steve O'Neill	85	69	2nd	12
48	Steve O'Neill	78	76	5th	18.5
49	Red Rolfe	87	67	4th	10
1950	Red Rolfe	95	59	2nd	3
51	Red Rolfe	73	81	5th	25
52	Red Rolfe	23	49	(8th)	
	Fred Hutchinson	27	55	8th	45
53	Fred Hutchinson	60	94	6th	40.5
54	Fred Hutchinson	68	86	5th	43
55	Bucky Harris	79	75	5th	17
56	Bucky Harris	82	72	5th	15
57	Jack Tighe	78	76	4th	20
58	Jack Tighe	21	28	(5th)	
	Bill Norman	56	49	5th	15
59	Bill Norman	2	15	(8th)	
	Jimmie Dykes	74	63	4th	18
1960	Jimmie Dykes	44	52	(6th)	
	Billy Hitchcock	1	0	(6th)	
	Joe Gordon	26	31	6th	26
61	Bob Scheffing	101	61	2nd	8
62	Bob Scheffing	85	76	4th	10.5
63	Bob Scheffing	24	36	(9th)	
	Chuck Dressen	55	47	5th T	25.5
64	Chuck Dressen	85	77	4th	14
65	Bob Swift	24	18	(3rd)	
	Chuck Dressen	65	55	4th	13
66	Chuck Dressen	16	10	(3rd)	
	Bob Swift	32	25	(3rd)	
	Frank Skaff	40	39	3rd	10
67	Mayo Smith	91	71	2nd	12
68	Mayo Smith	103	59	1st	—h
				AL East	
69	Mayo Smith	90	72	2nd	19
1970	Mayo Smith	79	83	4th	29
71	Billy Martin	91	71	2nd	12
72	Billy Martin	86	70	1st	—i
73	Billy Martin	71	63	(3rd)	
	Joe Schultz	14	14	3rd	12

Continued

Year	Manager	W	L	AL East	Games Behind
74	Ralph Houk	72	90	6th	19
75	Ralph Houk	57	102	6th	37.5
76	Ralph Houk	74	87	5th	24
77	Ralph Houk	74	88	4th	26
78	Ralph Houk	86	76	5th	13.5
79	Les Moss	27	26	(5th)	
	Dick Tracewski	2	0	(5th)	
	Sparky Anderson	56	50	5th	18
1980	Sparky Anderson	84	78	4th T	19
81	Sparky Anderson	60	49	4th	2
82	Sparky Anderson	83	79	4th	12
83	Sparky Anderson	92	70	2nd	6
84	Sparky Anderson	104	58	1st	_j
85	Sparky Anderson	84	77	3rd	15
86	Sparky Anderson	87	75	3rd	8.5
87	Sparky Anderson	98	64	1st	_k
88	Sparky Anderson	88	74	2nd	1
89	Sparky Anderson	59	103	7th	30
1990	Sparky Anderson	79	83	3rd	9
91	Sparky Anderson	84	78	2nd T	7
92	Sparky Anderson	75	87	6th	21
93	Sparky Anderson	85	77	3rd T	10
94	Sparky Anderson	53	62	Season not completed	
95	Sparky Anderson	60	84	4th	26
96	Buddy Bell	53	109	5th	39
97	Buddy Bell	79	83	3rd	19
				AL Central	
98	Buddy Bell	52	85	(5th)	
	Larry Parrish	13	12	5th	24

[a]Lost to Chicago in World Series
[b]Lost to Chicago in World Series
[c]Lost to Pittsburgh in World Series
[d]Lost to St. Louis in World Series
[e]Defeated Chicago in World Series
[f]Lost to Cincinnati in World Series
[g]Defeated Chicago in World Series
[h]Defeated St. Louis in World Series
[i]Lost to Oakland in ALCS
[j]Defeated Kansas City in ALCS; defeated San Diego in World Series
[k]Lost to Minnesota in ALCS

Manager Summary

Most seasons—Anderson 17

Most games—Anderson 2,579

Continued

Most wins–Anderson 1,331

Most losses–Anderson 1,248

AL pennants–Jennings 3, Cochrane 2, Anderson 1, Baker 1, O'Neill 1, Smith 1

Division titles–Anderson 2, Martin 1

Multiple terms as manager–Baker 4, Cochrane 3, Dressen 2, Harris 2, Swift 2

Fewest games managed–Hitchcock 1

Number of different managers–32

KANSAS CITY Royals 1969–98

Year	Manager	W	L	AL West	Games Behind
1969	Joe Gordon	69	93	4th	28
1970	Charlie Metro	19	33	(5th)	
	Bob Lemon	46	64	4th T	33
71	Bob Lemon	85	76	2nd	16
72	Bob Lemon	76	78	4th	16.5
73	Jack McKeon	88	74	2nd	6
74	Jack McKeon	77	85	5th	13
75	Jack McKeon	50	46	(2nd)	
	Whitey Herzog	41	25	2nd	7
76	Whitey Herzog	90	72	1st	–[a]
77	Whitey Herzog	102	60	1st	–[b]
78	Whitey Herzog	92	70	1st	–[c]
79	Whitey Herzog	85	77	2nd	3
1980	Jim Frey	97	65	1st	–[d]
81	Jim Frey	30	40	(2nd)	
	Dick Howser	20	13	4th	11[e]
82	Dick Howser	90	72	2nd	3
83	Dick Howser	79	83	2nd	20
84	Dick Howser	84	78	1st	–[f]
85	Dick Howser	91	71	1st	–[g]
86	Dick Howser	40	48	(4th)	
	Mike Ferraro	36	38	3rd T	16
87	Billy Gardner	62	64	(4th)	
	John Wathan	21	15	2nd	2
88	John Wathan	84	77	3rd	19.5
89	John Wathan	92	70	2nd	7
1990	John Wathan	75	86	6th	27.5
91	John Wathan	15	22	(7th)	
	Bob Schaefer	1	0	(7th)	
	Hal McRae	66	58	6th	13
92	Hal McRae	72	80	5th T	24

Continued

Year	Manager	W	L	AL West	Games Behind
93	Hal McRae	84	78	3rd	10
				AL Central	
94	Hal McRae	64	51	Season not completed	
95	Bob Boone	70	74	2nd	30
96	Bob Boone	75	86	5th	24
97	Bob Boone	36	46	(4th)	
	Tony Muser	31	48	5th	19
98	Tony Muser	72	89	3rd	16.5

[a]Lost to New York in ALCS

[b]Lost to New York in ALCS

[c]Lost to New York in ALCS

[d]Defeated New York in ALCS; lost to Philadelphia in World Series

[e]Lost to Oakland in AL West split-season playoff

[f]Lost to Detroit in ALCS

[g]Defeated Toronto in ALCS; defeated St. Louis in World Series

Manager Summary

Most seasons—Howser 6

Most games—Howser 770

Most wins—Herzog 410

Most losses—Howser 365

AL pennants—Frey 1, Howser 1

Division titles—Herzog 3, Howser 3

Multiple terms as manager—none (thru Boone)

Fewest games managed—Schaefer 1

Number of different managers—14

MINNESOTA Twins 1961–98
WASHINGTON Senators 1901–60

(Also often known as Washington Nationals, 1901–56.)

Year	Manager	W	L	AL Rank	Games Behind
WASHINGTON					
1901	Jimmy Manning	61	73	6th	21
02	Tom Loftus	61	75	6th	22
03	Tom Loftus	43	94	8th	47.5
04	Mal Kittredge	1	16	(8th)	
	Patsy Donovan	37	97	8th	55.5
05	Jake Stahl	64	87	7th	29.5
06	Jake Stahl	55	95	7th	37.5

Continued

Year	Manager	W	L	AL West	Games Behind
07	Joe Cantillon	49	102	8th	43.5
08	Joe Cantillon	67	85	7th	22.5
09	Joe Cantillon	42	110	8th	56
1910	Jimmy McAleer	66	86	7th	36.5
11	Jimmy McAleer	64	60	7th	38.5
12	Clark Griffith	91	61	2nd	14
13	Clark Griffith	90	64	2nd	6.5
14	Clark Griffith	81	73	3rd	19
15	Clark Griffith	85	68	4th	17
16	Clark Griffith	76	77	7th	14.5
17	Clark Griffith	74	79	5th	25.5
18	Clark Griffith	72	56	3rd	4
19	Clark Griffith	56	84	7th	32
1920	Clark Griffith	68	84	6th	29
21	George McBride	80	73	4th	18
22	Clyde Milan	69	85	6th	25
23	Donie Bush	75	78	4th	23.5
24	Bucky Harris	92	62	1st	—a
25	Bucky Harris	96	55	1st	—b
26	Bucky Harris	81	69	4th	8
27	Bucky Harris	85	69	3rd	25
28	Bucky Harris	75	79	4th	26
29	Walter Johnson	71	81	5th	34
1930	Walter Johnson	94	60	2nd	8
31	Walter Johnson	92	62	3rd	16
32	Walter Johnson	93	61	3rd	14
33	Joe Cronin	99	53	1st	—c
34	Joe Cronin	66	86	7th	34
35	Bucky Harris	67	86	6th	27
36	Bucky Harris	82	71	3rd T	20
37	Bucky Harris	73	80	6th	28.5
38	Bucky Harris	75	76	5th	23.5
39	Bucky Harris	65	87	6th	41.5
1940	Bucky Harris	64	90	7th	26
41	Bucky Harris	70	84	6th T	31
42	Bucky Harris	62	89	7th	39.5
43	Ossie Bluege	84	69	2nd	13.5
44	Ossie Bluege	64	90	8th	25
45	Ossie Bluege	87	67	2nd	1.5
46	Ossie Bluege	76	78	4th	28
47	Ossie Bluege	64	90	7th	33
48	Joe Kuhel	56	97	7th	40

Continued

Year	Manager	W	L	AL Rank	Games Behind
49	Joe Kuhel	50	104	8th	47
1950	Bucky Harris	67	87	5th	31
51	Bucky Harris	62	92	7th	36
52	Bucky Harris	78	76	5th	17
53	Bucky Harris	76	76	5th	23.5
54	Bucky Harris	66	88	6th	45
55	Chuck Dressen	53	101	8th	43
56	Chuck Dressen	59	95	7th	38
57	Chuck Dressen	4	16	(8th)	
	Cookie Lavagetto	51	83	8th	43
58	Cookie Lavagetto	61	93	8th	31
59	Cookie Lavagetto	63	91	8th	31
1960	Cookie Lavagetto	73	81	5th	24
MINNESOTA					
1961	Cookie Lavagetto	19	30	(8th)	
	Sam Mele	2	5	(9th)	
	Cookie Lavagetto	4	6	(9th)	
	Sam Mele	45	49	7th	38
62	Sam Mele	91	71	2nd	5
63	Sam Mele	91	70	3rd	13
64	Sam Mele	79	83	6thT	20
65	Sam Mele	102	60	1st	_d
66	Sam Mele	89	73	2nd	9
67	Sam Mele	25	25	(6th)	
	Cal Ermer	66	46	2nd T	1
68	Cal Ermer	79	83	7th	24
AL West					
69	Billy Martin	97	65	1st	_e
1970	Bill Rigney	98	64	1st	_f
71	Bill Rigney	74	86	5th	26.5
72	Bill Rigney	36	34	(3rd)	
	Frank Quilici	41	43	3rd	15.5
73	Frank Quilici	81	81	3rd	13
74	Frank Quilici	82	80	3rd	8
75	Frank Quilici	76	83	4th	20.5
76	Gene Mauch	85	77	3rd	5
77	Gene Mauch	84	77	4th	17.5
78	Gene Mauch	73	89	4th	19
79	Gene Mauch	82	80	4th	6
1980	Gene Mauch	54	71	(6th)	
	John Goryl	23	13	3rd	19.5
81	John Goryl	11	25	(5th)	

Continued

MINNESOTA (continued)

Year	Manager	W	L	AL West	Games Behind
	Billy Gardner	30	43	7th	23
82	Billy Gardner	60	102	7th	33
83	Billy Gardner	70	92	5th T	29
84	Billy Gardner	81	81	2nd T	3
85	Billy Gardner	27	35	(6th)	
	Ray Miller	50	50	4th T	14
86	Ray Miller	59	80	(7th)	
	Tom Kelly	12	11	6th	21
87	Tom Kelly	85	77	1st	—g
88	Tom Kelly	91	71	2nd	13
89	Tom Kelly	80	82	5th	19
1990	Tom Kelly	74	88	7th	29
91	Tom Kelly	95	67	1st	—h
92	Tom Kelly	90	72	2nd	6
93	Tom Kelly	71	91	5th T	23
				AL Central	
94	Tom Kelly	53	60	Season not completed	
95	Tom Kelly	56	88	5th	44
96	Tom Kelly	78	84	4th	21.5
97	Tom Kelly	68	94	4th	18.5
98	Tom Kelly	70	92	4th	19

[a]Defeated New York in World Series

[b]Lost to Pittsburgh in World Series

[c]Lost to New York in World Series

[d]Lost to Los Angeles in World Series

[e]Lost to Baltimore in ALCS

[f]Lost to Baltimore in ALCS

[g]Defeated Detroit in ALCS; defeated St. Louis in World Series

[h]Defeated Toronto in ALCS; defeated Atlanta in World Series

Manager Summary

Most seasons–Harris 18

Most games–Harris 2,772

Most wins–Harris 1,342

Most losses–Harris 1,407

AL pennants–Harris 2, Kelly 2, Cronin 1, Mele 1

Division titles–Kelly 2, Martin 1, Rigney 1

Multiple terms as manager–Harris 3, Lavagetto 2, Mele 2

Fewest games managed–Kittredge 18

Number of different managers–28

(Also known as New York Highlanders, 1903–12.)

Year	Manager	W	L	AL Rank	Games Behind
BALTIMORE					
1901	John McGraw	68	55	5th	13.5
02	John McGraw	26	31	(7th)	
	Wilbert Robinson	24	57	8th	34
NEW YORK					
1903	Clark Griffith	72	62	4th	17
04	Clark Griffith	92	59	2nd	1.5
05	Clark Griffith	71	78	6th	21.5
06	Clark Griffith	90	61	2nd	3
07	Clark Griffith	70	78	5th	21
08	Clark Griffith	24	32	(6th)	
	Kid Elberfeld	27	71	8th	39.5
09	George Stallings	74	77	5th	23.5
1910	George Stallings	78	59	(3rd)	
	Hal Chase	10	4	2nd	14.5
11	Hal Chase	78	76	6th	25.5
12	Harry Wolverton	50	102	8th	55
13	Frank Chance	57	94	7th	38
14	Frank Chance	60	74	(7th)	
	Roger Peckinpaugh	10	10	6th T	30
15	Bill Donovan	69	83	5th	32.5
16	Bill Donovan	80	74	4th	11
17	Bill Donovan	71	82	6th	28.5
18	Miller Huggins	60	63	4th	13.5
19	Miller Huggins	80	59	3rd	17.5
1920	Miller Huggins	95	59	3rd	3
21	Miller Huggins	98	55	1st	—[a]
22	Miller Huggins	94	60	1st	—[b]
23	Miller Huggins	98	54	1st	—[c]
24	Miller Huggins	89	63	2nd	2
25	Miller Huggins	69	85	7th	28.5
26	Miller Huggins	91	63	1st	—[d]
27	Miller Huggins	110	44	1st	—[e]
28	Miller Huggins	101	53	1st	—[f]
29	Miller Huggins	82	61	(2nd)	
	Art Fletcher	6	5	2nd	18
1930	Bob Shawkey	86	68	3rd	16
31	Joe McCarthy	94	59	2nd	13.5
32	Joe McCarthy	107	47	1st	—[g]
33	Joe McCarthy	91	59	2nd	7

Continued

Year	Manager	W	L	AL Rank	Games Behind
34	Joe McCarthy	94	60	2nd	7
35	Joe McCarthy	89	60	2nd	3
36	Joe McCarthy	102	51	1st	—h
37	Joe McCarthy	102	52	1st	—i
38	Joe McCarthy	99	53	1st	—j
39	Joe McCarthy	106	45	1st	—k
1940	Joe McCarthy	88	66	3rd	2
41	Joe McCarthy	101	53	1st	—l
42	Joe McCarthy	103	51	1st	—m
43	Joe McCarthy	98	56	1st	—n
44	Joe McCarthy	83	71	3rd	6
45	Joe McCarthy	81	71	4th	6.5
46	Joe McCarthy	22	13	(2nd)	
	Bill Dickey	57	48	(3rd)	
	Johnny Neun	8	6	3rd	17
47	Bucky Harris	97	57	1st	—o
48	Bucky Harris	94	60	3rd	2.5
49	Casey Stengel	97	57	1st	—p
1950	Casey Stengel	98	56	1st	—q
51	Casey Stengel	98	56	1st	—r
52	Casey Stengel	95	59	1st	—s
53	Casey Stengel	99	52	1st	—t
54	Casey Stengel	103	51	2nd	8
55	Casey Stengel	96	58	1st	—u
56	Casey Stengel	97	57	1st	—v
57	Casey Stengel	98	56	1st	—w
58	Casey Stengel	92	62	1st	—x
59	Casey Stengel	79	75	3rd	15
1960	Casey Stengel	97	57	1st	—y
61	Ralph Houk	109	53	1st	—z
62	Ralph Houk	96	66	1st	—aa
63	Ralph Houk	104	57	1st	—bb
64	Yogi Berra	99	63	1st	—cc
65	Johnny Keane	77	85	6th	25
66	Johnny Keane	4	16	(10th)	
	Ralph Houk	66	73	10th	26.5
67	Ralph Houk	72	90	9th	20
68	Ralph Houk	83	79	5th	20
	AL East				
69	Ralph Houk	80	81	5th	28.5
1970	Ralph Houk	93	69	2nd	15
71	Ralph Houk	82	80	4th	21

Continued

Year	Manager	W	L	AL East	Games Behind
72	Ralph Houk	79	76	4th	6.5
73	Ralph Houk	80	82	4th	17
74	Bill Virdon	89	73	2nd	2
75	Bill Virdon	53	51	(3rd)	
	Billy Martin	30	26	3rd	12
76	Billy Martin	97	62	1st	—dd
77	Billy Martin	100	62	1st	—ee
78	Billy Martin	52	42	(3rd)	
	Dick Howser	0	1	(3rd)	
	Bob Lemon	48	20	1st	—ff
79	Bob Lemon	34	31	(4th)	
	Billy Martin	55	40	4th	13.5
1980	Dick Howser	103	59	1st	—gg
81	Gene Michael	48	34	(5th)	
	Bob Lemon	11	14	3rd	2hh
82	Bob Lemon	6	8	(4th)	
	Gene Michael	44	42	(5th)	
	Clyde King	29	33	5th	16
83	Billy Martin	91	71	3rd	7
84	Yogi Berra	87	75	3rd	17
85	Yogi Berra	6	10	(7th)	
	Billy Martin	91	54	2nd	2
86	Lou Piniella	90	72	2nd	5.5
87	Lou Piniella	89	73	4th	9
88	Billy Martin	40	28	(2nd)	
	Lou Piniella	45	48	5th	3.5
89	Dallas Green	56	65	(6th)	
	Bucky Dent	8	22	5th	14.5
1990	Bucky Dent	18	31	(7th)	
	Stump Merrill	49	64	7th	21
91	Stump Merrill	71	91	5th	20
92	Buck Showalter	76	86	4th T	20
93	Buck Showalter	88	74	2nd	7
94	Buck Showalter	70	43	season not completed	
95	Buck Showalter	79	65	2nd	7ii
96	Joe Torre	92	69	1st	—jj
97	Joe Torre	96	66	2nd	2kk
98	Joe Torre	114	48	1st	—ll

[a]Lost to New York in World Series
[b]Lost to New York in World Series
[c]Defeated New York in World Series
[d]Lost to St. Louis in World Series
[e]Defeated Pittsburgh in World Series

Continued

[f]Defeated St. Louis in World Series

[g]Defeated Chicago in World Series

[h]Defeated New York in World Series

[i]Defeated New York in World Series

[j]Defeated Chicago in World Series

[k]Defeated Cincinnati in World Series

[l]Defeated Brooklyn in World Series

[m]Lost to St. Louis in World Series

[n]Defeated St. Louis in World Series

[o]Defeated Brooklyn in World Series

[p]Defeated Brooklyn in World Series

[q]Defeated Philadelphia in World Series

[r]Defeated New York in World Series

[s]Defeated Brooklyn in World Series

[t]Defeated Brooklyn in World Series

[u]Lost to Brooklyn in World Series

[v]Defeated Brooklyn in World Series

[w]Lost to Milwaukee in World Series

[x]Defeated Milwaukee in World Series

[y]Lost to Pittsburgh in World Series

[z]Defeated Cincinnati in World Series

[aa]Defeated San Francisco in World Series

[bb]Lost to Los Angeles in World Series

[cc]Lost to St. Louis in World Series

[dd]Defeated Kansas City in ALCS; lost to Cincinnati in World Series

[ee]Defeated Kansas City in ALCS; defeated Los Angeles in World Series

[ff]Defeated Boston in one-game playoff for AL East title; Defeated Kansas City in ALCS; defeated Los Angeles in World Series

[gg]Lost to Kansas City in ALCS

[hh]Defeated Milwaukee in AL East split-season playoff; defeated Oakland in ALCS; Lost to Los Angeles in World Series

[ii](AL Wild Card) Lost to Seattle in ALC first round

[jj]Defeated Texas in ALC first round; defeated Baltimore in ALCS; defeated Atlanta in World Series

[kk](AL Wild Card) Lost to Cleveland in ALC first round

[ll]Defeated Texas in ALC 1st round; defeated Cleveland in ALCS; defeated San Diego in World Series

Manager Summary

Most seasons—McCarthy 16

Most games—McCarthy 2,345

Most wins—McCarthy 1,460

Most losses—McCarthy 867

AL pennants—Stengel 10, McCarthy 8, Huggins 6, Houk 3, Lemon 2, Martin 2, Torre 2, Berra 1, Harris 1

Division titles—Lemon 2, Martin 2, Torre 2, Howser 1

Multiple terms as Manager—Martin 5, Berra 2, Houk 2, Howser 2, Lemon 2, Michael 2, Piniella 2

Fewest games managed—Fletcher 11

Number of different managers—33

Year	Manager	W	L	AL Rank	Games Behind
PHILADELPHIA					
1901	Connie Mack	74	62	4th	9
02	Connie Mack	83	53	1st	–
03	Connie Mack	75	60	2nd	14.5
04	Connie Mack	81	70	5th	12.5
05	Connie Mack	92	56	1st	—a
06	Connie Mack	78	67	4th	12
07	Connie Mack	88	57	2nd	1.5
08	Connie Mack	68	85	6th	22
09	Connie Mack	95	58	2nd	3.5
1910	Connie Mack	102	48	1st	—b
11	Connie Mack	101	50	1t	—c
12	Connie Mack	90	62	3rd	15
13	Connie Mack	96	57	1st	—d
14	Connie Mack	99	53	1st	—e
15	Connie Mack	43	109	8th	58.5
16	Connie Mack	36	117	8th	54.5
17	Connie Mack	55	98	8th	45.5
18	Connie Mack	52	76	8th	24
19	Connie Mack	36	104	8th	52
1920	Connie Mack	48	106	8th	50
21	Connie Mack	53	100	8th	45
22	Connie Mack	65	89	7th	29
23	Connie Mack	69	83	6th	29
24	Connie Mack	71	81	5th	20
25	Connie Mack	88	64	2nd	8.5
26	Connie Mack	83	67	3rd	6
27	Connie Mack	91	63	2nd	19
28	Connie Mack	98	55	2nd	2.5
29	Connie Mack	104	46	1st	—f
1930	Connie Mack	102	52	1st	—g
31	Connie Mack	107	45	1st	—h
32	Connie Mack	94	60	2nd	13
33	Connie Mack	79	72	3rd	19.5
34	Connie Mack	68	82	5th	31
35	Connie Mack	58	91	8th	34
36	Connie Mack	53	100	8th	49
37	Connie Mack	39	80	(7th)	
	Earle Mack	15	17	7th	46.5
38	Connie Mack	53	99	8th	46

Continued

Year	Manager	W	L	AL Rank	Games Behind
39	Connie Mack	25	37	(6th)	
	Earle Mack	30	60	7th	51.5
1940	Connie Mack	54	100	8th	36
41	Connie Mack	64	90	8th	37
42	Connie Mack	55	99	8th	48
43	Connie Mack	49	105	8th	49
44	Connie Mack	72	82	5th T	17
45	Connie Mack	52	98	8th	34.5
46	Connie Mack	49	105	8th	55
47	Connie Mack	78	76	5th	19
48	Connie Mack	84	70	4th	12.5
49	Connie Mack	81	73	5th	16
1950	Connie Mack	52	102	8th	46
51	Jimmie Dykes	70	84	6th	28
52	Jimmie Dykes	79	75	4th	16
53	Jimmie Dykes	59	95	7th	41.5
54	Eddie Joost	51	103	8th	60
KANSAS CITY					
1955	Lou Boudreau	63	91	6th	33
56	Lou Boudreau	52	102	8th	45
57	Lou Boudreau	36	67	(8th)	
	Harry Craft	23	27	7th	38.5
58	Harry Craft	73	81	7th	19
59	Harry Craft	66	88	7th	28
1960	Bob Elliott	58	96	8th	39
61	Joe Gordon	26	33	(8th)	
	Hank Bauer	35	67	9th T	47.5
62	Hank Bauer	72	90	9th	24
63	Eddie Lopat	73	89	8th	31.5
64	Eddie Lopat	17	35	(10th)	
	Mel McGaha	40	70	10th	42
65	Mel McGaha	5	21	(10th)	
	Haywood Sullivan	54	82	10th	43
66	Alvin Dark	74	86	7th	23
67	Alvin Dark	52	69	(10th)	
	Luke Appling	10	30	10th	29.5
OAKLAND					
1968	Bob Kennedy	82	80	6th	21
				AL West	
69	Hank Bauer	80	69	(2nd)	
	John McNamara	8	5	2nd	9
1970	John McNamara	89	73	2nd	9

Continued

Year	Manager	W	L	AL West	Games Behind
71	Dick Williams	101	60	1st	—i
72	Dick Williams	93	62	1st	—j
73	Dick Williams	94	68	1st	—k
74	Alvin Dark	90	72	1st	—l
75	Alvin Dark	98	64	1st	—m
76	Chuck Tanner	87	74	2nd	2.5
77	Jack McKeon	26	27	(7th)	
	Bobby Winkles	37	71	7th	38.5
78	Bobby Winkles	24	15	(6th)	
	Jack McKeon	45	78	6th	23
79	Jim Marshall	54	108	7th	34
1980	Billy Martin	83	79	2nd	14
81	Billy Martin	64	45	1st	—n
82	Billy Martin	68	94	5th	25
83	Steve Boros	74	88	4th	25
84	Steve Boros	20	24	(4th)	
	Jackie Moore	57	61	4th	7
85	Jackie Moore	77	85	4th T	14
86	Jackie Moore	29	44	(6th)	
	Jeff Newman	2	8	(7th)	
	Tony LaRussa	45	34	3rd T	16
87	Tony LaRussa	81	81	3rd	4
88	Tony LaRussa	104	58	1st	—o
89	Tony LaRussa	99	63	1st	—p
1990	Tony LaRussa	103	59	1st	—q
91	Tony LaRussa	84	78	4th	11
92	Tony LaRussa	96	66	1st	—r
93	Tony LaRussa	68	94	7th	26
94	Tony LaRussa	51	63	Season not completed	
95	Tony LaRussa	67	77	4th	11
96	Art Howe	78	84	3rd	12
97	Art Howe	65	97	4th	25
98	Art Howe	74	88	4th	14

[a]Lost to New York in World Series
[b]Defeated Chicago in World Series
[c]Defeated New York in World Series
[d]Defeated New York in World Series
[e]Lost to Boston in World Series
[f]Defeated Chicago in World Series
[g]Defeated St. Louis in World Series
[h]Lost to St. Louis in World Series
[i]Lost to Baltimore in ALCS
[j]Defeated Detroit in ALCS; defeated Cincinnati in World Series

Continued

kDefeated Baltimore in ALCS; defeated New York in World Series

lDefeated Baltimore in ALCS; defeated Los Angeles in World Series

mLost to Boston in ALCS

nDefeated Kansas City in AL West split-season playoffs; lost to New York in ALCS

oDefeated Boston in ALCS; lost to Los Angeles in World Series

pDefeated Toronto in ALCS; defeated San Francisco in World Series

qDefeated Boston in ALCS; lost to Cincinnati in World Series

rLost to Toronto in ALCS

Manager Summary

Most seasons—C. Mack 50

Most games—C. Mack 7,466

Most wins—C. Mack 3,582

Most losses—C. Mack 3,814

AL pennants—C. Mack 9, LaRussa 3, Williams 2, Dark 1

Division titles—LaRussa 4, Williams 3, Dark 2, Martin 1

Multiple terms as manager—Bauer 2, Dark 2, C. Mack 2, E. Mack 2, McKeon 2

Fewest games managed—Newman 10

Number of different managers—26

SEATTLE Mariners 1977–98

Year	Manager	W	L	AL West	Games Behind
1977	Darrell Johnson	64	98	6th	38
78	Darrell Johnson	56	104	7th	35
79	Darrell Johnson	67	95	6th	21
1980	Darrell Johnson	39	65	(7th)	
	Maury Wills	20	38	7th	38
81	Maury Wills	6	18	(7th)	
	Rene Lachemann	38	47	6th	20
82	Rene Lachemann	76	86	4th	17
83	Rene Lachemann	26	47	(7th)	
	Del Crandall	34	55	7th	39
84	Del Crandall	59	76	(7th)	
	Chuck Cottier	15	12	5th T	10
85	Chuck Cottier	74	88	6th	17
86	Chuck Cottier	9	19	(6th)	
	Marty Martinez	0	1	(6th)	
	Dick Williams	58	75	7th	25
87	Dick Williams	78	84	4th	7
88	Dick Williams	23	33	(6th)	
	Jimmy Snyder	45	60	7th	35.5
89	Jim Lefebvre	73	89	6th	26

Continued

SEATTLE (continued)

Year	Manager	W	L	AL West	Games Behind
1990	Jim Lefebvre	77	85	5th	26
91	Jim Lefebvre	83	79	5th	12
92	Bill Plummer	64	98	7th	32
93	Lou Piniella	82	80	4th	12
94	Lou Piniella	49	63	Season not completed	
95	Lou Piniella	79	66	1st	—a
96	Lou Piniella	85	76	2nd	4.5
97	Lou Piniella	90	72	1st	—b
98	Lou Piniella	76	85	3rd	11.5

aDefeated California in one-game playoff for AL West title; defeated New York in ALC first round; lost to Cleveland in ALCS
bLost to Baltimore in ALC first round

Manager Summary

Most seasons—Piniella 6
Most games—Piniella 903
Most wins—Piniella 461
Most losses—Piniella 442
AL pennants—None
Division titles—Piniella 2
Multiple terms as manager—None
Fewest games managed—Martinez 1
Number of different managers—11

TAMPA BAY Devil Rays 1998

Year	Manager	W	L	AL East	Games Behind
1998	Larry Rothschild	63	98	5	56.5

TEXAS Rangers 1972–97
WASHINGTON Senators 1961–71

Year	Manager	W	L	AL Rank	Games Behind
WASHINGTON					
1961	Mickey Vernon	61	100	9th T	47.5
62	Mickey Vernon	60	101	10th	35.5
63	Mickey Vernon	14	26	(10th)	
	Eddie Yost	0	1	(10th)	

Year	Manager	W	L	AL Rank	Games Behind
	Gil Hodges	42	79	10th	48.5
64	Gil Hodges	62	100	9th	37
65	Gil Hodges	70	92	6th	38
66	Gil Hodges	71	88	8th	25.5
67	Gil Hodges	76	85	6th T	15.5
68	Jim Lemon	65	96	10th	37.5
				AL East	
69	Ted Williams	86	76	4th	23
1970	Ted Williams	70	92	6th	38
71	Ted Williams	63	96	5th	38.5
TEXAS				**AL West**	
1972	Ted Williams	54	100	6th	38.5
73	Whitey Herzog	47	91	(6th)	
	Del Wilber	1	0	(6th)	
	Billy Martin	9	14	6th	37
74	Billy Martin	84	76	2nd	5
75	Billy Martin	44	51	(4th)	
	Frank Lucchesi	35	32	3rd	19
76	Frank Lucchesi	76	86	4th T	14
77	Frank Lucchesi	31	31	(4th)	
	Eddie Stanky	1	0	(2nd)	
	Connie Ryan	2	4	(4th)	
	Billy Hunter	60	33	2nd	8
78	Billy Hunter	86	75	(2nd)	
	Pat Corrales	1	0	2nd T	5
79	Pat Corrales	83	79	3rd	5
1980	Pat Corrales	76	85	4th	20.5
81	Don Zimmer	55	48	2nd	5
82	Don Zimmer	38	58	(6th)	
	Darrell Johnson	26	40	6th	29
83	Doug Rader	77	85	3rd	22
84	Doug Rader	69	92	7th	14.4
85	Doug Rader	9	23	(7th)	
	Bobby Valentine	53	76	7th	28.5
86	Bobby Valentine	87	75	2nd	5
87	Bobby Valentine	75	87	6th T	10
88	Bobby Valentine	70	91	6th	33.5
89	Bobby Valentine	83	79	4th	16
1990	Bobby Valentine	83	79	3rd	20
91	Bobby Valentine	85	77	3rd	10
92	Bobby Valentine	45	41	(3rd)	
	Toby Harrah	32	44	4th	19

Continued

TEXAS (continued)

Year	Manager	W	L	AL West	Games Behind
93	Kevin Kennedy	86	76	2nd	8
94	Kevin Kennedy	52	62	Season not completed	
95	Johnny Oates	74	70	3rd	4
96	Johnny Oates	90	72	1st	_a
97	Johnny Oates	77	85	3rd	13
98	Johnny Oates	88	74	1st	_b

aLost to New York in ALC first round
bLost to New York in ALC first round

Manager Summary

Most seasons—Valentine 8
Most games—Valentine 1,186
Most wins—Valentine 581
Most losses—Valentine 605
AL pennants—none
Division titles—Oates 2
Multiple terms as manager—none
Fewest games managed—Stanky 1, Wilber 1, Yost 1
Number of different managers—20

TORONTO Blue Jays 1977—98

Year	Manager	W	L	AL East	Games Behind
1977	Roy Hartsfield	54	107	7th	45.5
78	Roy Hartsfield	59	102	7th	40
79	Roy Hartsfield	53	109	7th	50.5
1980	Bobby Mattick	67	95	7th	36
81	Bobby Mattick	37	69	7th	23.5
82	Bobby Cox	78	84	6th T	17
83	Bobby Cox	89	73	4th	9
84	Bobby Cox	89	73	2nd	15
85	Bobby Cox	99	62	1st	_a
86	Jimy Williams	86	76	4th	9.5
87	Jimy Williams	96	66	2nd	2
88	Jimy Williams	87	75	3rd T	2
89	Jimy Williams	12	24	(6th)	
	Cito Gaston	77	49	1st	_b
1990	Cito Gaston	86	76	2nd	2
91	Cito Gaston	66	54	(1st)	
	Gene Tenace	19	14	(1st)	
	Cito Gaston	6	3	1st	_c

Continued

TORONTO (continued)

Year	Manager	W	L	AL East	Games Behind
92	Cito Gaston	96	66	1st	—d
93	Cito Gaston	95	67	1st	—e
94	Cito Gaston	55	60	Season not completed	
95	Cito Gaston	56	88	5th	30
96	Cito Gaston	74	88	4th	18
97	Cito Gaston	72	85	(5th)	
	Mel Queen	4	1	5th	22
98	Tim Johnson	88	74	3rd	26

aLost to Kansas City in ALCS
bLost to Oakland in ALCS
cLost to Minnesota in ALCS
dDefeated Oakland in ALCS; defeated Atlanta in World Series
eDefeated Chicago in ALCS; defeated Philadelphia in World Series

Manager Summary

Most seasons—Gaston 9
Most games—Gaston 1,322
Most wins—Gaston 686
Most losses—Gaston 636
AL pennants—Gaston 2
Division titles—Gaston 4, Cox 1
Multiple terms as manager—Gaston 2
Fewest Games managed—Queen 5
Number of different managers—8

Sixteen-year Yankee pilot **Joe McCarthy** first managed in the majors with the Cubs. Here, at the 1936 All-Star Game, McCarthy visits with one of his Chicago successors, **Charlie Grimm**, winner of three Cubs pennants. (*Transcendental Graphics*)

En route to the Hall of Fame, Yankee manager **Miller Huggins**, *left*, and the Philadelphia Athletics' **Connie Mack** won nine of the American League's 11 pennants from 1921 through 1931. (*Transcendental Graphics*)

Adrian Anson, known as "Cap" when player-managers were actually team captains, won five NL pennants at Chicago from 1879 to 1897. Anson was outspoken against black players in organized baseball. Some historians cite his strong stance as a major reason the color barrier was not broken sooner. (*Transcendental Graphics*)

Sparky Anderson is the only manager to pilot World Series winners in both leagues (Cincinnati NL 1975–76, Detroit AL 1984). His 17 straight years at Detroit rank second to Connie Mack's 50 seasons as a consecutive American League managing run with one team. (*Transcendental Graphics*)

Loquacious **Tom Lasorda**, perhaps baseball's most visible ambassador, led Los Angeles to four NL pennants and two World Championships during his 20-year managership. He's the sixth Hall of Fame manager who was once a Dodger pilot. The others: Ned Hanlon, Wilbert Robinson, Casey Stengel, Leo Durocher, and Walt Alston. (*Transcendental Graphics*)

Uniform numbers of these popular pilots were retired by their teams. The Number 37 of **Casey Stengel** will never be worn again by any Yankee or Met. **Walt Alston** was the last Dodger to don Number 24. Cincinnati retired **Fred Hutchinson's** Number 1 shortly after his death at age 45. (*Transcendental Graphics*)

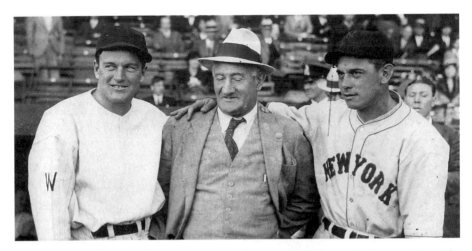

At the 1933 World Series, two first-time title-winning managers—Washington's **Joe Cronin**, *left*, and the New York Giants' **Bill Terry**, *right*—talk with Hall of Famer **Honus Wagner**, a veteran of numerous Pittsburgh pennant campaigns. (*Transcendental Graphics*)

Is **Casey Stengel** flashing signs or merely soothing an itch? Here, in his Yankee managing prime, Casey gave full attention to the flow of the game. Only Stengel and his Giants mentor John McGraw managed 10 pennant winners. (*Transcendental Graphics*)

A "boy wonder" skipper at age 24, **Lou Boudreau** led Cleveland to a World Series crown six years later in 1948. He is the most recent pennant-winning player-manager. (*Transcendental Graphics*)

A longtime catcher with the scrappy 19th-century Baltimore Orioles, **Wilbert Robinson** later managed Brooklyn to two pennants (1916 and 1920). So popular was he that, during his 18-year managership, the Brooklyn club was often known as the Robins in "Uncle Robby's" honor. (*Transcendental Graphics*)

Three-time pennant winner **Bucky Harris** could be delivering a train platform goodbye here to a former team, or a hello to a new one. This Hall of Famer was hired eight different times—three by the Senators alone and twice by Detroit—during his 29-year managing career. (*Transcendental Graphics*)

Tony LaRussa has been a pennant winner and World Series champ at Oakland and a division-winning skipper at his two other big-league posts—first with the Chicago White Sox and now at St. Louis. (*Transcendental Graphics*)

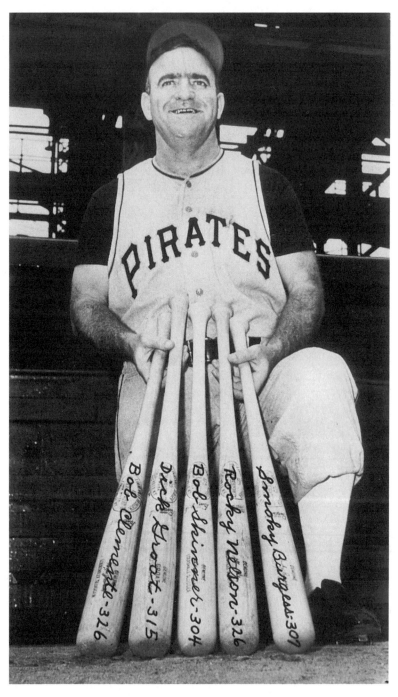

Four-time Pirate pilot **Danny Murtaugh** guided Pittsburgh to two NL championships and then to seven-game World Series triumphs over New York (1960) and Baltimore (1971). Here Murtaugh displays five of his Bucs' 1960 midseason war clubs. (*Transcendental Graphics*)

Player-Managers:
A Vanished Breed

To anyone born less than a generation ago, the term "player-manager" must be as foreign as "swell," "nifty," "dandy," and "Kilroy Was Here." The bench boss plays? Come on, now. That would be like Marv Levy in football pads and a helmet. Or basketball coach Pat Riley in short pants at courtside! A "player-manager?" What's that?

In the 1990s he's a dinosaur, a legendary character who once was a central figure in major league baseball. With the departure of Pete Rose from Cincinnati's active playing roster in 1986, the player-manager is nothing more than a footnote in the game's evolution.

Calling signals from the field, marshalling his troops behind him, leading them by example—that was the player-manager. A clear-cut field general. Often his team's best player. The National Baseball Hall of Fame is peppered with no fewer than 58 of them. With a handful of exceptions, they earned their Cooperstown stripes primarily for their excellence as players: . . . Ty Cobb, George Sisler, Tris Speaker, Rogers Hornsby, Lou Boudreau, Joe Cronin, Bill Terry, Mel Ott, Frankie Frisch, Frank Robinson, Frank Chance, Mickey Cochrane. Under the Hall of Fame's category of "manager," the most prominent player-manager of this century is Bucky Harris. Legendary Clark Griffith could likely have qualified for the Hall under several headings—player, manager, or executive (in which category he is officially enshrined). Likewise, Frank Chance, a Hall of Famer in the players' section, could just as well be in the managers' wing for his luminous won-lost percentage and his four Chicago Cubs pennants.

In the very early 1900s—then again in the Depression days of the 1930s—there were often as many, and sometimes more, player-managers than strictly bench skippers. Financial concerns were major factors in the early days, when roster limits were more severe than now, and then again during the nation's deflated economy of the 1930s, when attendance waned at most major league ballparks. If a club owner could replace one player on his roster with a combination player and manager (one salary for two jobs), all the better to help balance wobbly ledgers. Many of the men chosen for dual duty became legitimate leaders for several years, as evidenced by lengthy and successful managing careers after their playing days ended. Most had been spark plugs on the field as well as in the dugout.

The 1934 season, at mid-Depression, is a good example. Nine of big-league baseball's 16 teams that year employed player-managers. Seven of them are in the Hall of Fame in recognition of their playing credentials. Two, Frankie Frisch of the Cardinals and Mickey Cochrane at Detroit, opposed each other in the 1934 World Series, as had two others—Bill Terry (Giants) and Joe Cronin (Senators)—the preceding year. The other player-managers of 1934 were Charlie Grimm, Chicago Cubs; Pie Traynor, Pittsburgh; Jimmie Wilson, Philadelphia Phillies; Rogers Hornsby, St. Louis Browns; and Jimmie Dykes, Chicago White Sox. Most of them managed for many years after they last penciled their own names on lineup cards.

Back in 1901, the first year of the American League at the major level, and the second in which the National had restructured as an eight-team unit, fully half the pilots were player-managers. And, as in 23 subsequent seasons, the pennant winners that year—White Sox under Clark Griffith, Pirates directed by Fred Clarke—were tutored by player-managers. Their 1901 counterparts were Patsy Donovan of St. Louis and George Davis at New York in the National League, and Boston's Jimmy Collins, Cleveland's Jimmy McAleer, Milwaukee's Hugh Duffy, and Baltimore's John McGraw in the American's initial big-league season. In total, 32 pennants have been won by player-managers—all of them between 1901 and 1948, the last time a player-manager, Lou Boudreau at Cleveland, was a flag winner. Seven times—1903, 1906, 1907, 1909, 1933, 1934, and 1935—player-managers squared off against each other in the World Series. Frank Chance is the only player-manager to direct World Series teams four times. Twice, Clarke, Hughie Jennings, Bill Carrigan, Bucky Harris, Grimm, Cochrane, and Terry were player-pilots in seasons in which their troops advanced to the Series. (Clarke also won Pittsburgh pennants in 1901 and 1902 before the World Series was instituted after the 1903 regular season.) So predominant were player-managers that 98 of them were rostered between 1901 and 1950.

But since the time of Boudreau's 1948 championship season, only 15 men have been employed for double duty as player and manager. Most of them played sparingly, generally serving as occasional fill-ins or pinch hitters. Exceptions are Boudreau, himself, at Cleveland, Phil Cavarretta (Cubs), Rose (Reds), and designated hitter Frank Robinson (Indians). The only other player-managers from 1950 forward have been Hank Bauer, Solly Hemus, Tommy Holmes, Fred Hutchinson, Eddie Joost, Don Kessinger, Marty Marion, Eddie Stanky, Elvin Tappe, Joe Torre, and Harry Walker. Rose, at Cincinnati from 1984 through 1986 before he relinquished his player status to become a full-time bench manager in 1987, is baseball's only player-manager since 1979, when the White Sox dismissed Kessinger.

In the late 1800s, when "club teams" had evolved into baseball's first formal professional leagues, the best players were usually assigned to be managers. At that time "manager," rather than another title such as "head coach," fit the job description quite accurately, because the "manager" was generally a combination business manager, publicity chairman, traveling secretary, and, on field, his team's playing captain. Harry Wright served in all those capacities with the first official baseball professionals, the Cincinnati Red Stockings. With the National League's founding in 1876, and its brief competition from other organizations that billed themselves as "major league" between 1882 and 1891, baseball's popularity increased rapidly, and owners wanted their teams to be directed by men with a combination of skills. The foremost requirement would be their excellence on field, for "superstars"—then as now—were important drawing cards. Additionally, because owners usually had been successful in business or politics—but were not known for their baseball acumen, they recognized the importance of engaging baseball people to run their baseball operation. Who better, then, than those on-field captains to help attract fans? Now and then, in those early days, an owner would sometimes catch the good fortune to hire a manager who was adept at teaching his troops the finer points of the game, too. Such a man was Harry Wright. Cap Anson, Charlie Comiskey, John Morrill, Bob Ferguson, Monte Ward, and Ned Hanlon were also bona fide stars with the leadership qualities and teaching abilities needed to develop successful teams for their owners, and successful careers—many on into the modern baseball of the 20th century—for themselves.

Baseball of the late 19th century was a far less complicated enterprise than it was soon to become. Its attendance figures, measured by today's standards, were shockingly low; a crowd of six to eight thousand back then was a stellar day at the box office. Managers, about half of whom doubled as players, were deemed expendable unless they displayed a clear ability to advance their clubs quickly in the standings. James Thomas (Deacon) McGuire, himself a player-manager for six years between 1898 and 1911, played under a ridiculous number of managers— 23 of them in 26 seasons beginning in 1884. Of course he played for an inordinate number of teams, too. Serving in three leagues—the National, American Association, and American—the widely traveled McGuire stepped to the plate for no less than a dozen different clubs.

Overall this century the average tenure of a manager with one team has been roughly 3.2 seasons. A hundred and more years ago that would have been considered comfortably stable. The National League alone employed 111 different managers—the vast majority of them player-managers—during the relatively short span of 1876, its initial season, through 1900. Its St. Louis club had five different pilots in 1892 alone, and for the 25 years 23 managerial changes had been made by owner Chris Von Der Ahe, who himself stepped in three short times with only slightly less success (3–15) than his other St. Louis pilots. One of those skippers was Tim Hurst. His managing career consisted of just one long year, 1898. Shortly thereafter he became a prominent National League umpire for more than a dozen seasons. The year Hurst managed St. Louis the club had changed its nickname from Browns to Perfectos. Perfectos? With a record of 39 wins and 111 losses? Talk about misnomers. Wisely, the team installed its new mascot, a Cardinal, the following year.

Some of the successful player-managers of the 1890s continued as pilots into the modern era of the 20th century. Notable among them are Ned Hanlon, Connie Mack, and John McGraw; all are in the Hall of Fame's managers' wing. Hanlon, the best player of the trio when he patrolled the Detroit Wolverines' outfield in the 1880s, was player-manager for three years at Pittsburgh before taking over Baltimore in 1892, where he got the credit he deserved for developing the powerful Old Orioles and their successful style of aggressive inside baseball. McGraw was one of Hanlon's players there after Hanlon had become solely a bench skipper. When Hanlon departed to take the Brooklyn dugout post before 1899, McGraw succeeded him at Baltimore. But the team folded after that season, so McGraw played one year at St. Louis before returning to Maryland to guide the Orioles' first American League team in 1901. However, continual strife with the front office and league headquarters prompted him to quit at midseason of 1902, and he immediately signed on as player-manager of the New York Giants, with whom he would be a celebrated, dominating figure for three decades.

Mack is widely heralded for his 50 years of managing the American League's Philadelphia Athletics. Most photographs depict him as the elder statesman that he had become by the 1920s, but rarely chronicled is Mack's 11 year playing career, albeit mediocre statistically. Primarily a catcher with a .245 batting average and little power, he developed into an on-field leader with Washington, with Buffalo for one season when he jumped to the short-lived Players League, then back again to the National League at Pittsburgh where he was player-manager for three seasons from 1894 through 1896, when his playing career ended. Mack then moved to Milwaukee to manage in the Western League, a high minor circuit that was the forerunner of the American League (so renamed for the 1900 season and then elevated to major league status for 1901 and henceforth).

Of the 111 National League managers from 1876 through 1900, only 14 would later manage in the modern American and National leagues. Aside from Hanlon, Mack, and McGraw, the others who had served as player-managers were Patsy Donovan and "Miracle" George Stallings. Ironically, in that era when player-managers dominated baseball, six of the 14 carryovers into the new century of managing—like Joe McCarthy and Earl Weaver years later—had never played major league baseball. They were Frank Bancroft, Al Buckenberger, Horace Fogel, John McCloskey, Frank Selee, and Bill Shettsline. The most prominent and successful was Selee.

During Selee's 12 years as dugout director of the Boston club, then known as the Beaneaters, the team enjoyed the most successful National League run in its 77-year Boston history, which preceded a 1953 transfer to Milwaukee and a 1966 shift to Atlanta. Selee, at age 30, took his first Boston team (1890) to a fifth-place finish before landing five titles and two runner-up spots. He was highly regarded as a motivator and a first-rate instructor. At least 16 of his players in Boston, and later at Chicago, became major league managers. Three of them—Jimmy Collins, Pat Moran, and Frank Chance—won multiple championships.

Selee was induced to sign on with league rival Chicago for the 1902 season. In three-plus years there he directed 280 victories against only 213 losing games and ended his noteworthy managing career in mid-1905, five years before his death at age 49. For his 16-year career the highly regarded Selee posted a brilliant .598 winning percentage. Of all of the 20th century's managers to date, only Joe McCarthy's .615 exceeds Selee's mark.

In retrospect, perhaps team owners should have studied more closely the exploits of Selee, who never made the majors as a player; of Hanlon, whose greatest managing accomplishments occurred after he retired from the Old Orioles' active roster; and of Mack, who led Philadelphia to frequent contention. But in those early days of the 20th century, most clubs still chose player-managers as their field leaders. Often it was for their box office lure, but it likely also reflected the old "team captain" concept. The best players were the on-field captains, so they were considered prime candidates for managing posts. Jimmy Collins, Frank Chance, Clark Griffith, Fielder Jones, Fred Clarke, McGraw, and Hugh Jennings—in addition to the recently retired-as-a-player Mack—soon won pennants as the new American League–National League format proceeded through its first decade. McGraw, despite his rapidly aging appearance, still entered his Giants' lineup occasionally through the 1906 season.

If evolution from team captain–field leader to this century's proliferation of player-managers was a natural development, then the reduction in their number was bound to follow eventually. Age, as it always does in athletics, would encroach on playing time and baseball skills. But not necessarily on these managers' leadership abilities or their baseball acumen. The player-manager—the Clarkes, McGraws, Griffiths, Chances, Joneses, and a few others—would then become, solely, the manager. The player-manager concept would not disappear for many decades, but after 1920 there was at first a gradual and then a rapid decline to the point that only one man after 1979—Pete Rose—would both play and manage at the same time.

Thirty-two player-managers directed major league teams from 1901 through 1909. A total of 37—many of them carried over from the previous decade—held dual posts between 1910 and 1920. Then came the drop-off: 19 player-managers in the 1920s, 16 in the 1930s, 11 in the 1940s (some of them filling in for wartime absentees), just nine in the 1950s, and since 1960 a total of only six double-duty leaders.

The American League's most recent was Don Kessinger of the 1979 Chicago White Sox. Kessinger, a shortstop, had long been a mainstay on the north side of Chicago with Leo Durocher's Cubs when they were East Division contenders in the late 1960s and early 1970s. He eventually went to St. Louis for a year and a half before the White Sox traded for him in mid-1977. Late in 1978, when it was clear that Don's playing career was ebbing, Sox owner Bill Veeck probed Kessinger's interest in managing the club.

"I told him that, honestly, I had no urge to manage," recalls Kessinger. "I said that I wouldn't dream of talking about it now anyway because I thought our manager at the time, Larry Doby, deserved a chance to go to spring training as manager again in 1979.

"During the winter, though, the front office decided that Doby would not be rehired. So when they offered me the job again as player-manager, I accepted."

Kessinger, who is now associate athletic director at the University of Mississippi, reminisced about Veeck and his admiration for him. "He was a brilliant promoter, as everyone knew, but he was also an astute baseball man. He had fun.

The people around him did, too. And so did the Sox fans. He felt his main role was to entertain fans—until the game began. Then it was time for only baseball."

After 106 games of the 1979 season, with Kessinger having played in 56 of them, the White Sox were in fifth place when he was replaced by Tony LaRussa. (LaRussa was unable to advance the team during the season's final third, a situation generally typical of a new manager's inability to improve a team's standings position for at least a year or two.)

Kessinger looks back on 1979 as a pleasant, interesting episode of his baseball career but talks of some of the drawbacks that face player-managers. "For me—and it was my own psychological makeup, I guess—the hardest thing to do was to put my own name on the starting lineup card. I was always concerned that some of the other players would think I was pulling rank and considering myself better than they were. I was so reluctant, in fact, that our coaches got together and told me that, for the sake of the team, I needed to play more. I started about half of our games after that.

"I found that, on offense, there would be a communications problem in giving signs whenever I was on base. But we soon worked that out. Bobby Winkles, one of our coaches, was the guy I relied on to let the other runners and the batter know what we wanted. I want to give a lot of credit to our other coaches of that year, too, especially Joe Sparks and Freddie Martin. Sadly, Martin was on board for only a short time. He was diagnosed with cancer during spring training, and he died in early June. Ron Schueler, now the White Sox general manager and then one of our spot pitchers, served double duty as our pitching coach when Martin left the club. He was a big help.

"It's probably better if a player-manager is an infielder or catcher. From shortstop I could give signs to our catchers to relay to the mound; that was relatively easy. But one of the problems—and you might not have thought about this—is that league rules prohibit a manager from going to the mound more than once an inning unless he removes the pitcher. Well, at shortstop, it's natural to talk with your pitcher once in a while—whether or not you're the manager. Exactly what constitutes a trip to the mound, or how near you can get to it, is not really clear. After a few games I tried to keep that rule foremost in my mind and truly made efforts not to circumvent it. And I must say the umpires were very considerate, too. They seemed to give me a little leeway when it was evident to them that I honestly tried to stay within the rules and regulations. Still, it was tough not to holler out a message to the pitcher, even if it's just a word of encouragement.

"Yet, even with all the help a man gets from his coaches and, in my case, consideration from the umpires, I would not recommend having a player-manager in this day and age. There are so many more demands on a manager's time now than there was back in those earlier years when a lot of men played and managed at the same time. Making public appearances isn't so tough, because they don't occur during game time, anyway. Nowadays, though, media obligations immediately before and after games take more time than they used to. But in my case, again, I was lucky. Because, just as the umpires understood the odd circumstances surrounding player-managing, the press seemed to recognize the necessity of my working out prior to games, and they tried not to intrude on that."

A half decade has elapsed since a player-manager was a pennant winner. Interestingly, that manager's playing heroics were largely responsible. Lou Boudreau's 1948 Cleveland Indians were deadlocked with Boston at the end of the regulation 154-game season, the first time in American League history that a pennant play-off was required. The Red Sox won the coin flip for home park advantage. When Boudreau's Tribe took the field at Fenway Park, they featured a lineup altered significantly from its regular season norm. (That situation is chronicled in this book in the controversial decisions section.) Boudreau, however, took his regular position at shortstop that day. It didn't take long for him to set the tone.

His first-inning home run gave Cleveland a 1–0 lead that was never relinquished. In the fourth inning he led off with a single that ignited a four-run burst. At game's end Boudreau had gone 4-for-4 with two home runs, three runs scored, and a pair of RBI. The Indians' 8–3 victory propelled them to their first World Series in 28 years. That Series, which Cleveland won in six games against the Boston Braves, represents the team's last World Championship up to the time of this book's writing. Boudreau delivered 10 hits in his seven-game postseason (including the play-off game): four singles, four doubles, and two home runs. His regular-season batting average of .355, 18 homers, 106 runs batted in, consistently solid fielding, and dugout leadership earned him the American League's 1948 Most Valuable Player Award.

Boudreau had already been Cleveland's regular shortstop for two full seasons when, prior to the 1942 campaign, he was appointed player-manager at age 24. He continued doing double duty for the remainder of his Indians career (through 1950) and later entered the lineup four times in 1952 when he was the Red Sox skipper.

"Overall I didn't find that playing and managing at the same time was very difficult," says Boudreau, who stayed active in baseball as a manager (Athletics and Cubs following his Cleveland and Boston tenures) and a Chicago Cubs broadcaster until the mid-1980s. "First of all there wasn't nearly the time needed with press and radio people that's required of today's managers. We had two or three beat writers at each game. They'd have a few questions before games and maybe ask for a comment or two afterwards, but that was it most of the time.

"It would be awfully hard to do both jobs today, but back then it worked out all right. When a player-manager is a shortstop, as I was most of the time, you're deeply involved in the game anyway. Your head's right in the action, where a manager's should be. In my case a very good group of coaches made my job so much easier. Bill McKechnie, Steve O'Neill, Oscar Melillo, George Susce, and my old teammate Mel Harder did a great job with the players. And in spring training we had fellows like Tris Speaker, Hank Greenberg, and Muddy Ruel helping out. If my coaches had personnel moves to recommend or certain strategy in mind they talked it over with me. They served as go-betweens between me and the players. They'd tell the players what I wanted. Then, if the players started to dispute it, the coaches were instructed by me to have the player see Number Five. The coach and the player usually resolved the matter!

"There's no question that, for me, the toughest part of being a player-manager was my decision not to socialize with the guys on the team—particularly my old friends who were teammates from when I first joined the Indians late in 1938. I knew that if I'd go to dinner with one guy the other 23 would probably figure I was playing favorites. I certainly didn't want that. I really missed my social friendships with teammates once I became manager."

As we have seen, a large number of player-managers populated baseball shortly before Boudreau's time. One of them, Frankie Frisch, won a St. Louis Cardinals pennant (1934). By 1937, his penultimate season as Redbirds pilot, he seldom played anymore, and he firmly believed that his importance to the team was diminished. He felt that a player-manager of good playing ability was far more inspirational than a straight bench manager. Talking with baseball writer Bob Broeg, Frisch said, "I'm afraid I was not as good a manager when [after leaving the active list] I could no longer lead the gang over the top. I plead guilty to impatience and mediocrity."

A 1930s contemporary, the Giants' Bill Terry, evidently subscribed to Frisch's theory. Terry in 1936, at age 39, was troubled with sore, aching knees. With his club over a half dozen games out of first place in mid-July, Terry was urged to take himself out of the lineup. He refused, saying his greatest value to the team was as a player. The Giants immediately embarked on a 15-game winning streak, Terry wound up hitting .310 in the 79 games he played, and New York won the first of two successive pennants, finishing five games in front of the Cubs and Cardinals. It was Terry's last year as a player, but his on-field presence was considered a prime factor in that year's championship.

Frank Robinson, another believer in inspirational leadership, penciled in his name as designated hitter upon his debut as Cleveland pilot on opening day of 1975. He hit a home run in the first inning. Inspirational though the roundtripper might have been, it wasn't nearly enough to turn around the sad-sack Indians of that era.

Pete Rose was another pilot who apparently felt that his potential to deliver as a player outweighed his managing contributions to the Reds. When asked about any problems adjusting to playing and managing simultaneously, Rose said that finding time to "keep my skills sharp by working out and preparing to play that night's game" was something he simply had to do to perform at his customary high level to help the Reds win. Some close observers note that Rose composed the lineup card, then directed the coaches to handle the games' details and take responsiblity for virtually all teaching matters. Whether or not Rose totally abstained from these typical managing duties is debatable, but it was quite clear that he underwent a kind of a funk in the early days of strictly bench managing. For several weeks, once the game began, he seldom left the dugout except to question umpires' decisions and for rules interpretations. Cincinnati's pitching coach was sent to the mound to remove pitchers when necessary. After 25 years of active participation game after game, Rose seemed almost embarrassed to be seen on a major league diamond in—what he might have perceived as simply a bystander's role. Eventually Cincinnati coaches and players convinced Pete to be more visible. He never grew completely satisfied to be out of the lineup, but by most accounts he ultimately became more acclimated and comfortable with bench managing.

Just as the public address announcer's megaphone and the knotholes in outfield fences are among baseball's faded memories, so is the player-manager. Even at minor league levels today it is extremely rare to find one. By the 1950s, with very few player-managers in existence, skippers still would sometimes handle first- or third-base coaching. Leo Durocher, Tom Lasorda, Charley Dressen, and Gene Mauch would frequently step into the coach's box in an effort to be part of the action again, to superstitiously try to snap losing streaks, or simply to get a different view of the game or of the opposing pitchers. Before this century's midpoint, most teams carried only two, and no more than three, coaches. Sometimes other duties precluded coaches' appearance on the lines, so the manager went out there instead.

The three-man coaching staff has given way to six and seven lieutenants now. A veteran owner of a major league club recently said he sees no need for that many aides. Of course, he's the man who must pay them! Most managers today disagree with that owner. We live in an age of specialization. In terms of progress, and despite any disadvantages of specialization, baseball's player-manager—like the hula-hoop, disco nights, and the buck-and-a-half box seat— is relegated to the back shelves of baseball's archives.

THE PLAYER-MANAGERS, 1901–86

Player-Manager	Years	Team	Primary Position
Jimmy Austin	1913, '18, '23	St. Louis (AL)	3B
Dave Bancroft	1924–27	Boston (NL)	SS
Jack Barry	1917	Boston (AL)	2B
Hank Bauer	1961	Kansas City A's	OF
Joe Birmingham	1912–14	Cleveland	OF
Lena Blackburne	1929	Chicago (AL)	P (1)
Jim Bottomley	1937	St. Louis (AL)	1B-PH
Lou Boudreau	1942–50	Cleveland	SS
Lou Boudreau	1952	Boston (AL)	INF
Frank Bowerman	1909	Boston (NL)	C
Roger Bresnahan	1909–12	St. Louis (NL)	C
Roger Bresnahan	1915	Cincinnati	C
Jimmy Burke	1905	St. Louis (NL)	3B
Donie Bush	1923	Washington	3B
Nixey Callahan	1903–4, 1912–13	Chicago (AL)	OF
Bill Carrigan	1913–16	Boston (AL)	C
Phil Cavarretta	1951–53	Chicago (NL)	1B
Frank Chance	1905–12	Chicago (NL)	1B
Frank Chance	1913–14	New York (AL)	1B
Ben Chapman	1945–46	Philadelphia (NL)	OF-P
Hal Chase	1910–11	New York (AL)	1B
Fred Clarke	1901–15	Pittsburgh	OF
Ty Cobb	1921–26	Detroit	OF
Mickey Cochrane	1934–37	Detroit	C
Eddie Collins	1924–26	Chicago (AL)	2B
Jimmy Collins	1901–06	Boston (AL)	3B
Gavvy Cravath	1919–20	Philadelphia (NL)	OF
Joe Cronin	1933–34	Washington	SS
Joe Cronin	1935–45	Boston (AL)	SS
Bill Dahlen	1910–11	Brooklyn	PH
George Davis	1901	New York (NL)	SS
Harry Davis	1912	Cleveland	1B
Bill Dickey	1946	New York (AL)	C
Patsy Donovan	1901–03	St. Louis (NL)	OF
Patsy Donovan	1904	Washington	OF
Patsy Donovan	1906–07	Brooklyn	OF
Wild Bill Donovan	1915–16	New York (AL)	P
Red Dooin	1910–14	Philadelphia (NL)	C
Hugh Duffy	1901	Milwaukee (AL)	OF
Hugh Duffy	1904–06	Philadelphia (NL)	OF
Leo Durocher	1939–41, '43, '45	Brooklyn	SS
Jimmie Dykes	1934–39	Chicago (AL)	INF

Continued

THE PLAYER-MANAGERS (continued)

Player-Manager	Years	Team	Primary Position
Kid Elberfeld	1908	New York (AL)	SS
Johnny Evers	1913	Chicago (NL)	2B
Lew Fonseca	1932–33	Chicago (AL)	OF-1B
Frankie Frisch	1933–37	St. Louis (NL)	2B
John Ganzel	1908	Cincinnati	1B
Clark Griffith	1901–02	Chicago (AL)	P
Clark Griffith	1903–07	New York (AL)	P
Clark Griffith	1909–10	Cincinnati	P
Clark Griffith	1912–14	Washington	P
Charlie Grimm	1932–36	Chicago (NL)	1B
Heinie Groh	1918	Cincinnati	3B
Bucky Harris	1924–28	Washington	2B
Bucky Harris	1929,'31	Detroit	2B
Gabby Hartnett	1938–40	Chicago (NL)	C
Solly Hemus	1959	St. Louis (NL)	PH
Billy Herman	1947	Pittsburgh	2B
Buck Herzog	1914–16	Cincinnati	INF
Tommy Holmes	1951	Boston (NL)	PH
Rogers Hornsby	1925–26	St. Louis (NL)	2B
Rogers Hornsby	1927	New York (NL)	2B
Rogers Hornsby	1928	Boston (NL)	2B
Rogers Hornsby	1930–32	Chicago (NL)	2B
Rogers Hornsby	1933–37	St. Louis (AL)	2B
Miller Huggins	1913–16	St. Louis (NL)	2B
Fred Hutchinson	1952–53	Detroit	P
Hughie Jennings	1907, '09, '12, '18	Detroit	INF
Fielder Jones	1904–08	Chicago (AL)	OF
Eddie Joost	1954	Philadelphia (AL)	SS
Joe Kelley	1902–05	Cincinnati	OF
Joe Kelley	1908	Boston (NL)	OF
Don Kessinger	1979	Chicago (AL)	SS
Bill Killefer	1921	Chicago (NL)	C
Mal Kittredge	1904	Washington	C
Johnny Kling	1912	Boston (NL)	C
Nap Lajoie	1905–9	Cleveland	2B
Fred Lake	1910	Boston (NL)	PH
Bobby Lowe	1904	Detroit	2B
Harry Lumley	1909	Brooklyn	OF
Ted Lyons	1946	Chicago (AL)	P
Rabbit Maranville	1925	Chicago (NL)	SS
Marty Marion	1952–53	St. Louis (AL)	SS
Christy Mathewson	1916	Cincinnati	P

Continued

THE PLAYER-MANAGERS (continued)

Player-Manager	Years	Team	Primary Position
John McGraw	1901–2	Baltimore	3B
John McGraw	1902–6	New York (NL)	INF
Deacon McGuire	1907–8	Boston (AL)	C
Deacon McGuire	1910	Cleveland	C
Stuffy McInnis	1927	Philadelphia (NL)	1B
Marty McManus	1932–33	Boston (AL)	INF
Clyde Milan	1922	Washington	OF
Kid Nichols	1904–5	St. Louis (NL)	P
Bob O'Farrell	1927	St. Louis (NL)	C
Bob O'Farrell	1934	Cincinnati	C
Mel Ott	1942–47	New York (NL)	OF
Roger Peckinpaugh	1914	New York (AL)	SS
Branch Rickey	1914	St. Louis (AL)	PH
Frank Robinson	1975–76	Cleveland	DH
Wilbert Robinson	1902	Baltimore	C
Pete Rose	1984–86	Cincinnati	1B
Ray Schalk	1927–28	Chicago (AL)	C
Luke Sewell	1942	St. Louis (AL)	C
George Sisler	1924–26	St. Louis (AL)	1B
Harry Smith	1909	Boston (NL)	C
Heinie Smith	1902	New York (NL)	2B
Billy Southworth	1929	St. Louis (NL)	OF
Tris Speaker	1919–26	Cleveland	OF
Chick Stahl	1906	Boston (AL)	OF
Jake Stahl	1905–6	Washington	1B
Jake Stahl	1912–13	Boston (AL)	1B
Eddie Stanky	1952–53	St. Louis (NL)	2B
George Stovall	1911	Cleveland	1B
George Stovall	1912–13	St. Louis (AL)	1B
Gabby Street	1931	St. Louis (NL)	C (1)
Billy Sullivan	1909	Chicago (AL)	C
Elvin Tappe	1962	Chicago (NL)	C *
Fred Tenney	1905–7, '11	Boston (NL)	1B
Bill Terry	1932–36	New York (NL)	1B
Joe Tinker	1913	Cincinnati	SS
Joe Tinker	1916	Chicago (NL)	INF
Joe Torre	1977	New York (NL)	1B
Pie Traynor	1934–35, '37	Pittsburgh	3B
Bob Unglaub	1907	Boston (AL)	1B
Honus Wagner	1917	Pittsburgh	INF
Harry Walker	1955	St. Louis (NL)	PH
Bobby Wallace	1911–12	St. Louis (AL)	SS

Continued

THE PLAYER-MANAGERS (continued)

Player-Manager	Years	Team	Primary Position
Bucky Walters	1948	Cincinnati	P
Jimmie Wilson	1934–38	Philadelphia (NL)	C
Ivy Wingo	1916	Cincinnati	C
Kaiser Wilhelm	1921	Philadelphia (NL)	P
Harry Wolverton	1912	New York (AL)	3B
Cy Young	1907	Boston (AL)	P
Chief Zimmer	1903	Philadelphia (NL)	C

(1)Indicates man played in only one game while managing his team
*Elvin Tappe was a member of Chicago Cubs "college of coaches" in 1962

Pennant Winning Player-Managers

1901[a]	Clark Griffith, Chicago AL; Fred Clarke, Pittsburgh NL
1902[a]	Fred Clarke, Pittsburgh NL
1903	Jimmy Collins, Boston AL; Fred Clarke, Pittsburgh NL
1904[a]	Jimmy Collins, Boston AL; John McGraw, New York NL
1905	John McGraw, New York NL*
1906	Fielder Jones, Chicago AL; Frank Chance, Chicago NL
1907	Hughie Jennings, Detroit AL*; Frank Chance, Chicago NL
1908	Frank Chance, Chicago NL
1909	Hughie Jennings, Detroit AL*; Fred Clarke, Pittsburgh NL
1910	Frank Chance, Chicago NL
1912	Jake Stahl, Boston AL
1915	Bill Carrigan, Boston AL
1916	Bill Carrigan, Boston AL
1920	Tris Speaker, Cleveland AL
1924	Bucky Harris, Washington AL
1925	Bucky Harris, Washington AL
1926	Rogers Hornsby, St. Louis NL
1931	Gabby Street, St. Louis NL*
1932	Charlie Grimm, Chicago NL
1933	Joe Cronin, Washington AL; Bill Terry, New York NL
1934	Mickey Cochrane, Detroit AL; Frankie Frisch, St. Louis NL
1935	Mickey Cochrane, Detroit AL; Charlie Grimm, Chicago NL*
1936	Bill Terry, New York NL
1938	Gabby Hartnett, Chicago NL
1941	Leo Durocher, Brooklyn NL*
1948	Lou Boudreau, Cleveland AL

*Player-manager during season, but did not participate as active player during World Series
[a]No World Series played in 1901, 1902, and 1904

Managing by Committee!
Trading Managers!
Managers for a Day!

Wrigley's Experiment

It happened only once, and it lasted only a few seasons—thank goodness. Baseball purists protested that it was sacrilegious, while veteran Chicago sportswriters shrugged that it was just Phil Wrigley being Phil Wrigley. Nobody was neutral, though, when the owner of the Chicago Cubs, distressed by his perpetual also-rans, decided that the function of manager might be handled better by a committee instead of by one man. As we'll see, Mr. Wrigley was mistaken.

The Cubs haven't always been hapless. It just seems that way to anyone born since World War II. Chicago was a charter member of the National League and, in fact, one of the league's most formidable and successful operations during the 20th century's first half. The Cubs won 10 pennants in the first 45 years of the 1900s and, even though their most recent World Championship was as far back as 1908, they captured eight more league titles in the subsequent 37 years and were often contenders when they didn't wind up in first place. Earlier, the Bruins' NL flag-winning club of 1906 set a still-standing major league single-season victory total record—116 wins in only 152 games.

Since 1945, however, when they went to the seventh game of the World Series before bowing to Detroit, the Cubs have been anything but the forceful powerhouse that typfied the franchise until then. No pennants have flown over Wrigley Field in the meantime (although, with the advent of division play, the Cubs were twice East Division winners—1984 and 1989—under Jim Frey and Don Zimmer, respectively, before suffering League Championship Series losses to San Diego and San Francisco).

Following the 1945 title, field manager Charlie Grimm's club placed a distant third in 1946. The Cubs' return to the first division would not take place until 21 years later, when, led by Leo Durocher in his second year in charge, they ranked third in 1967. As acutely frustrating as the team's annual failures were to its loyal followers, the most discouraged was owner Philip K. Wrigley. At the conclusion of the 1960 season, after 14 consecutive second-division finishes and an average of nearly 88 losses per year over those 14 summers, Phil Wrigley decided a new approach was needed.

Records confirm that Wrigley's unique concept proved fruitless. Nevertheless, he had decided that his baseball team would no longer have one manager in charge. Instead, he introduced the idea of rotating managers or, as he called them, his "college of coaches." Wrigley planned to hire several coaches to run his ball club. One of them would be the "head coach" for awhile. Then, after a couple of weeks or maybe a long road trip, he would relinquish the assignment to another of the coaches, who would direct the proceedings until time for yet another man to step in. The first two seasons of this bizarre arrangement resulted in seventh- and ninth-place finishes and a grand total of 193 losses against only 123 victories. (Those 1906 Cubs, remember, won almost that many—116—in one season.) Mercifully for Chicago players, fans, and even most of the coaches who were involved, the experiment lasted only five seasons—just two of them in its original format.

Against tradition, yes, but also against the standard administrative concept of one leader at whose desk the buck stops. The obvious question was Why, Mr. Wrigley?

The late Hall of Fame outfielder Rich Ashburn, who was Chicago's player representative in 1961, was convinced he knew the answer. "He [Wrigley] hated to fire managers. Over the years he had to let some of his favorites go, fellows like Charlie Grimm and Gabby Hartnett. He figured that, with the system of rotating coaches, if the top man was in a long losing stretch, he'd just shift positions with another one of the college's coaches. He wouldn't be directing things anymore—for awhile, at least—but he'd still be a key member of the coaching staff. He would be shifted around, but not fired."

The idea made no sense to the majority of baseball men, including Ashburn and the Cubs' 1960 manager, the veteran Lou Boudreau, who had traded roles with Grimm during that season's first month. Boudreau went to the dugout from the broadcast booth; Grimm took Lou's place at the microphone.

"Soon after our 1960 season ended Mr. Wrigley and John Holland, the general manager, told me about their plan to have rotating coaches run the ball club," recalls Boudreau. "It meant, of course, that I was out of my job as manager. No one, in fact, would have that title. They asked me to sign on as a member of the coaching staff." But I declined to put my name on the list. I knew it wouldn't work—it's just not good to take directions from one man, one personality, and follow his strategy for a week, then try to get used to another coach's style the next week, and so on through the season. I went back to the radio booth for the next 20 years."

Player representative Ashburn, by then a 13-year major league veteran, was invited to the mid-winter meeting at which Wrigley outlined his plans. "Mr. Wrigley explained how the system would work. One fella would manage for a week or two, we'd see how things were going, then another man would be rotated in for a while. All the coaches, of course, thought it was a great idea. I didn't think it would work because there would be a lack of stability. And that's just what happened. The coaches became competitive against each other; each had his own ideas about different lineups and tactics. The result was a lot of unhappiness among the players. Three or four, including Ernie Banks and Billy Williams, played all the time. Most of the rest of the team didn't know if they'd be playing or not the next day, in fact didn't know for sure which one of the coaches would be in charge the next game.

"There was no stability. After several weeks of this, Don Zimmer, the team captain, and I called a team meeting in Pittsburgh one night. Only the players; no coaches were invited. We pointed out the fact that everybody was aware this was a bad situation, but let's make the best of it. We are professionals. Stop griping about the situation; stop going to the press about it all the time. Well, we cleared the air and went on to win eight games in a row. When we ended the road trip and returned to Chicago, John Holland, who was the one who decided when the coaches would rotate, called Zim and me into his office. Turned out he was mad about our closed-door meeting at Pittsburgh; some of the coaches must have complained. Anyway, he didn't say anything about the eight-game win streak. Just said that if we did that again it would cost us $500 apiece. In those days, the early '60s, that was a lot of money."

The Cubs of 1961 and 1962 could field a respectable nucleus of players, including Banks, Williams, Zimmer, and Ashburn along with Ron Santo, George Altman, Ken Hubbs, Lou Brock (the future Hall of Famer deemed expendable by Chicago, which traded him to St. Louis in 1964), and promising pitchers

Don Elston, Dick Ellsworth, Don Cardwell, and Glenn Hobbie. But under the rotating-manager set up, the team never developed into a cohesive unit.

During that unsettled 1961 campaign, Vedie Himsl, who had previously worked in the front office as a payroll administrator, and Elvin Tappe were the designated head coaches three times each. Harry Craft was in charge for two stints totaling 16 games, and Lou Klein was in command for one 11-game stretch. On a percentage basis Klein's 5–6 record was the best among the four rotators. Tappe, whose three terms covered about two-thirds of the season, was 42–54, Craft had a 7–9 log, and Himsl was 10–21. Himsl never wore a major league uniform again, and before the 1962 season got under way Craft was hired as the expansion Houston club's first manager. Tappe and Klein remained with Chicago for 1962 when they were joined in the command post by Charlie Metro. The format was then altered from the previous year; instead of changing leaders every few games, as in 1961, each coach was the head man only one time. Tappe (4–16) opened the season, Klein (12–18) followed, then Metro (43–69) completed the year.

Although the so-called "college of coaches" continued through 1965 as an official designation, the arrangement drastically changed after the 1962 campaign. Instead of rotating coaches, Bob Kennedy was, in effect, "head coach" for the full 1963 and 1964 seasons, and for the first third of 1965, until Lou Klein replaced him. The 1963 club, at 82–80 under head coach Kennedy, registered the Cubs' first winning season in 17 years.

When owner Wrigley decided to employ Leo Durocher as his field leader in 1966, the "college of coaches" was scrapped for good. After the announcement of Leo's hiring, a Cubs official commented, "We've found from long experience that it doesn't make any difference what title a team leader has as long as he has the ability to take charge."

Durocher's unsurprising reply: "I just gave myself a title. I'm not the head coach here. I'm the manager!"

Jimmie Dykes for Joe Gordon

Some headlines of yesteryear: "Frank Robinson Swapped for Milt Pappas," "Cubs Exchange Brock for Cardinals' Broglio," "Home Run King Colavito Switches Uniforms with Batting Champ Kuenn," "Series-Winning Player-Manager Rogers Hornsby Sent to New York Giants for Frankie Frisch."

Baseball trades have often excited the fans—and sometimes disappointed them, too. Trades have been known to turn fair teams into solid contenders, and they traditionally have fueled hot-stovers with high hopes for the following summer. Sadly, they were a more important part of baseball during the many decades before free agency and astonomical salaries and no-cut contracts dictated the way baseball's front offices construct their rosters.

Until two decades ago the annual trading deadline was in mid-June. Toward June 15 office workers would gather at water coolers to speculate about possible player transactions. Young boys, would argue the merits of swapping their favorite team's second-line shortstop and an aging reliever for, say, 29-year-old Stan Musial. The more creative and imaginative among them would hypothesize multiplayer, three-team deals.

There's no record, however, of any fan's dreaming up the Jimmie Dykes for Joe Gordon trade of 1960!

One manager for another.

It is the only time in major league history that managers have traded places. Occasionally a manager has been permitted to terminate his contract to sign on with another club—or *not permitted* to, as when Dick Williams, still under contract to the Athletics but having departed his dugout post, was legally restrained by owner Charley Finley from becoming the Yankees' pilot. Interestingly, Finley eventually softened his stance and allowed Williams to take on another managing job—with the Angels.

Finley, hardly idolized by any of his numerous short-term skippers, actually managed to trade one of them. But it was manager for player, not one manager for another.

Chuck Tanner, the sixth manager under Finley's command at Oakland, was permitted to depart after just one season [1976, when his A's posted an 87–74 log and a strong second place finish behind Kansas City]. The Pittsburgh Pirates, for whom Tanner would win the 1979 World Series, had courted Chuck's services, but Finley insisted upon a member of the Pirates in exchange—Manny Sanguillen, a former All-Star catcher. Sanguillen's career was winding down when he joined the 1977 Athletics, although he did lead the club in at bats while hitting .275. Tanner, meanwhile, began a 10-season managing tenure with Pittsburgh. Later he piloted Atlanta for three years to complete his 19-year managing career.

The Tanner-Sanguillen arrangement was dull, though, compared with the bizarre 1960 Dykes for Gordon affair, which was orchestrated by Frank Lane, known then and remembered now as "Trader" Frank Lane, and by Detroit's new general manager Bill DeWitt. Wherever Lane did time as general manager—White Sox, Indians, Kansas City A's, Cardinals—his team's fans could be certain that as much as half of the roster would be railroaded, bused, or flown out of town within a year. Often the replacements stayed only long enough for the proverbial cup of coffee.

Perhaps the Dykes-Gordon transaction would never had occurred had not Lane created a public relations fiasco earlier that year. On the very eve of the 1960 season, as teams prepared to break spring-training camps, Lane traded off one of the most popular players in Cleveland history, Rocky Colavito.

Colavito was coming off a 1959 season in which he led the American League in home runs, 42. Lane traded him to Detroit for shortstop Harvey Kuenn, who was the defending batting champion. Kuenn's .353 in 1959 was the best average of his 15-year career, which concluded with a .303 lifetime mark. Fans in both Cleveland and Detroit were disgusted, distraught, and, in fact, enraged. In each city the franchise lost one of the era's premier drawing cards. Besides that, the overall mix of talent on each club suggested that Cleveland needed Colavito's longball capabilities more than Detroit did. Conversely, the Tigers' offense was more balanced with Kuenn's doubles and singles than with another power man.

Cleveland, under Joe Gordon's managership and with Colavito's 42 home runs, had ranked a solid second in 1959. Detroit, with Kuenn on board that year, was fourth. While Kuenn and Colavito registered creditable numbers after the swap (albeit figures that failed to match their preceding season marks), both teams' chemistry and offenses became unbalanced. It was evident by late July that both clubs were on a win one–lose one course, and that championships were extremely unlikely. By midseason the fans' disenchantment with management was reflected not only through letters to the editor, but at the box office as well.

"Trader" Lane, in concert with his Detroit counterpart DeWitt, concocted a way to re-ignite baseball interest in their towns. At least that was their intention. The Gordon for Dykes transaction was made. At the time, Detroit was in sixth place, where it would finish the season under Gordon. When Dykes replaced Gordon at Cleveland, the Tribe ranked fourth. That's where it stayed.

The Dykes-Gordon headliner followed, by only two months, another "trade" involving a baseball manager. That time it was a manager for an announcer!

Charlie Grimm had been managing, off and on, for 28 years in the National League. He had led the Cubs to three pennants (1932, 1935, and 1945) during two tenures in Chicago and had been the Braves' last manager in Boston and, after the franchise transfer, their first in Milwaukee. Now, by 1960, he was in his third Chicago term at Wrigley Field, after Bob Scheffing was dismissed following the 1959 campaign.

One of the Cubs' radio broadcasters at the time was Lou Boudreau, who, three years earlier, had wrapped up 15 years as an American League manager at Cleveland, Boston, and Kansas City. Boudreau was comfortable in the radio booth, even though the early-season Cubs of 1960 seldom gave him much in the way of successful exploits to describe to his listeners.

Boudreau sets the trade's scene this way: "Charlie Grimm was a great guy, a good friend of mine. But, when he took over in 1960, his spring training was a bit lackadaisacal. Then, when the season started, the team never appeared to get fired up. In early May we had just come home from a bad road trip, and Grimm immediately made an appointment to visit with owner Phil Wrigley and general manager John Holland. He told them he was resigning as manager. 'I knew it was time to quit,' he told them, 'on the last night of the trip. It was three o'clock in the morning and I'm sitting in my hotel room reading the sports page. With the lights out! Time to get out, gentlemen.' "

Within minutes the Chicago front office invited Boudreau to take over as manager. Lou, however, was under contract with WQAL Radio for the season. But Cubs management, with the nodding, somewhat puzzled approval of Boudreau and Grimm, negotiated a trade—Boudreau to the dugout, Grimm to take over on radio. Chicago ranked eighth in the National League that day. At season's end, and after 139 games of Boudreau's leadership, the club had advanced only to seventh—just one game above the basement.

Charlie Grimm, in the darkness of that spring night back in 1960, apparently had a pretty clear vision of the Cubs' potential.

Nationally prominent baseball announcer Jerry Coleman was another microphone man who went directly to the field. However, in Coleman's case there was no trade. San Diego Padres manager Roger Craig had been ousted after his team finished fifth in NL West, and management looked to Coleman as the replacement. Despite occasional announcing malaprops, Coleman was considered an astute baseball man. He had been a San Diego announcer for several seasons. Before that, following a brief but successful tenure as a Yankees second baseman, Jerry had broadcast Yankee games and had been associated with CBS Radio baseballcasts.

After several meetings designed to persuade him to become San Diego's field manager, Coleman finally agreed to a contract for the 1980 season. It would be his first and last year as a manager. What prompted Jerry to depart the relative comfort of the radio booth for the daily stress of a manager's job?

"Bob Fontaine was one of the top officials of the Padres then," Coleman explained. "He and I grew up together, and we'd sometimes sit together and discuss the ball club. One day in late '79 he asked, 'Why don't you manage the team?' I thought he was kidding, so I said I would if he'd be my pitching coach. Later the talks got more serious and I said, okay, I'll try it. Then I made another foolish statement. Said that, since I'd been with the team day in and day out as a broadcaster, at least I know these guys. Wrong. I'd been out of uniform for 23 years at that point and didn't realize how things had changed. You just don't know a team until you're with them on the bench and understand what's going on there. Things happen. It brought me up-to-date.

"The game and the people had changed since I was a player. At New York, when my managers Bucky Harris and Casey Stengel said jump, you'd say, 'How high?' It's not that way anymore. And it's because of the money and free agency. Sparky Anderson had a good observation. I mentioned to him one time that one of his players used to be okay when he was young, but now he's a kind of a jerk. Sparky said, 'No, he was always a jerk. Money just gave him a chance to prove it.' Not everybody in baseball's that way, of course, but, overall, the players are much more independent.

"Looking back, though, on 1980, it was a great experience for me even though we came in last and I got fired. It brought me up-to-date. I got a feel for the way they think on the bench, and that helped me with my broadcast work. When I took over the team we had a lot of older players. I would have been better off with a young group where you can teach and express your philosophies. The group I had thought I was 55 when I arrived on this earth! I enjoyed the game, still enjoy the game of baseball. But I didn't enjoy the politics in the clubhouse. Truly, I was glad to get back to broadcasting after that one year. It gives me a chance to stay a part of baseball. I enjoy the game. But not the rest of what went on. Even though I was still around the Padres in 1981, I had no problems with the players. Most of the team's hard-core problems, in fact, had been traded away by then."

Jerry Coleman. Not exactly a trade. Rather a one-year hiatus in the dugout before his return to the microphone.

Charlie Grimm to the booth for Lou Boudreau. An internal trade, indeed, but only temporarily. Neither of the two ever managed again. Grimm continued to do goodwill work for baseball in general and the Cubs in particular for many years. He passed away at age 84 in 1983. Boudreau returned to announcing immediately following 1960 when he declined the team's invitation to be one of the many representatives on Chicago's "college of coaches." He remained at the mike for another 28 years.

Jimmie Dykes and Joe Gordon. Until Dick Williams and John McNamara matched them several years later, Dykes and Rogers Hornsby were the only men to have managed as many as six different major league clubs. Dykes's longest one-club tenure, beginning as player-manager, was 13 seasons with the White Sox. Subsequently he became only the second Philadelphia Athletics pilot, having been handpicked by his mentor Connie Mack. Dykes was the Orioles' first skipper after their move from St. Louis in 1954. Later he led the Reds, Tigers, and Indians. When the 1961 season was one day from its conclusion he was fired by Cleveland. He never managed again but was in uniform later as a coach with the Milwaukee Braves and Kansas City A's. When Dykes was finished as a manager, his 21 years with no pennants represented a dubious record that was eventually surpassed when Gene Mauch completed 26 managing seasons without a visit to the winner's circle.

Dykes had been a standout infielder with the Philadelphia Athletics throughout the 1920s, and he was one of the team's spark plugs during its pennant-winning seasons of 1929, 1930 and 1931. He was one of Connie Mack's favorites. When Mack was forced to sell key players after 1932 in order to remain financially solvent, Dykes was dispatched to the White Sox with team-mates Al Simmons and Mule Haas. At first Dykes was angry with Mack, but he later acknowledged that the transaction made good business sense. In less than two years Dykes became Chicago's player-manager. His club never finished higher than third, yet Jimmie was widely respected and well liked—even by most umpires, whom he often harrassed. Veteran American League umpire Johnny Stevens was once hospitalized in the off season for back surgery. Dykes, then retired, sent a get-well card with this message: "Get better soon. I was surprised to hear about your back operation. I assumed you were in there to get your eyes repaired!" On the other hand, Jimmie was often the target of umpires' put-downs. Playing third base in his early career with the A's, he took a throw from the cutoff man just as Yankee Joe Dugan was sliding into the bag. It was a close play and might have been called either way. When the umpire hesitated in announcing his decision Dykes looked up and asked, "Well, is he out or safe?" Replied the arbiter, "He ain't nothin' til I tell you what he is!"

When the 1963 season ended, Dykes had been in baseball for 47 years. He resigned his coaching position at Kansas City then and spent his remaining 13 years as a radio baseball talk-show host and a popular after-dinner speaker. Born in Philadelphia in 1896, he died there just a few months before his 80th birthday.

Joe Gordon, who managed in only five seasons [Cleveland, Detroit, Kansas City A's, and Royals], was better known as an All-Star second baseman who was outstanding defensively and who could be counted on for the long ball. Five times he appeared in the World Series with the Yankees, for whom he was American League MVP in 1942. He also helped spark Cleveland to the 1948 pennant, leading the team in home runs with 32.

His managing record is undistinguished—305 victories, 308 defeats. Ironically, his best finish was second place in 1959 at Cleveland, the season before the "trade" with Detroit for Dykes. Technically, that transaction was not a trade, but in reality that's what it was. The contracts of both Dykes and Gordon were both terminated within 24 hours. Officially, then, both were available at the same time. The following day they joined their new teams. Both knew they were to be signed within hours. But a trade, in essence, is what it was, signifying the only occasion on which managers have been dealt for one another.

Interim Managers

Short-term job security for baseball managers is a certainty. Some last longer than others, of course, but "temporary" and "provisional" are two words that come to mind in discussing a managing career's longevity. For most, the position can be described, technically, as "interim."

Connie Mack was an interim manager—50 years.

So were John McGraw, the New York Giants pilot for 31 seasons, Walter Alston and Tom Lasorda with the Dodgers for 20 and more years each, and such other well-known longtimers as Joe McCarthy, Casey Stengel, Tom Kelly, Fred Clarke, Miller Huggins, Earl Weaver, Hughie Jennings, and Sparky Anderson.

Every manager we know of, with the exceptions of Mack and McGraw, who were major shareholders of their teams' ownership, would subscribe to the adage that "managers are hired to be fired." Mack and McGraw would likely concur, too—when it came to everybody else.

Don Zimmer, one of only two men (Dick Williams was the other) to manage teams from all four of the divisions that existed at the time, was piloting the NL East Chicago Cubs after tenures at San Diego (NL West), Boston (AL East), and Texas (AL West). Someone asked him why he always arrived at the ballpark early.

"I wanted to make sure no one was in my uniform," he replied.

The colorful Casey Stengel managed five minor league teams in addition to his major league assignments with the Brooklyn Dodgers, the Boston Braves, and the New York Yankees and Mets. He was terminated by management from most of them, including the Yankees, who implied that Stengel's age was a prime factor in their decision. Said Casey, who led the team to another pennant that season (1960), "I'll never make the mistake of being 70 years of age again!" Whenever he discussed his firings Stengel used the term "discharged" instead of "dismissed," "terminated," or "fired." "Yes, discharged," he said, "because there was no question that they wanted me to leave."

Perhaps the most ironic baseball "discharging" occurred on a September evening in 1992 when the Padres fired manager Greg Riddoch. It happened to be Unemployment Night at San Diego's Jack Murphy Stadium!

Despite the average of a slim 3.15 years in a managing tenure this century, and even though no lifetime guarantees are offered, managers embark on their jobs with the intention and the front office's understanding that the situation's designed as a full-time position. Unstated is both sides' recognition that an estrangement is only a few years, or less, away. And when a parting of the professional ways occurs, especially in midseason, an "interim manager" is often beckoned as a short-term caretaker. Generally that fellow is a coach, often a longtime associate who's been loyal to the organization for many years as player, minor league manager, perhaps scout, or coach. Mel Harder at Cleveland twice, Mike Gonzalez on two occasions with the Cardinals, George Myatt who was called in for interim duty two successive years with the Phillies, Eddie Popowski of the Boston Red Sox, and even Earle Mack, one of Connie's sons and an Athletics coach at the time, are good examples.

Sometimes the interim interval has been only a day or two, while the newly hired full-timer is closing personal affairs out of town. Most of the one-game managers this century fall into that category. Among them are Billy Hitchcock at Detroit and Cleveland's Jo-Jo White, active coaches then, who took over for a day while the celebrated "trade" of managers Jimmie Dykes and Joe Gordon was being completed. Burt Shotton became Cincinnati's official manager for one day in 1934, between the terms of Bob O'Farrell and Chuck Dressen. Dressen lasted there for three undistinguished seasons. Eventually, both Shotton and Dressen earned full-time managing positions many years later with the Dodgers, and each won a pair of pennants for Brooklyn—Shotton in 1947, after replacing Leo Durocher who had been suspended for that season, and 1949, and Dressen in 1952 and 1953. One summer day back in 1977 the man hired by the Texas Rangers to replace skipper Frank Lucchesi turned out, in effect, to be the equivalent of an interim manager. Eddie Stanky had been a player-manager with the Cardinals in the early 1950s and later had guided the White Sox for 2½ years, including 1967 when the team was in pennant contention into the season's final weekend. Stanky was out of professional baseball for nearly a decade (he'd done some coaching at the University of South Alabama) when the Rangers invited him back into uniform. With a 31–31 record at the time, Texas posted a win in Stanky's first game there. The team jumped to second from fourth place that day, when three teams had been in a virtual standings deadlock. Stanky's first game was his last, by his own choosing. In less than 24 hours Stanky realized that he had no desire at all to be a big-league manager again. He thanked the Rangers for their confidence and their invitation, then packed up and headed back to Alabama. His replacement? An interim, of course. It was coach Connie Ryan who handled the club for six games until the new regular manager, Billy Hunter, signed on.

Some of the one-game interim pilots—Shotton, Billy Hitchcock, Gabby Street, Harvey Kuenn, Dick Howser, Cal Ripken Sr., and Bob Skinner—enjoyed full-time managing terms before or since. For the others, their single day in the sun was all they needed to gain admittance into the archives of major league managers.

Most of the one-gamers knew their time in the director's chair would be brief, and that they might go right back to the coaching lines or to their interrupted scouting assignments. Other interim managers, however, had hoped their elevations portended of lengthy careers. One such midseason replacement was Bobby Wine at Atlanta. Wine had been a standout shortstop defensively for nearly a decade in the National League under manager Gene Mauch in both Philadelphia and Montreal. He later was dugout assistant when Phillies general manager Paul Owens came downstairs to replace the abruptly dismissed Pat Corrales as manager in midseason of 1983.

Wine subsequently signed on with Atlanta as a coach. Joe Torre had been replaced as manager by Braves minor league veteran Eddie Haas for the 1985 season. Haas, however, seemed to have problems motivating his players, who in turn showed little confidence in him. With the Braves in fifth place 21 games under .500 in August, owner Ted Turner terminated the contract of Haas and replaced him with Wine, under whom the team posted a 16–25 record for the rest of the season.

"At the time Ted Turner hired me to manage," recalled Wine, "he indicated that I would continue as manager, at least into 1986, unless any one of three specific people became available. He was very honest about that. The three were Tom Lasorda, Bobby Cox [a previous and future Braves pilot then managing Toronto], and Chuck Tanner. Tanner became available. I became the Braves' advance scout.

"Looking back on what was really an interim managing assignment, I knew there was a problem taking over so late in the year. The club had already been pretty well molded, and by then the players knew there was no realistic chance to get back into contention. Still, I was pleased with our players under those circumstances. They gave me no aggravation. They're professionals, and, under me or any interim manager, players will perform as well as they can. Their careers are at stake, too."

In reminiscing about his 41-game major league managing career, Wine often speaks of Mauch, his old mentor. "I was a young rookie in 1962, and he was my first manager. Players really had problems at first trying to figure why he did things—in-game strategy, lineup decisions, platooning—the way he did. After awhile, though, you begin to understand. As a young player you felt like he was overlooking you if you weren't in the lineup. But in retrospect, some of the lessons I eventually learned from him were very valuable in my managing. For instance, he taught me that you play the men you think can do the best job that day against the team you're playing that day. When the manager makes out the lineup card it represents your best chance to beat that opponent in that game."

I can attest to Bobby Wine's initial unhappiness with Mauch. During Wine's first or second full season with Mauch's Phillies, I happened upon him in the Phillies clubhouse one evening before a game. He was disgusted and despondent, and very soon into our conversation he inquired if a job was open in the sports department of the daily newspaper by whom I was employed at the time. "I don't think so, Bob," I answered. "But I'll be happy to look into it. By the way, who's it for?" "For me," came the swift reply. "This guy's [Mauch] driving us nuts. You come to the park not knowing if you're gonna play, and if so where [what position] you'll play, or how long you might be on the bench until he notices you again. Let me know about the sports department." Fortunately Bobby Wine soon thought better of seeking work outside of baseball. From that night forward he has been in almost continous baseball employ. As time passed, Wine gained respect for Mauch, and credits him as a brilliant teacher.

At Port St. Lucie, Florida, during spring training in the mid-1990s, when Wine was coaching for Mets manager Dallas Green, the Kansas City Royals were the exhibition game visitors one day. Before the game Wine and Green were chatting with Royals pilot Bob Boone and his dugout assistant, Gene Mauch, whom Boone had enticed from retirement to help build the team. After cheerfully reminiscing about this happenstance or that game of decades earlier, and chuckling about Mauch's intensity, impatience, and sharp tongue of those days, Wine recalls Mauch asking, "Did I really do some of the things they wrote about me? Was I so hard to get along with? Was I that bad?"

Wine, grinning: "Do you have time to sit down for a few hours, Gene?"

John Vukovich, another former National League infielder with exceptional defensive skills, has twice served as an interim manager. Both times he was summoned from the coaching ranks—first with the Cubs for two games in 1986 between managers Jim Frey and Gene Michael, then for the 1988 season's final nine games after the Phillies axed Lee Elia. His overall interim managing record was 6 and 5.

"When you know that your role is that of interim manager," relates Vukovich, "and there's no question that you're just filling in, there isn't much you try to change with the team because if you've been there right along as a coach, and you're loyal to the guy you replace, then why didn't you give him your recommendations when he was still the manager? The best thing you can do for the short time you're going to be running things is to keep the status quo. You try to maintain the same relationship with the players that you had before and probably will again. Players have a tendency to come to a coach with certain problems that they hesitate to discuss with the manager. Managers don't need nit picking; coaches can take that off the manager's shoulders. The best advice I could give is, don't change your approach or relationships when you're the interim [manager]."

Danny Ozark is sometimes remembered for malaprops and for one particular 1977 League Championship Series game when he failed to insert his usual defensive replacement in left field prior to a Dodgers game-winning rally. He is less noted for his exemplary six-season record: He had led the Phillies to three successive division titles from 1976 through 1978, but when the 1979 club appeared lethargic and developed some clubhouse cliques that griped and groused, Ozark was dismissed in favor of farm director Dallas Green, whom the front office counted on to be a drill sergeant who could get the troops back in shape—or else! Philadelphia's potential and its recent accomplishments forecast success for several years, and Green was deemed to be the stopgap who would return the club to winning ways.

Green's new post was planned as a short-term assignment designed to get the club back on track. But when the team rebounded rapidly (albeit a little too late to catch Pittsburgh, which eventually went on, under Chuck Tanner, to win the World Series), it was decided that Green would stay on in Philadelphia's dugout permanently. His 1980 Phillies produced the franchise's only World Series championship in history by downing Kansas City in six games after coming from behind to defeat Houston in one of the most exciting League Championship Series ever played. "Permanently," as we've seen, is a misnomer. And after the 1981 season Green was off to Chicago as president and general manager of the Cubs. Later he would manage the Yankees and the Mets, the latter for just over three seasons, from midyear 1993 through most of the 1996 campaign.

The man hired to succeed Green at Shea Stadium was a veteran pilot embarking on his second major league managing assignment. Bobby Valentine, a New York-area native (Stamford, Connecticut) who has continued to reside there, was promoted from the Mets' Triple-A team in Norfolk. Before joining the Mets' organization in 1993, he had directed the Texas Rangers to middivision finishes for seven-plus seasons until the summer of 1992.

Valentine described some of the situations that confront a midseason replacement manager, generally more pronounced than those greeting a pure interim fill-in. "Depending on where the man comes from, circumstances will be different for the new manager. By that, I mean sometimes he'll come right from the team's ranks—a coach, maybe a vice president who's seen the team play all year, someone that's very familiar with the talent. Then there's the situation where the newcomer has been with another team in your league. He, too, already knows the opposition—the rest of the league—and has some familiarity with his new team's pros and cons. In both of these cases, the new manager still has a good deal of acclimation that will be required.

"The situation is compounded though, and is more difficult, when the new manager is brought up from the minor leagues or from the other major league. He must quickly figure out what the expectations for your squad are and what the competition is all about.

"When a new pilot comes on board at midstream, an inherent problem always surfaces. And it's simply this: Human beings don't like change. Any change that the manager implements, a physical change such as inserting a new player at a position or finding a new position for someone else, is usually met with some skepticism and resistance."

As Valentine studied his New York roster in late 1996 he found that nine members of it had played for him in the Mets' minor league system a year or two earlier. Knowing something about them and their capabilities was one of the positive factors in his joining a club that had been molded by Dallas Green. Valentine admits that" my familiarity with those nine players helped to lend a relaxing moment or two in a game for me."

Terry Bevington came directly to his team's top dugout job from a different angle than did Valentine to the Mets. Bevington had been serving as a Chicago White Sox coach when the team terminated the employ of manager Gene Lamont. Lamont's situation was a classic example of "what have you done for me lately?" thinking. In his first season at Comiskey Park, 1992, he led the Sox to a third-place finish at 10 games over .500. The following season Chicago won the American League West for the first time since 1983 before losing to Toronto in the ALCS. The next year was the season in which the lamentable work stoppage occurred, but until that dark day in early August Lamont had his team playing at an even better pace than his 1993 winners—a .582 percentage against the previous year's solid .580. However, when the White Sox left the gate in 1995 with only 11 victories in their first 31 games, Lamont got an early-season thumb from his bosses, and Bevington was elevated from the coaching staff to take charge. Chicago played at over .500 for the remainder of the season and finished second with an 85–77 mark in 1996.

"Although it's tough to take over in the middle of things," said Bevington, "it would have been a lot harder if I was not acquainted with the situation. But being a coach there under Gene, and having been directly involved with the operation and the personnel from spring training on, I knew a lot about the players and they were familiar with me. We didn't have to take two or three weeks to get to know each other. Instead, those first weeks gave us all time to work together in establishing strategy and plans for the rest of the season. I think that the fact I was a minor league manager for eight years made it so much easier for me to step in than if I had no managing experience at all. I'd recommend that anyone who wants to manage in the big leagues get some minor league managing experience first. It's so important to understand the manager's relationships with his players. It would be difficult to step right in [as a major league pilot] without earlier managing experience."

Just a little over a year after Bevington took over, White Sox ownership dealt away nearly half of its respected pitching staff, effectively removing the team from its position of legitimate contention at midseason. And, you guessed it, manager Bevington was soon sacked. He immediately surfaced as a Triple-A manager in the Toronto system.

Surely less hectic but also less satisfying than interim managing or taking over in midseason is the truly temporary assignment given to an "acting manager." Acting managers are neither credited with their team's official wins nor charged with losses. Their status can be equated to that of a substitute teacher. They take command, at the club's behest, when the regular skipper cannot be on hand due to circumstances such as illness or injury, important family matters, or, of course, when an umpire decrees his prompt departure from the premises. At those times the acting manager is in full charge, but the game's official result goes on the absentee's record. In late June 1996 the Dodger manager, Tom Lasorda, was sidelined with heart surgery. Longtime coach Bill Russell took over the team. At that point it was not certain if Lasorda's health would permit his return, although it was generally assumed that he would be back in the dugout eventually. Roughly a month later, recuperating and feeling relatively well, Lasorda decided to retire from managing, and the Dodgers immediately signed him to a vice presidency. Russell, at the same time, was named permanent Dodgers manager. The club ruled that, from the time of Lasorda's June hospital visit to the date of his official resignation, the 30 or so games that Russell ran would go in the books with "interim manager" after his name. Because Lasorda's manager title had not been revoked during that month, he felt he should get credit for the Dodgers' games during that period. The club, however, disagreed. So Tom Lasorda ends his career with 1,599 victories, 13th on the all-time list. Had the games Los Angeles won during those four weeks been posted on Lasorda's log, he would have advanced past Fred Clarke into 12th place and have been only a handful of wins in back of Ralph Houk's 1,619 victories, which rank 11th all-time.

Unlike the player-manager heyday that is unlikely to return soon, if ever, the average career curve of the bench manager will probably be a constant— the same short-lived tenure that it has been over this century-plus of professional baseball. Whenever managing's inevitable "dischargings" occur abruptly during the season, the midyear replacements and the loyal interims will be standing by, eagerly awaiting their "temporary, provisional" days, months, or maybe even a few seasons in the spotlight.

Family Matters

6

A Young Man's Game?

Some of us still file away sandlot baseball memories among the special high-lights of our youth. The late Roy Campanella, a three-time Most Valuable Player as the Brooklyn Dodger catcher in the early 1950s, said, "It takes a man to be a big-league ballplayer, but you still have to have a lot of little boy in you."

By the time most professional baseball players have reached their mid-30s, they're about ready to call it a career—or have their career short-circuited by their employers. Those who intend to continue in the game as coach or man-ager or executive usually start that new phase of their baseball life before age 40. Except in the early part of the 20th century when a majority of teams hired young player-managers, big-league skippers—on average—have taken on their first piloting assignments in their late 30s or early 40s.

That part of baseball is similar to U.S. industry, which places talented ad-ministrators in top management positions at roughly those same ages. In baseball, though, managers soon realize that their profession is, indeed, a young man's game—even for the field generals. True, the daily physical ex-ertion required of an active player is no longer part of his job description (player-managers being another matter, of course), but rarely can an elderly fellow stand up to very many seasons of six months' worth of plane travel, 26 hotel check-ins per summer (and a few more if his club advances to post-season competition), daily media quizzes before and after each game, evening meals often eaten after midnight, reviews to be written and scouting reports to be analyzed, attentiveness to administering his management's policies, and daily responsibilities for a 25-man work force—at the same time continuously scrutinizing the performance and productivity of his personnel and building strategy based on its capabilities. And toss in the occasional Chamber of Commerce luncheon speech, the pregame radio program (for which he is usually well remunerated), preseason goodwill meetings with sponsors and marketers, and service as a veritable punching bag for the radio call-in show "experts."

Jim Fregosi was 36 when the California Angels tapped him to manage for the first time. That was in the summer of 1978. By age 54 Fregosi was still skippering, was not yet burned out, and had two division titles and one league championship (Phillies 1993) to his credit before his dismissal by Philadelphia after the 1996 season.

He now smiles about the 1978 incident that made him wonder about what he was getting into. "It was right at the beginning of my time as Angels manager," he recalls. "We'd lost two out of three at home in my first series, then headed up to Oakland for a Monday night game. I really wanted to win that one, because it would have evened our record at 2–2, and also I'm from the Bay area and several members of my family would be in attendance. I hoped we'd play well. After a few innings our pitcher got in trouble, but I decided to stay with him a little longer. All of a sudden, from near our dugout, this loud-mouthed fan, who started to call me every name in the book, yelled, 'Who said you could manage! Don't you know when to get that bum out of there?'—things like that. I tried to stay composed, but pretty soon I couldn't take it any longer. I jumped out of the dugout, looked for the culprit, and just before I shouted back, I got a good look at him. It was my dad! I knew right then that managing was going to be a lot tougher than I thought!"

From age 36 to 54 Fregosi weathered the grind and the abuses that come with the territory, and he was hoping for yet another managing assignment. But whether a man could *start* managing at 54 and still be a dugout director 18 years later is doubtful. Quite exceptional are men who managed after age 70 at the tail end of lengthy careers. Connie Mack (87 when he retired) and Casey Stengel 74) are prominent examples. Leo Durocher, Tom Lasorda, Wilbert Robinson, and Jimmie Dykes each managed in several decades and continued doing so well into their sixties.

Even more rare are men who were past 60 when hired for their *first* major league managing job. None was a headliner in the mold of Mack, Stengel, Durocher, or Dykes, but the fact that they were selected at that age as pilots for the first time is noteworthy. Some were interim skippers and some were stop-gap caretakers, such as the eldest of the group, Tom Sheehan (66), a longtime Giants scout, who handled the final 98 San Francisco games in 1960. However, Bobby Mattick, age 62 when Toronto tapped him, was chosen because of his patience and mentoring ability, as the expansion Blue Jays were attempting to solidify their young talent foundation. Mattick held the job for two full seasons, 1980 and 1981.

At the other extreme of managers' age range is Roger Peckinpaugh, age 23, a 20-game fill-in for the 1914 New York Yankees. Fourteen years later, following a long career as a shortstop on Yankee and Senator pennant winners, he became a full-time manager at Cleveland for five years. Eventually, in 1941, he served as a one-year pilot at Cleveland again after the infamous Oscar Vitt mutiny. Peckinpaugh's successor there was young Lou Boudreau. Tabbed the "Boy Wonder," Boudreau was only 24 when the Indians named him as their manager in 1942. Cleveland gambled that Lou's apparent leadership ability would blossom. Evidently it did. Boudreau lasted nine seasons as Indians pilot (winning the 1948 World Series) and later was hired by the Red Sox, Athletics, and Cubs as their field leader.

The accompanying lists focus on the eldest of big-league managers when first hired and on the very youngest of this century's dugout directors. Most of the latter group were player-managers who had previously exhibited leadership characteristics on the field. One of them, Bucky Harris, became a Hall of Fame manager; several others—Boudreau, Joe Cronin, Roger Bresnahan, Rogers Hornsby, Frank Chance, Joe Kelley, Nap Lajoie, Mickey Cochrane, Jimmy Collins, Johnny Evers, George Sisler, Tris Speaker—enjoyed Hall of Fame playing careers.

Retired Uniform Numbers

The oft-heard stadium vendors' call, "You can't tell the players without a scorecard," has been shouted throughout ball parks for generations, at least since the late 1920s. Until then professional baseball players wore no numbers on their uniform shirts. In fact it was not until well into the 1930s that all teams were mandated to have numerals sewn on their flannels.

At first a player's number related to his customary position in the batting order. Babe Ruth, for instance, generally batted third for the Yankees. He wore Number 3. The Babe was usually followed at the plate by Lou Gehrig, Number

BASEBALL'S ELDEST MANAGERS When Hired for First Managing Assignment			BASEBALL'S YOUNGEST MANAGERS When Hired for First Managing Assignment		
Name	**Age**	**Team and Year**	**Name**	**Age**	**Team and Year**
Tom Sheehan	66	San Francisco 1960	Roger Peckinpaugh	23	New York AL 1914
Bobby Mattick	64	Toronto 1980	Lou Boudreau	24	Cleveland 1942
Red Corriden	62	Chicago AL 1950*	Bob Unglaub	25	Boston AL 1907*
Luke Appling	60	Kansas City A's 1967*	Joe Cronin	26	Washington 1933
Jack Onslow	60	Chicago AL 1949	Jake Stahl	26	Washington 1905
Bill Adair	57	Chicago AL 1970*	Ivy Wingo	26	Cincinnati 1916*
Felipe Alou	57	Montreal 1992	Bill Bradley	27	Cleveland 1905*
Hank Gowdy	57	Cincinnati 1946*	Frank Chance	27	Chicago NL 1905
Joe Morgan	57	Boston AL 1988	Hal Chase	27	New York AL 1910
Dave Garcia	56	California 1977	Bucky Harris	27	Washington 1924
Don Gutteridge	56	Chicago AL 1969	Joe Birmingham	28	Cleveland 1912
Hans Lobert	56	Philadelphia NL 1938*	Buck Herzog	28	Cincinnati 1914
Billy Meyer	56	Pittsburgh 1948	Harry Lumley	28	Brooklyn 1909
Eddie Popowski	56	Boston AL 1969*	Jack Barry	29	Boston AL 1917
Andy Cohen	55	Philadelphia NL 1960*	Roger Bresnahan	29	St. Louis NL 1909
Jerry Coleman	55	San Diego 1980	Nixey Callahan	29	Chicago AL 1903
Don Heffner	55	Cincinnati 1966	Heinie Groh	29	Cincinnati 1918 *
Connie Ryan	55	Atlanta 1975*	Rogers Hornsby	29	St. Louis NL 1925
Jimmy Snyder	55	Seattle Mariners 1988	Bill Carrigan	29	Boston AL 1913
George Myatt	54	Philadelphia NL 1968*	Jimmy Burke	30	St. Louis NL 1905
Salty Parker	54	New York Mets 1967*	Red Dooin	30	Philadelphia NL 1910
Del Wilber	54	Texas 1973*	Joe Kelley	30	Cincinnati 1902
Larry Doby	53	Chicago AL 1978	Nap Lajoie	30	Cleveland 1905
Joe Frazier	53	New York Mets 1976	Bob O'Farrell	30	St. Louis NL 1927
Billy Gardner	53	Minnesota 1981	Heinie Smith	30	New York Giants 1902*
			Mickey Cochrane	31	Detroit 1934
			Jimmy Collins	31	Boston AL 1901
		*Interim manager	Johnny Evers	31	Chicago NL 1913
			Clark Griffith	31	Chicago AL 1901
			Branch Rickey	31	St. Louis AL 1913
			George Sisler	31	St. Louis AL 1924
			Tris Speaker	31	Cleveland 1919

4. But a few years after numbered shirts became commonplace, the coincidence of numerals with batting-order slots was discontinued. Take Rickey Henderson, a consummate lead-off hitter. He's worn Number 24 for virtually all of his successful career. Today, most teams also affix players' names to their shirts, a practice instituted by Bill Veeck for his Chicago White Sox in the late 1950s and soon after encouraged by televisers, whose audience normally did not have scorecards in their living rooms.

The custom of retiring uniform numbers was inaugurated in 1939 with a ceremony honoring Gehrig at New York's Yankee Stadium. Since then the Yankees have saluted 14 more of their luminous alumni with the official retiring of their numbers. Two of those honored were New York managers—Casey Stengel and Billy Martin. Another pair of former Bronx skippers are on that distinguished list of 15 Yankees—Yogi Berra and Bill Dickey—but they are cited essentially for their accomplishments as players and not as Yankee managers. Interestingly, both were primarily catchers, and both wore Number 8 for most of their careers. That Number 8 was eventually retired in both of their names. It is noteworthy that the Yankees' ultra-successful Joe McCarthy was never so honored; he chose not to wear a number, and no one told him he had to. Six-time pennant winner Miller Huggins was not recognized either, but the Yankees were just beginning to wear numbers when Huggins died during the 1929 season. Huggins, however, is memorialized with one of the special granite markers at Yankee Stadium's "Monument Park," an attractive enclosure in center field. And at least McCarthy has a memorial plaque there.

Even though 12 American League franchises (including the Brewers) and 13 National League clubs have retired certain uniform numbers, the practice is rare and, therefore, special. Of the thousands of men who've worn major league uniforms this century, and a handful of executives with honorary numbers placed forever in the archives, only 125 (by late 1998) have had their numbers retired. A mere 15 of them were saluted for their managing, and three of those—Lou Boudreau, Joe Cronin, and Bill Terry—were player-managers whose outstanding playing careers led to their honor-roll selections as much as, if not more than, their title-winning managing did.

Casey Stengel is the only manager whose number (37) has been retired by two teams—the Yankees and New York Mets.

Ironically, one manager on the retired-numbers list didn't have a number! John McGraw, who directed the New York Giants for 31 years, was in command during that early era before uniform numbers were required. The Giants organization feels certain his number would have been retired had he worn one, so he is appropriately honored with an outfield plaque that adjoins the retired-number citations at San Francisco's 3-Com Park at Candlestick Point. Its graphics are "McGraw, NY."

Another member of the exclusive retired-number roster is Pittsburgh's Billy Meyer. The Pirates were the only major league team he managed, and during his five years at their helm the Bucs finished in the first division only once (fourth place in 1948) and posted an overall log of 317–452. In researching this section of the book I asked Pirates officials to cite any special circumstances that led to Meyer's number retirement. They knew of none, other than to note that he was highly regarded as a competent baseball man and a first-class gentleman. Evidently he touched many lives in a positive way; the minor league park in Meyer's hometown of Knoxville, Tennessee, was named in his honor many years ago.

Meyer's Pittsburgh club is one of only five teams—the Yankees, Giants, Dodgers, and Mets are the others—with more than one manager's uniform number retired. Meyer is joined by one of his former players, Danny Murtaugh, who piloted the Pirates to two World Championships. Three teams, in posthumously honoring managers who died at early ages, retired the uniform num-

RETIRED UNIFORM NUMBERS of Big League Managers

American League

BALTIMORE	Earl Weaver	4
BOSTON	Joe Cronin	4 *
CLEVELAND	Lou Boudreau	5*
KANSAS CITY ROYALS	Dick Howser	10
NEW YORK	Billy Martin	1
	Casey Stengel	37

National League

BROOKLYN/LOS ANGELES	Tom Lasorda	2
	Walter Alston	24
CINCINNATI	Fred Hutchinson	1
NEW YORK GIANTS/SAN FRANCISCO	John McGraw†	
	Bill Terry	3*
NEW YORK METS	Gil Hodges	14
	Casey Stengel	37
PITTSBURGH	Billy Meyer	1
	Danny Murtaugh	40
ST. LOUIS	Red Schoendiest	2*

The following teams retired uniform numbers of other men who played for and later managed them. These retired numbers mainly salute playing careers.
American League: ANAHEIM, Jim Fregosi, 11; BALTIMORE, Frank Robinson, 20; CHICAGO, Ted Lyons, 16; CLEVELAND, Mel Harder, 18; DETROIT, Ty Cobb†; NEW YORK, Yogi Berra, 8, Bill Dickey, 8.
National League: BOSTON/MILWAUKEE/ATLANTA BRAVES, Eddie Mathews, 41; NEW YORK GIANTS/SAN FRANCISCO, Mel Ott, 4; PITTSBURGH, Pie Traynor, 20, Honus Wagner, 33; St. LOUIS, Ken Boyer, 14

*Enjoyed lengthy career as both player and manager
†Career ended before uniform numbers were commonly worn

bers of Fred Hutchinson (Cincinnati), Dick Howser (Kansas City Royals), and Gil Hodges (Mets).

Fathers and Sons

Baseball, like many other businesses and professions, has often been a family affair.

The first professional team, the Cincinnati Red Stockings, was managed and fully operated by Harry Wright, whose brother George was a star shortstop. Both brothers, in fact, are members of the National Baseball Hall of Fame. Even casual fans know of the three DiMaggio brothers, first Vince, then Joe and Dominic. Among other prominent baseball siblings are Paul and Lloyd Waner, the Alou trio, Dizzy and Paul Dean, battery mates Rick and Wes Ferrell and Mort and Walker Cooper, Dixie and Harry "the Hat" Walker, Hank and Tommy Aaron, right-handed pitching standouts Gaylord and Jim Perry, Bob and Emil Meusel, and Tony and Chris Gwynn.

The more than 400 managers this century include only one set of brothers. Marcel Lachemann piloted the California Angels in 1994, 1995, and part of 1996. Younger brother Rene held the top posts at Seattle (1981–83), Milwaukee (1984), and Florida, where he was the expansion Marlins' first manager from 1993 into the 1996 All-Star break.

Two men named Stahl managed in the American League in its earliest years, but no evidence exists that they were relatives. Garland "Jake" Stahl was the skipper at Washington before moving to Boston, where his Red Sox won the 1912 World Championship. Charles "Chick" Stahl had directed Boston in its final 40 games of the 1906 campaign. Tragedy struck when, shortly before the 1907 season began, Stahl ingested a toxic liquid, or a combination of fluids, and died within minutes. Journalistic reports of the time suggest that Stahl, who was a standout National League outfielder a decade earlier with the Boston Beaneaters, had eagerly looked forward to managing the Red Sox again in 1907. Whether the 34-year-old manager mistakenly picked up a glass containing the lethal concoction, was forced by someone else to drink it, or did in fact commit suicide is still an unsolved mystery. Six years after Chick's demise, Jake Stahl piloted Boston to a pennant.

Over the years sons have followed famous fathers into baseball. Terry and dad Tito Francona, and Todd Hundley and his father, Randy, come to mind, as do the three generations of Gus, Buddy, and David Bell, and Ray, Bob, Bret, and Aaron Boone. Terry Francona, Buddy Bell, and Bob Boone advanced to managerships in the 1990s, although their fathers never managed in the major leagues. Only one father-and-son duo, in fact, is listed among full-time managers this century: George Sisler was player-manager with the 1924–26 St. Louis Browns; his son Dick directed Cincinnati in two seasons four decades later. Another Sisler, Dick's brother Dave, pitched in the American League in the 1950s but never took up managing. (Connie Mack's son Earle was in charge of the Philadelphia Athletics during parts of the 1937 and 1939 campaigns, but he served only in the capacity of interim manager.)

Connie and Earle Mack share a distinction with only four other families. Back in 1910, 1911, and 1914, when Earle played in five games for the Athletics, it marked the first time this century that a father managed his son. Earle's performance was unspectacular. The fact that his father was the boss might have been the only reason Earle's name appeared in a box score. He was 2-for-16 at bat in just five games over three seasons! The five combinations of fathers managing sons are:

Father	Son	Team	Years
Connie Mack	Earle	Athletics	1910–11, 1914
Yogi Berra	Dale	Yankees	1985
Cal Ripkin Sr.	Cal Jr., Bill	Orioles	1985, 1987–88
Hal McRae	Brian	Royals	1991–94
Felipe Alou	Moises	Expos	1992–96

The 1985 season, when Yogi and Dale were together at Yankee Stadium, was only 16 games old when Yogi was dismissed in favor of the fourth coming of Billy Martin, so there was really no time for father and son to have established much of a working relationship. Dale, as one would suspect, was upset for his dad and angry with the front office. But Martin immediately upon his appointment approached Dale. He had known Dale since he was a toddler, for Billy and Yogi had been Yankee teammates under Casey Stengel then. Martin sympathized with Dale's natural concern for Yogi, and, according to Martin, he assured the young man that he had not undermined Yogi. The peripatetic Martin was gone again, after the 1985 season, but Dale remained with the club through 1986 and completed his 11-year career the following season at Houston.

The manager fathers and their player sons talked freely about the unique and sometimes ticklish circumstances confronting them when suiting up in the same locker room.

"From my standpoint," says Felipe Alou, "I was very fortunate here [Montreal] in that Moises had always been one of the team's top players. It was easy for me, because nobody questioned that he was an everyday player, so I didn't have to ax somebody so my son can play. I thank God for that. There is some pressure, though. When the father's the manager, you feel you have to be a little tougher. The manager wants the game to be played perfectly; we expect players to know the game. So if he's the child of the manager, he's expected to know the game a little more than someone who hasn't grown up in a baseball environment.

"It was different when another of my sons played for me in Class A ball. Sometimes I had to get him out of the lineup to give someone else a chance to play. That's not the case with Moises. Unfortunately the other boy just didn't have Moises's talent."

Moises appears to have a firm grasp of his father's position. "Dad treats me pretty much the same as everyone else except when I make mistakes. Then he's a little tougher on me. But I understand that. He wants me to do well."

When a family group largely consisting of, say, carpenters gets together for a social outing, conversations will likely touch on hammers, leaky roofs, and power saws. So, too, is baseball apt to enter the discussions among a family of ballplayers. Felipe and Moises try to get some fishing in together during the off-season, and they agree that perhaps 60 percent of their casual conversation is about fishing. Most of the rest of it is baseball.

Moises, then a free agent, signed a healthy contract with Florida after the 1996 campaign, so he and Felipe had to part professional company. With baseball's nomadic character in the 1990s, the younger Alou has since moved to the Astros. Still, he has pleasant memories of the Alous' five seasons together in Canada.

Referring to Felipe, Moises says, "He is one of the best around, and I don't say that just because he's my father. As a baseball teacher he really helped me a lot. My father is a good communicator. I admit that he doesn't always agree with some of the things I've done [on the field], but that's beside the point as far as I'm concerned. Playing for him meant a lot to me, because I grew up idolizing him. My parents had divorced when I was only two, so for years I didn't see much of him. Now I was able to be with him every day—spring training, flying around the league together, having dinner now and then on road trips. You know, it's clear that we've been blessed—the Ripkens, McRaes, Dad and me. We were lucky to be major league players and to be there with our dads."

Brian McRae reminisced about the four seasons he and his father, Hal, were together on the Royals. Hal's manager's contract was terminated after the 1994 campaign, and Brian joined the Cubs' outfield for 1995 before a trade to the New York Mets two summers later. Hal went over to the National League, too, where he's been the hitting coach with the Reds and Phillies.

"When we were first together at Kansas City, many people wondered if a man managing his son would find the situation to be difficult," Brian said. "Well, everybody made a bigger deal of it than we did. Of course one advantage we had is that I was there before he was named manager; it might be harder the other way around—if he'd been the manager for awhile before I arrived. So I didn't notice any problems from the other players. They made me feel comfortable. Talked the same way in front me that they would no matter who the manager was."

Brian McRae, like many youngsters whose fathers are professional ballplayers on the road much of the year, seldom had his dad on hand for his Little League games. "So playing for him later, sharing the same dugout, was a wonderful opportunity to be together. Even now we still try to meet for dinner whenever my team plays the Phillies. It's true that he rarely had the chance to coach me back when I was a kid, but he did give me good guidelines. And after we teamed up in Kansas City he worked with me [teaching baseball's fine points] the same as with the other players. He didn't treat me any differently than the others. He expected all of us to play hard!

"Playing for my father was a unique experience that I'll look back on at the end of my career with a lot of pleasure. What a thrill to have a chance to do something like that at this [major league] level."

The father, Hal McRae, independently concurred with much of what Brian said about their days together in Kansas City. "It was indeed a challenging experience for me," he remembers, "because I was a rookie manager and he [Brian] wasn't fully established yet at that time. But it was an experience I truly enjoyed and something Brian and I will tell the grandkids about someday. There was early pressure, though. There was criticism, or at least concerns, from the press. Would it work? Could I manage a team right if my son is on it? Would he get preferential treatment? How would the other players react? I knew we, especially me as the manager, would be under a microscope. I don't know if it was apparent to others or not, but I really worked hard to make certain that, when all was said and done, our careers would reflect that we had a good working relationship together.

"I think I was a little harder on Brian than I might have been if he were not my son. I guess I tried to go overboard in making certain he didn't get special treatment. Eventually, if I was displeased about something he did or didn't do on the field, I'd have one of the coaches speak to him—as we did with other players, too. Coaches often communicate better—at least some players think so—than the manager. And it's a fact that, on every team, a special rapport does develop between certain players and coaches. Players often take what a coach says as constructive criticism. Since my son was one of the players, we handled things that way [through the coaches], and Brian and I built a strong relationship that continues to grow.

"I encouraged him to socialize with his teammates, do the things that players do, go where they go. We would chat at the ballpark, and Brian knew he could come to me whenever he wanted to, usually if he was in a slump. Still does, even though we're not in the same clubhouse anymore. But we usually saved our own time together for after the season. In fact, we already have a ski trip planned for next winter, and we'll have a big family get-together for Thanksgiving."

Of the five father-son/manager-player families, the Ripkens are unique in that Cal Ripken Sr. managed not one, but two, of his sons at the same time. There was a one-game interim assignment in 1985. Later Cal Sr. was the full-season Orioles director in 1987, before his unceremonious and abrupt firing after only six games, all losses, in 1988. (Baltimore, under Frank Robinson, continued its horrible start by losing another 13 in a row.) The O's' 21 successive defeats at the beginning of a season surpassed the previous record, 13 straight, with plenty of room to spare. By season's end, which came none too soon for the Orioles, their 108 setbacks were the franchise's most since Fred Haney's hapless 1939 St. Louis Browns lost 117 times.

Senior, as he was and continues to be known since Cal Jr.'s notoriety burgeoned, had been an Orioles organization man for well over two decades, serving as a minor league instructor and manager, and then as a coach with the major league club. When Earl Weaver's managing career ended after the 1986 season, Senior was among the men considered a likely successor. From some quarters it was suggested that the club would, indeed, sign Senior to assure that Cal Jr. would remain an Oriole. Comments to that effect had even been attributed, accurately or not, to Junior. A vehement denial, regarding Junior's stance was issued by all of the Ripken baseball men, including Bill, who had just completed his fourth full season in Baltimore's minor league system. After his appointment as manager Cal Sr. is reported to have said, "Now that I'm hired, there was nothing for him [Cal, Jr.] to have said about that anyway. His job is to get to the ballpark and play. He doesn't have time to get caught up in anything else."

The sporting press soon blew another situation out of logical proportion. Before 1987's spring training, a handful of experienced infielders, including Rick Burleson, Ray Knight, and minor league standout Craig Worthington, had signed on. Would the new manager consider shifting his famous son to third base to help balance the lineup? Senior did not rule out the possibility. Eventually, however, the most formidable Orioles roster featured Junior's continuing at shortstop. The next controversial question posed to Senior was, "Would you keep your son in the lineup just to prolong his playing streak?" His diplomatic answer was one any smart manager might give: "Any team could use a guy who hits 25 home runs and drives in 80 to 100 runs a year. I wish I had 24 of them, whether it's Cal Ripken or anyone else."

Senior had dutifully waited his turn, and when it materialized he clearly relished the chance to manage in the big leagues. Best of all was the opportunity to have his own sons on the squad. Yet he told writer Harvey Rosenfeld for the book, *Iron Man: The Cal Ripken, Jr. Story,* "In both managing and coaching I didn't think of it as a father-son relationship. I'd always considered all the men playing for me as sons."

Offering his comments and recollections for this book, Bill Ripken said, "We were family, and we'll always relate to each other as family. But here [at the ballpark] he's the manager and you're the player. Hey, he's the guy that cut me, sent me back to the minors! Fortunately I had some good numbers then in Triple-A, and I eventually came back that season."

Young Bill returned in time to help make history on July 11, 1987. It was the first game in which a manager had two sons in the lineup. No special results ensued however: Cal Jr. 0-for-4; Bill 0-for-3; Orioles lose to Minnesota, 2–1. About two months later Senior's managerial decision midway through the eighth inning resulted in another historical moment. The O's were losing, 17–3, at Toronto. Cal, Sr. removed Junior from the game at that point, snapping a string of 8,243 consecutive innings played, going back more than five years. "I'd been thinking about doing that for a long time," said the manager. "I wanted to take the monkey off his back. It was my decision, not his."

Bill Ripken still speaks of his concern and worry when his father became Baltimore's manager. "He was very businesslike, seemed to have a good rapport with most of the players, he knew baseball, and he knew what he had to do to lead our team. But I recognized the pressure that's on a manager, any manager, and hoped that the stress wouldn't get to him. I knew, though, that he couldn't pass up the opportunity, and I guess we really wanted him to get the manager's job. Later everybody knew the team would be rebuilding for '88 after we were 67 and 95 in 1987. [The year before that, Weaver's final season, had been the first time since moving to Baltimore in 1954 that the Orioles, aging and bereft of a productive farm system, finished in last place.] So what happened next took us by surprise."

What happened was the dismissing of Senior after only six games. Naturally, his sons were disturbed, distraught, and angry. Then Cal Ripken Sr., the baseball veteran of 3,000 and more games from the Tri Cities Atoms to the Baltimore Orioles, approached his sons as the father, not their manager anymore: "Go back out there, bust your rears, keep your heads up, and play baseball."

Another prominent baseball figure had high hopes that he might manage his son one day, but it was not to be. When Pete Rose was managing the Cincinnati Reds (1984–89) his eldest son, Pete Jr.—or Petey—was considered by some observers to have professional baseball potential. Whether or not the Reds thought so, they declined to sign him.

"I think they [the Reds] figured there'd be too much pressure on Petey and me," mused Rose for his book, *Pete Rose: My Story*. "But as far as I know, Petey could take the pressure fine, and the situation wouldn't have bothered me at all. I mean, if I was filling my roster and I had to pick between Petey and another kid, be sure Petey would have to be a whole hell of a lot better before he was the one I'd pick."

Pete Rose Jr. signed with the Orioles organization, played nearly a decade in the minors, eventually was signed on by the Reds system, and appeared sparingly in Cincinnati as a late-season call-up in 1997. Pete Sr. was pleased that his son landed somewhere as a professional, even if not with him.

This footnote on fathers, the managers, and their sons, the players: Remember the notation about Earle Mack's entering the lineup between 1910 and 1914 for his dad's Philadelphia A's? Well, Earle served as a coach from time to time after that and was an interim pilot twice during his father's illnesses. In 1948, when Connie Mack, at age 85, last managed the Athletics to a first-division finish, it was suggested that he could use Earle, then 58, as one of his coaches. "I don't think that's a good idea," remarked Connie. "After all, the boy's getting up in years."

Nicknames

Baseball, probably more than other U.S. games, has provided a wide variety of colorful nicknames over the years. Most common, of course, are such monickers as Lefty, Red, and Slim, for the obvious reasons: They throw baseballs with their portside arm, or their hair is a particular color, or their bones are a little bare.

Then we had Schnozz or Monk or Dummy, but that was a few decades ago, before it was widely accepted as in poor taste to call attention to a physical peculiarity or a handicap. For instance, William Ellsworth Hoy, a .288 hitter over 14-big league seasons from 1888 to 1902, was clinically deaf and dumb. Naturally, he became known forever as Dummy Hoy. Two-time National League batting champion Ernie Lombardi was often called Schnozz; the Hall of Famer happened to have an unusually large nose.

Managers, many of whom acquired their nicknames long before their playing days, have had some of baseball's more unusual nicknames. Most of them who appear in this section have been cited by James K. Skipper Jr. in his 1992 book, *Baseball Nicknames: A Dictionary of Origins and Meanings.* (Speaking of names, how about excerpts from an author named Skipper for a managers' book?)

Following is a cross-section of managers' nicknames:

Walter "Smokey" Alston as a young sandlot pitcher, had a good fastball that was said to smoke.

George Lee "Sparky" Anderson in sandlot, high school, and legion baseball was the spark plug of his teams. Later he was often called "Captain Hook" due to his penchant for replacing pitchers when trouble began brewing.

Adrian "Cap" Anson was the captain and manager of great Chicago White Stocking clubs of the National League's earliest years.

Johnnie B "Dusty" Baker, had a dog named Dusty; Johnnie was given the same name because, whenever the dog was called to come home from playing with his master in the dirt—not the grass—Johnnie B would come, too! (By the way, the "B" stands alone; it does not designate a name.)

Dave "Beauty" Bancroft got his name from teammates who would often shout, "Beauty!" when Bancroft made one of his consistently classy fielding plays.

John Francis "Shano" Collins was called by this seldom-used Gaelic equivalent of "John."

Charles "Old Roman" Comiskey sported patrician characteristics and a mane of white hair.

Russell "Bucky" Dent was named by his grandmother, who said he looked like a little Indian boy, an Indian buck.

Howard Rodney "Doc" Edwards was a U.S. Navy medic during the 1950s.

Norman "Kid" Elberfeld stood 5'5" and weighed 134 pounds.

William "Kid" Gleason early in his career consistently wore his baseball cap on the back of his head, like a "little boy."

Clark "The Old Fox" Griffith, considered a wily administrator later in his career, was a standout major league pitcher in his younger days when the nickname was applied . It was reported that he often engaged in chicanery on the mound with such actions as spiking and scuffing the baseball.

Stanley "Bucky" Harris "bucked like a bronco" in a basketball game one night as he shook two defenders off his back.

Dorrell Norman Elvert "Whitey" and "White Rat" Herzog would probably have welcomed most any nickname. "Whitey" was a natural because of his light hair color; "White Rat," because he resembled southpaw Bob Kuzava, who also was known as White Rat.

Mike "Pinky" Higgins had a rosy complexion as a youngster.

Arthur "Cut Rate" Irwin reportedly would work for less money than other skippers, and thus he had several jobs as manager in the late 1800s.

Walter "Big Train" Johnson had a fastball that was likened to an express locomotive. Another nickname was "Barney," because Barney Oldfield was setting speed records at the time in auto racing.

Fielder Jones, the 1906 Chicago White Sox pennant-winning manager, was indeed born Fielder Allison Jones.

Michael Joseph "King" Kelly, a Hall of Fame member, was, arguably, baseball's first super star. He attracted widespread public attention in the late 1800s as the "king" of baseball.

Marty "Slats" Marion, the 1944 National League MVP, was tall and thin.

Alfred Manuel "Billy" Martin, the five-time Yankee manager, as a baby was called "Belli" by his grandmother, which, she said, means "beautiful." Belli, of course, became Billy.

John "Mugsy" McGraw back in his days as an original Oriole, was said to resemble a notorious Baltimore politician called Mugsy. He detested that name. McGraw was also known as "Little Napoleon" because of his small stature and autocratic manner.

John Phalen "Stuffy" McInnis, on sandlots as a youngster, would often hail a good play with the words, "That's the stuff, kid."

Carl Harrison "Stump" Merrill walked off the field between two 6'5" pitchers, when his manager beckoned the diminutive Merrill by calling out, "Hey, Stump."

John Francis "Honest John" Morrill was an early National League pilot (1876–89) widely regarded as honest, honorable, affable, and courteous.

Francis "Salty" Parker, when working in a grocery store as a teenager, liked to eat salted peanuts.

Clarence "Pants" Rowland once had to borrow his older brother's over-sized knickers in a minor league game.

Herold "Muddy" Ruel as a young boy fell into a puddle of murky water.

James Edward "Pete" Runnels reportedly had the same nickname as all the men in his family. (Confusion surely reigned when the phone rang for Pete.)

Charles Dillon "Casey" Stengel was a native of Kansas City, or "K.C."

James Wren "Zack" Taylor is believed to have been a relative of the United States' 10th president, Zachary Taylor.

Robert Ferguson—Bob "Death to Flying Things" Ferguson—may be the most creative nickname on the list. The name has stuck for more than a century, but its origin is somewhat in doubt. In one version he is so nicknamed because of his adroit fielding as a third baseman and middle infielder. Another, more dubious, explanation is this one: He was an exceptionally good fly swatter in his traveling team's hotel lobbies.

Other managers have been known as Nixey and Pud, Bid and Baldy, Cracker and Stud. And, in the privacy of the locker room and the opposing dugout, managers have been called many names we prefer not to print on these pages. Yet, as far as we know, nicknames have had no bearing or effect on the abilities—or the deficiencies—with which their carriers managed. What nicknames have done, however, is add to the aura and the character of major league baseball's colorful past and present. It's incomprehensible that any other sport would designate one of its super heroes "Death to Flying Things"!

Where They Came From

California has a lot of space and millions of people. So it's not all that surprising that more of baseball's managers are natives of California than of any other state.

There's the good weather, too. High school, college, Legion, and other amateur baseball organizations are active there most of the year. For decades now, California has annually sent dozens of its young men into professional baseball. Among the notables have been Lefty O'Doul, the brothers DiMaggio, Billy Martin, Dave Stewart, and Joe Cronin from the Bay Area; Tom Seaver, Bob Boone, and numerous others from California college rosters; San Diego's splendid Ted Williams; and scrappy Los Angeles athletes such as Joe Gordon, Eddie Murray, and Eric Davis.

Thirty-nine California native sons have been elevated to major league managerships over the years; the latest was Los Angeles's 1998 rookie pilot Glenn Hoffman, who was born in Orange. Perhaps someday he'll join the ranks of Californians who have directed their clubs into the World Series—from Frank Chance, who won the first of his four Cubs' pennants in 1906, through the October achievements of Joe Cronin, Billy Martin, Bob Lemon, and John McNamara, to, most recently, Jim Fregosi. With its expanding population and its overall mild climate, California is likely to continue to be a prime supplier of baseball talent.

The East and the Midwest, though, produced most of the early 20th-century managers. Pennsylvania, Illinois, Ohio, and New York State head that list. Massachusetts ranks sixth among states supplying big-league pilots. From East Brookfield came Cornelius Alexander McGillicuddy, later known as Connie Mack. He was born there three days before Christmas in 1862. Nearly 88 years later he was still managing the Philadelphia Athletics. Tiny Rhode Island was home to six men who became skippers in the majors, most of them in the first half of the century.

Only five states of the current 50 have failed to contribute any favorite sons to major league managing posts. As one would suppose, they are among the nation's least populous—Alaska, Hawaii, Nevada, Idaho, and Wyoming. Yet sparsely populated South Dakota is the birthplace of *two* managers, following the 1997 appointment of Terry Francona as Phillies dugout leader. The other South Dakotan? Future Hall of Fame member Sparky Anderson.

Seven states, in sending off their natives to direct big-league dugouts, have accounted for more than 50 percent of this century's skippers: California, 39; Pennsylvania, 36; Illinois, 35; Ohio, 33; New York, 28; Massachusetts, 23; and Missouri, 20.

Rounding out the top 10 are Texas, 15; Alabama, 12; Georgia, Michigan, and Florida, 11 each; Louisiana and North Carolina, 9 apiece; Indiana, Kansas, New Jersey, and Wisconsin, 8 each; Maryland, 7; Rhode Island and Tennesse, 6; Connecticut and Iowa 5 each; Colorado, Maine, and Oklahoma, 4 each; Nebraska and Oregon, 3 each; Arkansas, Delaware, Kentucky, Minnesota, Mississippi, New Hampshire, South Carolina, South Dakota, Virginia, and West Virginia, 2 each; and Arizona, Montana, New Mexico, Utah, Vermont, and Washington, 1 each. Manager Maury Wills was born in the District of Columbia.

Nine foreign countries are the birthplaces of 14 20th-century managers. Cuba leads that list with five—Preston Gomez, Mike Gonzalez, Marty Martinez, Tony Perez, and Cookie Rojas. Canada is the home country of George Gibson and Fred Lake. In addition to Rojas, who had a brief interim assignment with the Marlins in 1996, two other 1990s pilots were born abroad—Felipe Alou in the Dominican Republic, and Bruce Bochy in France. From other nations came Jimmy Austin (Wales), Hugo Bezdek (Czechoslovakia), Patsy Donovan (Ireland), Judge Emil Fuchs (Germany), and Harry Smith (England).

Bezdek was a two-sport notable long before the era of Bo Jackson, Deion Sanders, and Brian Jordan. He is the only man ever to manage a major league baseball club (Pittsburgh 1917–19), coach a National Football League team (Cleveland Rams 1937–38), and serve as head coach of three Rose Bowl teams—Oregon State 1917, Mare Island Navy gridmen 1918, and Penn State 1923. Following his 1919 departure from the Pirates he was Penn State's head football coach and athletic director through 1936.

One foreign-born manager, pre-1900, is honored in the Hall of Fame's Meritorious Service section. The innovative Harry Wright, baseball's first professional manager with the 1869 Cincinnati Red Stockings and later a successful National League pilot, is a native of England. Of the 14 men honored as Hall of Fame managers, the states best represented are Massachusetts (Leo Durocher, Connie Mack, and Wilbert Robinson) and Pennsylvania (Tom Lasorda, Joe McCarthy, and Bill McKechnie), then New York (Bucky Harris and John McGraw), Missouri (Casey Stengel and Earl Weaver), and Ohio (Walter Alston and Miller Huggins). Ned Hanlon was born in Connecticut, Al Lopez in Florida.

Missouri and Pennsylvania also rank high as the birth states of pennant-winning managers; with eight World Series pilots each. Quaker Staters were, in order of their first Series appearances, Fielder Jones (White Sox '06), Hughie Jennings (Tigers '07, '08, '09), Bill McKechnie (Pirates '25; Cardinals '28, Reds '39, '40), Joe McCarthy (Cubs '29; Yankees '32, '36, '37, '38, '39, '41, '42, '43), Steve O'Neill (Tigers '45), Danny Murtaugh (Pirates '60, '71), Tom Lasorda (Dodgers '77, '78, '81, '88), and Chuck Tanner (Pirates '79). The flag winners born in Missouri were Clark Griffith (White Sox '01), Charlie Grimm (Cubs '32, '35, '45), Casey Stengel (Yankees 1949–53, 1955–58, '60), Johnny Keane (Cardinals '64), Yogi Berra (Yankees '64, Mets '73), Dick Williams (Red Sox '67, A's 1972–73, Padres '84), Mayo Smith (Tigers '68), and Earl Weaver (Orioles 1969–71, '79).

A geographic shift, in terms of managers' birthplaces, has shown up in the past two decades. From 1980 forward the only northeast natives who've been Series managers are Dallas Green from Delaware (author's license permits us to list the "First State" as northeast instead of south), Pennsylvania's Lasorda, and New York's Paul Owens and Joe Torre. During this period four Floridians—Dick Howser, Davey Johnson, Tony LaRussa, and Lou Piniella—have won pennants. So have three Californians (John McNamara, Bob Lemon, and Jim Fregosi) and a pair of Texans (Cito Gaston and Mike Hargrove). They have been joined, since 1980, by Whitey Herzog of Illinois birth; Ohio's Jim Frey and Jim Leyland; Joe Altobelli, from Michigan; Wisconsin native Harvey Kuenn; Oklahoma's Bobby Cox; three-team winner Dick Williams of Missouri; South Dakotan Sparky Anderson; Roger Craig of North Carolina; Tom Kelly, who has directed his own home state's Minnesota Twins to two World titles; and Bruce Bochy, who was born in France.

Multiple Tours with the Same Team

When Billy Martin was managing the Twins, Tigers, Rangers, and Athletics, he constantly believed that "Yankee" red blood filled his veins. Oh, he consciensciously drove those other clubs hard and took every edge he could to achieve the upper hand against all comers, including New York. The fruits of his labor were quite evident, in fact, as he improved team standings, and usually the box office numbers, everywhere he managed. His Minnesota, Detroit, and Oakland clubs won division championships, and all of them dramatically heightened their victory totals in their first seasons under his guidance. And even though the Rangers were not title winners during his brief tenure in Texas, they posted the franchise's best record up to that time in his first full year as their manager.

His tours of duty were generally short-lived, however, because of his notorious off-field collisions with fans, with John Barleycorn, with constables and magistrates, and sometimes with his own teammates or an owner or general manager who intruded on his personnel decisions. These latter arguments, more often than not, ultimately confirmed that Martin's assessments of player talent were more astute than his bosses'.

No matter where he was employed, and regardless of how devoted he was to satisfying the task at hand, Billy Martin in his heart and head was forever a New York Yankee. The pinstripers, after all, had brought him to the major leagues as a 22-year-old utility infielder in 1949. Martin would later refer to himself as the original Mr. October for his World Series achievements in the mid-50s. For many years he held the record for most hits in a six-game Series, with 12 against Brooklyn in 1953.

When New York traded him to the Kansas City Athletics in June 1957 he openly wept, feeling the Yankees meant to embarrass him and that his mentor and father figure, manager Casey Stengel, had betrayed him. He would not speak to Stengel for years; happily, they eventually reconciled. History shows that general manager George Weiss, who never cared for Martin and felt he was a negative influence on his teammates, was solely responsible for the trade. Stengel, in fact, had argued against it. Still, Martin felt shunned, for the Yankees were family and he could not understand why they would turn him away. (On the day following the trade he homered against New York!)

By 1975, with Weiss long retired from baseball, new Yankee owner George Steinbrenner invited Billy Martin back home. Although he would claim to hesitate about accepting the offer, there is no evidence that he delayed for an instant in dashing to the nearest airport for a flight to New York to sign on again with his beloved Yankees.

Mirroring his successes with his previous managing assignments, Martin's team improved immediately. By 1976 they won their first American League pennant in 12 years, then topped that achievement a year later with the World Series championship via a six-game triumph over Los Angeles, when the second Mr. October, Reggie Jackson, delivered his famous three celebrated home runs in the finale.

The seasons of 1975 through mid-1978 represent Martin's first of a record-setting five separate managing terms with the same team. Once, in 1978, he resigned. On later occasions he was terminated by Steinbrenner. Their feuds are legendary. Yet, four times they kissed and made up. Martin's popularity with Yankee fans was not lost on Steinbrenner, who likes a constant spotlight on him and his Yankees—in the standings, as a box office competitor of the cross-town Mets, and on New York's sports pages. And even though Martin, until his 1989 death in a traffic accident, criticized Steinbrenner's "football mentality"—often directly to the owner's face—it can be assumed that Steinbrenner recognized Martin's talent for inspiring teams when they most needed motivation.

After 1977 Martin never again led the Yankees to a pennant. But his overall record in New York is formidable—556 wins against 473 losses, a .540 percentage. Despite their five professional divorces, Billy was sincerely grateful to George for keeping the Yankee family's porch light on for him.

Martin is the only one of this century's 400-plus managers to have served five terms with the same team. But the concept of family, the comfortable feeling of familiarity with known quantities and successful track records, has also compelled most of the other baseball organizations to bring back previous leaders from time to time.

Pittsburgh, for example, hired Danny Murtaugh four times to perk up its team. He directed the Pirates to pennants, and Series titles, in two of those terms. Prominent longtimers Bucky Harris and Charlie Grimm were returned to their original folds twice. Harris, who led the Washington Senators to successive flags in 1924 and 1925, never elevated the team to championship levels again, but over three terms he totaled 18 seasons as Washington manager. Charlie Grimm won with the Chicago Cubs in his first year, 1932, repeated three seasons later, then, in his second term at Wrigley Field, guided the Bruins to their most recent title in 1945.

In total, 62 men have managed the same team for more than a single term. Many of them—Mel Harder at Cleveland, Cincinnati's Tommy Helms, the Red Sox's Eddie Popowski, and a dozen or so others—were coaches or other organizational loyalists who served as interim fill-ins briefly on two or more occasions. Others, such as Baltimore's Earl Weaver, the White Sox's Al Lopez, Gene Mauch at California, and Yankee Ralph Houk were persuaded out of loyalty— and, of course, with a suitable pay check—to restore order to teams that had fallen into decline since they had managed them some years earlier.

Many will be surprised to learn that Connie Mack did *not* manage the Philadelphia Athletics for 50 consecutive years. Or that John McGraw's 31-year run in the New York Giants' dugout was not continuous. Officially, both are multiple-term managers. Mack suffered from severe stomach ailments at midseason of both 1937 and 1939. During his sidelining he turned over managing duties to his son, Earle, who had been serving as one of the team's coaches. Connie Mack, of course, retained his position as principal owner of the A's and eventually reassigned himself to the bench when his health improved.

Between 1902 and his retirement at midyear 1932, McGraw twice assigned other men to substitute for him as Giants pilot. Both of them—Hughie Jennings and Rogers Hornsby—had previously won pennants with other clubs. McGraw stepped aside for awhile in 1924, in favor of his Old Orioles teammate Jennings, but returned for season's end and a World Series appearance against Harris's first Washington winner. Three years later, feeling burned out both physically and emotionally, McGraw left the dugout at midyear and tabbed Hornsby interim manager for the remainder of the season. McGraw, like Mack, was a major shareholder in his team and was in a position to manage—or not— as he pleased. He renamed himself pilot for the 1928 season and remained as head man at the Polo Grounds until abruptly departing for good in 1932 when he handpicked Bill Terry as his successor.

RETURN ENGAGEMENTS

Manager	Team	Seasons	Pennants
Jimmy Austin	St. Louis AL	1913, 1918, 1923	
Del Baker	Detroit	1933, *1936–42**	1
George Bamberger	Milwaukee AL	1978–80, 1985–86	
Hank Bauer	Kansas City/Oakland	1961–62, 1969	
Yogi Berra	New York AL	*1964*, 1984–85	1
Nixey Callahan	Chicago AL	1903–04, 1912–14	
Bill Carrigan	Boston AL	*1913–16*, 1927–29	2
Mickey Cochrane	Detroit	*1934–38*	2
Bobby Cox	Atlanta	1978–81, *1990–98*	4
Alvin Dark	Kansas City/Oakland	1966–67, *1974–75*	1
Leo Durocher	Brooklyn	*1939–46*, 1948	1
Johnny Evers	Chicago NL	1913, 1921	
	Chicago AL	1924–24	
Jim Fanning	Montreal	1981–82, 1984	
George Gibson	Pittsburgh	1920–22, 1932–34	
Mike Gonzalez	St. Louis NL	1938, 1940	
Charlie Grimm	Chicago NL	*1932–38, 1944–49*, 1960	3
Mel Harder	Cleveland	1961, 1962	
Bucky Harris	Washington	*1924–28*, 1935–42, 1950–54	2
	Detroit	1929–33, 1955–56	
Tommy Helms	Cincinnati	1988, 1989	
Pinky Higgins	Boston AL	1955–59, 1960–62	
Rogers Hornsby	St. Louis AL	1933–37, 1952	
Ralph Houk	New York AL	*1961–63*, 1966–73	3
Dick Howser	New York AL	1978, 1980	
Fred Hutchinson	Cincinnati	*1959–64*, 1964	1
Jack Krol	St. Louis NL	1978, 1980	
Harvey Kuenn	Milwaukee AL	1975, *1982–83*	1
Nap Lajoie	Cleveland	1905, 1905–9	
Bob Lemon	New York AL	*1978–79, 1981–82*	2
Hans Lobert	Philadelphia NL	1938, 1942	
Al Lopez	Chicago AL	*1957–65*, 1968, 1968–69	1
Connie Mack	Philadelphia AL	*1901–37*, 1938–39, 1940–50	9
Earle Mack	Philadelphia AL	1937, 1939	
Billy Martin	New York AL	*1975–78*, 1979, 1983, 1985, 1988	2
Gene Mauch	California	1981–82, 1985–87	
John McGraw†	New York NL	*1902–24, 1924–27*, 1928–33	10
John McNamara	California	1983–84, 1996	
Gene Michael	New York AL	1981, 1982	
Les Moss	Chicago AL	1968, 1968	
Danny Murtaugh	Pittsburgh	*1957–64*, 1967, *1970–71*, 1973–76	2
George Myatt	Philadelphia NL	1968, 1969	

Continued

177

RETURN ENGAGEMENTS (continued)

Manager	Team	Seasons	Pennants
Paul Owens	Philadelphia NL	1972, *1983–84*	1
Roger Peckinpaugh	Cleveland	1928–33, 1941	
Johnny Pesky	Boston AL	1963–64, 1980	
Lou Piniella	New York AL	1986–87, 1988	
Eddie Popowski	Boston AL	1969, 1973	
Paul Richards	Chicago AL	1951–54, 1976	
Bill Rigney	New York/San Francisco NL	1956–60, 1976	
Cal Ripken Sr.	Baltimore	1985, 1987–88	
Eddie Sawyer	Philadelphia NL	*1948–52*, 1958–60	1
Red Schoendienst	St. Louis NL	*1965–76*, 1980, 1990	2
Burt Shotton	Brooklyn	*1947, 1948–50*	2
Dick Sisler	Cincinnati	1964, 1964	
Billy Southworth	St. Louis NL	1929, *1940–45*	3
Gabby Street	St. Louis NL	1929, *1930–33*	2
George Strickland	Cleveland	1964, 1966	
Zack Taylor	St. Louis AL	1946, 1948–51	
Fred Tenney	Boston NL	1905–7, 1911	
Earl Weaver	Baltimore	*1968–82*, 1985–86	4

Note: List includes interim managers.

Italics denote term(s) in which titles were won.

†John McGraw took two lengthy leaves of absence due to illness. In 1924 coach Hughie Jennings and in 1927 second baseman Rogers Hornsby were in charge in the interim. The *Baseball Encyclopedia* lists both men as official managers of the New York Giants; thus, McGraw is technically a multiple-term manager.

From 1961 to 1965 the Chicago Cubs had several head coaches, many of whom served multiple terms in that capacity. See the Cubs' year-by-year history for details.

Interim managers Del Baker, Earle Mack, and Dick Sisler officially filled in for managers who eventually returned from illness or injury (Mickey Cochrane, Connie Mack, and Fred Hutchinson, respectively). Baker and Sisler later served full terms when Cochrane's and Hutchinson's returns were brief.

While some of the multiple-term managers were able to achieve equal or better success on return engagements, most forged loftier records in their initial tenures with the same team. A notable exception is one of the current decade's most distinguished pilots, Bobby Cox. When he was at Atlanta from

1978 through 1981, his team finished no better than fourth place. Then, after four seasons at Toronto's helm, with the Jays winning a division crown in 1985, Cox returned to Atlanta as general manager, then went into the Braves' dugout again in 1990. His four pennants and one World Series championship have all been posted during his second time around.

Race and Ethnicity

A century ago professional baseball was densely populated by men of Germanic, Irish, and British-Welsh-Scottish backgrounds. Their families had settled in the eastern part of the United States, largely in industrial areas, working in factories, in foundries, with railroads, on docks, and in construction trades. Several others lived in farming regions that fanned out from the East's and Great Lakes' centers of heavy industry, and from the Midwest's river cities.

Growing up in blue-collar environments where baseball was spawned (New York City, New Jersey's Hudson River communities, Brooklyn—then an independent borough—and New England's mill towns), the young men of that time engaged in baseball as their primary form of group athletics and organized recreation. Industrial league rosters featured men who worked together in factories.

By their nature, town teams, or neighborhood "clubs," were composed of players of similar backgrounds, interests, and ethnic heritage, for European immigrant families typically clustered in a particular section of their adopted cities. A correlation with today's amateur soccer can be made: In many major cities it's common to find Sunday's sandlot soccer schedule featuring the Ukrainian outfit against the crosstown Italian club, the Lithuanian booters facing the 12th Street Hungarians, and an exciting brand of Latin American soccer creating rapidly expanding participant and spectator interest.

So it was with baseball a century ago. Young men of German and Irish backgrounds developed an early interest in the game and encouraged their brothers and cousins, workmates and neighborhood pals, to participate. These two ethnic groups would dominate baseball for a half century or more. Cliques and clans are facets of baseball that seem hard to eradicate.

Naturally, baseball's early professional managers evolved from these players. The Irish were particularly prominent dugout leaders, even into the 1930s, with such noted managers as Connie Mack (McGillicuddy), Bill Carrigan, John McGraw, Pat Moran, Hugh Duffy, Jimmy Collins, Patsy Donovan, Ned Hanlon, and Wild Bill Donovan. Of the 16 managers who opened the 1906 major league season, for example, fully 50 percent answered to Duffy, McGraw, Donovan, Hanlon, McCloskey, Mack, McAleer, or Collins. Before long, men named Cronin, O'Neill, McCarthy, and Cochrane—among others of Irish descent—would follow.

By the 1940s the ethnic backgrounds of managers would vary far more, as the nation assimilated its citizenry mainly through educational institutions, mobility, mass communication, and world wars. But not until 1975 did a black man advance to a big-league managership—Frank Robinson at Cleveland. The first skipper of Latin background was Mike Gonzalez, a longtime Cardinals coach. But he served only as an interim fill-in twice at St. Louis, in 1938 and 1940.

Baseball had advanced into this century's second half before an Italian American became a manager. Eighty-one games into the 1951 season the Chicago Cubs replaced veteran pilot Frankie Frisch (a German American) with longtime hometown hero Phil Cavarretta who remained on the job through 1953. Some historians suggest that baseball's establishment practiced an unwritten bias against southern and Slavic Europeans in the late 1800s and into this century, but Italian Americans finally gained good standing in the game after a mother lode of talent was discovered in the San Francisco Bay area. The first of note among them was Francesco Stephano Pezzolo, a 10-season American League outfielder for the White Sox, A's, and Yankees who hit .275, stole about 10 bases a summer, and averaged 20 outfield assists per season. Never heard of him, you say? That's because he felt compelled to change his name to Ping Bodie in order to gain admittance to the big leagues. Soon after Pezzolo/Bodie's career ended, though, such well-known players as Tony Lazzeri, Ernie Lombardi, Augie Galan, the three DiMaggio brothers, Frank Crosetti, and Cookie Lavagetto emerged from the Bay region. Lavagetto later managed, as did Billy Martin and Jim Fregosi several years later. Martin, of course, is not typically a name of Italian derivation; however, his mother was born of Italian parents. His given name was Alfred Manuel Martin.

After the Cubs signed Cavarretta to manage, other men of Italian background were given similar assignments. Cookie Lavagetto replaced Chuck Dressen at Washington in early 1957; Sam Mele followed, succeeding Lavagetto in 1961 after the Senators had been transplanted to Minnesota. The first Italian American to manage a World Series entry was Yogi Berra, of the 1964 Yankees. A notable succession followed—Tom Lasorda, with four pennants; Tony LaRussa, three; Berra again, Martin, and now Joe Torre, two; and Mele, Joe Altobelli, Lou Piniella, and Jim Fregosi with one league title apiece. As the 1998 season got underway, managerships were held by five men of full or partial Italian heritage: Terry Francona, LaRussa, Piniella, Torre, and Bobby Valentine.

Only three black men were at the helm then—Dusty Baker, Jerry Manuel, and Don Baylor—and just one manager of Latin background, Felipe Alou, had a manager's post. All have performed remarkably. At Colorado, Baylor's Rockies (he was their only manager until his dismissal in October 1998) won a postseason wild-card berth in only their third season. Manuel was second in his first White Sox year. Baker had twice been Manager of the Year. His Giants won their division in 1997, and his 1993 San Francisco club posted 103 victories, its most ever in a 162-game season since the franchise moved west from New York in 1958. Alou, at Montreal, is credited with enticing overachievement year after year from his good—but not great—squads. During strike-shortened 1994, in fact, his National League East club ranked first by a sizeable margin when the plug was pulled on the season. Despite the excellent managing performances turned in by some minority members, the ratio of black managers to black players, and of the one Latin man to the large number of Latino big leaguers, is unbalanced.

Nearly a quarter century has passed now since Frank Robinson was hired by the Indians as major league baseball's first black manager. That was more than 25 years after Jackie Robinson debuted in Brooklyn as a first baseman. If baseball seems to move slowly now on matters of affirmative action and equal employment opportunity, remember the tightly wired German and Irish baseball network of years ago? Not much different. Nor much better.

Dusty Baker, widely regarded as both a baseball strategist and a thoughtful leader, offers these reflections and observations. "I knew that it wasn't long after Frank Robinson was signed by Cleveland that [Larry] Doby and Maury Wills got managers' jobs. They didn't last long, though, and then there was a big drought until recent seasons. A couple of years ago Baylor, Hal McRae, Cito Gaston in Toronto, and I were all active managers at the same time. And Felipe Alou, a Latin American, was managing along with us. Still is. But these changes seem to last less than half a decade. Right now [1998] Baylor, Jerry Marvel, and I are the only African American managers. It's almost as if teams wanted to show the public that Al Campanis [Dodgers official who delivered disparaging, controversial opinions in 1987 about black intellect] was wrong. So they went out and hired some black managers and executives. But after a few years things reverted back. I'm hopeful, though, that when openings occur in the future, that highly qualified fellas like Willie Randolph, Ron Washington, and Chris Chambliss get fair consideration. They'd be good managers."

Baker and Baylor had far surpassed baseball's average longevity (roughly three years) of managing one team. Each had completed six full seasons when the 1998 campaign concluded. Gaston was discharged by the Blue Jays late in 1997 when the team was ending a fourth straight losing season after many of its World Series heroes of 1992 and 1993 were lured away by free-agency dollars. As managers' tenures go, though, it was a good run for Gaston. Eight-plus years in the command post.

Whether another team will hire him, or in fact whether Cito himself would choose to return to the dugout, is another matter. Of history's eight black managers—only seven since Frank Robinson's Cleveland tenure—just one of them, Robby himself, has been given a second chance with another team.

After two years and a few months, mostly in the second division at Cleveland Stadium, Robinson was dismissed. Soon thereafter the Giants signed him. He stayed in San Francisco for a little over three full seasons and, eventually, was engaged for a third managing stint when Baltimore invited him to replace Cal Ripken Sr. in 1988. He was on duty in Baltimore for slightly more than three years.

Baker and Baylor were still at their original posts as 1998 began, but four of the five deposed pilots had not been hired yet for a second go-round. Hal McRae managed Kansas City for nearly four seasons and posted a .517 winning percentage. Gaston was the most successful of the group, having led Toronto to two World Championships while winning 52 percent of its regular-season games. Two others had short terms. Larry Doby, in effect an interim manager with Bill Veeck's 1978 White Sox, directed only 87 games (and finished fifth). He is now beyond the age that would lend him realistic consideration for another managing assignment. Maury Wills, at Seattle with mediocre personnel and a submediocre 26–56 seventh-place record, also is no longer a likely candidate. Doby, the American League's first black player when Veeck signed him to play for the 1947 Indians three months after Jackie Robinson's first NL appearance, was recently honored with a 1998 Hall of Fame induction.

Sports Illustrated magazine, in a 1997 study, reported that major league baseball's playing population was 17 percent black and 20 percent Latino.

Baker, Baylor, and Alou represented just 10 percent of field managerships. Baker believes that significantly greater inroads will not occur quickly. "A few years ago, when I began considering the possibility of a career in coaching and managing, I thought about where I might like to work. I quickly determined that some cities were just not ready for a black manager. And that still holds true. Think about the towns that have been or would be most receptive. Look at who they are. Two of them aren't even in this country—Montreal and Toronto are cosmopolitan Canadian cities. Another town is my city. San Francisco's one of the most liberal places in the world. Two Black managers there so far. Sad to say that many other cities still aren't ready.

"When I played for the Dodgers I talked a lot with Junior Gilliam, one of our coaches then. One day I asked him why he hadn't applied to manage someplace, because I thought he'd be a great manager. But he said, 'I'll never be a manager. You have to be a spokesman, and I don't speak the king's English well enough.' It's true that he wasn't especially glib or a great articulator. And it's also true what he said. No matter what color you are, a manager has to be able to say what he means the first time. Saying something wrong, then trying to explain what you meant in the first place, makes it worse. One wrong statement could cost you. Gilliam was a good man. He taught me a lot. I think he was sympathizing with all managers when he said you had to be able to speak well. But I know that he was especially fearful of black managers making misstatements or using poor grammar. He felt that would hurt the cause of other men aspiring for managers' jobs. Yogi—hey, I love you Yogi—could get away with some of that stuff. Gilliam figured that a black manager couldn't."

Controversial Managerial Decisions

Every time your favorite team's manager replaces a pitcher, sends in a pinch hitter for a regular, or makes (or neglects to make) a defensive change, some fans are certain that it's the wrong move. Chances are good that the pinch hitter won't come through (because even the best hitters fail more than 60 percent of the time), that no ball will be hit anywhere near the special defensive replacement, or that the relief pitcher can't zero in on home plate. "Dumb move!" cry the grandstand critics.

In a fair number of instances, though, the manager's strategy succeeeds. Whether it was clairvoyance, the result of astute analysis of a scouting report, the law of averages, or merely a lucky hunch, the pilot comes away looking like a genius. Managers' strategies and personnel manipulations foster second-guessing in virtually every game played by every team all season. Nearly every fan has a personal list of disagreements with the skipper and can clearly recall controversial managerial decisions made by their favorite targets. Here are some of the most rehashed.

Dressen, Branca—and Bobby Thomson

Chuck Dressen, who managed big-league teams in 16 seasons and twice went to the World Series, remains the most prominent managerial "goat" nearly a half century after the 1951 "shot heard round the world." His Brooklyn Dodgers and the New York Giants were tied for first as the regular season ended, and a best-of-three play-off for the National League championship was scheduled. The Giants won the opener, besting Dodger right-hander Ralph Branca, an eight-year veteran who had posted 13 wins with a 3.26 earned run average that year. The next day Brooklyn deadlocked the series with a 10–0 win that set up the rubber game at the Polo Grounds in New York.

Behind big Don Newcombe, a 20-game winner, the Dodgers had built a 4–1 lead by the ninth inning and appeared headed to their third World Series in five years. However, with the edge reduced to 4–2 and two runners on base for New York in the bottom of the ninth, manager Dressen removed a tiring Newcombe. He called in Branca to face right-hand-hitting Bobby Thomson. Thomson had homered off Branca in Game 1 of the play-off, but, overall, Branca had been generally successful against him during recent regular seasons. In what has been categorized as baseball's most famous single incident this century, Thomson homered into the lower left-field stands to win the game and the pennant, and to earn baseball immortality.

It follows that Dressen was criticized severely, in fact still is, for that particular personnel move. In piecing together the few seconds he took to decide what to do, we find that Dressen phoned bull-pen coach Clyde Sukeforth to learn which of the relievers then warming up seemed ready to pitch. Sukeforth said, "Preacher [Roe] can't get loose, [Carl] Erskine just bounced a curve ball into the dirt, but Branca's throwing pretty good." So Branca took center stage and is remembered more for that one pitch to Thomson than for any of his 88 pitching wins over a creditable 12-year career. His uniform number, by the way, was 13.

After the game Dressen tore off his own uniform shirt without unbuttoning it. And, much later, Erskine, whose bull-pen hook was bouncing on the ground, joked that if he had been sharper it might have been he, rather than Branca, who was victimized by Thomson. "That's the best curveball I ever threw!"

Boudreau's Williams Shift

It was mid-1946 and Ted Williams, who went on to MVP honors that year, had been menacing every pitching staff in The American League. Lou Boudreau, then in his fifth year as Cleveland manager (and later a Williams skipper at Boston), devised the "Boudreau shift" one July afternoon at Fenway Park. With no runners on base and Williams at the plate, Boudreau placed three infielders to the right of second base, had his three outfielders aligned from center field to the right-field foul line, and positioned his third baseman, Ken Keltner, just to the left of second base.

"I knew that Ted, a powerful pull hitter, would want to challenge it rather than try to poke a hit to left," remembers Boudreau. "At first I got a lot of criticism for the strategy, but we found that we got him out 35 percent more with the shift than without it. Ted, of course, could do anything with the bat, but I figured he wouldn't try to cross up the defense; he'd try to overpower the shift. One time, though, at old League Park in Cleveland, he did hit an inside-the-park home run to left field to beat us, 1–0. Of course we usually played the shift only when the bases were empty—and never with a runner on second, and third base unoccupied."

Since 1946, when the Boudreau shift was moderately effective, many other teams have devised similar, but less drastic, defensive alignments against powerful pull hitters.

Fenway Park Again

Boudreau was involved with another criticized maneuver in Boston two years later. And so was his counterpart with the Red Sox, manager Joe McCarthy.

Cleveland and the Sox, tied for first place at the conclusion of the regular season, met at Fenway Park for a one-game pennant playoff. Despite the short distance to Fenway's left-field wall, Boudreau selected knuckleballing southpaw Gene Bearden, a rookie with 19 wins, to pitch against the hard-hitting home team.

"I knew Gene had only two days' rest," Boudreau said, "but I also realized there wasn't much strain on a knuckleballer's arm. And I knew that our right-handers—Bob Feller, Bob Lemon, and Steve Gromek—had not been especially effective at Fenway Park that season. We had a one-hour meeting in the clubhouse to discuss my decision. Johnny Berardino argued loud and long against my plan that also included starting one of our reserve outfielders, Allie Clark, at first base. Clark was a right handed hitter, and I had expected that left hander Mel Parnell would start for Boston. Our regular first baseman, Eddie Robinson, hit from the left side. Anyway, after a lot of discussion, Joe Gordon [All-Star second baseman] spoke up. 'Look, Lou took us this far for 154 games; I'll go along with him for the 155th.'"

This was one of those cases in which unorthodox strategy paid off. The Indians, with Boudreau leading the offense via two home runs and two singles, Ken Keltner's three hits, including a home run and double, and Bearden's six-strikeout complete game, recorded an 8–3 victory. They stayed over in Boston to face the National League Braves, whom they would defeat, four games to two, in the World Series.

Controversy also surrounded Red Sox manager McCarthy's pitching selection. Most Boston players, according to third baseman Johnny Pesky, assumed, as Boudreau had, that Parnell would be the Red Sox starter. Instead, McCarthy called on 36-year-old right hander Denny Galehouse, who had been considered a reliable second-level starter for the previous 14 seasons at Cleveland, St. Louis and Boston. In 1948 he ranked no better than Boston's fourth starter behind Parnell, Ellis Kinder, and Jack Kramer. Galehouse was only 8–7 with a 4.00 ERA going into the play-off game but had been brilliant against Cleveland in a six-inning relief outing two weeks earlier. McCarthy's hunch backfired for the Red Sox. Galehouse allowed only Boudreau's first solo home run through three innings but lost his effectiveness—and the game—when the Tribe scored four times in the fourth.

"McCarthy," said Pesky nearly 50 years later, "was the best manager I ever played for. We all thought Parnell would pitch that game, but I guess Joe had his reasons. It just didn't work out."

Donie Bush Benches Kiki Cuyler

Hazen Shirley "Kiki" Cuyler, at age 24, became a regular in the Pittsburgh Pirates' outfield in 1924. He hit .354 that rookie season, followed by .357 and .321. His 26 triples led the National League in 1925 as he helped the Pirates to the pennant and a seven-game World Series win over Washington. Four times he paced the NL in stolen bases en route to 328 thefts in his 18-year career.

During the 1927 campaign Cuyler was disabled briefly with an injury. When he was able to play again, manager Donie Bush, in his first of three seasons at Pittsburgh, decided to keep Cuyler on the bench. There was no doubt that the Waner brothers (Paul with a league-leading .380 average and rookie Lloyd at .355) deserved everyday duty. Clyde Barnhart, a capable journeyman, had taken over Cuyler's post, however, and Bush continued to play him after Cuyler's return to the active roster. When Cuyler questioned him, Bush became enraged and sent Kiki into the doghouse for the remainder of the year. Pittsburgh fans, at first curious, became outraged about the situation.

Bush maintained his stance. Some called him stubborn and arrogant. When the Pirates won the pennant, Bush felt vindicated. Still, he refused to play Cuyler for even one inning in the World Series. His absence—or his presence in the lineup—would likely have meant little to the overall outcome, because the great 1927 Yankees swept the four-game series. However, two games were decided by just one run. Pittsburgh's team batting average was only .223

for the four games, so would Cuyler's participation in those games have swayed the outcome? Probably not, but who can tell for certain?

Bush's refusal to make peace with Cuyler might have cost the Pirates additional championships. Kiki was traded to the Cubs for the 1928 season. He starred for them for eight years, including their title season of 1932. In the meantime, Pittsburgh finished second—without Cuyler—three times during that period. Cuyler, with a lifetime batting average of .321 in a career that continued through 1938, was eventually enshrined at the Hall of Fame.

Two Philadelphia Pitchers

The Philadelphia Athletics of 1929–31 are ranked as one of the century's best teams. They won three pennants and two World Series under manager Connie Mack's direction. With 104 victories they won the 1929 title by 16 games over second-place New York, as big right-hander George Earnshaw led the American League with 24 pitching wins. Hall of Famer Lefty Grove posted a 20–6 record, and four other A's hurlers logged double figures in victories. None of them was Howard Ehmke.

Ehmke was a journeyman right-handed pitcher whose career had started at Buffalo in the Federal League in 1915. Ultimately he registered a lifetime 166–166 major league record. By 1929 he was in his penultimate season. As seventh man on Mack's staff Ehmke started only eight games, finishing with a creditable 7–2 record.

Other members of that formidable pitching corps, especially Earnshaw, Grove, and Rube Walberg, were assumed to be Philadelphia's key World Series starters against the National League's 1929 champs, the Cubs. But to the surprise of virtually everyone who followed baseball—including his own teammates—Ehmke was chosen by Mack to open the Series. Ehmke had not pitched for two weeks and, in fact, had not been with the team during that period. It turned out that he was on a special travel assignment from Mack—following the Cubs and scouting them. Chicago featured sluggers such as Rogers Hornsby, Hack Wilson, and Kiki Cuyler, who were accustomed to facing hard-throwing National League pitchers. Ehmke, a curveballer with changes of speed, was Connie Mack's secret weapon. The manager's decision, which was criticized as a mockery of baseball and its showpiece event, baffled Earnshaw, Grove, and their mates. But it proved to be a master stroke.

The 35-year-old veteran scattered eight Chicago hits in a 4–1 complete-game victory. En route he established a World Series single-game strikeout record of 13, which stood for 24 years. Thirteen strikeouts in his first postseason appearance! During the regular year, in 54⅔ innings, Ehmke had fanned only 20 batters.

Mack started Ehmke again in the fifth game. The A's won it to finalize the Series, but Ehmke was replaced by Walberg, the winning pitcher, in the fourth inning. Howard had no strikeouts in his second outing of the 1929 World Series. He never won another major league game, retiring early in 1930 after he posted an 0–1 record in three games and only 10 innings.

Twenty-one years after Mack's fortuitous decision to pitch Ehmke, another Philadelphia manager pulled a similar surprise as a World Series started. Eddie Sawyer, skipper of the "Whiz Kids"—the 1950 Phillies—called on the National League's Most Valuable Player to open the first game against New York's powerful Yankees.

No surprise, you figure, to start off with an MVP hurler. Except this man, Jim Konstanty, had not been the starting pitcher in even one game all year. He earned his MVP laurels for his then record-setting 74 relief appearances, a league-leading 22 saves, and 16 victories—all, of course, in relief. His ERA that year was an excellent 2.66.

Philadelphia's pitching ace, Robin Roberts, had toiled for 10 innings in a grueling Sunday battle that clinched the Phillies' first pennant in 35 years. It was no shocker, then, that Sawyer would choose someone other than Robbie for the Series opener. Bob Miller, Ken Heintzelman, and Russ Meyer had been frequent starters throughout the year. So when the manager selected Konstanty, eyebrows rose and critics bellowed. Konstanty, after all, would best serve his team by holding a late-game lead, wouldn't he? Wasn't that why he was so valuable to the Phillies? Sawyer thought differently, and, as it developed, his "controversial" decision was a good one except for one small matter: Konstanty lost the game.

Had there been some offensive support for him, the result might have been different. The final score was 1–0. The 33-year-old Konstanty, one of the older members of Sawyer's young squad, pitched eight strong innings and permitted just five hits. The only run of the game was scored in the fourth inning after Bobby Brown, later an American League president, doubled. He advanced to third on a fly ball by Hank Bauer, then scored when Jerry Coleman delivered a sacrifice fly. Konstanty's solid performance was overshadowed by the Yankees' Vic Raschi who allowed only two singles in his complete-game outing.

Fans Manage Zack's Browns

The St. Louis Browns, formerly the first Milwaukee Brewers and later the second-edition Baltimore Orioles, seldom finished in the first division during their 52 years in Missouri. They won only one pennant (1944 under skipper

Luke Sewell) and were usually out of contention by Memorial Day. Managers came and went; very few of them ever had much in the way of all-star-caliber players to direct. When the team's last St. Louis owner, Bill Veeck—an astute baseball man and innovative promoter—took command in 1951, he recognized the ball club's deficiencies in terms of both its American League competitiveness and its drawing power.

St. Louis fans frequently complained about the manager, Zack Taylor, even though he hadn't much talent available. Fan discontent with managers was no better or worse then than it is now, although radio talk-show critics back then were virtually nonexistent. Veeck, as he usually did, seized the situation as an opportunity to build some interest in his drab team.

In conjunction with a local newspaper's promotion, he invited the fans to manage a game.

This chapter has focused on moves made by legally employed managers. But this section is about the night in 1951 that Taylor sat not in, but atop, the dugout in a rocking chair supplied by Veeck. (Eventually umpires banished him to a box seat because he was wearing civilian clothes, not a proper uniform.)

Upon entering Sportsman's Park, fans holding a Grandstand Managers form from the St. Louis newspaper were presented with placards printed with "yes" on one side, "no" on the other. When a game situation dictated the possibility of a bunt, hit-and-run, intentional walk, stolen base, or replacement of the Browns' pitcher, public relations director Bob Fishel would hold up a poster that read "Bunt?" for example. Grandstand Managers responded with the yes or no side of their placards. Unofficial research suggests that about half of the fans answered in the affirmative, the other half the opposite. A coach in the dugout, on a walkie-talkie with Fishel, would give the Browns' players the appropriate signals.

Whether it was the fans' strategies or the luck of the draw, the on-field result was a rare St. Louis victory, a 5–3 triumph over the visiting Philadelphia Athletics. Interestingly, the man who managed more major league games than anyone else took part in directing baseball maneuvers this one more time. Connie Mack was in his first season of managerial retirement in 1951. As principal owner, though, he still traveled with the Athletics frequently. He was in a box near the A's dugout on this particular night, and his host, Veeck, invited him to help the other fans tell Taylor how to run his ball club. Mack displayed his "yes" or "no" judgments a couple of times and appeared to enjoy himself greatly. His congratulations to Veeck for the unique promotion were genuine. Mack liked Veeck and had admired him for years.

For the record, this controversial promotion, which Athletics general manager Art Ehlers derided and threatened to protest, entered the official record books as a victory for Taylor—one of only 235 wins against 410 setbacks in his five seasons as manager.

And Now, Playing Right Field . . .

Back in 1918 one of baseball's brightest young stars, for whom a lengthy pitching future was predicted, already had two seasons with more than 20 wins. In one of those years he led the American League with a 1.75 ERA in 323 innings at age 22. By the end of the 1917 campaign, this Boston left-hander had logged a remarkable 67–33 won-lost record. So what did his newly installed manager, Ed Barrow, do the following year? He inserted his brilliant pitcher in the outfield on about half the days he wasn't pitching. Many Red Sox fans feared an injury to their youthful pitching hero, who had become instrumental in the 1916 World Championship and whose pitching, they believed, would lead to another title in 1918. (Boston did, indeed, win.)

But Ed Barrow was soon applauded for his personnel maneuver, and the controversy quickly subsided. As glorious as the phenom's pitching potential was, Babe Ruth's bat was meant to be in the lineup everyday.

The Luxury of the Second Guess

Golfers offer this lament: "should'a, could'a, would'a, if." Sounds pretty much like the open-mike radio callers the morning after. By then, hours after the game, they've figured out all the mistakes made by the home team's manager. The task wasn't difficult at all, because they had plenty of time for the second guess. Or the third. And more.

Only the manager is duty bound to make split-second decisions in the heat of battle.

And shame on him when his ninth-inning pinch hitter, entering the contest with a .345 batting average, fouls out to end the game. Your friendly neighborhood baseball skipper should've known better, shouldn't he? What a dope!

All right, then—you make the call. Pretend, for a moment that it's many years ago—no second-guessing allowed here—and you're running the dugout. You are Bucky Harris and Rogers Hornsby and Dusty Baker and John McNamara and Danny Ozark and Tony LaRussa and Tom Lasorda, transported back in time.

Dodger Stadium, October 15, 1988—Ninth inning, Game 1 of the World Series. A's lead Dodgers, 4–3. LaRussa brings in All-Star reliever Dennis Eckersley to replace Oakland starter Dave Stewart, who's been pitching well. Two out, one on, now. In a last-ditch effort to win the game, Lasorda sends up an injured man, Kirk Gibson, to pinch-hit. Gibson can only limp to the plate, having suffered a severe leg injury a few weeks earlier. Eck fires a slider that Gibson drives into the right-field stands to win the dramatic game. It's only the first game of the Series, but the underdog Dodgers, behind two complete-game Orel Hershiser victories, lose just one game en route to the World Championship. Did Gibson's heroics provide the momentum they needed? Ironically, that Game 1 home run came in his only plate appearance in the entire five-game series.

Forbes Field, October 15, 1925—Game 7, World Series. Pittsburgh, four days earlier, down three games to one, battled back against Washington to deadlock the series at three wins apiece. Future Hall of Famer Walter Johnson, nearing his 38th birthday, was tapped by Senators manager Bucky Harris to pitch this rubber game. Johnson already had posted two complete-game wins (Games 1 and 4). Now, working with three days' rest, he held Pittsburgh scoreless for two innings as Washington built a four-run lead. But the Pirates scored three in the third, then continued to light up Johnson for a total of nine runs on 15 hits. Manager Harris allowed Johnson to pitch the entire eight innings in his team's 9–7 loss. With his club putting runs on the board, should Harris have relieved his star pitcher early? Or, despite sentimentality, never started him in the first place? A year earlier Johnson was the winner as a relief pitcher in Game 7 against New York. That 1924 triumph was the original Senators' lone World Championship during their 60 years in Washington.

Yankee Stadium, October 10, 1926—Game 7, World Series. Whether it was sentimentality, a lucky guess, or brilliant strategy, Cardinals pilot Rogers Hornsby pushed the right buttons with another Hall of Fame pitcher who had a pair of complete-game wins to his credit earlier in this World Series. Grover Alexander, born nine months before Walter Johnson, was nearly 39. He had permitted just two New York runs in each of Game 2 and Game 6 victories. A heavy drinker, he celebrated the Game 6 win well into the night, not expecting to pitch again. But with two out in the seventh inning, and St. Louis leading 3–2, Hornsby signaled the bull pen to send in Alexander. The bases were loaded, but the veteran right-hander fanned dangerous Tony Lazzeri, then held New York scoreless the rest of the game. Imagine the catcalls that would have been directed toward Hornsby had Alexander failed. That game, by the way, ended not with a controversial managerial decision, but with some unwise player strategy. The final out: Babe Ruth's failed attempt to steal second base.

Candlestick Park, October 3, 1993— The Giants aim for their first division crown in four years. After leading the NL West most of the season they've slumped toward the end but still have 103 wins—their most in regulation play since moving from New York 35 years earlier. One more victory would clinch the division title. But manager Dusty Baker, with 20-game winners John Burkett and Billy Swift tired from recent outings down the stretch, chooses to start young Solomon Torres in this crucial regular-season-ending contest. Torres is shelled by the visiting Dodgers, becomes, according to some witnesses, an emotional basket case, and seldom thereafter showed signs of his earlier potential. Should Baker have started him? In retrospect, no. But the NL Manager of the Year had little choice. Atlanta, in the meantime, won its third straight division flag.

Veterans Stadium, October 7, 1977—It was only Game 3, but in those days the League Championship Series was best of five, and the Phillies and Dodgers had split the first two in Los Angeles. Now the winner would have a significant 2–1 edge. Philadelphia had what it considered a comfortable 5–3 lead with two outs and none on in the top of the ninth inning. After a pinch-hit single, Manny Mota, a second Dodgers pinch hitter, drilled a long drive to deep left where Greg Luzinski bobbled, then dropped, the ball. That was just the beginning. The rally continued after a Mike Schmidt misplay, a controversial safe call at first base, and a wild pickoff attempt. Phillies pilot Danny Ozark is still criticized for not replacing Luzinski with defensive specialist Jerry Martin, a move Ozark frequently made during the season. Unable to score in its half of the ninth, Philadelphia lost the game, 6–5, and the LCS the next night, when LA , with Dusty Baker the offensive star, logged a 4–1 victory.

Shea Stadium, October 25, 1986—The Bill Buckner game. Red Sox manager John McNamara is ridiculed for not replacing Buckner at first base with utility man Dave Stapleton, who often took over in late innings with the Sox ahead. This night, in Game 6 of the World Series, Boston had taken a 5–3 lead in the top of the 10th and held that margin with two out and nobody on base in the bottom of the inning. Then three singles, a wild pitch by reliever Bob Stanley, and Mookie Wilson's grounder through Buckner produced a miraculous comeback victory. Don't forget, though, it was only Game 6. Boston blew a 3–0 lead the next night when the Mets won the World Series. Critics, noting Buckner's achy, injured legs, second-guessed Stapleton's nonappearance. Yet, Buckner's legs weren't the culprits. They got him into proper position to field the ball. He didn't get the mitt down in time. If McNamara's to be criticized, how about his replacing Roger Clemens, pitching effectively with the lead after seven innings, with Calvin Schiraldi, whose World Series ERA was to become 13.50?

Maybe you vividly recall some other controversial managerial decisions. Surely you have your own arguments with your home team manager for the boner he pulled just last Tuesday. And if you don't, your neighbor on the radio call-in show will.

Be grateful that the first guess goes to the manager. And not you.

Baseball pioneer **Harry Wright** is memorialized in the Hall of Fame's Meritorious Service section. He managed the first professional baseball team, the legendary Cincinnati Red Stockings, and later, for 18 seasons, was a successful 19th-century National League manager. (*Transcendental Graphics*)

New York Giants manager **Leo Durocher**, *left*, with part-time coach **Frankie Frisch** in 1953. A former Cardinals, Pirates, and Cubs pilot, Frisch was a Giants rookie in 1919. Durocher, manager of New York's final two pennants before the Giants' transfer to San Francisco, was the fiery shortstop on Frisch's 1934 Cardinal champs. (*Transcendental Graphics*)

Earl Weaver (Baltimore 1969–71), *left*, and **Ralph Houk** (Yankees 1961–63) join Frank Chance and Hughie Jennings as the only managers in history to guide teams to league pennants in their first three full years. (*Transcendental Graphics*)

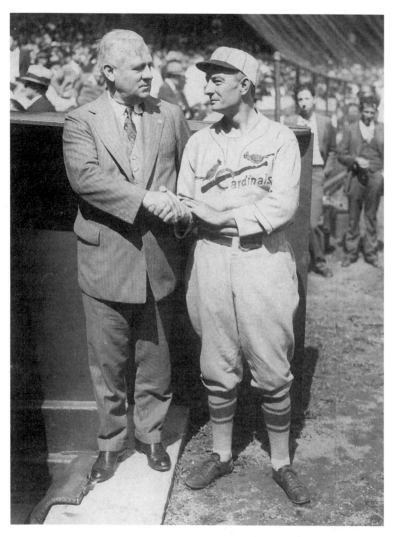

During the 1928 pennant drive, contending managers **John McGraw**, *left*, of the New York Giants, and St. Louis's **Bill McKechnie** exchange pregame greetings. St. Louis eventually won the title, the second of McKechnie's three pennant-winning teams to do so. Pittsburgh (1925) and Cincinnati (1939–40) were the others. (*Transcendental Graphics*)

In 1944 **Luke Sewell** managed the St. Louis Browns to the team's only pennant during its 52 seasons in Missouri prior to the franchise's transfer to Baltimore. Under his leadership, St. Louis posted a six-year 432–410 record. Later he managed at Cincinnati. Golfing in his early eighties, Sewell often carded his age—or lower. (*Urban Archives, Temple University, Philadelphia, PA*)

Tom Kelly has managed Minnesota for a longer single stretch than any other skipper in the 98-year history of the Senators/Twins franchise. And of the 42 managers with three or more postseason matchups, he is the only pilot who's never lost an October series. His Twins won the ALCS and then the World Series in both 1987 and 1991. (*Minnesota Twins*)

Since 1962 four men, including **Dallas Green**, have managed both the New York Yankees and New York Mets. Casey Stengel, Yogi Berra, and Joe Torre were the others. Here at Philadelphia, Green's first managing stop, he led the 1980 Phillies to the franchise's only World Championship. (*Philadelphia Phillies*)

Gene Mauch, here in 1960 as baseball's youngest skipper at age 34, managed more games than anyone else without winning a pennant. Nevertheless, he is recognized as one of baseball's brightest innovators and strategists. (*Philadelphia Phillies*)

Walter Johnson, *left,* and **Steve O'Neill** are two of the all-time "nice guy" managers. Here, as Cleveland skipper Johnson is replaced by O'Neill, one of his coaches, they wish each other well. O'Neill managed four teams over 14 years and never had a losing season. He and Johnson are among baseball's most underrated managers. (*Urban Archives, Temple University, Philadelphia*)

Billy Southworth, *left,* "the best manager not in the Hall of Fame," greets Yankee pilot **Joe McCarthy.** The two split the 1942 and 1943 World Series. McCarthy's .615 winning percentage is baseball's best this century. Southworth's .597 ranks second. (*Urban Archives, Temple University, Philadelphia*)

Giants manager **John McGraw** left little to chance. He paid close attention to details in an effort to gain an edge on an opponent. Here he closely studies shortstop **Travis Jackson** during batting practice. (*Transcendental Graphics*)

Ted Williams in something other than a Boston Red Sox uniform? Often forgotten is his four-year managing career—three seasons with the second-edition Washington Senators and one more, here in 1972, when that club became the Texas Rangers. (*Texas Rangers*)

It began in 1985 when his Blue Jays advanced to the ALCS. **Bobby Cox** has managed more postseason games than anyone else in history. During his extremely successful 1990s reign in Atlanta, the Braves' four pennants equal the franchise's title total for the preceding nine decades. (*Atlanta Braves*)

The Giants' two-time NL Manager of the Year, **Dusty Baker**, earns high marks for his awareness of player strengths and weaknesses— and for his decisiveness. No question here that a relief pitcher is being summoned. (*San Francisco Giants/Stanton*)

On Opening Day 1916, manager **Pat Moran** displays floral congratulations that salute his Phillies' 1915 NL pennant, the team's first. Joining Moran at pregame ceremonies was **Wilbert Robinson**, visiting Brooklyn's skipper. Moran later led Cincinnati to a 1919 World Series win over the infamous Chicago Black Sox. (*Urban Archives, Temple University, Philadelphia*)

Jimmie Dykes managed six clubs during 21 seasons from 1934 through 1961. Here, after three years at Philadelphia, he discards an A's cap in favor of new headgear upon being named Orioles pilot, when the St. Louis Browns franchise was transferred to Baltimore for the 1954 season. (*Urban Archives, Temple University, Philadelphia*)

Dad and son, manager **Hal McRae**, *left*, and his son **Brian**, Royals outfielder, were together for four seasons in Kansas City. Only four other baseball families—the Alous, Berras, Macks, and Ripkens—have experienced this "sons playing for manager fathers" major league relationship. (*Permission granted by the Kansas City Royals*)

Billy Martin, not always the owner's pet, was clearly a favorite of New York fans. Here he acknowledges their cheers. He managed Minnesota, Detroit, Texas, and Oakland—and, five different times, the Yankees. (*Transcendental Graphics*)

Frank Robinson became major league baseball's first black manager when he was signed to direct the 1975 Cleveland Indians. He is the only black manager to be hired subsequently by other teams—San Francisco and Baltimore. (*Urban Archives, Temple University, Philadelphia*)

Al Lopez, the Hall of Fame's oldest living member, managed the 1959 Chicago White Sox to the club's most recent American League pennant. Earlier, in six seasons at Cleveland, Lopez's Indians won the 1954 flag and never finished below second place. (*Urban Archives, Temple University, Philadelphia*)

Dick Williams is one of just four men (Jimmie Dykes, Rogers Hornsby, and John Mc-Namara are the others) to manage six different teams. Montreal, here, was his fourth assignment. Williams (at Boston, Oakland, San Diego) and Bill McKechnie are the only managers to guide three franchises into the World Series. (*Urban Archives, Temple University, Philadelphia*)

Hall of Famers

"Dean" Al Lopez

The National Baseball Hall of Fame in Cooperstown, New York, houses bronze plaques citing 14 men for their remarkable achievements as managers. All of them guided their teams to championships at one time or another, although longevity and widespread respect for their abilities also had substantial bearing on the nominating committees' selections of several of them. Connie Mack and Bucky Harris, for instance, were "locks" for the Hall, even though each finished his lengthy and distinguished career with more losses than victories.

At least two Cooperstown inductees could have earned Hall admittance in more than one category. Clark Griffith, honored in the Hall's executive branch, was one of the top pitchers in the late 19th century, took the mound for another dozen or so years as a player-manager in the 1900s, and then earned distinction as the owner and president of the Washington Senators for more than three decades. Connie Mack, a three-year pilot at Pittsburgh in the 1890s, was the only full-time manager of the American League's Philadelphia Athletics during their first 50 years of existence. For more than half of his Philadelphia tenure Mack was the club's major shareholder and chief executive. John McGraw, whose Giants won 10 pennants under his tutelage, was simultaneously the manager and his team's key front-office decision maker during most of his 31 years in New York, just as Mack was in Philadelphia.

The hallowed Hall features men born well over a hundred years ago, but it also contains the plaques of recent managers who still look forward to their annual reminiscences and midsummer reunions on induction weekend at Cooperstown. Mack's, McGraw's, and Ned Hanlon's managing assignments spanned from the 1890s into the 20th century. As of 1998's Cooperstown inductions, Tom Lasorda is the most recently active manager, having wrapped up his notable Los Angeles leadership duties in 1996.

Lasorda and Earl Weaver are two of just three Hall of Fame skippers still living. The other is Al Lopez, one of baseball's most highly respected and widely admired men for both his managing accomplishments and his gentlemanly demeanor. Congenially commenting for this book at his Tampa, Florida, home, Al Lopez modestly yet proudly acknowledged his standing as the oldest living member of the Hall of Fame when he reminisced about his lengthy career and his famous associates.

"A lot of people have said some nice things about my managing." Lopez smiles. "But I was lucky enough to have some pretty good training for it. After all, every one of the six managers I played for when I was catching is in the Hall of Fame. Robby [Wilbert Robinson], Casey [Stengel], and Bill McKechnie are in the managers' wing of the Hall. My other managers—Max Carey, Frank Frisch, and Lou Boudreau—are at Cooperstown as players. Most of the time they made me the playing captain, so I was pretty much involved with the details of a game before I became a manager."

Al Lopez's big-league playing career began in 1928 at Brooklyn when he appeared in three games. He was just 19 years old then, and he "told Uncle Robby I'd like to go back to the minors for seasoning rather than sit on the Dodgers' bench." By 1930 Al was back to the majors, where he played through the 1947 season and, along the way, established a record for most games caught (1,981). That standard was eventually surpassed by Bob Boone in 1988, then again later by Carlton Fisk and Gary Carter. When Boone was the first to exceed the 41-year-old record, Lopez sent a congratulatory note to him. Al turned in solid offensive figures during his playing days, a .261 lifetime batting average, but it was his defensive skills and his handling of pitchers that earned him notoriety. Over those 1,981 games he caught, his fielding average was an excellent .984. After Robinson retired after 18 years as Brooklyn pilot, Lopez played under Max Carey and Casey Stengel with the Dodgers, Bill McKechnie then Stengel again in Boston with the Braves, Frankie Frisch in Pittsburgh for more than six years, and, in his final active season (1947), Lou Boudreau at Cleveland.

"Actually, I was only 16 years old when I started in the minors in the Brooklyn organization," Lopez said. "That was right after I had the chance to catch the great Walter Johnson. Washington, the team Johnson played his entire career for, was in spring training right here in my hometown of Tampa. Teams didn't bring a lot of extra players to Florida like they do now, so somebody found out that I was a catcher here in town and asked me if I wanted to earn $45 dollars a week as a bull-pen and batting-practice catcher for the Senators. Sometimes Johnson—and he was a big gate attraction—pitched to me, including once in an actual exhibiton game. I remember that Walter was so easy to catch. In the strike zone all the time."

After Lopez, then 21, became a fixture in the Dodgers' lineup, manager Robinson turned over much of the signal calling to Al. Robby was winding down his career at the time and was not as attentive to game details as he once had been. Lopez soon became the playing captain and was the acknowledged on-field defensive leader after Carey followed Robinson to the manager's post, and when Stengel succeeded Carey in 1934.

Lopez chuckles about one incident in particular of that Brooklyn era, but it was not amusing to him at the time. "Bob Quinn was the Dodgers' general manager, and he tried to cut my salary after I hit .301 in 1933 and followed up with .273 in 140 games the next year. That made me mad, so for the only time in my life I held out. The team was training in Clearwater then, right across the bay from here, and we finally got together. Eventually Quinn traded me to the Boston Braves, but in the meantime I had worked with Casey Stengel for the first time. He was something, Casey was. They've said he was nothing but a clown, but Casey was a smart baseball man. He tried to emulate John McGraw. Casey had played for him with the Giants. McGraw ran those Giants with great authority, and Casey learned a lot from him. When he [Stengel] became a manager, he was in charge. No question about it. And, like McGraw, he liked to teach and talk fundamentals. The spring that we were in Clearwater some of the fellows thought Casey was overdoing it in the classroom. Every morning we had a long meeting about fundamentals. One of the fellows finally spoke up one day and said, 'Hey, how about some hitting practice, too?'"

When Lopez joined the Braves in 1936, Bill McKechnie was Boston's manager. The two formed a warm friendship and combined to improve the Braves' pitching substantially. The 1935 club had lost a then National League record of 115 games. As McKechnie and Lopez worked closely with the Boston pitchers, the Braves improved by 33 games. Next came a winning year in 1937 when

Lou Fette and Jim Turner both posted 20-victory seasons. "McKechnie was a great manager," Lopez has often said. "After '35 he recommended a lot of changes." Lopez and McKechnie would join forces 10 years later at Cleveland as Al completed his playing career and McKechnie served as a Boudreau coach. Bob Lemon became a full-time pitcher that season (he had begun his career as an infielder-outfielder), and McKechnie and Lopez are given a great deal of credit for Lemon's rapid conversion toward the Hall of Fame pitcher he became. The 6-foot right-hander, of course, would be a major ingredient in the outstanding Cleveland teams Lopez was soon to mold as manager.

"During that 1947 season at Cleveland, when I was 39 years old, I asked the owner, Bill Veeck, to help me get a coaching or managing job in the minor leagues," recalls Lopez. "I wanted to stay in baseball, and if I ever wanted to become a major league manager I figured that minor league managing experience was necessary and would help me decide. Donie Bush had been after me to manage his team in Indianapolis. He was a native there, and after his big-league career was over he held ownership shares in minor league clubs at Indianapolis. Well, Cleveland had a working relationship with Indianapolis at the time, so I went there in 1948 and managed the club for three years. One thing I found out right away: I couldn't socialize with the players anymore. I would think that has to be tough on player-managers, too. You used to sit down, maybe have a beer or a meal with them, but all of a sudden you can't do that. It might appear that you're playing favorites."

By the end of the 1950 season Boudreau had been Cleveland's pilot for nine years. A change was in order. Boudreau, nearing the end of his playing career, signed with the Red Sox (whom he would manage soon after), and the Indians and Lopez agreed to a managing contract in Cleveland. Seldom has any manager enjoyed such an extended run of success. In six seasons at Cleveland Stadium Lopez's Tribe won one league title and finished second the other five times (all as runner-up to Stengel's Yankees). Cleveland *averaged* 97 wins a year over those half-dozen seasons and won the 1954 pennant with 111 victories, an American League record that stood until 1998. And it was achieved during a 154-game schedule, not the 162 in effect now. The Indians' pitching staff that year featured four future Hall of Famers—Lemon, Bob Feller, Early Wynn, and spot-starter Hal Newhouser. Most of their mound mates—such as Mike Garcia, Art Houtteman, Ray Narleski, and Don Mossi—also carried quality credentials.

"In looking back," says Lopez, "naturally the main thing is winning. And it sure helps if the manager has the kind of players we had on that Indians team. We also had a pretty fair pitcher in the minor leagues that year over at Indianapolis, and Hank Greenberg [Cleveland GM at the time] wanted me to bring him up during the '54 season. His name was Herb Score, and you know how outstanding he became right from the start of his rookie year in 1955 until he was hit in the eye with a batted ball a couple of years later. Anyway, I told Hank I didn't need pitchers with that great staff we already had. Besides, Score would have been under pressure. But I guaranteed Hank that Score would definitely be on the '55 staff." All the brilliant young southpaw did then in 1955, as Cleveland finished second, was to go 16–10 with a 2.85 earned run average and a league-leading strikeout total of 245, a major league rookie standard not broken until Dwight Gooden surpassed it 30 years later.

A few months before Score's arrival, Lopez and the Indians suffered the great disappointment of a 1954 World Series sweep by the underdog New York Giants of Leo Durocher. "Not enough credit has ever been given to the Giants," laments Lopez. "They had a pretty good team that year. On the other hand, if we had started the series in Cleveland, instead of the Polo Grounds with its funny configurations, I still think we'd have won it. But that's water over the dam. Give New York credit. We didn't hit at all [Cleveland's World Series batting average was only .190 for the four games], and the Giants came through in the clutch, especially when that Dusty Rhodes hit two home runs. That killed us. For me it wasn't the end of the world; I knew a short series could go either way. Still, it was a big disappointment that we didn't have a better showing. On the other hand, winning the pennant meant that we finally got past my old pal Casey Stengel. The funny thing was, the Yankees won more games [103] that year than at any time in the 12 seasons Casey was at New York. But, of course, we had the 111 that season."

As his Indians engaged in down-to-the-wire battles with New York year after year, Lopez's reputation as a manager grew. It was quickly conceded that he was an adroit handler of pitchers (remember his team captaincies of a generation earlier when he was a durable catcher, and his close work with McKechnie) and a patient, comparatively quiet man who led generally strife-free clubhouses. Other clubs sought his services when they had manager openings. Finally, after the 1956 season, Al talked with Greenberg and said that he wanted out of Cleveland, that he had achieved about as much as he thought possible, that he was beginning to feel a little stale in the job there, and that he didn't plan to sign on again. "It was nothing personal," Lopez recalls. "In fact I got along well with Hank. I just thought I needed a change."

It didn't take long for a big-league change of address to materialize. The Chicago White Sox had been annual contenders for a few years, were benefiting from a solid farm system at the time, and had a job opening if Lopez would accept. He did, and the same pattern as Cleveland's developed—two runner-up finishes to New York and then Chicago's first American League pennant (1959) in four decades. When Chicago finished third in 1960, 20 games over .500, it was the first time in the 10 seasons that Stengel and his former pupil Lopez managed against each other that someone other than the two of them landed as high as second place (it was Paul Richards with the rapidly improving Orioles). Stengel's Yankee career stretched over 12 seasons, during which time his club won 10 pennants. Teams managed by Al Lopez won the other two.

Lopez continues to express great admiration for Stengel. "He was a great manager, no question about it. When I managed against him it was always a challenge. But we remained great friends even then. Looking over at the other dugout you could always learn something about managing from Casey. And beside his abilities as a manager, he was just a great guy. I remember one time when I was playing with the Pirates. We went to spring training in California. Casey was out of the major leagues then [handling minor league managing jobs between big-league posts with the Braves and the Yankees], and he invited some of us to his house in Glendale for a meal, some socializing, and baseball reminiscences.

"I recall another West Coast incident, too. It didn't involve Casey, but Ty Cobb as a manager plays a major role in this story. A charity exhibition game was scheduled in Hollywood, and Cobb, long retired by then, was one of the managers that day. There were about four big-league clubs in spring training out there, so they picked several players from each team for this exhibition game. I was on Cobb's team, and one of our pitchers was Satchel Paige [still a Negro League star then, but not yet signed to his first major league contract]. Well, it was always pretty well known that Satch marched to his own drummer, and as the game was about to start Cobb said, 'Okay, who's our starting pitcher? Get him warmed up.' 'It's Satchel Paige,' came a reply, 'but he's not here.' 'Then,' Cobb growled, 'get somebody else.' After about the fourth inning here comes Satchel Paige into the dugout. 'Hello, Mr. Cobb,' he grins. 'Who are you?' asked Cobb, knowing full well who he was speaking with. 'I'm Satchel Paige.' 'Well, go over there and sit down,' says Ty. 'Maybe I'll use you later!'

"When I was managing the White Sox several years later, Bill Veeck, who built our '59 club that won the pennant, kept after me to sign Paige for our bull pen. I couldn't bring myself to do it, though, and I tried to explain why to Veeck even though I'm not sure he ever understood. See, I knew Satch could still pitch. The guy had a rubber arm. And I liked him a lot, enjoyed being around him. But I also knew you couldn't count on him to be there. He'd show up at the ballpark when he wanted to; sometimes made the team train, sometimes didn't. The manager can't have that. The same rules have to apply to everybody. If you don't have discipline you can't have a winning baseball team.

"I guess that touches on the subject of the toughest part of managing. It applied in my day, and I'm sure it still does. Discipline is a key factor. So is the ability to handle—or try your best to handle—different personalities. Then there's a manager's relationship with the front office. They have to recognize that you're doing a good job and have confidence that you know baseball and your team. Nobody knows more about the ball club than the manager. He knows who's doing the job and who isn't. You're with them every day, around them all the time. Regardless of how many scouting reports and anybody else's observations, it's the manager who's supposed to be the most knowledgeable about the ball club. If not, then he shouldn't be the manager anymore."

Just as Lopez was associated with experienced teachers and baseball veterans along his playing career path, some of Lopez's players themselves proceeded on to major league managing posts. Larry Doby piloted the White Sox for most of the 1978 season, Bob Kennedy headed the Cubs' offbeat "college of coaches" format and also managed the Athletics, and Bob Lemon was the dugout director of three clubs—the Royals, the White Sox, and the Yankees, whom he led into two World Series.

"I would hope they learned some things about managing from me," Lopez said. "Maybe even some things not to do. For me, one of the things I enjoyed most about the job was helping young players. I got a big kick out of that. Jim Landis is a good example. Jim was a great kid but needed a lot of polish when he came up to the White Sox. It was gratifying to see him develop into one of the best defensive center fielders in the league at the time. He was a big reason we won the pennant in '59."

Catchers Jim Hegan and Sherman Lollar, both deceased now, are said to have expressed admiration for Lopez's baseball skills, and an appreciation for his working with them. Interestingly, both men were big-league veterans when Lopez signed on to manage their teams—Hegan's Indians and Lollar's White Sox. The admiration was mutual. "I was truly lucky to manage those two," says Lopez of Hegan and Lollar. "Two great catchers, two fine men."

Lopez suspects managing today presents more problems than it did in his heyday. "I suppose I could figure out the designated hitter all right," he said, "but it must be depressing not to know who might be with you next year because of free agency and the salary situation of today. It must be awfully hard to build for much of a future. It also seems that a lot of men are advanced to the big leagues now before they've had much minor league experience. That means more teaching of fundamentals after they arrive. That's a big change in baseball. When Bill McKechnie managed the old Braves I think he had only one coach. Now there's, what, six or seven to help with the teaching that's required. The subject of teaching, though, is a two-edged sword. No question that it's necessary somewhere along the line, but I think teaching can be overdone. I've known some players who got to the point of depending on you and your coaches instead of learning and practicing for themselves. You can often learn more by observing and doing it yourself."

Apparently Al Lopez observed and absorbed well, as evidenced by that Hall of Fame plaque with his name on it. No manager is more qualified to review a century of baseball than this "dean" of Cooperstown. Few if any other managers in this book had direct associations with teammates of the legendary Mc-Graw, sat in dugouts next to Stengel and McKechnie, and filled in lineup cards with the names of players who will continue to serve baseball in managing or front-office capacities in the next millennium. Along his way to Cooperstown he posted the fifth-highest winning percentage of any full-time manager this century. In the face of Leo Durocher's reported slur about nice guys finishing last, Al Lopez—born, bred, and still playing golf in Tampa—proved a decisive exception.

Other Managers' Routes to Cooperstown

We issue this advisory to any young managers aspiring to Hall of Fame coronation: Don't waste much time searching out a common denominator for success.

There simply are not many common threads binding the 14 men already enshrined in Cooperstown's managers' wing, nor the six other former managers inducted in the Hall's executive section. Stay healthy and focused though, for there is this one constant: a tenure far surpassing the average major league manager's career of under six seasons. It follows, then, that a man's first piloting assignment should occur relatively early in life, as witness the 10 of the 14 who were running teams before age 40, and the eldest starter among them, Tommy Lasorda, who was 49 when he was signed to manage Los Angeles in late 1976.

It might help to have been an infielder, because only one pitcher (Lasorda), three catchers (Connie Mack, Lopez, Wilbert Robinson), and just two outfielders (Casey Stengel and Ned Hanlon) are Hall of Fame managers. Two of the distinguished managers—Joe McCarthy and Earl Weaver—never played major league ball, but they did perform as minor league infielders. Walt Alston, a first baseman, recorded a single major league at-bat. We suggest you not be tall and lanky. Alston, at 6 feet, 2 inches, is the Hall's tallest manager. Connie Mack, 6 feet, 1 inch, is the only other one who stood six feet or more. None hailed from anyplace farther west than Missouri, and no Hall of Fame manager was born overseas.

Remembering the stay-healthy admonition, long careers (a 10-year minimum) constitute one official qualifying requisite for Cooperstown consideration. Demographically speaking, a long life has been a typical characteristic, too. As we have seen, Al Lopez, Lasorda, and Weaver are the Hall's only living managers as this book is written. Mack and McCarthy, though, died after their 90th birthdays. Only John McGraw and Miller Huggins failed to reach age 70. Huggins, who died youngest, was 50 and seemingly in his prime as Yankees skipper when blood poisoning sidelined him with just 11 regular-season games remaining in 1929. He was dead before the season was over.

Elsewhere in the book you'll find highlighted the managing careers of Al Lopez, Bill McKechnie, Joe McCarthy, and Ned Hanlon, along with those of two former managers now in Cooperstown's Meritorious Service branch, Harry Wright and Charlie Comiskey. Here is a summary of the careers of other Hall of Fame managers, who surface again from time to time in this book's review of managing highlights, trends, and noteworthy incidents.

Walter Alston. Managed 23 years, all with the Dodgers (first in Brooklyn, then Los Angeles),1954–76; seven pennants, four World Championships; first managing job at age 42; native of Venice, Ohio; died at age 72; was retired seven years upon his Hall of Fame induction.

Who in the world was this obscure fellow the Brooklyn Dodgers named to succeed popular Chuck Dressen as manager before the 1954 season? Dressen, a prominent baseball figure for 20 years, was just coming off his second consecutive Brooklyn pennant. When he demanded a multiyear contract, (some say at his wife's persistent urging), Brooklyn said no. Dressen promptly departed, although he later piloted Washington, the Milwaukee Braves, and Detroit.

Alston had been a successful but generally unknown manager in the Dodgers' minor league system for several years but had no big-league coaching experience nor, in fact, any major league playing background except for a single time at-bat (he fanned and committed an error at first base) for the Cardinals in 1936. Opening Day of 1954, as dugout boss in Brooklyn, would be his next official appearance in major league flannels. The Dodgers finished a competitive second in Walt's first season and then ran off two pennants in a row, including the 1955 flag that propelled them toward the franchise's first World title after it had lost seven World Series. Brooklyn's earlier pennant winners— Wilbert Robinson, Leo Durocher, Burt Shotton, Dressen—had all failed to capture Series laurels. After the team's 1958 transcontinental transfer to Los Angeles, Alston directed it to five more pennants and three World Series crowns (1959 over Chicago, 1963 over New York, 1965 over Minnesota). Alston produced a first-place finish about every three years, on average, and usually contended during the intervening seasons. And, perhaps remembering Dressen's failed negotiations, he signed one-year contracts year after year after year.

Alston's first taste of managing came in 1940 at Portsmouth, Ohio, a Cardinals farm club in the Middle Atlantic League. He was a minor league player-manager for three years, a good long-ball hitter, and a sometime pitcher. His Cardinals boss, Branch Rickey, took over Brooklyn in 1943, remembered Alston from the St. Louis system, and hired him in 1945 to manage Dodgers farmhands. Alston did so for the next nine seasons before the Brooklyn invitation was extended.

His managing style was not flamboyant, and he rarely spent much time teaching his players the fine points of the game or reviewing fundamentals. He could become angry on occasion and was known to chew out individuals, or the entire squad, if he perceived that laziness or carelessness were eroding performances. Alston was an advocate of the set lineup, and, after all, who among managers wouldn't pencil the names of Campanella, Robinson, Reese, Furillo, Snider, et al. onto lineup cards every day? He should not be considered static, however. When the aforementioned group and their mates played for Alston at Brooklyn, he leaned toward a long-ball, big-inning style of offense. When the sluggers' careers had run out, and exceptional pitching was the team's strong point instead, Alston adapted to the one-run-at-a-time strategy that relied on basepath speed and tight defense.

He also reversed the cool clubhouse reception he got when he replaced Dressen. Roughly half the squad was made up of established and successful veterans—most of them well-known starters. Combined, they had earned dozens of World Series rings going back into the 1940s and on to their 1952 and 1953 championship seasons. How could this newcomer, Alston, command them with authority? After all, he wasn't really a major league guy—didn't know anything about life in the National League. A few of them would never be completely comfortable with Alston. But half of his 1954 club consisted of men he had known and managed on minor league farms at St. Paul and Montreal. They were aware of the new man's talents and were at ease with his leadership. He, in turn, was pleased to see at least some friendly faces at Ebbets Field. Eventually, even most of the grizzled veterans grudgingly conceded that the selection of Walter might have been okay after all.

Sparky Anderson, himself an odds-on favorite for Hall of Fame induction someday, managed the Cincinnati Reds against Alston's Dodgers for seven seasons. Speaking of Alston and another contemporary, Gene Mauch, Anderson offered this compliment: "If their teams were better than yours, and they made the right moves, they'd win. If your team was better, you'd usually win, but not without a struggle." Of all his managerial opponents in the early 1970s, Anderson singled out those two for commendation. He also thanked Alston for some off-field advice. Early in the week at one of the first league meetings Sparky attended, Alston, the stoic midwesterner who was never accused of chasing bright lights, approached a somewhat bewildered and reticent Anderson and made a quiet suggestion. He told Sparky, "You don't have to be in the middle of traffic telling everybody how important you are. Leave that to the pretenders. They won't be around long anyway."

Leo Durocher. Managed 23 years (Dodgers 1939–46, 1948; Giants 1948–55; Cubs 1966–72; Astros 1972–73); three pennants, one World Championship; first managing job at age 33; native of West Springfield, Massachusetts; died at age 86; was retired 21 years upon posthumous Hall of Fame induction.

Teammate of Babe Ruth and Lou Gehrig, and manager of men who played major league baseball into the 1980s, Leo Durocher is one of the most colorful and controversial of all the managers in the Hall of Fame. As a Yankee rookie in the mid-20s he was dubbed Lippy Leo, or Leo the Lip. The moniker remained appropos for the nearly 50 years that he was an important figure in baseball.

Leo was barely 20 when he appeared in two games for the 1925 Yankees. Three years later he was a semiregular at shortstop and served as a defensive replacement in four 1928 World Series games under Miller Huggins. Soon after, Durocher was the Reds' and Cardinals' regular shortstop, and eventually he would manage four National League clubs off and on for 35 seasons. The first team he skippered, Brooklyn, won the first of his three pennants in his third season.

By 1938 the highly energized executive Larry MacPhail had taken over the front office in Brooklyn, and he went looking for a man to replace field manager Burleigh Grimes. General manager Branch Rickey, for whom Durocher was then playing in St. Louis, recommended Leo. In 1941 Brooklyn won the pennant and then nearly made it two in a row. But a serious injury to 1941 rookie standout Pete Reiser, incurred when he collided with the concrete outfield wall in St. Louis, derailed the 1942 Dodgers toward season's end. They posted 104 victories but fell two games short of the Cardinals. Durocher had then been in charge for four seasons. By Leo's own count MacPhail had fired him—then rehired him—40 times. According to longtime Dodger official

Harold Parrott in his book *The Lords of Baseball,* it was *only* 27. Both men were volatile. Each craved the spotlight. Many times their tempers flared into shoving and even punching matches. The numerous "firings" were always verbal and unofficial. Within 24 hours MacPhail invariably reinstated Leo—until the next "misunderstanding."

During the war years Durocher, nearing 40, played occasionally but usually penciled in the name of some teenager—Gene Mauch, Tommy Brown, Eddie Basinski, some others—to fill in at shortstop until bona fide veterans returned from the military. MacPhail, himself, had left the Dodgers to serve as an army colonel. After the war he assumed the presidency of the New York Yankees. His replacement at Brooklyn was Durocher's one-time St. Louis boss, Branch Rickey.

Rickey rebuilt the Dodgers quickly, but when they won the 1947 flag Durocher was not on board. After Leo had taken the club to spring training, baseball commissioner Happy Chandler suspended him for a full year. His edict was issued just a few days before the 1947 season opener. Interim pilot Clyde Sukeforth thus became Jackie Robinson's first major league manager, for two games, before Rickey's longtime aide from St. Louis days, Burt Shotton, settled in to run the team during Durocher's suspension.

Leo's off-field activities had concerned his employers and others for many years. It was no secret that he fancied himself a dandy of a ladies' man. He was usually accompanied by a trunkful of suits and silk shirts on his teams' road trips. Durocher was a big spender and lavish tipper but seldom had much of a bank account. He was easily persuaded—and probably persuaded others as well—to engage in high-stakes games of chance involving cards, cubes, and horses. That was his undoing in 1947. Leo charged that MacPhail, by then with the Yankees, falsely accused him of providing exhibition-game box seats to a quartet of underworld figures. (Later investigations seemed to suggest that the foursome might actually have been MacPhail's guests.) The commissioner's office was already tracking Leo's alleged association with professional gamblers and Hollywood high rollers, including actor George Raft, in whose home Leo lived during the off-season. The commissioner's official sanction against Leo centered on "activities not in the best interest of baseball."

When the suspension was lifted, Leo returned to the Dodgers to displace Shotton in 1948. But with Brooklyn under .500 and in fifth place near the All-Star break, a bombshell burst in New York. Mel Ott, the popular but ineffective manager of the Giants, was fired. Horace Stoneham, the Giants' owner, asked Rickey if Shotton was available to replace Ott. Rickey said, "Yes, but how about my giving you a choice—Shotton or Leo?" Stoneham, as Rickey expected he would, chose Durocher. There was instant chaos among fans of both teams. No more heated rivalry existed in all of sports than that between the Dodgers and Giants. For New York fans, their acerbic, churlish, mortal enemy—Durocher—was in their camp now. But a mere three years later he was their hallowed hero when New York overcame a massive deficit to force a 1951 three-game play-off, won by the Giants over Brooklyn on Bobby Thomson's dramatic ninth-inning home run. The Polo Grounders lost the World Series to the neighboring Yankees in Joe DiMaggio's final official appearances before retirement, but 36 months later Durocher would guide the Giants, against Cleveland, to their first World Championship since 1933. It was to be their last Series title in New York and the franchise's most recent—even after four decades in San Francisco.

When his 1954 World Champs faded to a mediocre third the following season, Leo resigned. Out of baseball for the first time in 30 years (except for the 1947 suspension), Durocher continued to be attracted to the bright lights and attractive to many of the people who lit them. For a time he was a special-events announcer with NBC and one season hosted its weekly bowling telecasts. In the early 1960s he was enticed back to baseball by his old team. The Dodgers hired him as a coach under Walt Alston, whose character was as unflamboyant as Leo's was animated, and the two endured an arms-length relationship for about three years.

In 1966 Leo would surface in Chicago, where he was the Cubs' pilot until late in 1972. They challenged for the East Division title at least twice, including 1969 when their nine-game lead disappeared after August. A few days after his eventual Chicago dismissal Leo was hired to manage Houston, his final stop, where he stayed through 1973. He was then 68, the fifth eldest major league manager this century. It was rumored that Walter O'Malley discussed Leo's return as Dodgers manager shortly after the Houston assignment, but a mutual agreement never materialized.

Durocher was proud of and boastful about his baseball accomplishments. But he also was forthright in admitting his personal foibles. Disputes with some of his employers aside, he much preferred badgering and antagonizing his opponents on the baseball field. Few, if any, managers were as vitriolic in abusing and castigating opposing teams and umpires. Hall of Fame outfielder Monte Irvin, a key member of the 1951 and 1954 champion Giants, provides this insight into Leo's intensity: "One night Ewell Blackwell, Cincinnati's sidewinding, hard-throwing right-hander, struck out our side early in the game. Leo was hollering at him all along. Somebody on our bench said to go easy on Blackwell. Durocher said, 'I know what I'm doing.' He called Blackwell every name in the book—limp-arm s.o.b., everything.

"Leo was hoping he'd overthrow, groove one trying for another strikeout. I came up with the bases loaded and hit one out, a grand slam. Boy, did Blackwell cuss me out. Back in the dugout Leo grinned, 'See, I told you.' It helped win the game for us, but Leo didn't do me any favors. Next time up, with a count of three-and-oh, Ewell drilled me in the left side. As I stumbled down to first Leo is yelling, 'Don't rub; don't rub.' I knew not to rub, but I also knew I hurt. They sprayed some pain killer on me to deaden the soreness. With play back in, Leo's in the dugout still riding Blackwell by shouting at me to 'show him up. Steal it.' I took one step, fell flat on my face, and passed out. I had three broken ribs and didn't play again for a few weeks!

"I'll sum up Durocher this way. He was an excellent teacher. By the time I played for him, he had seen a lot. He might want you to change your stance or your grip. He'd nicely say, 'Give it a try this way.' He would gamble for the extra base or call pitchouts, and they usually worked. Leo was always thinking four or five batters ahead—sometimes a couple innings ahead. I found him to be way ahead of most opposing managers, and he was a great student of the rule book. As in the Blackwell example, he knew how to get the best of opponents. Umpires, too. And Leo had great intuition. In 1951 and 1954 he seemed to move fielders into just the right position at every critical time in a game, and to remove pitchers at just the right time and replace them with the right reliever for that situation. That was Leo Durocher. And those were magical years."

Clark Griffith. Managed 20 years (White Stockings 1901–2; Highlanders/Yankees 1903–8; Reds 1909–11; Nationals/Senators 1912–20); one pennant (1901 White Stockings before World Series was instituted); first managing job at age 31; native of Clear Creek, Missouri; died at age 85; was retired 26 years from managing upon Hall of Fame induction, but still active as president of Senators. (Although Griffith is officially placed in the Hall's Meritorious Service to Baseball section, he belongs among these notable managers in recognition of his contributions to baseball for more than 60 years, many of them as a successful manager. Until his death in 1955, Griffith was still front-office boss of the Washington Senators.)

When the American League gained major status in 1901, Griffith was persuaded to manage the Chicago entry, then known as the White Stockings. He simply moved across town from Chicago's National League club, where he had averaged more than 21 wins in the previous seven seasons as one of the league's top-shelf right-handers. Griffith's new club immediately won the American League's first major league pennant. (The AL had been formed in the 1890s as the Western League, a crack high minor league. In preparing for major ranking, the league, still operating as a minor circuit, changed its name to American League for the 1900 season.) Chicago's top pitcher in that 1901 pennant-winning season? Player-manager Clark Griffith with a 24–7 record, a 2.67 earned run average, and a league-leading five shutouts. And in 89 at bats he chipped in with a .303 average. Among his 27 hits were two home runs.

The Baltimore franchise was transferred to New York for the 1903 season, and Griffith was enticed to leave Chicago and become its manager. The club flirted with a .500 record during most of Clark's five-plus seasons there, with highpoints of second-place finishes in 1904 and 1906. It was in the 1904 campaign that one of Griffith's hurlers, Jack Chesbro, won an astonishing 41 games, a single-season pitching record still standing and likely to be unmatched.

Philosophical differences with new management prompted Griffith to re-sign his New York job in 1908, and the next season he was in Cincinnati trying to build up a lackluster Reds franchise. After three seasons there his club did, indeed, show a little improvement, but it could never finish better than three or four games over or under breaking even. As the 1914 season approached, Clark Griffith headed off to the nation's capital where he would be manager through 1920 and Washington's chief baseball officer until his death more than three decades after that. By 1920 the ball club was beginning to show a profit, and after appointing Bucky Harris as a "boy manager," Griffith saw Washington post its first championships (1924 and 1925).

He was always considered loyal to his uniformed personnel, and when Hall of Fame pitcher Walter Johnson finally retired in 1927, Griffith arranged a minor league managing job as training for the Senators' post awarded to him in 1929. Johnson's Senators played well, ranking right below the powerful Athletics and Yankees of the early 1930s. However, Griffith felt a change would be good for his team after 1932, so he elevated his shortstop—also his son-in-law—Joe Cronin, to the managership. Cronin brought the team home first in his initial season. Eventually Cronin also managed a Red Sox title winner, and he later became president of the American League. The Great Depression and low attendance sapped Griffith's financial resources by the mid-1930s, yet he was able to stay borderline solvent, although pennantless, for the remainder of his ownership.

An old derogatory saying made fun of Griffith's Senators: "Washington: first in war, first in peace, last in the American League." Cute, but largely untrue. During the 42 years that Clark Griffith was in the command post, Washington finished last only three times. From the time he took over the dugout in 1914 through the 1933 championship season, Washington posted 14 first-division finishes. Clark Griffith's managing, then his front-office administering, were major factors in this overall success.

The "Old Fox" could legitimately have been placed in any one of three Hall of Fame categories—player, manager, or in the meritorious service's executive branch, where he is forever enshrined.

Bucky Harris. Managed 29 years (Senators 1924–28; Tigers 1929–33; Red Sox 1934; Senators 1935–42; Phillies 1943; Yankees 1947–48; Senators 1950–54; Tigers 1955–56); three pennants, two World Championships; first managing job at age 27; native of Port Jervis, New York; died at age 81; was retired 19 years upon Hall of Fame induction.

Stanley "Bucky" Harris was hired to manage major league teams on eight different occasions. Only one man this century—Billy Martin with nine such signings—was recycled more frequently. Both of them seemed to have a "home team." Martin's was the Yankees, and Harris's was the Washington Senators, with whom he broke in as an infielder and for whom he managed its first two pennant winners.

Ironically, this fellow who was hired time and again by a variety of owners for nearly 30 years played a major, if inadvertent, role in the permanent disbarment of one of his employers. In Harris's only venture into the National League—in 1943 following completion of his second Washington term—he was saddled with a typically dreary second-division Phillies club coming off five consecutive basement finishes. The team's new owner that year was 33-year-old William Cox, who would later hold ownership shares in the NFL's Brooklyn Dodgers of the 1940s and in professional soccer. Even though Harris advanced the Phillies to fifth place at midyear, Cox was a continual irritant with his clubhouse interference and offhand remarks to writers. The owner and manager squabbled often, and in July Cox, leaking his intentions to the press, fired Harris. The entire 24-man roster immediately came to Bucky's defense and threatened to strike if he were not reinstated. When Cox apologized to Harris for mishandling the affair, Harris convinced his players to take the field. In rehashing the incident with reporters a day or two later, according to *The New Phillies Encyclopedia*, Harris casually mentioned Cox's taste for betting on Phillies games. The remark prompted an investigation by the National League and the Commissioner's Office and resulted in Cox's banishment from baseball. Cox lasted one year in the major leagues; Harris managed 29.

With Harris leading the Phillies for awhile, two Hall of Fame managers—he and Mack of the A's—were operating in the same city at the same time. Several similar situations have occurred in New York (including Brooklyn)—

McGraw-Griffith/Huggins/McCarthy; McCarthy-Robinson/Stengel/Durocher; Robinson-Huggins/McCarthy/McGraw; Durocher-McCarthy/Harris/Stengel/ Alston; Alston-Stengel.

Bucky was called the "boy manager" as a rookie pilot in 1924 and was dubbed the nation's capital's miracle man when Washington defeated the New York Giants of legendary John McGraw in the World Series. It was the last of McGraw's 10 National League championships, but the first of Harris's two straight American League titles. In that Series, Bucky got more credit for his famous base hit than for his managing. With his club trailing 3–1 in the eighth inning of Game 7, he delivered a bad-hop, two-run single. Washington won it in the 12th when Earl McNeely's grounder hit a pebble, bounced over the third baseman's head, and provided relief pitcher Walter Johnson with the victory. Under Harris, Washington took American League honors again in 1925, but this time, after opening a big lead, the Nats (as they were generally known then) earned dubious distinction as the first club to lose a World Series after leading three games to one. Pittsburgh, directed by another Hall of Fame skipper, Bill McKechnie, pulled off the comeback.

Harris is one of the few Hall of Fame pilots to have more games in the loss column than on the victory side of his ledger. The margin is slim, standing at 2,157–2,218—a .493 percentage. His most successful streak came with his first of three managing terms at Washington (1924–28). The Senators ranked in the first division all five of those seasons. Unfortunately for Harris and his career statistics, only once more was he able to put together back-to-back first-division finishes. Those were his two seasons in New York when the Yankees won a seven-game 1947 World Series from Brooklyn—Remember the Al Gionfriddo catch of DiMaggio's long drive, and Cookie Lavagetto's two-out ninth-inning double to beat New York and break up Bill Bevens's no-hitter at the same time?—and then the next year when Cleveland and Boston tied for the American League title, forcing a one-game play-off as the Yankees stayed in the race until the final weekend.

Harris is not known to have received widespread credit either as a particularly inspirational leader or as an instructor of special ability. His in-game strategy was considered to be textbook, rather than innovative. Many of the men who played for him, however, are reported to have genuinely liked the manager and his easygoing manner. And Bucky was careful to treat his men with respect, to avoid confrontations except in private one-on-one meetings, and to prefer a businesslike and calm clubhouse. He was general manager of the Red Sox for a few seasons after retiring from the dugout in 1956, but he will be remembered best for his remarkable longevity as a field manager. Only Connie

Mack and John McGraw ran major league teams longer than Harris's 29 seasons. The fact that Bucky Harris was invited to manage on nine different occasions, including three stints with Washington and two at Detroit, testifies to the confidence that his peers placed in him.

Miller Huggins. Managed 17 years (Cardinals 1913–17; Yankees 1918–29); six pennants, three World Championships; first managing job at age 34; native of Cincinnati, Ohio; died at age 50; deceased 35 years before Hall of Fame induction..

The New York Yankee dynasty began under the managership of Miller Huggins, the shortest (5 feet, 5 inches) manager in the Hall of Fame, but a behemoth in terms of historical significance. New York had not won a title in the franchise's first 20 years under 10 different pilots. The best the club had done was three second-place finishes sandwiched between stretches of mediocrity. But in 1915 the team was purchased by Jacob Ruppert and Tillinghast L'Hommedieu Houston, who immediately earmarked funds to purchase top talent and to employ a winning manager. Some of the players they soon corraled were Waite Hoyt, Carl Mays, Wally Schang, Frank "Home Run" Baker, and a budding young Red Sox slugger named Babe Ruth. To mold their group of "new look" Yankees, they engaged the managing services of Miller Huggins.

The well-educated and reserved midwesterner had been a National League infielder with exceptional defensive abilities before landing his first managing assignment, a dual player-manager position, with the St. Louis Cardinals in 1913. For years St. Louis regularly finished near the bottom of the league, but in Huggins's second season in charge they advanced dramatically from eighth to third place. Two losing seasons followed, but Huggins had his team third again in 1917. However, new ownership took command at that time, and general manager Branch Rickey decided he'd like to revise control of the dugout. Huggins resigned after that 1917 campaign, and when the Yankees learned he was available, the two parties promptly agreed to contract terms. Huggins took over in 1918 and, with the exception of one season,1925, never finished out of the first division in his 12 years at New York. Were it not for his fatal blood poisoning in 1929, when Huggins was only 50, it is probable that he would have added significantly to his remarkable records.

Beginning in 1921, as Ruth was entering the prime of his offensive career, Huggins's club won six pennants in eight years. Until then the Yankees were the poor relatives of the well-entrenched New York Giants, at whose ballpark, the Polo Grounds, the Yankees had been tenants since 1913. But as Ruth's heroics increased and the team's standings position accelerated, the Yankees were soon outdrawing their landlords, even though the Giants won the all–New York World Series of 1921 and 1922.

Having been issued an eviction notice a year or two year earlier, the Yankees had begun construction on Yankee Stadium, which opened in 1923. Again the two New York clubs met in a third straight Series, but now it was the Yankees' turn to capture the October laurels, and they won the first of their 23 World Championships. Bucky Harris's Washington Senators outdistanced the rest of the American League pack in 1924 and 1925, but here came Huggins's club again with three successive crowns from 1926 through 1928. Huggins's old club, the Cardinals, won the 1926 Series under manager Rogers Hornsby, who coincidentally had supplanted Huggins at third base in St. Louis nine years earlier.

Two unprecedented World Series four-game sweeps by New York followed— over Pittsburgh in 1927 and St. Louis in 1928—and Huggins appeared primed to remain in the spotlight for at least another decade. Ruth was still at the top of his game, the club had good pitching and solid defense to complement its powerhouse hitting attack, and it seemed to attract one or two promising young players each year in the late 1920s. Among them were Lou Gehrig, Bill Dickey, Earle Combs, and Tony Lazzeri. These men contributed to numerous pennants over the next decade and more. Sadly, Huggins was not around to enjoy them.

Although small in stature, Huggins was a forceful leader. At first Ruth, perhaps due to his size advantage and his daily headlines, ridiculed his new manager and was reluctant to take orders. A conflict came to a head during a western road trip in 1925. Ruth, apparently after a long night of carousing, arrived late and in ragged shape for the next afternoon's game in St. Louis. He had been warned frequently by Huggins about breaking team rules, and this time Huggins took drastic action. After privately consulting by phone with Ruppert and general manager Ed Barrow back in New York, where the two officials assured their manager of their full backing, Huggins suspended Ruth and fined him $5,000 (a figure greater than a season's salary for some of his teammates). The slugger protested vehemently, and when Huggins would not back down Ruth grabbed the next train for New York. Upon his arrival he immediately called on Ruppert and Barrow to overrule Huggins. When they firmly supported the manager, Ruth somewhat meekly returned to the club, apologized to Huggins, and never again gave him any significant problems.

When Huggins died, Babe Ruth wept unashamedly.

Tommy Larsorda. Managed in 21 consecutive seasons, fourth-longest string with one team this century (Dodgers 1976–96); signed Los Angeles managing contract at age 49; four pennants; two World Championships (1981,

1988); native of Norristown, Pennsylvania; was retired for one year upon Hall of Fame induction.

Precisely one week after celebrating his 49th birthday in late September of 1976, Tom Lasorda was appointed as the second manager of the Los Angeles Dodgers. Two decades later, nearly one year to the day after announcing his 1996 retirement as Dodgers manager, he was installed in the managers' wing of the National Baseball Hall of Fame.

As famous for his vocal support for Italian Americans as for his pride in having "Dodger *Blue* blood" coursing through his veins, Lasorda is the first manager of Italian descent to earn a Cooperstown plaque. He's also the only former pitcher among Hall of Fame managers, and he joins his Dodger predecessor Walt Alston and the Orioles' Earl Weaver as the Hall's only three men to have managed just one major league team during their lengthy careers.

If a manager has hopes for Hall of Fame enshrinement, he might consider piloting the Dodgers, should such a rare opportunity arise. Of the 14 men in the managers' wing, six—Alston, Lasorda, Leo Durocher, Ned Hanlon, Casey Stengel, and Wilbert Robinson—directed the Brooklyn or Los Angeles Dodgers or both. The only other franchise with similar history is the Yankees'. Technically, they also have six Cooperstown managers, but two of them, John McGraw and Robinson, skippered the old Baltimore Orioles before they transferred to New York in 1903. Since then, Yankee pilots Miller Huggins, Joe McCarthy, Bucky Harris, and Stengel have been honored in Cooperstown.

Lasorda lists other firsts among his Hall credentials. He is the only man there whose career began as late as the 1970s, and the only one who managed into the 1990s. And, by six years, he was older (49) than any other Hall of Fame manager when first assigned a managership. Prior to Tom's admittance, Stengel had been the eldest starter, at age 43. Perhaps Lasorda's most important first is this: Among the 14 Hall skippers only Lasorda and Bucky Harris managed pennant winners in their first year on the job. Not only that: Lasorda and Harris both won again the very next season. (Technically, that's stretching a point, for Tom succeeded Alston for the final four games of the 1976 season. Weaver was a pennant winner in 1969, his first *full* year, after he came on board for the entire second half of the previous season.)

For his 19 full seasons, and parts of two others, Lasorda managed Los Angeles to two World Series championships, four National League titles, and seven division (National League West) crowns. The 61 postseason games he managed rank third—all time—behind Bobby Cox and Stengel. Tommy's 31 postseason victories merit an all-time fourth behind Cox's 43 games won, Stengel's 37, and Sparky Anderson's 34. Successful early-century managers, of course, such as

Mack, McGraw, Frank Chance, and Fred Clarke, never had the additional October opportunities that today's expanding play-off rounds offer.

As an active player, young Lasorda was a southpaw hurler. More than 40 years have elapsed since he last toed a big-league rubber, but Tom still admits to disappointment and frustration that his major league career was less than successful. An 0-and-4 lifetime record is, indeed, lackluster. He appeared in eight games for Brooklyn in 1954 and 1955, starting one, neither winning nor losing any, and totaling 13 innings pitched. A year later, with Lou Boudreau's Kansas City A's, Tom was 0-and-4. His big-league pitching career then ended.

But the persistent, optimistic Lasorda wouldn't give in. The Dodgers gave him another contract to pitch and coach for Montreal, their top farm club, where he had already spent the better parts of four seasons. Now, however, it was 1957, and even Tommy recognized that his dreams to be a big-league regular had pretty well evaporated. He discovered, though, that he enjoyed working with young pitchers. And between his tutorial duties he continued to post winning seasons as a spot starter. Lasorda's 107 mound victories constitute a still-standing International League record of most career pitching wins.

When Montreal's 1960 season ended, Lasorda was invited to remain with the Dodger family—as a scout. Scouting, then winter league managing in Central America, and eventually rookie league managing in the Los Angeles system convinced Tom that he was, clearly, a career baseball man. He enjoyed managing, and he decided he would concentrate on gaining experience. When the Dodgers promoted him to guide their Triple-A club in Spokane (subsequently transferred to Albuquerque), he was ready for the challenge. Four years later he was back in a major league uniform again. As the Dodgers' newly appointed third-base coach, Lasorda would be working under his former Montreal and one-time Brooklyn manager, Walt Alston.

It was during his four-year coaching tenure in Los Angeles that Lasorda first gained national attention. Continually peppery and animated, seemingly all over the field during pregame drills, Lasorda was a lively chatterbox at his third-base coaching post. One Saturday, during a telecast of the Game of the Week, NBC attached a microphone to him. His remarks, pretty much in the form of nonstop commentary, combined humor with some sage inside baseball and even a prediction or two that destiny (or perhaps a key clutch hit by Ron Cey) fulfilled.

About half of the Los Angeles players, among them most of the regulars, had apprenticed under Lasorda's minor league managership. Included in this group were Steve Garvey, Davey Lopes, Bill Russell, and Cey, a quartet who formed a Dodger infield that played together for more years than any other in baseball history, nine consecutive seasons. Because of a close relationship that developed between Lasorda and these players, and because of his increasing popularity, it was widely expected that he would be the leading candidate for the Dodgers' managing post whenever Alston completed his distinguished tenure. And so he was. The two of them—Alston (23 seasons) and Lasorda (21)—rank third and fourth, behind Connie Mack and John McGraw, in number of consecutive years managing the same team.

Tom Lasorda exhibited world-class gregariousness during his managing career—and beyond. He has frequently been saluted, aptly, as baseball's goodwill ambassador. He's also recognized for his showmanship—on the field; in the clubhouse, where he entertained family, politicians, Hollywood luminaries, and casts of thousands of what he refers to as "my very good friends"; and in broadcast and print advertisements for a variety of products and services. Clownish on occasion, as was Stengel, Lasorda emulated Stengel in this important characteristic, too: Both were deadly serious about the business of baseball managing, and about their love for the game.

Since his 1996 retirement from the Dodgers' dugout, following a health scare relating to heart problems, Tom has continued a heavy travel schedule of speaking engagements for school, church, civic, and business organizations. At every one of them (and, in fact, at any impromptu gathering of a bellman or two, or a couple of passersby at a newsstand), he espouses the values and the pure joy of baseball. And these audiences, no matter the size, hear about his relatively poor but warm family background back in his beloved Norristown, Pennsylvania, along with hilarious but mostly whimsical stories of his baseball travels and the interesting people crossing his path along the way.

If one managerial quality of Lasorda's stands out, it might be this: With a vast number of his players he was able to maintain both a fatherly or brotherly relationship while commanding their allegiance to his stature as the team's boss. Of course, turning out annual contenders helps foster that kind of fellowship. Lasorda seemed to know just when to critique, cajole, or encourage his charges. Take the oft-recited story of Joe Ferguson's switching positions. Ferguson, who would be a mainstay on several of Lasorda's division championship clubs, came to camp as a young outfielder. Lasorda felt he could be converted to catcher, and told him so. Ferguson loudly disagreed. So Tom reminded Joe that All-Star catchers Gabby Hartnett, Mickey Cochrane, and Ernie Lombardi began their careers as outfielders. Ferguson consented to give the move a try (and eventually became a successful catcher). Later, someone said to Lasorda, "Tom, why did you tell him Hartnett and those other guys started as outfielders? They never played there. Catcher was their only position." Replied Lasorda, "I know that. And so do you. But Joe doesn't!"

When I asked a prominent baseball owner about changes he's seen over the years, he made this comment: "We don't hire managers for their box office appeal any more like they used to, especially back in the days of the player-managers. I guess the last big box office draw, as manager, was Casey Stengel, particularly with the Mets. No, that's not quite true. There's been another one in the meantime. We never hear press releases touting a big game with such-and-such team, managed by so-and-so anymore—with one exception. And that's 'Order your tickets now, fans, because Tommy Lasorda and the Los Angeles Dodgers are coming to town this weekend!'"

A tribute, indeed, to a man and his profession.

Connie Mack. Managed three years in National League in 1890s, then 50 years (1901–50) with Philadelphia Athletics; one of American League's founders; nine pennants, five World Championships; first managing job at age 31 in 1894, Pittsburgh NL; native of East Brookfield, Massachusetts; died at age 93; member of Hall of Fame's first class of inductees, 1937, when still active as manager.

No one will ever again manage a team as long as Connie Mack did. You can bet the estate on it. For one thing, owners invariably terminate managers sooner or later. And, unlike the circumstances in Mack's day, baseball owners are no longer permitted to be field managers. Mack was principal owner of his team, the Philadelphia Athletics, for most of the time he was associated with it. It just so happened that he declined to fire himself.

Terms such as "venerable," "Tall Tactician," "beloved," "Grand Old Man," "respected," "Mr. Baseball," "revered," and of course "durable" have been associated with his name seemingly forever. Admittedly, forever is a bit of a stretch, but we're talking here about someone who was born in Massachusetts during the Civil War and was still with us 93 years later, after the Korean Conflict had been concluded.

His became one of the most famous names in America. Ironically, it's not the name that Mr. Baseball was born with. He entered the world as Cornelius Alexander McGillicuddy on December 22, 1862, at East Brookfield, Massachusetts. He left his hometown and his job in a shoe factory there at age 21 to pursue professional ball, and he unofficially changed his name to Connie Mack because it identified him far better in a boxscore than Mc'G'l'c'dy would. As it would develop, "Mack" fit nicely into many thousands of newspaper headlines in the decades ahead.

Connie was a catcher throughout his active career, which began at Meriden in the Connecticut State League. He proceeded to Hartford and then advanced to the New York Metropolitans (not the same club that occupies Shea Stadium now). After less than two full seasons of pro baseball, Mack joined the 1886 Washington Senators, then of the National League, and caught there for three years. Mack has often been described as a dignified solid citizen, and little evidence suggests otherwise. So It might surprise you to learn that he was part of an early baseball revolt. In the late 1880s several players banded together to form the Players League, sometimes called the Brotherhood League. They objected to low pay and severe restrictions that prevented them from moving to other teams (sound familiar a century later?). Mack signed on with Buffalo. But the league disbanded after its one season, and he returned to the National League, this time with Pittsburgh. There he played for Ned Hanlon, whose managing career was young but whose philosophy of tight defense behind strong pitching Mack adopted when he became the Pittsburgh manager soon after Hanlon had departed for Baltimore and great fame with the Old Orioles.

Hanlon was the first Hall of Fame pilot that managed or played against manager Mack. But surely not the last. Of Mack's 13 manager counterparts in Cooperstown, nine were his big-league opponents at one time or another, either as players or managers. The exceptions are Alston, Lasorda, McKechnie, and Weaver.

Connie's Pittsburgh managing record offered no hint of his later successes. His club ranked no higher than sixth during his three years there. However, Western League president Ban Johnson and his chum Charlie Comiskey foresaw Mack's leadership talents and invited him to manage Milwaukee in their strong minor circuit which would evolve into the American League. By 1901 the league was ready to claim major status, and Mack was asked to establish one of its entries—Philadelphia. He stayed there for awhile! His 1902 Athletics won the AL championship but went no further because World Series competition would not start until after the next season. Boston, Chicago, and Philadelphia, then Detroit for one three-year stretch, dominated the new league by winning its first 19 pennants. (The mighty Yankees didn't claim their first title until the league's 21st season.) Mack's A's not only captured six of those flags; they also won three World Series—1910 against Frank Chance's Cubs, and in 1911 and 1913 opposite the dynastic New York Giants. Ironically, one of Philadelphia's Series losses came against what was perhaps history's all-time Series underdogs, George Stallings's Miracle Boston Braves of 1914. It was a four-game sweep, to boot. The loss was, of course, disappointing to Mack. But more disheartening was his perception of the situation.

Reminiscing many years later, Mack wrote, "Baseball fans throughout the country did not realize what was behind our collapse; neither did many of the sportswriters. They said the 'wonder team' was taking it lying down. I knew that the 'wonder team' was engaged in a civil war, fighting one another." The crisis at hand was a situation akin to 1890's, when Mack jumped to Buffalo. The Federal League, an upstart group of eight teams, had raided the American and National leagues for top players. Its first season was 1914, and, although the Athletics were not victims of significant defections, Mack knew that the promise of bigger paychecks from the Federals was at best distracting his players and at worst a demoralizing element in the clubhouse. "If the players were going to cash in [as many A's planned to do in 1915] and leave me to hold the bag, there was nothing for me to do but to cash in too." So Mack broke up the powerful Athletics by selling most of his headliners to other major league clubs.

It took nearly a decade to rebuild the A's. They ranked second in 1925, third the next year, then second again for two seasons before running away with three straight championships (1929, 1930, 1931), featuring more than 100 victories each year. Many baseball historians cite Mack's Athletics of those years as the greatest team in league history. Mickey Cochrane, Jimmie Foxx, Al Simmons, and Lefty Grove eventually went to Cooperstown. The Yankees, coming off their outstanding 1927 season, remained a powerful aggregation, but the A's, for those three years, left them in the dust. Just two years later Connie decided to break up a great team again. There was no player revolt this time, but economics provided the impetus. The Great Depression was nearing its height, and baseball turnstiles most everywhere slowed down. Attendance slipped badly, especially in Philadelphia where, in addition to fans' reduced income, the populace had become somewhat bored with the A's and the ease with which they'd been winning. It was a tough combination to combat, so Mack sold off his stars again. He would return to the first division only once more (fourth place, 1948) before his retirement in 1950.

During Mack's final dozen or so years as manager his energy level waned—after all, he was nearly 75 years old in 1937—and his sharp mind and quick decision-making capacities began to ebb a bit.

His coaches got more involved with running the club. In 1937 and again in 1939 Earle Mack, one of Connie's sons and then a coach, served as interim manager for nearly a half season while his father recuperated from serious stomach ailments. But the elder Mack returned each time and, in fact, appeared greatly recharged heading into the 1940s. One brief incident, of consequence mainly for what it revealed about Mack's image, occurred on Sunday, August 27, 1948—a brutally steamy day in Philadelphia. For as long as anyone could remember, Connie was fastidious in his attire, and unfailingly he wore a stiff-collared shirt, always a necktie, and usually his suit coat. Early in the second game of a doubleheader that day, he broke tradition. Connie Mack removed his collar and tie! (By the way, the A's won both games to move within three of the league lead.)

Leonard Koppett has carefully analyzed baseball's top managers and focused on their special attributes. He wrote at length about Mack in *The Man in the Dugout.* "Mack concentrated on defense, which is fundamentally pitching. He was more conscientious about giving pitchers proper rest than most of the managers of his time. He showed self-control, had a feel for people, and was concerned about the feelings of others. Today every team has reams of diagrams and computer printouts." Not so in Mack's day. "He made detailed notes on where particular hitters hit the ball off particular pitchers (and pitches), and positioned his fielders accordingly. [When instructing players] Mack knew the answer but wanted you to learn it too, and to do it on your own."

Among his player-pupils were a number of college men, rare for baseball in the first half of the century. Mack was the first manager to even consider scouting colleges for ballplayers, and he put a platoon of scouts on that assignment as long ago as the early 19-teens. That's how the likes of Mickey Cochrane, Eddie Plank, Eddie Collins, and Chief Bender were brought to Mack's attention.

Even casual fans are familiar with some of Connie's bottom-line statistics—50 years managing the A's; nine pennants, five World Series crowns: eight Hall of Famers—himself and Cochrane, Foxx, Simmons, Collins, Ty Cobb, Grove, Tris Speaker—on his 1928 team. They know he directed far more games (7,755) than any other manager in history. And that he won more than anybody else (3,731). In an era of mostly daytime games, Mack's 75 tie games are probably a record, too. But along his brilliant path this remarkable man was charged with more losses than any other manager—3,948.

That last figure is but an inconsequential footnote to the exemplary life and legendary Hall of Fame career of the Grand Old Man of baseball.

John McGraw. Managed NL Orioles in 1899, then 32 years with Orioles AL 1901–2 and Giants 1902–32; 10 pennants, three World Championships; first managing job at age 26 (1899); native of Truxton, New York; died at age 60; was retired five years upon his posthumous Hall of Fame induction.

He was just a teenager when he left his small hometown near Elmira, New York, to play professional baseball. Twenty-five years later John J. McGraw could well have run for the office of mayor of New York City—and might have won. He was a certified toast of the town for most of the 31 years that he managed the New York Giants, the most renowned and formidable professional sports franchise of the time. Until Babe Ruth took New York—and all of base-ball—by storm, McGraw had been the game's foremost celebrity for nearly two decades. He defined baseball managing in almost textbook fashion. Myriad successors patterned their styles after his, perhaps refining this element or that, sometimes adding a tint to the mosaic here or maybe toning it down a little there. Would-be protégés studied McGraw carefully, many admitting that their analysis was a prerequisite for successful managing. Some of the more clinical among them would conclude that McGraw's concepts, precepts, and strategies led to the very core of sound baseball; but many would determine early that the man's character, personality, and temperament were not the ideal ones re-quired to earn respect and support from a 25-man baseball team day after te-dious day—even though those traits might have worked in McGraw's time.

His vitriolic outbursts at umpires, opponents, and baseball executives are legendary. But so are John McGraw's 10 pennants at New York, his unequaled four straight National League flags (1921–24), his league-record 31 consecu-tive seasons piloting the same club, and his assignment, in retirement, to man-age in the first All-Star Game. Even now, going on eight decades later, only one other National League manager (Sparky Anderson, Cincinnati 1975–76) has been able to accomplish two consecutive World Championships since the 1921 and 1922 achievements of John McGraw's Giants. John McGraw *was* the New York Giants. They were his: John McGraw's New York Giants.

Only a handful of teams since Mack's and McGraw's days are so closely as-sociated in print and on the tongue with their managers. Their names were vir-tually adjectives. For awhile we knew Casey Stengel's New York Yankees, maybe Jimmie Dykes's Chicago White Sox, and recently "Tom Lasorda's Los Angeles Dodgers." Earl Weaver's Orioles, perhaps. But you're hard-pressed to connect many another manager's name with a team, although Cleveland's nickname for a short spell was Naps (Lajoie) and the Brooklyn club was known as the Robins when Wilbert Robinson managed there.

The Giants were managed by a giant of a personality, but one of the short-est men in the Hall of Fame. McGraw was listed at 5 feet, 7 inches and weighed 155 pounds in his playing days. He was only 16, but even then brash and self-assured, when he left little Truxton, New York, to join the Olean club of a low minor league classification. He was at first a pitcher but was soon shifted to in-field posts for Olean and a succession of three other minor teams before catch-ing the eye of the 1891 Baltimore Orioles, then a member of the American As-sociation operating with major status. When he was 18, his talent was still raw. He had no formal experience with high-level professional baseball, although he barnstormed in Florida and Cuba during two winters with teams containing some major leaguers. By 1892 the American Association was out of business, but the Baltimore club was absorbed into the then 12-team National League. Its new manager was future Hall of Famer Ned Hanlon. He knew McGraw was not ready to play regularly in the National League. But Hanlon was impressed with the young man's spunk and decided to keep him on the roster. McGraw's managing would one day emulate Hanlon's, as Mack's did—special importance on fundamentals, tight defense supporting strong pitching, smart baserunning, and, in those days of low-scoring games, the moving of runners one base at a time. The hit-and-run and bunt were vital offensive weapons. (Although both Hanlon and McGraw generally eschewed sacrifice bunts: why give up an out on purpose?).

McGraw was not the only scrappy agitator on Hanlon's club. Heinie Reitz, Wee Willie Keeler, and Joe Kelley were known to aggravate opponents, umpires, and their own teammates on occasion, and were key instruments in the Old Orioles' reputation for feistiness and chicanery (with only one umpire in those early days it wasn't too difficult to cheat by shortening the distance between first and third or grabbing onto a runner's belt to impede his journey home). Their reputation for fundamental soundness and alertness was widely known too, as Baltimore won three league titles. Years later oldtimers would retell tales of the "wonderful Old Orioles." After three straight Baltimore pennants and a pair of seconds Hanlon decided to take the manager's post offered by Brooklyn. McGraw, only 26, succeeded him at Baltimore. A year later the National League reduced its rolls to eight teams, and Baltimore, whose attendance had withered despite its on-field success, was evicted. Its player-manager, McGraw, had just come off a season when he hit .391 in 117 games. Cincinnati sought his services as player-manager, but he hesitated to leave Baltimore. Two or three years earlier he and teammate Wilbert Robinson, the Orioles' catcher, entered into partnership as owners of a Baltimore restaurant, the Diamond Cafe. It was popular among the city's sports crowd and was turning a nice profit. Ultimately McGraw signed up with the Cardinals for the 1900 season, but with a contract provision that did not bind him to St. Louis beyond that one year. The following winter then, McGraw, who was to become the most celebrated manager in National League history, helped formulate the American circuit's first major league season.

Planning to reestablish baseball in Baltimore, league president Ban Johnson and cohort Charlie Comiskey persuaded McGraw to join with them, Clark Griffith, and Connie Mack (among others) to get the American League off on a solid footing. That first season, 1901, saw the new Orioles finish fifth, three games over .500. McGraw would not be there, though, when the second season finished.

Continually at odds with Ban Johnson, and with a second-division team on his hands, McGraw learned of an opportunity to manage in New York. He bolted the Orioles at midseason, signed with the Giants a few days later, and for years would characterize the American League as inferior, even though frequently proven incorrect on that point. McGraw's own Giants would gain more of a national following than any other club—National or American—for 20 years.

They were in last place when he took over with 65 games to go in the 1902 season. And they finished eighth. Thirty years later, ill and much older looking than his 59 years, he resigned with his team where it was when he had arrived. Eighth. In the intervening three decades the Giants had finished below the first division just twice. Of all the descriptions of McGraw, both the positive and the many negative, "autocratic" is perhaps the most appropos. John McGraw was the Boss. No question about it.

In order to field a successful baseball team, he had concluded many years earlier, the manager *must* be clearly in command. McGraw, an ardent student of the game who forever planned ways to get any edge on an opponent, was convinced that his strategies and personnel decisions were correct. His players, he was certain, must have unquestioned faith in their manager at all times. And since he, McGraw, was the Giants' manager and in his own mind always right, then his players' adherence to his commands would result in success.

He, of course, would be the first to admit that the players must have the talent to carry out orders. He was a harsh but good judge of talent. Over the years he signed many boys still in their teens and men just past 20. If not farmed out for seasoning, they played sporadically but mostly sat on the bench for a year or so to learn the game from McGraw and observe the veteran players. McGraw might have been remembering his own beginnings when, at a young age, he played irregularly for Hanlon before earning his stripes as a Baltimore regular. Mel Ott, then 16, Fred Lindstrom, and Frankie Frisch are examples of the many young players who eventually achieved brilliance with McGraw's Giants.

After McGraw had been with New York just two years, his team won the 1904 pennant. At the insistence of owner John Brush, the Giants declined to meet Boston in what would have been the second World Series. Some criticized McGraw for the decision, but it was Brush's call (although McGraw might have been relieved not to chance a loss to the "junior circuit").

In 1905, though, Hall of Fame pitcher Christy Mathewson led the Giants to a World Series triumph over Connie Mack's Athletics. Then, after some near misses, New York went to the Series again in 1911, 1912, 1913, and 1917, experienced a brief lapse, then won four consecutive pennants beginning in 1921. Babe Ruth was beginning to take some New York headlines away from

McGraw and the Giants by then. His long-ball magic changed the style of play. McGraw preferred the old "inside baseball," but he knew he must adapt to the new strategy. When he spotted the potential of the teenaged Ott in the mid-20s he knew he had his own New York power hitter. Ott's 511 career homers were a National League record for many years.

It was often suggested that McGraw had a Napoleonic complex. He was small in stature, as was the similarly autocratic French leader. He demanded perfection and complete attention, although he believed in providing his players with first-class travel, commodious locker rooms, and salaries above baseball's norm of the day. After all, they were *the* New York Giants. McGraw frequently suffered from various physical ailments that might well have fostered his irritability. Most of them were annoyances, although he experienced almost annual sinusitis attacks that led to absences from his team. And he died at 60 of prostate cancer. The fact that his father was widowed early and paid little attention to young John has been cited as another factor that contributed to McGraw's brash nature.

Conversely, or perhaps subconsciously reflecting on his youth, he was a generous man who often gave cash or arranged jobs for old friends, even friends' friends, who had fallen on hard times. Yet, despite his notoriety and high standing among New York's elite, McGraw was not a wealthy man. He'd become a holder of substantial stock in the Giants before the 1920s but had often invested poorly in business ventures as well as in the thoroughbred races he attended regularly.

His baseball acumen was superb, his managing brilliant. The trades he initiated invariably benefited the Giants. Several of his players later managed successfully for many years—his handpicked successor, Bill Terry, Frisch, Billy Southworth, and Casey Stengel among them. And, as writer Leonard Koppett has reported, those men begot others, and they still others, whose managing styles carried the McGraw influence all through the century.

Except for the initial All-Star Game when he was invited to manage the 1933 National League squad, McGraw's latter days in baseball were mainly unpleasant, even bitter. After 1922 his Giants never achieved World Champ status; from 1924 they did not win another pennant for him, although they contended often. Twice illness forced him to step aside for interim managers—first his Old Orioles chum Hughie Jennings and later Rogers Hornsby. Despite the disappointments of his final decade, John McGraw is remembered for his achievements, and for the legacy he bequeathed to managers of the future. When the Hall of Fame opened in 1937, no one questioned John McGraw's right to be there.

Wilbert Robinson. Managed 19 years (Orioles 1902; Dodgers 1914–31); two pennants; first managing job at age 39; native of Bolton, Massachusetts; died at age 71; was retired 14 years upon his posthumous Hall of Fame induction.

The Dodgers' franchise, first in Brooklyn and then representing Los Angeles, has employed the fewest managers of any major club that's been operating throughout this century. Only 14 full-time pilots, about half the average for other teams, have been in control of Dodgers dugouts. In Los Angeles only four managers have run things during the club's 40 years there—Walt Alston, 1958–76; Tom Lasorda, late 1976–mid-1996; Bill Russell; and then Glenn Hoffman.

Wilbert Robinson, known better to baseball players of his time as Uncle Robby, was the first of the Dodgers' longtimers. Under his leadership Brooklyn appeared in its first two World Series. His 1916 club, featuring first baseman Jake Daubert, Zack Wheat, Casey Stengel, and 41-game pitchers Larry Cheney and Jake Pfeffer, lost out to Boston (and 23-win pitcher Babe Ruth) in the Series. Four years later, after nabbing its second National League flag under Robinson, Brooklyn ran up against player-manager Tris Speaker's Indians, who overmatched the Dodgers five games to two in a best-of-nine World Series (a format used from 1919 through 1921 and in 1903). That 1920 Series is still remembered for the unassisted triple play registered at old League Park by Cleveland second baseman Bill Wambsganss. It's been the only triple play, unassisted or otherwise, ever accomplished in postseason baseball.

Uncle Robby's overall managing record is not particularly impressive in terms of wins and losses. He barely surpassed .500 lifetime (1,399 wins, 1,398 losses, 21 tie games). Just one more victory apiece would have elevated Robby and one of his successors, Tom Lasorda, to another milestone. Robinson fell one win shy of 1,400. Lasorda finished his career with 1,599 Dodger victories.

Seldom blessed with an abundance of superstars, Uncle Robby's teams wound up in the first division on only a half dozen occasions. Never a cellar finisher, Brooklyn ranked fifth or sixth 12 times during his tenure.

Statistics aside, Wilbert Robinson was considered one of the most knowledgeable baseball men—and one of the game's best-liked members—during his 16 seasons as a player (mostly in the late 1800s) and throughout his managerships in the 20th century. A catcher in his playing days, Robby was highly regarded as a handler and tutor of pitchers, a quality that served him and his employers well when he later coached and managed. He started his big-league career with the American Association's Philadelphia team in 1886, but he earned widespread prominence as the principal catcher with the Old Orioles managed by Ned Hanlon (who, incidentally, became another Brooklyn skipper of modest longevity—seven years). One of Robinson's teammates at Baltimore was John McGraw. They were fast friends and became business partners in a successful Baltimore restaurant venture. When the Baltimore club was resurrected as one of the original American League entries with McGraw as its pilot, Robinson joined in as a backup catcher, team captain, and part-time pitching coach. It was at Baltimore that Robby signed his first big-league managing contract. McGraw had abruptly departed for the Giants in mid-1902, and Robinson replaced him as skipper. The team won fewer than a third of its remaining games and was uprooted to New York (to be known first as the Highlanders and then the Yankees) for the 1903 season when Clark Griffith would manage it. Robby's first managing assignment was over, and, based solely on its statistics, his future as a manager did not appear especially bright.

So Robinson went to the sidelines for a few years. Upon McGraw's move to New York Robby was the sole proprietor of the Baltimore restaurant. He did some consulting with minor league operators during the next several seasons. Now and then McGraw invited him to Giants spring training as an instructor. Rube Marquard, a youthful pitcher with potential (eventually fully realized), was with the Giants in 1911, and McGraw called on his old friend and associate Robinson to be a full-time New York coach with the nurturing of Marquard as his special assignment. Robby had assumed that the old McGraw-Robinson friendship and camaraderie would pick up where it had left off in Baltimore, but he was mistaken. McGraw had changed; he was more autocratic and acerbic than Robby remembered. The warm friendliness of their earlier association could not be rekindled, and, when McGraw blamed his old friend for a costly coaching error in the 1913 World Series lost to Mack's A's, he fired Robinson.

The Brooklyn and New York clubs were bitter rivals throughout their National League coexistence in the nation's largest city. So when the Dodgers hired Robinson to manage them immediately upon his rejection by McGraw, eyebrows popped up everywhere. But it didn't take long for Robinson to feel welcome at Ebbets Field. Soon after his arrival the team became popularly known as the Robins, in his honor, and it did not revert back to the Dodgers until his retirement. By nature he was a pleasant, congenial fellow—the direct opposite of McGraw in that regard—and a cordial companion of New York writers and most of his own players. Today his managing style would be described as laid back. He wrote out the lineup card and let his players play. One of them, as we have seen, was Stengel. Several decades later Casey was credited with the strategy of platooning, but it was a tactic he learned way back in his playing days under Robinson; Casey, himself, was a platoon outfielder during most of his career, when he generally faced only right-handed pitching. Three managers at that time—Robby, McGraw, and the Braves' George Stallings—regularly engaged in the southpaw pitcher vs. right-handed hitter lineup juggling.

Robinson was the butt of his players' practical joke one afternoon during spring training in Daytona, Florida. The story is still told from time to time. Robby, the former catcher, knew that Senators catcher Gabby Street had recently caught a baseball dropped from the top of the Washington Monument. Robinson figured the feat was not particularly difficult, so it was decided to drop a ball to him from a low-flying single-engine airplane during a spring-training lull. But instead of a baseball, the pranksters dropped a small grapefruit. Robby positioned himself for the reception, reached for the sphere as it neared land, and almost caught it. But it glanced off his mitt, connected with his neck and shoulder, and virtually exploded. Keeling over, the manager shouted that he'd been killed. Not until he fingered the liquid dripping down his body did he realize that it was citrus juice, not blood.

Catching was Robinson's forte as a player, and at teaching the fine points of the position he was masterful. During his Brooklyn managership, catching was always one of the team's strengths. Otto Miller was an accomplished backstop there for many years. Then Al Lopez came along as a rookie during Robinson's later years. Robby groomed Lopez in the fine art of catching, of calling pitches and knowing the opposition, and recognized Lopez's leadership potential by making him, in effect, the team's playing captain.

When he wrapped up his lengthy baseball career after the 1931 season, Robinson was 68 years of age, the fourth-eldest manager this century after Mack, Stengel, and—by six months—Lasorda. (Robby was a month older than Durocher was when Leo retired.) By then Uncle Robby had turned over the daily running of the club to coaches and young leaders such as Lopez, and he was ready to call it quits. His long career as Brooklyn manager, his popularity throughout baseball (at 5 feet, 7 inches and eventually well more than 250 pounds he was a stereotypical jolly fat man), and his ability to teach catching were major factors in his selection to the Hall of Fame.

Casey Stengel. Managed 25 years (Dodgers 1934–36, Braves 1938–43, Yankees 1949–60, Mets 1962–65); 10 pennants, seven World Championships; first managing job at age 43; native of Kansas City, Missouri; died at age 85; was retired one year upon his Hall of Fame induction.

When baseball is reviewed after another 100 years—I hope people will still talk about it then—a handful of names from the 20th century will continue to be discussed. They are the immortals, men whose contributions to baseball must certainly survive. Babe Ruth, John McGraw, and Connie Mack will surely be among them. Bank on Joe DiMaggio, Jackie Robinson, Willie Mays, Walter Johnson, and Hank Aaron too, and on Ted Williams, Cy Young, Ken Griffey Jr., Stan Musial, and Ty Cobb.

And, of course, Casey Stengel.

Often it has been suggested that Stengel ranks right behind Ruth as the most popular of baseball's celebrated personalities. In the 1950s a unique lingo—it's inaccurate to call it a new language—was christened "Stengelese" in honor of manager Casey Stengel. To the uninitiated or poorly informed, the double-talk he often spouted confirmed their assessment of this man as simply a clown, a show-off. But to knowledgeable baseball people it was quickly apparent that Casey Stengel was anything but a clown or a caricature when it came to everything vital about baseball. Strategy. Personnel. Instruction. Judging potential. Team unity. And (very important) public relations.

On the last matter Stengel carefully studied the roles of press representatives. He knew who the feature writers were as well as the daily newspaper writers with their tight deadlines. Casey had the ability to gain the confidence of writers so that when he went off the record his remarks remained private. He also knew just how, and for whom, to manipulate the press. If he thought one of his players, for example, was a little depressed for whatever reason, he might mention that man's heads-up baserunning that helped to win a key game during the last road trip. Usually the player, after reading Casey's quotes in the paper, would soon perk up. It was the same kind of psychology that Casey frequently employed on the bench during, before, and after his headline seasons with the Yankees.

A case in point was recalled by Hall of Fame member Rich Ashburn, a veteran outfielder on Stengel's first Mets club in 1962. "Casey got some amazing results from pinch hitters. When he was with the Yankees, of course, he always had that great bench. If Casey had something to manage, as he did back then, he managed a game very well. The Mets didn't have that kind of talent, but we turned in some great pinch-hitting records there anyway. When a situation obviously called for a pinch hitter, Casey'd walk up and down the dugout kind of mumbling, talking to himself. But he did it just loud enough for us to hear him. He'd be saying things like, 'Mr. Hodges . . . no we'll use him for the long ball. Well, Mr. Ashburn maybe, but, no, I'll save him for later to move a base runner over.' Then he'd stop in front of somebody else and say something about getting on base now. See, what he was doing was making the guy he finally chose feel special about the assignment—to feel that Casey had confidence in only him to get this particular job done. I remember pinch hitter Hobie Landrith [a journeyman catcher] going to the plate one night filled with confidence. All he did was hit a ninth-inning, game-winning home run off Warren Spahn. Casey made you feel you were just the right guy at the right time. He was, what, 72 years old when I played for Casey, but he was the best I ever saw at handling players. There wasn't any finger pointing on Stengel's teams. We had harmony on the Mets, and I credit him for it."

Ashburn paraphrased an eternal truism about managing when he talked of the star performers at Casey's command with the Yankees. The smartest and best-prepared managers can produce winning results if they have several good players. Stengel was 43 when he signed his first major league managing contract in 1934, and he didn't have many outstanding players at Brooklyn then. His three Dodger teams finished sixth, fifth, and seventh; then he was gone. The Boston Braves, who were then completing two generally futile decades, hired Casey in 1938. But he couldn't stir up any better results than he had in Brooklyn. He was given plenty of time (six seasons) to improve the Braves, but their playing talent was thin. Had new owner Lou Perini and his construction business associates stayed the course with him, Stengel might not have been available to the Yankees six years later. Perini poured money into his new venture, made fortuitous player transactions, hired the proven Billy Southworth as manager, began to develop a farm system, and wound up with a National League pennant winner in 1948.

Meanwhile Casey took a managing job at then Triple-A Milwaukee where, coincidentally, the Braves would move in 1953 and tangle with Stengel's Yanks in the 1957 and 1958 World Series. He hadn't planned to manage in 1944. He'd worn big-league and minor league flannels for 34 seasons (beginning in 1910) and wondered if, perhaps, that was a long enough career. But an old friend from National League managing days, Charlie Grimm, was invited to return to the Cubs for his second term as their skipper. Grimm had been dugout boss at Milwaukee (American Association) and in early May asked Casey to step in to clear the way for Grimm to take the Chicago job. Casey did, and by season's end Milwaukee was in first place. However, Stengel resigned due to perceived friction between him and absentee owner Bill Veeck, who was in the Pacific with the Marines at the time. (Some years later Stengel and Veeck would become good friends.) Old pals keep reappearing, though, and for the 1945 season Casey was urged by New York farm director George Weiss to manage the Yankees' AAA team in Kansas City. Weiss, at New Haven, and Stengel had met in 1925 during Casey's first managing job at Worcester, Massachusetts. Kansas City was Casey's hometown and also the site of Casey's long ago minor league team. After a year there, with undistinguished players, Casey signed to manage Oakland in the strong Pacific Coast League. By then he and his wife lived in Southern California, and at Oakland he'd be closer to home. His Oaks capped Stengel's three seasons there with the 1948 PCL pennant. A week later he was the surprise choice to manage the New York Yankees.

The glib baseball veteran, famous for his quick quips and humorous anecdotes, suddenly turned dead serious. He recognized the enormity of the task of replacing popular Bucky Harris at baseball's most visible managing post. And until Joe DiMaggio would eventually retire after the 1951 World Series, Stengel was aware that New York was DiMaggio's team, not Casey's.

Five straight World Championships changed that. Stengel was in exalted managing company. The pennants continued almost yearly. Only Casey and one of his former managers and mentors, McGraw, have ever won 10 pennants. Casey's seven Series crowns tie him with Joe McCarthy for best in that category. Careful attention to detail and planning—traits learned primarily from McGraw—contributed greatly to his managing success. Knowing his players' capabilities, and their weaknesses too, enabled him to put the right man in the right circumstance at the right time. His ability to teach the rudiments of smart baseball was another of Stengel's major attributes. A case in point: young Mickey Mantle's first appearance at Brooklyn's Ebbets Field for a 1951 preseason exhibition game against the Dodgers. Casey, Mantle's manager, had been a Brooklyn outfielder when Ebbets Field was new. Stengel knew all about the tricky caroms that could result from balls hit against the beveled lower portion of the right-field wall. Before the game he took Mantle to the fence and showed him how weird bounces could occur. Often grumpy and sarcastic, Casey was amused at Mantle's reaction to the manager's hopping around spearing pregame caroms. "He looked at me kinda funny," said Stengel. "Like he thought I was born 60 years old!"

When the Yankees replaced their celebrated manager after the 1960 World Series in which Casey had admitted a mistake in planning his Series pitching rotation—the Yankees lost to Pittsburgh in seven games—he was 70. It was widely assumed he would stay fully retired. But when his old friend Weiss became general manager of the newborn Mets, Stengel was persuaded to come back. Admittedly, his box office popularity in New York was one important reason for the invitation. ("Casey Stengel and the New York Mets are open for business.") With aging veterans the Mets always finished last during Casey's 3½ years there, but they usually outdrew his former employers in the Bronx. Casey suffered a broken hip midway through the 1965 season and was forced to retire for good. Shortly thereafter the Mets retired Number 37, just as the Yankees had done earlier. Retired number or not, the exploits of Hall of Famer Casey Stengel will remain vivid for as long as baseball is chronicled and discussed.

Earl Weaver. Managed 17 years (Orioles 1968–82, 1985–86); four pennants, two World Championships; first managing job at age 38; native of St. Louis, Missouri; was retired 10 years upon his Hall of Fame induction.

"Earl Who?" the nation's headlines bellowed in July 1968, when the Baltimore Orioles dismissed manager Hank Bauer and replaced him with first-year coach Earl Weaver. Less than two years before, Bauer had skippered the Orioles to their first pennant (and then a four-game World Series sweep of Los Angeles) since they had set up shop in Maryland after the St. Louis Browns franchise was transfered there in 1954.

Orioles fans knew of Weaver's successes in the Baltimore minor league system, but the rest of the country wondered, Who's he?

With Baltimore just a shade above .500 at the 1968 All-Star break, general manager Harry Dalton—never a strong supporter of Bauer—decided it was a good time to terminate him. No major surprise there. But his successor was a puzzlement. Weaver had joined the team only that spring as Bauer's first-base coach. Yes, he had long been a loyal organization man and had managed in Baltimore's farm system for a dozen seasons, the previous two at Triple-A Rochester. But because Weaver was new to the American League, and third-base coach Billy Hunter was well acquainted with the Orioles and the rest of the league, it was assumed that Hunter would replace Bauer.

Whether or not the Orioles would have enjoyed the remarkable success under Hunter that Weaver achieved is not certain. Fact is, Weaver directed the franchise to its most notable long run in history. Three consecutive American League flags (1969–71), another pennant in 1979, six East Division titles in 11 years, more victories than any other team in the league during that span, 13 first- or second-place finishes between 1968 and the 1982 completion of Earl's first of two Baltimore managing terms. When his 1969–71 champs posted three successive 100-plus-victory seasons Earl became the only manager since Connie Mack to accomplish what we'd now term a 100-win three-peat. Granted, Weaver had several standout ballplayers at his command, but so have other managers over the years. If Weaver was "supposed" to win with the likes of Frank and Brooks Robinson, Mark Belanger, Boog Powell, Davey Johnson, Paul Blair, and a young strong-armed pitching staff, then he deserves credit for accomplishing his task. Among his moundsmen was a quartet of 20-game winners in 1971—Mike Cuellar, Dave McNally, Pat Dobson, and Hall of Famer Jim Palmer. But players came and players went, and Weaver's teams continued to contend. By 1979, Earl's final pennant year, only Palmer and Belanger were significant holdovers from the champions of a decade earlier. No question that the farm system was productive during that time—Eddie Murray, Doug

DeCinces, Mike Flanagan, Al Bumbry, Rich Dauer, others. Every time, though, as old favorites left and the good rookies appeared, it was Weaver's ability to tailor new lineups, often via platooning, that enabled the O's to continue their ride into annual contention.

Like Hall of Fame manager Joe McCarthy before him, Weaver was a scrappy minor league infielder who simply lacked the talent for the majors. Both were short men—Weaver is about 5 feet, 7 inches—and both got to the finish line with champions their second seasons as American League pilots. Weaver, even as a youngster, had a feisty nature. Several sources report that he was not especially popular with his players. He did not hesitate to scold, loudly, and is said to have distracted some Orioles with constant hollering (pepping up the team, Earl says) during games. He seldom held grudges, though. When the shouting and beefing with umpires or opponents ended, Weaver usually put the conflict, whatever it was, behind him. That held true with his one-on-one critiques of his own players as well. Despite some internal differences of opinion, former Orioles hold Weaver in high esteem for his capacity to extract the utmost effort and performance from them. Ace pitcher Palmer and Weaver engaged in dozens of verbal battles over the years, but mutual respect survived. Both men are egoists when it comes to their professional talents, and both chuckle now about most of their tiffs, even if they can't forget them.

Earl Weaver was among the foremost talent judges of his time. Long before he became Orioles manager, he was a valued member of organization councils that met each winter to evaluate players. If opinions were deadlocked about whether to advance a player to the next level or cut him, Earl's recommendation usually proved accurate and insightful. He was often ridiculed for his alleged reliance on computer-generated reports detailing statistical strengths and weaknesses—so-and-so hit .545 against left-handers during day games in the Central Time Zone last year. But Weaver, with the exception of Lasorda, is the Hall of Fame's most recently active manager, and technology now enables managers to obtain performance updates more quickly and in more intricate detail than ever before. Had these evaluation tools been available to McGraw, for example, he surely would have taken advantage of them in hopes of getting another edge on the opposition. But valuable as this kind of assistance can be to a manager, Weaver insists that he didn't base his tactics and strategy solely on statistics. He said, shortly before his 1996 Cooperstown induction, "The manager's main job is to get the most out of his players. Sure, statistical information helps to decide personnel moves sometimes, but it's not the main thing. Know how your players work together, how they adjust to adversity, how they fit into the scheme of things—the right piece to fit the puzzle.

Great chemistry is very important in building a winning team. And it doesn't just happen." A manager needs to know much more about his players than simply their bat speed or bunting abilities.

Whenever complimented for his enormous achievements, Weaver gives some credit to others. He invariably salutes the Baltimore front office for its efficiency in developing young players through the farm system en route to Earl's dugout. For many years, of course, Weaver himself was one of the organization's most effective minor league tutors. There's no reason to suppose he forgot how to instruct when one of his major league Orioles required a refresher course.

Three seasons without a division championship had elapsed by the end of 1982 when Baltimore finished just one game behind the AL East–winning Brewers. Weaver retired. He was only 52 but appeared to be aging rapidly. He was not afflicted with any serious illness; he just seemed to be burned out—a phrase then entering popular jargon. His successor was Joe Altobelli, who had managed the Giants for a few seasons in the 1970s, and Altobelli's Orioles won the World Series in 1983. By then, however, it was obvious that the farm system's productivity had eroded, and in mid-1985 when Baltimore was no longer dominating its division, Altobelli was dismissed and Weaver was urged to return to revive the old glory. He couldn't restore the old successes, of course, because the talent was not as potent as before.

Earl's contagious enthusiasm was no longer there. He finished that 1985 campaign for the Orioles, then came back for the final year of his Baltimore encore. His 1986 club ranked seventh, last, in American League East. That was enough for Earl. This time his goodbyes were permanent. He left the dugout and headed toward Cooperstown.

Honorable Mention. Three men who managed major league teams in the 20th century, and three whose managing careers ended before 1900, have been inducted in the Hall of Fame's executive category under the special classification of Meritorious Service to Baseball. They are Edward "Ed" Barrow, who earned prominence as New York Yankees general manager; ground breaker Branch Rickey, general manager of the St. Louis Cardinals, Brooklyn Dodgers, and Pittsburgh Pirates; Clark Griffith, longtime owner of the Washington Senators; Charles Comiskey, one of the founders of the American League and then owner of the Chicago White Sox; Harry Wright, the innovator who organized and ran baseball's first professional team, the Cincinnati Red Stockings, and later was a National League pioneer; and his brother George Wright, an early star player, championship manager, and prominent developer of baseball equipment.

Earlier Barrow had managed the Detroit Tigers and Boston Red Sox (1918 World Champions); Rickey was manager of both St. Louis teams, the Browns and Cardinals; Griffith was the American League's first pennant-winning manager (Chicago,1901) before piloting the Highlanders (Yankees), Reds, and Senators; Comiskey managed solely in the 1800s in three leagues, primarily at St. Louis, compiling a .608 winning percentage for 12 seasons; Harry Wright directed Boston, Providence, and Philadelphia during the National League's first 18 years beginning in 1876 and finished in the first division in 15 of those seasons; and George Wright, in his one and only managing campaign, won the National League's 1879 pennant at Providence.

HALL OF FAME MEMBERS
Selected to Hall of Fame for Achievements as Managers

Name	Year Elected	Name	Year Elected
Walt Alston	1983	Connie Mack*	1937
Leo Durocher	1994	Joe McCarthy	1957
Ned Hanlon*	1996	John McGraw*	1937
Bucky Harris	1975	Bill McKechnie	1962
Miller Huggins	1964	Wilbert Robinson	1945
Tommy Lasorda	1997	Casey Stengel	1966
Al Lopez	1977	Earl Weaver	1996

Note: These 14 managers represent all 16 of the "original" franchises since 1901, in addition to two expansion teams (Durocher, Astros; Stengel, Mets)
*Managing career began before 1900 and continued into the 20th century

HALL OF FAME PLAYERS WHO ALSO SERVED AS MANAGERS

Name	Year Elected	Primary Position	Name	Year Elected	Primary Position
Cap Anson*	1939	1st base	Frank Chance	1946	1st base
Luke Appling	1964	Shortstop	Fred Clarke	1945	Outfield
Dave Bancroft	1971	Shortstop	Ty Cobb	1936	Outfield
Yogi Berra	1972	Catcher	Mickey Cochrane	1947	Catcher
Jim Bottomley	1974	1st base	Eddie Collins	1939	2nd base
Lou Boudreau	1970	Shortstop	Jimmy Collins	1945	3rd base
Roger Bresnahan	1945	Catcher	Roger Connor*	1976	1st base

continues

HALL OF FAME PLAYERS WHO ALSO SERVED AS MANAGERS (Continued)

Name	Year Elected	Primary Position	Name	Year Elected	Primary Position
Joe Cronin	1956	Shortstop	Eddie Mathews	1978	3rd base
George Davis	1998	Shortstop	Christy Mathewson	1936	Pitcher
Bill Dickey	1954	Catcher	Tommy McCarthy*	1946	Outfield
Larry Doby	1998	Outfield	Kid Nichols	1949	Pitcher
Hugh Duffy	1945	Outfield	Jim O'Rourke*	1945	Outfield
Johnny Evers	1939	2nd base	Mel Ott	1951	Outfield
Buck Ewing*	1946	Catcher	Frank Robinson	1982	Outfield
Frankie Frisch	1947	2nd base	Ray Schalk	1955	Catcher
Pud Galvin*	1965	Pitcher	Red Schoendienst	1989	2nd base
Burleigh Grimes	1964	Pitcher	George Sisler	1939	1st base
Gabby Hartnett	1955	Catcher	Al Spalding*	1939	Pitcher
Billy Herman	1975	2nd base	Tris Speaker	1937	Outfield
Rogers Hornsby	1942	2nd base	Bill Terry	1954	1st base
Hughie Jennings	1945	Shortstop	Joe Tinker	1946	Shortstop
Walter Johnson	1936	Pitcher	Pie Traynor	1948	3rd base
Joe Kelly	1971	Outfield	Honus Wagner	1936	Shortstop
King Kelly*	1945	Catcher	Bobby Wallace	1953	Shortstop
Nap Lajoie	1937	2nd base	Ed Walsh	1946	Pitcher
Bob Lemon	1976	Pitcher	Monte Ward*	1964	2nd base-Pitcher
Ted Lyons	1955	Pitcher	Ted Williams	1966	Outfield
Rabbit Maranville	1954	Shortstop	Cy Young	1937	Pitcher

•Entire managing career completed before 1901

Measures of Greatness

Joe McCarthy's Winning Ways

Except for a handful of interim managers who posted perfect records in one or two games, only one full-time major league pilot finished his notable career with an average of better than six wins out of every 10 games. Hall of Famer Joe McCarthy directed his Cubs, Yankees, and Red Sox to 2,125 regular season victories during a total of 24 years in their dugouts.

His winning percentage: .615. Never, remarkably over those two dozen summers, did he rank in the second division. And not once did his charges finish a season under .500. Only four times, in fact, did a McCarthy club place lower than third. He was a pennant winner nine times—once at Chicago, then eight championships at Yankee Stadium. His World Series record was an astounding 30 and 13, a .698 percentage that included seven Series titles. Three of them, in 1932, 1938, and 1939, were four-game sweeps.

Joe McCarthy first was referred to as a "push-button manager," first by Jimmie Dykes, then skipper of the White Sox. If true, his record reflects that he pushed the right buttons. His talented rosters offered him myriad options, although he was not much of a platoon pilot. He generally fielded a set lineup. One of just two Hall of Fame managers who never played major league baseball (Earl Weaver is the other, although Walter Alston had only one big-league at bat), McCarthy gained prominence early when, in his first major assignment, he brought the 1926 Chicago Cubs home fourth after they had finished in the National League basement a year earlier. Three years later Chicago, under Mc-Carthy, won its first league pennant in 11 years.

By an odd coincidence, Rogers Hornsby was connected with McCarthy's most-successful Chicago season, and then with his departure from Wrigley Field. After the Cubs, with 91 victories, finished third in 1928, McCarthy convinced owner Phil Wrigley and team president William Veeck Sr. that a trade for Hornsby, then with Boston, could help assure a pennant. That's precisely what happened when Hornsby arrived in 1929. But toward the end of the 1930 season, when the Cubs finished second, McCarthy felt certain that Hornsby was undermining him and wanted the manager's job for himself. McCarthy, with four games remaining and the team out of mathematical contention, resigned. Before a month had passed he was hired to manage the New York Yankees. And in the Bronx he would achieve his greatest renown.

The highly regarded Miller Huggins had died in office late in the 1929 season, and New York, under Bob Shawkey in 1930, finished an also-ran third, 16 games behind the champion Philadelphia A's. Yankee ownership, aware of Mc-Carthy's success at Chicago, signed him on for 1931 even though Babe Ruth had openly campaigned for the job. Yankee general manager Ed Barrow (the most recent man to manage Boston to a World Championship, 1918, when Ruth was a Red Sox headliner) had confidence that McCarthy could develop a reasonably comfortable working relationship with Ruth. He did, and he remained Yankee pilot for more than 15 seasons, the team's longest managerial tenure in history. McCarthy resigned his Yankee Stadium post 35 games into the 1946 campaign with the team in second place at 22–13. He cited ill health as the reason. To a degree there was some legitimacy to that. McCarthy's drinking had increased (he had been a continually heavy and often a private imbiber for some years). However, another and more likely factor for his resignation has been suggested. Prior to the 1946 season the flamboyant Larry MacPhail had been signed to run the Yankees' front office. He took the place of Barrow, a longtime confidant of McCarthy's. McCarthy believed that MacPhail's penchant for the spotlight would detract from McCarthy and the team, so he quit.

Not only did his Yankees win seven pennants, they ranked second on five other occasions during his tenure. Throughout his career he was deemed a master psychologist. This example was cited by Leonard Koppett in his book on the geneology of successful managing, *The Man in the Dugout:* "One day in the early 1930s McCarthy approached his excellent shortstop Frank Crosetti.

'I want you to do me a favor. Lou [Gehrig] has been dragging a bit lately. I don't want to talk to him about it, but I'd like to see something pep him up. When you do infield [practice] throw real hard to him, and talk it up. With your help, we can wake him up.' Crosetti did as he was told. After a few days Gehrig yelled at Crosetti, 'What's got into you?' Gehrig had a bunch of hits in those games (which was nothing unusual) and things went back to normal. The plan had worked, and Crosetti was proud of himself and of the confidence McCarthy had put in him. Many years later Crosetti and McCarthy met at an oldtimers' game and reminisced about the incident. McCarthy laughed. 'Now I can tell you,' he said. 'There wasn't anything wrong with Gehrig. You were the one who needed pepping up, and that was my way of doing it.'"

Following his resignation at New York McCarthy spent the next year and a half at his home, a small farm near Buffalo, New York. He had become acquainted with the area during his college days at Niagara University. Buffalo and environs would continue to be his home until his death in 1978, three months shy of his 91st birthday. Joe was born and raised in Philadelphia and, as a youngster, had been an admirer of Connie Mack—both the man and the manager.

McCarthy's health improved and his vigor returned during his nearly two-year hiatus from baseball. So when the Red Sox elevated 15-year skipper Joe Cronin to the general managership after the 1947 season, Boston called on McCarthy to replace Cronin. He was eager to accept, for Boston had a slugging ball club similar to the long-ball offenses he had directed in Chicago and New York. Besides that, Joe was not enamored of the MacPhail–Dan Topping–Del Webb operation of the Yankees, and he believed the Red Sox had an excellent chance to replace New York as the American League's top gun. They nearly did.

In 1948, his first season at Fenway Park, the Red Sox finished in a first-place deadlock with Cleveland. New York was third that year. Cleveland, however, won the single-game play-off when player-manager Lou Boudreau led the way with two home runs and pair of singles. That's the game in which each manager's starting pitching choice was controversial, as outlined more fully elsewhere on these pages. Boudreau's selection, rookie Gene Bearden, was the winning pitcher, besting Boston veteran Denny Galehouse.

McCarthy was nearly 61 when he took over the 1948 Red Sox. Before that, as Yankee pilot, he was reputed to be a no-nonsense disciplinarian. Among his New York rules and regulations was the edict that all players wear coats and ties on road trips and, in fact, anywhere the team appeared as a group in public. The Yankees, after all, were to be regarded as a "class" organization. What would happen, fans wondered, when Joe became Ted Williams's new boss at Boston? It was widely known that Ted had refused to wear a necktie throughout his sometimes contentious career. How would this conflict between the two national celebrities be handled? McCarthy immediately established the tone. On the first morning of spring training he arrived at the team's hotel dining room for breakfast before most of the players did. There he sat, reading the morning paper, wearing an open-collar shirt. Suitable apparel quickly became a nonissue.

After Boston's near miss in the 1948 pennant battle, McCarthy and his charges were heavy favorites to win the 1949 AL flag outright. Going into Yankee Stadium, scene of numerous McCarthy successes, the Red Sox held a one-game lead over New York with only two games remaining in the season's final weekend. The Boston lineup was feared throughout the league. Ted Williams and Vern Stephens each drove home 159 runs that year. Bobby Doerr had 109 RBI. Williams, Doerr, Dom DiMaggio, and Johnny Pesky all hit over .300. Standout pitchers were Mel Parnell (27 wins, 7 losses, 2.77 ERA) and Ellis Kinder (23–6, 3.36). By winning the Saturday afternoon game, New York had pulled into a first-place deadlock. The Yankees won again Sunday to clinch the crown.

Even though his Red Sox had won 96 games in both of his first two seasons, and each year had finished just a hair's breadth from the pennant, this second disappointment—especially since it was administered by the Yankees—seemed to drain enthusiasm from McCarthy. In 1950, with Boston a lethargic 31–28 and in fourth place, McCarthy resigned. He never managed again. As a matter of record, Steve O'Neill, Joe's Red Sox successor, advanced the team to third place by season's end, but a pennant would not adorn Fenway Park for another 17 years, until Dick Williams's "miracle season" of 1967.

In short order, after his retirement, McCarthy's health improved. For many years he attended oldtimers' ceremonies and visited spring training. He lived for nearly 28 years after hanging up his spikes. Half of this century's major league skippers have come and gone since McCarthy last managed. None of them, nor any of his predecessors or contemporaries, has been able to match his over-.600 winning percentage. Nearest to it is the .598 of Frank Selee, most of whose service to the National League was in the 1890s. Next is the underrated Billy Southworth at .597. The pilots who have come closest to McCarthy in the second half of this century are Hall of Famers Al Lopez, with a .584 mark for his distinguished career, and Earl Weaver, at .583. The best of the active managers in this category is Bobby Cox at .555 through 1998. Davey Johnson, who sat out 1998 before committing to L.A. for the '99 season, has a .575 record to his credit.

One perspective on the difficulty in achieving McCarthy's mark shows up in the managers' ranking which lists all of the men who managed at least 450 games (the equivalent of nearly three full seasons) this century. The list totals 190. Only McCarthy, on average, had a better than 6–4 record after every ten games. Another way to view his brilliant career: Thirty- five percent of these managers—and among them are dozens of men who are highly regarded, and deservedly so, for their exceptional achievements—would pretty much win one, lose one along the way. Sixty-five managers have posted career records of between .480 and .520—48 and 52. Or the other way around. An example is Chuck Dressen at .509 after 16 seasons—51 wins, 49 losses for every 100 games managed. Not much of a margin. When the very best of them, Joe McCarthy, loses nearly four games for each six that his team wins, the difficulty of winning baseball games consistently is clear.

McCarthy and the few others around .600, the half dozen or so with marks in the .400 range. Six-and-four, four-and-six. Just one loss—or merely one victory—away from .500. So close statistically, but, oh, so far apart on a career-success meter!

McKechnie and Williams

Several managers have guided their teams into the World Series. Ten of them directed two different franchises to league pennants. Only two men, however, from among the 84 who have skippered World Series teams, were in charge of *three* franchises that competed for the Series championship. Bill McKechnie is already enshrined in the Baseball Hall of Fame. Perhaps Dick Williams, the only other manager of three different World Series franchises, will join him in Cooperstown someday.

"Deacon" Bill McKechnie. The late "Fast Eddie" Lawson grew up on New York's Lower East Side. Eddie and several pals often enjoyed a summer afternoon of baseball in the old Polo Grounds center-field bleachers. They would usually situate themselves near the stairway leading from the visiting team's clubhouse to the playing field. According to Fast Eddie, the vast majority of uniformed visitors either ignored the teenagers or spewed profanity at them. One notable exception was Cincinnati manager Bill McKechnie.

"Without fail," Eddie recalled decades later, "McKechnie always gave us a warm smile and greeted us with, 'Gentlemen, how are ya!' Sure, we always backed our Giants. But because of the nice way McKechnie treated us we liked the Reds second best."

William Boyd McKechnie managed more major league franchises— three—to pennants than anyone else until Dick Williams accomplished the

Text continues on page 257

Manager	Percent	Won	Lost
Joe McCarthy	.615	2,125	1,333
Frank Selee*	.598	1,284	862
Billy Southworth	.597	1,044	704
Frank Chance	.593	946	648
John McGraw*	.587	2,784	1,959
Al Lopez	.584	1,410	1,004
Earl Weaver	.583	1,480	1,060
Mickey Cochrane	.579	361	262
Eddie Dyer	.578	446	325
Pants Rowland	.578	339	247
Fred Clarke*	.576	1,602	1,181
Davey Johnson	.575	985	727
Oscar Vitt	.570	262	198
Pat Moran	.561	748	586
Steve O'Neill	.559	1,040	821
Walter Alston	.558	2,040	1,613
Bobby Cox	.555	1,418	1,138
Miller Huggins	.555	1,413	1,134
Bill Terry	.555	823	661
Billy Martin	.553	1,253	1,013
Walter Johnson	.550	529	432
Nap Lajoie	.550	377	309
Jimmy Collins	.548	455	376
Bill Shettsline *	.548	367	303
Charlie Grimm	.547	1,287	1,067
George Gibson	.546	413	334
Sam Mele	.546	524	436
Sparky Anderson	.545	2,194	1,834
Dick Howser	.544	507	425
Mike Hargrove	.543	624	526
Tris Speaker	.543	617	520
Hughie Jennings	.542	1,163	984
Joe Cronin	.540	1,236	1,055
Leo Durocher	.540	2,008	1,709
Danny Murtaugh	.540	1,115	950
Eddie Kasko	.539	345	295
Herman Franks	.537	605	521
Del Baker	.536	412	357
Joe Morgan	.535	301	262
Ned Hanlon*	.533	1,253	1,096
Danny Ozark	.533	618	542

Continued

Manager	Percent	Won	Lost
Jimy Williams	.533	451	395
Bruce Bochy	.532	335	295
Whitey Herzog	.532	1,281	1,125
Johnny Keane	.532	398	350
Kevin Kennedy	.531	309	273
Jim Frey	.530	323	287
Pie Traynor	.530	457	406
Bill Murray	.529	240	214
Terry Collins	.528	398	352
Tom Lasorda	.526	1,599	1,439
Pete Rose	.525	412	373
Bill Armour	.524	382	347
Gabby Street	.524	365	332
Hal Lanier	.523	254	232
Tony LaRussa	.523	1,564	1,425
Bill McKechnie	.523	1,842	1,678
Hank Bauer	.522	594	544
Yogi Berra	.522	484	444
Clark Griffith	.522	1,491	1,367
Red Schoendienst	.522	1,041	955
Johnny Oates	.521	620	571
Red Rolfe	.521	278	256
Dusty Baker	.520	472	436
Lou Piniella	.520	940	866
Mayo Smith	.520	662	612
Dick Williams	.520	1,571	1,451
Felipe Alou	.519	535	496
Ty Cobb	.519	479	444
Kid Gleason	.519	392	364
Bill Virdon	.519	995	921
Joe Altobelli	.518	437	407
Cito Gaston	.518	683	636
Eddie Stanky	.518	467	435
Hal McRae	.517	286	267
Bob Lemon	.516	430	403
Birdie Tebbetts	.515	748	705
Red Dooin	.514	392	370
Frankie Frisch	.514	1,138	1,078
Ralph Houk	.514	1,619	1,531
Joe Kelley	.513	338	321
Gene Lamont	.513	406	386

Continued

MANAGERS RANKED BY WINNING PERCENTAGE (continued)

Manager	Percent	Won	Lost
Billy Hitchcock	.512	274	261
Harry Walker	.511	630	604
Alvin Dark	.510	994	954
Chuck Dressen	.509	1,008	973
Buck Showalter	.509	378	365
Casey Stengel	.508	1,905	1,842
Don Zimmer	.508	885	858
Paul Richards	.506	923	901
Buck Rodgers	.506	793	773
Clyde King	.505	234	229
Roger Peckinpaugh	.505	500	491
Tom Trebelhorn	.505	471	461
John Wathan	.505	326	320
Charlie Fox	.504	377	371
Mike Higgins	.502	560	556
Joe Torre	.502	1,196	1,186
Fred Hutchinson	.501	830	827
Roger Craig	.500	738	737
Jack McKeon	.500	589	589
Wilbert Robinson	.500	1,399	1,398
Bobby Valentine	.499	769	772
Dave Garcia	.498	307	310
Joe Gordon	.498	305	308
Jack Hendricks	.496	520	528
Bob Scheffing	.495	418	427
George Stallings*	.495	879	898
Chuck Tanner	.495	1,352	1,381
Bill Carrigan	.494	489	500
Frank Quilici	.494	280	287
Bucky Harris	.493	2,157	2,218
Jake Stahl	.493	263	270
Ed Barrow	.492	310	320
George Bamberger	.489	458	478
Jim Leyland	.489	997	1,041
Marty Marion	.489	356	372
Lum Harris	.488	466	488
Jim Lebebvre	.488	395	415
Lou Boudreau	.487	1,161	1,224
Dallas Green	.487	454	478
Bob Kennedy	.487	264	278
Tom Kelly	.486	923	977

Continued

Manager	Percent	Won	Lost
Connie Mack *	.486	3,731	3,948
Luke Sewell	.485	606	644
Don Baylor	.484	440	469
John McNamara	.484	1,168	1,247
Bill Rigney	.484	1,239	1,321
Gene Mauch	.483	1,902	2,037
Doug Rader	.482	388	417
Bobby Bragan	.481	443	478
Donie Bush	.480	497	539
Eddie Sawyer	.480	390	423
Jim Fregosi	.479	861	938
Phil Garner	.478	511	557
Jimmie Dykes	.477	1,406	1,541
Burt Shotton	.477	697	764
Fred Mitchell	.476	494	543
Frank Robinson	.475	680	751
George Sisler	.475	218	241
Pat Corrales	.474	572	634
Lee Fohl	.474	713	792
Branch Rickey	.473	597	664
Jeff Torborg	.472	492	551
Art Howe	.470	609	687
Gil Hodges	.467	660	753
Mel Ott	.467	464	530
Rogers Hornsby	.463	701	812
Dave Bristol	.462	657	764
Nixey Callahan	.462	394	458
Ken Aspromonte	.458	220	260
Bill Killefer	.457	524	622
Fred Haney	.454	629	757
Jim Riggleman	.454	419	503
Jimmy McAleer	.453	736	889
Wild Bill Donovan	.449	245	301
Hugh Duffy	.444	535	671
Darrell Johnson	.444	472	590
Lee Elia	.442	238	300
Billy Gardner	.442	330	417
Frank Lucchesi	.442	316	399
Patsy Donovan*	.438	684	879
Del Crandall	.437	364	469
Tom Loftus*	.436	416	538

Continued

5

MANAGERS RANKED BY WINNING PERCENTAGE (continued)

Manager	Percent	Won	Lost
Rene Lachemann	.434	428	559
Roger Bresnahan	.432	328	432
Dan Howley	.431	397	524
Ted Williams	.429	273	364
Ossie Bluege	.428	375	394
Harry Craft	.426	360	485
Stan Hack	.423	199	272
Deacon McGuire*	.423	210	287
Dave Bancroft	.415	238	336
Ben Chapman	.415	196	276
Wes Westrum	.415	260	366
Bill Dahlen	.414	251	355
Cookie Lavagetto	.414	271	384
Jim Marshall	.414	229	326
Billy Meyer	.412	317	452
Billy Herman	.408	189	274
Russ Nixon	.400	231	347
Buddy Bell	.399	184	277
Preston Gomez	.395	346	529
Art Fletcher	.382	237	383
Zack Taylor	.364	235	410
Joe Cantillon	.347	158	297
Roy Hartsfield	.343	166	318
Fred Tenney	.334	202	402
John McCloskey	.313	190	407
Doc Prothro	.301	138	320

Note: Tie games not included; list includes only men with 450 or more decisions, 1901–98
*Pre-1901 managing record included in this tabulation

same feat 45 years later. No one has matched their achievement. Twice Mc-Kechnie's league champions won World Series. He led Pittsburgh over Washington in 1925 and Cincinnati past Detroit in 1940. He managed 24 years in the National League, where his teams posted a .523 winning percentage (1,842 victories; 1,678 losses). Beginning in 1922, at Pittsburgh, his managing career included one championship season with the Pirates, another at St. Louis, eight years piloting the Boston Braves, then nine at Cincinnati, where the Reds finished in the first division seven times—twice first.

Bill McKechnie was 35 when he took on his first National League managing assignment at Pittsburgh 64 games into the 1922 season. Earlier, though, he had experienced the complexities of managing back in 1915 with Newark of the short-lived Federal League. As a player there he was elevated to manager with 99 games remaining and went 54–45 to finish in fifth place, one-half game beneath the first division.

A year later, after the Federal League folded, McKechnie was back in the National League as a player, at third base, with the Reds. Yet only briefly. After just 37 games he was involved in one of baseball's most publicized trades up to that time. The New York Giants sent their hallowed right-hander Christy Mathewson to Cincinnati for McKechnie and three other players. The following season Bill was returned to the Reds' infield. He then completed his modest nine-year playing career in 40 games at all four infield positions for the 1920 Pirates.

It is not certain whether McKechnie absorbed successful managing rudiments from two of his distinguished mentors. We can assume, however, that he studied both of them carefully. He played in 71 games as a New York Giant under cantankerous John McGraw in 1916. Surely, he did not adopt McGraw's feistiness or his propensity to prolong grudges. Earlier, beginning in 1910, McKechnie had played his first four seasons under the respected Fred Clarke at Pittsburgh. Clarke led the Pirates for 16 years at the start of the century. His four pennants are the most for any Pirate manager.

As young player, then big-league infielder, and finally as manager, McKechnie wore Pittsburgh flannels longer than any other uniform. The Bucs, in fact, were Bill's "home team"; he was born in Wilkinsburg, Pennsylvania, a Pittsburgh suburb. A Pittsburgh player in parts of six seasons, he later managed there for nearly five more. Four times his Pirates finished in third place. Then in 1925 they won the pennant and became the first team ever to overcome a three-games-to-one deficit to win a World Series, by downing the defending World Champion Washington Senators. When Pittsburgh "slipped" to 84 victories in 1926, Bill McKechnie was fired. A vocal minority of Pirate players and veteran officials had lobbied for old warhorse Fred Clarke—who, coincidentally, had returned as coach at McKechnie's invitation—to manage again. That didn't happen, but a rift had developed in the dugout, and the Pirates, to curtail growing dissention, chose to discard McKechnie. (Clarke's dugout duties were terminated, too.) The next season, 1927, was the only year between 1922 and 1946 that McKechnie did not manage in the major leagues.

The St. Louis Cardinals, who traditionally sacked managers with about the same frequency they laundered uniforms, hired McKechnie to manage in 1928. Bingo! Ninety-five victories and a National League pennant, his second. But by the next opening day McKechnie was demoted to manage Rochester, a top farm club, because Cardinals owner Sam Breadon was angry about St.

Louis's World Series sweep by the Yankees. Before the Cardinals' schizo-phrenic 1929 season would end, and with two managers—Billy Southworth and Gabby Street—in the interim, McKechnie was recalled from Rochester. The Redbirds won 33 of their final 62 games under him, but finished fourth. And with that Bill McKechnie was finished in St. Louis.

Sam Breadon's jockeying of St. Louis managers had frustrated Bill, so he accepted an offer to manage the Boston Braves despite their achieving just one first-division finish in the preceding 14 years.

Boston was the only one of the four clubs Bill managed that did not win a title. Yet some historians cite his Boston years as among his top achievements. Within two years he groomed the Braves into respectability. Twice in his eight full seasons there Boston finished in the first division; twice more the Braves were fifth, both times with a .500 or better log.

McKechnie's .486 Boston record may be considered dazzling compared with those of Braves teams of eight years previous and eight years later. Had it not been for one disastrous season when the Braves set a league record for most losses (115, broken by the infamous 1962 Mets), McKechnie's Boston fig-ures would have been even more respectable, especially considering that his Braves seldom rostered many legitimate All-Star candidates. A footnote to that 115-loss debacle in 1935: One of McKechnie's Braves was Babe Ruth, long past his productive prime. Ruth, in fact, retired from baseball early that year after only 72 at bats and a .181 average.

Even though pennantless in Boston, McKechnie, a former infielder, was adept at developing pitchers. Rookies Jim Turner and Lou Fette, both in their thirties, posted 20 wins each for the 1937 Braves, who were six games over .500 but one game shy of the first division. Back at Pittsburgh Lee Meadows and Remy Kramer had been 20-game winners for Deacon Bill. So, too, were Bill Sherdel and Jesse Haines with the pennant-winning Cardinals of 1928. Then, at the acme of McKechnie's managing career—the two titles and those five other first division seasons in Cincinnati—Paul Derringer and Bucky Walters each turned in three 20-plus victory seasons under Bill's leadership, and Johnny Vander Meer registered his double no-hitter.

Finishing no worse than fourth in his first seven years at Crosley Field, McKechnie and the Reds dropped to seventh in World War II's final year, then were sixth in 1946. McKechnie's luminous career as a major league manager ended. He was then 60 years old. But his on-field contributions continued. Af-ter leading three different teams—Pittsburgh, St. Louis, and Cincinnati—to league championships, McKechnie was widely, but unofficially, credited with "managing" yet a fourth pennant winner: the 1948 Cleveland Indians.

Lou Boudreau was the Tribe's player-manager then, and had been since 1942 when he was only 24 years old. Boudreau was a Hall of Fame shortstop and, as it developed, the 1948 American League MVP. Indians owner Bill Veeck, who bought the club in late 1946, was never enamored of Boudreau as a manager. In 1947 Veeck recognized the team's promise as a potential pennant contender and considered replacing his manager. Cleveland fans, however, who admired Boudreau as both player and pilot, loudly protested Veeck's proposal to trade their hero to the St. Louis Browns. So Veeck, who was not only a legendary promoter but an astute baseball administrator as well, collaborated with Boudreau on a plan that satisfied his constituents and was, to a significant degree, a key factor in bringing the 1948 pennant to Cleveland Stadium. Veeck kept Boudreau. Then he hired Bill McKechnie, who had been retired briefly as a coach.

McKechnie often coached at third base. But more important, he served as Boudreau's chief lieutenant. When the Tribe was on defense, with Lou stationed at shortstop, McKechnie ran the dugout. The title of "bench coach" was not in vogue in those days. Today it is standard nomenclature; virtually all teams now have a bench coach. Bill McKechnie, in 1948, might have been the first.

Perhaps it is more than coincidence that the 1948 Cleveland pitching staff, with McKechnie on hand, had two 20-game winners (Gene Bearden and Bob Lemon) and five pitchers with ERAs under 3.00. The Indians employed Satchel Paige for the second half of the season. Veteran All-Star Bob Feller posted 19 victories for them. With player-manager Boudreau in the field half the time, and on the basepaths an average of nearly twice per game, the dugout assistance and guidance of Bill McKechnie was a vital element in the team's championship season.

Bill retired a year later, but he returned again to coach briefly in Boston after Boudreau became the Red Sox pilot in 1952. In 1962 Bill McKechnie was elected to the Hall of Fame. No one questioned his credentials. The gentlemanly, soft-spoken McKechnie, nicknamed "Deacon Bill" for both his demeanor and his longtime role as a deacon in the Methodist church, died at Bradenton, Florida, in 1965. He was 79. Bradenton's ballpark, the spring-training home for many years of the Braves, and now of the Pirates, is named McKechnie Field.

Dick Williams. Dick Williams, whose major league playing career started just a year before Bill McKechnie put his final big-league uniform aside, has several statistics, accomplishments, and coincidences in common with Deacon

Bill. They both guided three different franchises into the World Series—the only two managers to accomplish that feat. Managing more than a generation apart, they registered nearly the same winning percentages after sitting in director's chairs for more than 3,000 games each.

Of the 3,023 regular-season games he managed, Williams's teams won 1,571 times, were defeated on 1,451 occasions, and tied once. McKechnie, whose 24 seasons were three more than Williams's total, directed his troops to 1,842 regular-season triumphs against 1,678 losses. McKechnie won at a .523 percentage; Williams had a .520 mark. Of the three different franchises each took to the World Series, McKechnie's teams won two series and lost two. So did Williams's. Both of these managing luminaries reached big-league pilot status in their thirties after relatively mediocre playing careers. And both concluded their managing at the same age—60. Williams's World Series teams were somewhat more successful than McKechnie's in terms of total games won; Dick's 12–14 Series log against Bill's 8–14. But the outcomes were the same—two Series winners apiece.

As with McKechnie, Williams's first managing assignment netted a league championship. In Williams's case it was his rookie season. In one of baseball's most celebrated reversals, Williams's 1967 Boston Red Sox rebounded from a 1966 ninth-place finish to outlast Minnesota, Chicago, and Detroit in the season's final series—a weekend that began with all four clubs still alive for the pennant. Going head-to-head with the Twins, who were American League champs just two years earlier, Boston won both weekend games at Fenway Park and then awaited the California vs. Detroit outcome, which eventually resulted in a Boston flag when the Angels won the first game of a damp, chilly doubleheader.

Unlike McKechnie, whose team (1925 Pirates) was a winner in Bill's first World Series, the Williams Red Sox of 1967 were seventh-game victims of St. Louis. Five years later Dick's 1972 Oakland A's were World Champions. It was the first of three straight Series titles for the Athletics, although Williams was not around for the last of those three. In 1973, however, in the Series against the New Yorks Mets and amid acrimonious controversy involving A's owner Charley Finley's edict to deactivate second baseman Mike Andrews, Oakland under Williams won its second consecutive seven-game Series. Williams's final World Series was in 1984 when his San Diego Padres were eliminated in five games by Sparky Anderson's Detroit Tigers. This Series marked the only time in history that *both* opposing managers had previously managed a World Series team from the "other" league (Williams with the American League's Red Sox and Athletics earlier; Anderson with Cincinnati four times, including 1972 when the Reds and Williams's A's met).

McKechnie was widely regarded as a mild-mannered man who generally spoke with civility and kindness. Richard Hirschfeld Williams was not gentle. In his 1990 book, *No More Mr. Nice Guy,* coauthored by Bill Plaschke, Dick Williams proudly and repeatedly admits that the public's general perception of him as aggressive and combative is pretty much on target. A line in the book's foreword gives some insight: "This book will not make me friends," he remarked. "But when I set out to write it I wasn't looking for friends."

Williams's competitive nature in baseball carried over from his childhood. It was said that he wanted to be the first kid on his block to touch the top of the clothes pole, and that when he was stoking furnaces and cleaning aisles and serving as part-time usher at a neighborhood cinema in his native St. Louis, this "high visibility" job gave him a feeling of power. Later, as a gifted athlete in baseball, football, basketball, and track, he continued to enjoy notoriety and visibility. Dick even gave amateur boxing a brief whirl.

Signed into the Brooklyn Dodger organization as a teenager, Williams had advanced through the Double-A level before his 1950 military induction during the Korean conflict. However, an ankle injury suffered a few years earlier in a junior college football game led to Dick's early dismissal from the army. Still Dodger property, he was immediately assigned to the Brooklyn roster at midseason of 1951. At that time a baseball "wartime waiver" rule stated, basically, that returning military personnel were to be placed on the team's active rolls, even if it meant increasing the roster size beyond 25. Otherwise, the player could be available to other teams via the waiver wire. With Williams now on board, Brooklyn had a 26-man team. He played in only 23 games, but his manager, Chuck Dressen, found Williams to be a valuable dugout ally. Dressen, a man who also had a strong competitive nature, encouraged Williams to be a bench jockey. According to Dressen, and to the opposing teams whom Williams irritated, he was a success at it.

He served most of his career as a utility player after a severe shoulder injury relegated him to part-time duty. Nevertheless, his ability and grit extended his career to 13 major league seasons. In just over 1,000 games Williams compiled a .260 lifetime batting average. It included 70 home runs (with a high of 16 for the 1959 Kansas City A's) , and featured time almost equally divided between the infield and outfield for the Dodgers, the Baltimore Orioles twice, Cleveland, the Athletics, and finally the Red Sox for 79 games in 1963 and 61 appearances in 1964. In World Series play Williams went 1-for-2 as a Dodger pinch hitter against New York in 1953. When his active career was ending, Dick told Red Sox officials of his penchant for managing, and in 1965 he was invited to manage the team's top farm club, Toronto, of the International League.

Two springs later he was in charge of the Red Sox, who were coming off a disastrous year in which they finished 26 games out of first place, and just a half game atop the basement. By early October 1967 the "Incredible Dream" had come true for Boston fans, and Williams was extolled as a regional hero. However, one of Dick's first decisions at Boston helped to jeopardize his long-range employment at Fenway Park. Red Sox icon Carl Yastrzemski had earlier been the Boston captain; Williams decided to eliminate the team's on-field captaincy. Yaz seemed less disappointed than the team's owner, the popular Tom Yawkey, who acknowledged a distrust and dislike for Williams thereafter. Yaz was a Yawkey favorite. However, after Yaz produced a triple-crown season in 1967, and Williams directed the club to the pennant, Yawkey retained his manager until the waning days of the 1969 season, when, with the team standing third in American League East, coach Eddie Popowski was asked to manage the Sox for the final nine games (Popowski's first of two interim terms).

Williams did not manage in 1970, the only year between his first season with Boston and his last piloting assignment (Seattle, 1988) that he wasn't heading a team. Instead, he served as a coach under Gene Mauch at Montreal and, according to Williams, refined his skills and learned a great deal more about managing under the equally intense Mauch.

Intensity was a Dick Williams trademark, and it led to disagreements with his players and with his management. He believed that hard work and concentration on baseball were primary ingredients of success. As a carryover from his days as Dressen's Brooklyn bench jockey, Dick tried to convince his players that relentless sarcasm and needling was a good way to show opponents how badly you wanted to beat them. One of Williams's former players, recalling the stress he felt under the intense pilot, said, "Dick Williams is the best manager I've ever played for, but as soon as he gets out of baseball I'm going to run him over with my car." At nearly all of his six managing stops—Boston, Oakland, California, Montreal, San Diego, Seattle—players eventually rebelled against him. One exception was Oakland, where owner Finley was the chief target of players' anger. The Athletics, who were notorious for scuffling among themselves while winning those world titles in the early 1970s, felt Finley was a cheapskate and a meddler. This was one time when the players looked upon Williams as their ally instead of their foe. Finley was the enemy. It was "Williams and us against him!"

Williams, weary of Finley's all-hours phone calls and lineup tampering, resigned after Oakland's second straight championship in 1973. Actually, he had expected to be named New York Yankees manager for the following season, but Finley would not agree to releasing Dick from his contractual obligations, which had another year to run. The failed opportunity to manage New York was a great disappointment to Williams. However, in mid-1974, after the Yankees had already hired Bill Virdon when Williams became unavailable, Finley consented to permit the California Angels to sign Williams. The Anaheim experience was a disaster for Dick. The roster was talent thin. For that second half of 1974, all of the following season, then to midway through 1976 before his departure, Williams's Angels never ranked in the first division. Everywhere else along Dick Williams's his 21-year managing tour, teams—with the exception of the final stop, Seattle—all posted at least one finish that was second place or better.

At Montreal (1977 through most of the 1981 season) the Expos finished second twice under Williams. The 1981 team won the East Division play-offs in the strike-aborted season, but Williams was gone at the end when general manager Jim Fanning stepped in for the final 27 regular-season games. By then Williams had become disenchanted with the attitudes of many players, and he was devastated by the substance abuse problem that infected several teams. The game seemed to lose its charm for him; players' egos became offensive to him; the Williams style of intimidation and pressure were no longer effective, he believed.

Williams assumed that his managing career was over after Montreal, but when San Diego beckoned during the next off-season, he signed on to manage the Padres. He directed the club for four full seasons, its most successful run up to then. The 1984 National League championship highlighted his tenure there. After departing following the 1985 campaign, the fourth straight year the Padres finished at .500 or better, Williams was off to Seattle for his final major league managing assignment. There, Williams and team owner George Argyros battled over expenditures required to improve talent, and Dick Williams, with his team in sixth place in mid-June of 1988, left a major league dugout for the final time. His 11 first-division finishes, four pennants, one other division title (Oakland 1971), and his teams' traditional characteristic of fundamental soundness earn Dick Williams distinctive notoriety among this century's major league managers.

Career Summaries

Bill McKechnie. Manager, 24 seasons; four National League pennants (Pittsburgh 1925, St. Louis 1928, Cincinnati 1939–40); World Series winner 1925, 1940; 524 overall winning percentage; first division 14 times; also managed Boston Braves, 1930–37, finishing at .500 or better four times; 1,842 total wins.

Dick Williams. Manager, 21 seasons; three American League pennants (Boston 1967, Oakland 1972–73) ; one National League pennant (San Diego 1984); World Series winner 1972, 1973; .520 overall winning percentage; first division 11 times; also managed California, Montreal, Seattle Mariners; 1,571 total wins.

MANAGING MORE THAN ONE FRANCHISE to a League Championship	
3 Teams	
Bill McKechnie	Pittsburg 1925
	St. Louis NL 1928
	Cincinnati 1931
Dick Williams	Boston AL 1967
	Oakland 1972, '73
	San Diego 1984
2 Teams	
Sparky Anderson	Cincinnati 1970, '72, '75, '76
	Detroit 1984
Yogi Berra	New York AL 1964
	New York NL 1973
Joe Cronin	Washington 1933
	Boston AL 1946
Alvin Dark	San Francisco 1962
	Oakland 1974
Leo Durocher	Brooklyn 1941
	New York NL 1951, '54
Bucky Harris	Washington 1924, '25
	New York AL 1947
Al Lopez	Cleveland 1954
	Chicago AL 1959
Joe McCarthy	Chicago NL 1929
	New York AL 1932, '36, '37, '38,
	'39, '41, '42, '43
Pat Moran	Philadelphia NL 1915
	Cincinnati 1919
Billy Southworth	St. Louis NL 1942, '43, '44
	Boston NL 1948

Pennants, Playoffs, and World Series

The Misters October

Here's a good baseball question for your next barroom or lunch table trivia session: Who has managed the most postseason games?

If a rapid response is forthcoming, it is apt to be Casey Stengel, who directed his Yankees to 10 World Series. Or perhaps Joe McCarthy or John Mc-Graw, with nine Series apiece. Maybe Connie Mack, whose Philadelphia Athletics appeared in eight World Series. (Mack's A's actually won nine American League pennants, but the first of them was in 1902, which was one year before the Series was established.)

All of these are good top-of-the head answers. But all would be incorrect.

Bobby Cox, the most successful of the 1990s managers, has directed his troops in 88 postseason games—seven in 1985 when his Toronto Blue Jays lost the American League Championship Series to Kansas City, and the remaining 81 at Atlanta since 1991. Stengel's 63 World Series games, then the Dodgers' Tom Lasorda, whose combined LCS and Series games totalled 61, are next in line after Cox's 79 October contests through the 1998 season.

Until 1969, of course, league champions moved directly into the World Series, which offered a maximum of seven games (not counting ties to be replayed or the 1903, 1919, 1920, and 1921 seasons when the Series was best-of-nine combat—although none of those matches went the full nine-game distance). However, since 1969 when the LCS was instituted, and then since 1995 when an additional round of games, which includes a wild-card entry, has been part of baseball's format, more managers qualify for postseason play. Cox and Lasorda, whose four World Series appearances each have been far fewer than Stengel's, McCarthy's, McGraw's, and Mack's, nevertheless have earned well-deserved positions within the upper echelon of this century's managers by guiding their teams to multiple division titles and on to frequent league championships after that.

Even with the expanded postseason now, and the greater opportunity for managers to enter it, only 102 of the 421 managers since 1901 have been there. (A 103rd would have been Clark Griffith of 1901 American League champ Chicago, had there been a World Series at the time. Other 1901, 1902, and 1904 winners Fred Clarke, John McGraw, Jimmy Collins, and Connie Mack did lead teams to the Series at one time or another.) Of the 102, only 27 pilots have been involved in 20 or more postseason games. Minnesota's Tom Kelly has a special place among them. Of all the men who have skippered teams to four or more October series—World Series and/or LCS—Kelly is the only one never to have lost a series. His Twins won the ALCS over Detroit (1987) and Toronto (1991), then were seven-game World Series victors against St. Louis and Atlanta.

Among the managers whose teams advanced to the World Series most frequently, McCarthy's brilliant record of seven championships in nine tries stands out. On the other hand, the innovative and highly-lauded McGraw was a Series loser in six of his nine appearances.

Of all managers who directed postseason teams, here are the top pilots in several important categories (The "most LCS" categories include LCS starting in 1969, LCS first-round/wild-card format since 1995, and the 1981 split-season play-offs between that season's first-half and second-half winners.):

Most Games. Bobby Cox 88; Casey Stengel 63; Tom Lasorda 61; John McGraw 56; Sparky Anderson 55.

Most Games Won. Cox 48; Stengel 37; Anderson 34; Lasorda 31; Joe McCarthy 30.

Most World Series (and w-l record). Stengel 10 (7–3); McCarthy 9 (7–2); McGraw 9 (3–6); Connie Mack 8 (5–3); Walter Alston 7 (4–3).

Most World Series Games Won. Stengel 37; McCarthy 30; McGraw 26; Mack 24; Alston 20.

Most LCS (and w-l record). Cox 12 (8–4); Davey Johnson 8 (4–4); Lasorda 8 (5–3); Anderson 7 (5–2); Mike Hargrove 7 (5–2); Tony LaRussa 7 (4–3); Whitey Herzog 6 (3–3); Billy Martin 6 (3–3); Earl Weaver 6 (4–2).

Most LCS games won. Cox 37; LaRussa 21; Hargrove 20; Johnson 19; Lasorda 19; Anderson 18; Herzog 16; Joe Torre 16.

World Series Managers

When fourth-year manager Bruce Bochy directed the San Diego Padres into the 1998 World Series against the Yankees, he became the 84th manager to appear in the Fall Classics that were first staged when American League champion Boston, under Jimmy Collins, faced Fred Clarke's Pittsburgh Pirates way back in 1903.

Of the elite 84 men piloting the 188 Series entries in 94 Octobers, the New York Yankees' Joe Torre, in 1996, was only the seventh to face off against a team he had previously managed. His Yankees, in Joe's first year in the Bronx, defeated Atlanta, whom he had managed from 1982 to 1984. Torre had also directed the Cardinals (1990–95) and the Mets (1978–81, where he was player-manager briefly) in earlier assignments.

The only other managers who at one time ran what turned out to be their eventual World Series opponents were John McGraw, Miller Huggins, Joe McCarthy, Casey Stengel, Whitey Herzog, and Bobby Cox.

John McGraw. His New York Giants of 1921, 1922, and 1923 met the New York Yankees in World Series competition. McGraw had managed the Yankees' franchise in its earliest days when it was located in Baltimore as the American League's original Orioles before transferring to New York for the 1903 season.

Miller Huggins. His 1926 and 1928 New York Yankees split those two series with St. Louis, which Huggins directed from 1913 through 1917.

Joe McCarthy. He led the Yankees to eight World Series. Two of them—1932 and 1938—were against the Chicago Cubs, a club McCarthy took to the 1929 National League pennant. Of the seven men on this list, he is the only one to have managed an October opponent in a previous World Series.

Casey Stengel. As Yankee skipper, he was the only man apart from McGraw to capture 10 league championships. Previously Casey had managed the Brooklyn Dodgers and Boston Braves. At New York he faced Brooklyn in five Series—1949, 1952, 1953, 1955 and 1956—and opposed the Braves, by then transplanted to Milwaukee, in 1957 and 1958.

Text continues on page 292

Manager	Year–Team	Games W	L	%	Opponent
Walter Alston					
World Series	1955 Brooklyn NL	4	3	.571	New York
(4–3)	1956 Brooklyn NL	3	4	.429	New York
	1959 Los Angeles NL	4	2	.667	Chicago
	1963 Los Angeles NL	4	0	1.000	New York
	1965 Los Angeles NL	4	3	.571	Minnesota
	1966 Los Angeles NL	0	4	.000	Baltimore
	1974 Los Angeles NL	<u>1</u>	<u>4</u>	<u>.200</u>	Oakland
		20	20	.500	
LCS	1974 Los Angeles NLW	3	1	.750	Pittsburgh
(1–0)					
Total Postseason Games (44)		23	21	.523	
Sparky Anderson					
World Series	1970 Cincinnati NL	1	4	.200	Baltimore
(3–2)	1972 Cincinnati NL	3	4	.429	Oakland
	1975 Cincinnati NL	4	3	.571	Boston
	1976 Cincinnati NL	4	0	1.000	New York
	1984 Detroit AL	<u>4</u>	<u>1</u>	<u>.800</u>	San Diego
		16	12	.571	
LCS	1970 Cincinnati NLW	3	0	1.000	Pittsburgh
(5–2)	1972 Cincinnati NLW	3	2	.600	Pittsburgh
	1973 Cincinnati NLW	2	3	.400	New York
	1975 Cincinnati NLW	3	0	1.000	Pittsburgh
	1976 Cincinnati NLW	3	0	1.000	Philadelphia
	1984 Detroit ALE	3	0	1.000	Kansas City
	1987 Detroit ALE	<u>1</u>	<u>4</u>	<u>.200</u>	Minnesota
		18	9	.667	
Total Postseason Games (55)		34	21	.618	
Del Baker					
World Series	1940 Detroit AL	3	4	.429	Cincinnati
(0–1)					
Total Postseason Games (7)		3	4	.429	

Continued

Manager	Year—Team	Games W	L	%	Opponent
Dusty Baker					
LC 1st Round (0–1)	1997 San Francisco NLW	0	3	.000	Florida
Total Postseason Games (3)		0	3	.000	
Ed Barrow					
World Series (1–0)	1918 Boston AL	4	2	.667	Chicago
Total Postseason Games (6)		4	2	.667	
Hank Bauer					
World Series (1–0)	1966 Baltimore AL	4	0	1.000	Los Angeles
Total Postseason Games (4)		4	0	1.000	
Don Baylor					
LC 1st Round (0–1)	1995 Colorado NLW	1	3	.250	Atlanta
Total Postseason Games (4)		1	3	.250	
Yogi Berra					
World Series (0–2)	1964 New York AL	3	4	.429	St. Louis
	1973 New York NL	3	4	.429	Oakland
		6	8	.429	
LCS (1–0)	1973 New York NL	3	2	.600	Cincinnati
Total Postseason Games (19)		9	10	.474	
Bruce Bochy					
World Series (0–1)	1998 San Diego NL	0	4	.000	New York
LCS (1–0)	1998 San Diego NLW	4	2	.667	Atlanta
LC 1st round (1–1)	1996 San Diego NLW	0	3	.000	St. Louis
	1998 San Diego NLW	3	1	.750	Houston
		3	4	.429	
Total Postseason Games (17)		7	10	.412	

Continued

Manager	Year–Team	Games W	L	%	Opponent
Lou Boudreau					
World Series (1–0)	1948 Cleveland AL	4	2	.667	Boston
Total Postseason Games (6)		4	2	.667	
Donie Bush					
World Series (0–1)	1927 Pittsburgh NL	0	4	.000	New York
Total Postseason Games (4)		0	4	.000	
Bill Carrigan					
World Series (2–0)	1915 Boston AL	4	1	.800	Philadelphia
	1916 Boston AL	4	1	.800	Brooklyn
		8	2	.800	
Total Postseason Games (10)		8	2	.800	
Frank Chance					
World Series (2–2)	1906 Chicago NL	2	4	.333	Chicago
	1907 Chicago NL	4	0	1.000	Detroit
	1908 Chicago NL	4	1	.800	Detroit
	1910 Chicago NL	1	4	.200	Philadelphia
		11	9	.550	
Total Postseason Games (21)*		11	9	.550	
*Includes one tie game in 1907 World Series					
Fred Clarke					
World Series (1–1)	1903 Pittsburgh NL	3	5	.375	Boston
	1909 Pittsburgh NL	4	3	.571	Detroit
		7	8	.467	
Total Postseason Games (15)		7	8	.467	

Continued

Manager	Year–Team	Games W	L	%	Opponent
Mickey Cochrane					
World Series	1934 Detroit AL	3	4	.429	St. Louis
(1–1)	1935 Detroit AL	4	2	.667	Chicago
		7	6	.579	
Total Postseason Games (13)		7	6	.579	
Jimmy Collins					
World Series	1903 Boston AL	5	3	.625	Pittsburgh
(1–0)					
Total Postseason Games (8)		5	3	.625	
Bobby Cox					
World Series	1991 Atlanta NL	3	4	.429	Minnesota
(1–3)	1992 Atlanta NL	2	4	.333	Toronto
	1995 Atlanta NL	4	2	.667	Cleveland
	1996 Atlanta NL	2	4	.333	New York
		11	14	.440	
LCS	1985 Toronto ALE	3	4	.429	Kansas City
(4–4)	1991 Atlanta NLW	4	3	.571	Pittsburgh
	1992 Atlanta NLW	4	3	.571	Pittsburgh
	1993 Atlanta NLW	2	4	.333	Philadelphia
	1995 Atlanta NLE	4	0	1.000	Cincinnati
	1996 Atlanta NLE	4	3	.571	St. Louis
	1997 Atlanta NLE	2	4	.333	Florida
	1998 Atlanta NLE	2	4	.333	San Diego
		25	25	.500	
LC 1st Round					
(4–0)	1995 Atlanta NLE	3	1	.750	Colorado
	1996 Atlanta NLE	3	0	1.000	Los Angeles
	1997 Atlanta NLE	3	0	1.000	Houston
	1998 Atlanta NLE	3	0	1.000	Chicago
		12	1	.923	
Total Postseason Games (88)		48	40	.545	

Continued

Manager	Year–Team	Games W	L	%	Opponent
Roger Craig					
World Series (0–1)	1989 San Francisco NL	0	4	.000	Oakland
LCS (1–1)	1987 San Francisco NLW	3	4	.429	St. Louis
	1989 San Francisco NLW	4	1	.800	Chicago
		7	5		
Total Postseason Games (16)		7	9	.438	
Joe Cronin					
World Series (0–2)	1933 Washington AL	1	4	.200	New York
	1946 Boston AL	3	4	.429	St. Louis
		4	8	.333	
Total Postseason Games (12)		4	8	.333	
Alvin Dark					
World Series (1–1)	1962 San Francisco NL	3	4	.429	New York
	1974 Oakland AL	4	1	.800	Los Angeles
		7	5	.583	
LCS (1–1)	1974 Oakland ALW	3	1	.750	Baltimore
	1975 Oakland ALW	0	3	.000	Boston
		3	4	.429	
Total Postseason Games (19)		10	9	.526	
Larry Dierker					
LC 1st Round (0–2)	1997 Houston NLC	0	3	.000	Atlanta
	1998 Houston NLC	1	3	.250	San Diego
Total Postseason Games (3)		1	6	.143	
Chuck Dressen					
World Series (0–2)	1952 Brooklyn NL	3	4	.429	New York
	1953 Brooklyn NL	2	4	.333	New York
		5	8	.385	
Total Postseason Games (13)		5	8	.385	

Continued

Manager	Year–Team	Games W	L	%	Opponent
Leo Durocher					
World Series	1941 Brooklyn NL	1	4	.200	New York
(1–2)	1951 New York NL	2	4	.333	New York
	1954 New York NL	<u>4</u>	<u>0</u>	<u>1.000</u>	Cleveland
		7	8	.467	
Total Postseason Games (15)		7	8	.467	
Eddie Dyer					
World Series	1946 St. Louis NL	4	3	.571	Boston
(1–0)					
Total Postseason Games (7)		4	3	.571	
Jim Fanning					
LCS	1981 Montreal NLE	2	3	.400	Los Angeles
(0–1)					
Div. Playoff	1981 Montreal NLE	3	2	.600	Philadelphia
(1–0)					
Total Postseason Games (10)		5	5	.500	
Charlie Fox					
LCS	1971 San Francisco	1	3	.250	Pittsburgh
(0–1)	NLW				
Total Postseason Games (4)		1	3	.250	
Jim Fregosi					
World Series	1993 Philadelphia NL	2	4	.333	Toronto
(0–1)					
LCS	1979 California ALW	1	3	.250	Baltimore
(1–1)	1993 Philadelphia NLE	<u>4</u>	<u>2</u>	<u>.667</u>	Atlanta
		5	5	.500	
Total Postseason Games (16)		7	9	.438	

Continued

Manager	Year–Team	Games W	L	%	Opponent
Jim Frey					
World Series (0–1)	1980 Kansas City AL	2	4	.333	Philadelphia
LCS (1–1)	1980 Kansas City ALW	3	0	1.000	New York
	1984 Chicago NLE	2	3	.400	San Diego
		5	3	.625	
Total Postseason Games (14)		7	7	.500	
Frank Frisch					
World Series (1–0)	1934 St. Louis NL	4	3	.571	Detroit
Total Postseason Games (7)		4	3	.571	
Cito Gaston					
World Series (2–0)	1992 Toronto AL	4	2	.667	Atlanta
	1993 Toronto AL	4	2	.667	Philadelphia
		8	4	.667	
LCS (2–2)	1989 Toronto ALE	1	4	.200	Oakland
	1991 Toronto ALE	1	4	.200	Minnesota
	1992 Toronto ALE	4	2	.667	Oakland
	1993 Toronto ALE	4	2	.667	Chicago
Total Postseason Games (34)		18	16	.529	
Kid Gleason					
World Series (0–1)	1919 Chicago AL	3	5	.375	Cincinnati
Total Postseason Games (8)		3	5	.375	
Dallas Green					
World Series (1–0)	1980 Philadelphia NL	4	2	.667	Kansas City
LCS (1–0)	1980 Philadelphia NLE	3	2	.600	Houston
Div. Playoff (0–1)	1981 Philadelphia NLE	2	3	.400	Montreal
Total Postseason Games (16)		9	7	.563	

Continued

Manager	Year–Team	Games W	L	%	Opponent
Charlie Grimm					
World Series	1932 Chicago NL	0	4	.000	New York
(0–3)	1935 Chicago NL	2	4	.333	Detroit
	1945 Chicago NL	<u>3</u>	<u>4</u>	<u>.429</u>	Detroit
		5	12	.294	
Total Postseason Games (17)		5	12	.294	
Fred Haney					
World Series	1957 Milwaukee NL	4	3	.571	New York
(1–1)	1958 Milwaukee NL	<u>3</u>	<u>4</u>	<u>.429</u>	New York
		7	7	.500	
Total Postseason Games (14)		7	7	.500	
Mike Hargrove					
World Series	1995 Cleveland AL	2	4	.333	Atlanta
(0–2)	1997 Cleveland AL	<u>3</u>	<u>4</u>	<u>.429</u>	Florida
		5	8	.385	
LCS	1995 Cleveland ALC	4	2	.667	Seattle
(2–1)	1997 Cleveland ALC	4	2	.667	Baltimore
	1998 Cleveland ALC	<u>2</u>	<u>4</u>	<u>.556</u>	New York
		10	8	.556	
LC 1st Round	1995 Cleveland ALC	3	0	1.000	Boston
(3–1)	1996 Cleveland ALC	1	3	.250	Baltimore
	1997 Cleveland ALC	3	2	.600	New York
	1998 Cleveland ALC	<u>3</u>	<u>1</u>	<u>.750</u>	Boston
		10	6	.625	
Total Postseason Games (47)		25	22	.532	
Bucky Harris					
World Series	1924 Washington AL	4	3	.571	New York
(2–1)	1925 Washington AL	3	4	.429	Pittsburgh
	1947 New York AL	<u>4</u>	<u>3</u>	<u>.571</u>	Brooklyn
		11	10	.524	
Total Postseason Games (21)		11	10	.524	

Continued

Manager	Year–Team	Games W	L	%	Opponent
Lum Harris					
LCS	1969 Atlanta NLW	0	3	.000	New York
(0–1)					
Total Postseason Games (3)		0	3	.000	
Gabby Hartnett					
World Series	1938 Chicago NL	0	4	.000	New York
(0–1)					
Total Postseason Games (4)		0	4	.000	
Whitey Herzog					
World Series	1982 St. Louis NL	4	3	.571	Milwaukee
(1–2)	1985 St. Louis NL	3	4	.429	Kansas City
	1987 St. Louis NL	3	4	.429	Minnesota
		10	11	.476	
LCS	1976 Kansas City ALW	2	3	.400	New York
(3–3)	1977 Kansas City ALW	2	3	.400	New York
	1978 Kansas City ALW	1	3	.250	New York
	1982 St. Louis NLE	3	0	1.000	Atlanta
	1985 St. Louis NLE	4	2	.667	Los Angeles
	1987 St. Louis NLE	4	3	.571	San Francisco
		16	14	.533	
Total Postseason Games (51)		26	25	.510	
Gil Hodges					
World Series	1969 New York NL	4	1	.800	Baltimore
(1–0)					
LCS	1969 New York NLE	3	0	1.000	Atlanta
(1–0)					
Total Postseason Games (8)		7	1	.876	
Rogers Hornsby					
World Series	1926 St. Louis NL	4	3	.571	New York
(1–0)					
Total Postseason Games (7)		4	3	.571	

Continued

Manager	Year—Team	Games W	L	%	Opponent
Ralph Houk					
World Series	1961 New York AL	4	1	.800	Cincinnati
(2–1)	1962 New York AL	4	3	.571	San Francisco
	1963 New York AL	<u>0</u>	<u>4</u>	<u>.000</u>	Los Angeles
		8	8	.500	
Total Postseason Games (16)		8	8	.500	
Dick Howser					
World Series	1985 Kansas City AL	4	3	.571	St. Louis
(1–0)					
LCS	1980 New York ALE	0	3	.000	Kansas City
(1–2)	1984 Kansas City ALW	0	3	.000	Detroit
	1985 Kansas City ALW	<u>4</u>	<u>3</u>	<u>.571</u>	Toronto
		4	9	.308	
Div. Playoff	1981 Kansas City ALW	0	3	.000	Oakland
(0–1)					
Total Postseason Games (23)		8	15	.348	
Miller Huggins					
World Series	1921 New York AL	3	5	.375	New York
(3–3)	1922 New York AL	0	4	.000	New York
	1923 New York AL	4	2	.667	New York
	1926 New York AL	3	4	.429	St. Louis
	1927 New York AL	4	0	1.000	Pittsburgh
	1928 New York AL	<u>4</u>	<u>0</u>	<u>1.000</u>	St. Louis
		18	15	.545	
Total Postseason Games (34)*		18	15	.545	
*Includes one tie game in 1922 World Series					
Fred Hutchinson					
World Series	1961 Cincinnati NL	1	4	.200	New York
(0–1)					
Total Postseason Games (5)		1	4	.200	

Continued

Manager	Year–Team	Games W	L	%	Opponent
Hughie Jennings					
World Series	1907 Detroit AL	0	4	.000	Chicago
(0–3)	1908 Detroit AL	1	4	.200	Chicago
	1909 Detroit AL	<u>3</u>	<u>4</u>	<u>.429</u>	Pittsburgh
		4	12	.250	
Total Postseason Games (17)*		4	12	.250	
*Includes one tie game in 1907 World Series					
Darrell Johnson					
World Series	1975 Boston AL	3	4	.429	Cincinnati
(0–1)					
LCS	1975 Boston ALE	3	0	1.000	Oakland
(1–0)					
Total Postseason Games (10)		6	4	.600	
Davey Johnson					
World Series	1986 New York NL	4	3	.571	Boston
(1–0)					
LCS	1986 New York NLE	4	2	.667	Houston
(1–4)	1988 New York NLE	3	4	.429	Los Angeles
	1995 Cincinnati NLC	0	4	.000	Atlanta
	1996 Baltimore ALE	1	4	.200	New York
	1997 Baltimore ALE	<u>2</u>	<u>4</u>	<u>.333</u>	Cleveland
		10	18	.357	
LC 1st Round	1995 Cincinnati NLC	3	0	1.000	Los Angeles
(3–0)	1996 Baltimore ALE	3	1	.750	Cleveland
	1997 Baltimore ALE	<u>3</u>	<u>1</u>	<u>1.000</u>	Seattle
		9	2	.818	
Total Postseason Games (46)		23	23	.500	
Fielder Jones					
World Series	1906 Chicago AL	4	2	.667	Chicago
(1–0)					
Total Postseason Games (6)		4	2	.667	

Continued

Manager	Year–Team	Games W	L	%	Opponent
Johnny Keane					
World Series (1–0)	1964 St. Louis NL	4	3	.571	New York
Total Postseason Games (7)		4	3	.571	
Tom Kelly					
World Series (2–0)	1987 Minnesota AL	4	3	.571	St. Louis
	1991 Minnesota AL	4	3	.571	Atlanta
		8	6	.571	
LCS (2–0)	1987 Minnesota ALW	4	1	.800	Detroit
	1991 Minnesota ALW	4	1	.800	Toronto
		8	2	.800	
Total Postseason Games (24)		16	8	.667	
Kevin Kennedy					
LC 1st Round (0–1)	1995 Boston AL	0	3	.000	Cleveland
Total Postseason Games (3)		0	3	.000	
Harvey Kuenn					
World Series (0–1)	1982 Milwaukee AL	3	4	.429	St. Louis
LCS	1982 Milwaukee ALE	3	2	.600	California
Total Postseason Games (12)		6	6	.500	
Gene Lamont					
LCS (0–1)	1993 Chicago ALW	2	4	.333	Toronto
Total Postseason Games (6)		2	4	.333	
Hal Lanier					
LCS (0–1)	1986 Houston NLW	2	4	.333	New York
Total Postseason Games (6)		2	4	.333	

Continued

Manager	Year–Team	Games W	L	%	Opponent
Tony LaRussa					
World Series	1988 Oakland AL	1	4	.200	Los Angeles
(1–2)	1989 Oakland AL	4	0	1.000	San Francisco
	1990 Oakland AL	<u>0</u>	<u>4</u>	<u>.000</u>	Cincinnati
		5	8	.385	
LCS	1983 Chicago ALW	1	3	.250	Baltimore
(3–3)	1988 Oakland ALW	4	0	1.000	Boston
	1989 Oakland ALW	4	1	.800	Toronto
	1990 Oakland ALW	4	0	1.000	Boston
	1992 Oakland ALW	2	4	.333	Toronto
	1996 St. Louis NLC	<u>3</u>	<u>4</u>	<u>.429</u>	Atlanta
		18	12	.600	
LC 1st Round	1996 St. Louis NLC	3	0	1.000	San Diego
Total Postseason Games (46)		26	20	.565	
Tom Lasorda					
World Series	1977 Los Angeles NL	2	4	.333	New York
(2–2)	1978 Los Angeles NL	2	4	.333	New York
	1981 Los Angeles NL	4	2	.667	New York
	1988 Los Angeles NL	<u>4</u>	<u>1</u>	<u>.800</u>	Oakland
		12	11	.522	
LCS	1977 Los Angeles NLW	3	1	.750	Philadelphia
(4–2)	1978 Los Angeles NLW	3	1	.750	Philadelphia
	1981 Los Angeles NLW	3	2	.600	Montreal
	1983 Los Angeles NLW	1	3	.250	Philadelphia
	1985 Los Angeles NLW	2	4	.333	St. Louis
	1988 Los Angeles NLW	<u>4</u>	<u>3</u>	<u>.571</u>	New York
		16	14	.533	
LC 1st Round	1995 Los Angeles NLW	0	3	.000	Cincinnati
Div. Playoff	1981 Los Angeles NLW	3	2	.600	Houston
Total Postseason Games (61)		31	30	.508	

Continued

Manager	Year–Team	Games W	L	%	Opponent
Bob Lemon					
World Series	1978 New York AL	4	2	.667	Los Angeles
(1–1)	1981 New York AL	2	4	.333	Los Angeles
		6	6	.500	
LCS	1978 New York ALE	3	1	.750	Kansas City
(2–0)	1981 New York ALE	3	0	1.000	Oakland
		6	1	.857	
Div. Playoff	1981 New York ALE	3	2	.600	Milwaukee
Total Postseason Games (24)		15	9	.625	
Jim Leyland					
World Series	1997 Florida NL	4	3	.571	Cleveland
(1–0)					
LCS	1990 Pittsburgh NLE	2	4	.333	Cincinnati
(1–3)	1991 Pittsburgh NLE	3	4	.429	Atlanta
	1992 Pittsburgh NLE	3	4	.429	Atlanta
	1997 Florida NLE (WC)	4	2	.667	Atlanta
		12	14	.462	
LC 1st Round	1997 Florida	3	0	1.000	San Francisco
(1–0)					
Total Postseason Games (36)		19	17	.528	
Al Lopez					
World Series	1954 Cleveland AL	0	4	.000	New York
(0–2)	1959 Chicago AL	2	4	.333	Los Angeles
		2	8	.200	
Total Postseason Games (10)		2	8	.200	
Connie Mack					
World Series	1905 Philadelphia AL	1	4	.200	New York
(5–3)	1910 Philadelphia AL	4	1	.800	Chicago
	1911 Philadelphia AL	4	2	.667	New York
	1913 Philadelphia AL	4	1	.800	New York
	1914 Philadelphia AL	0	4	.000	Boston
	1929 Philadelphia AL	4	1	.800	Chicago
	1930 Philadelphia AL	4	2	.667	St. Louis
	1931 Philadelphia AL	3	4	.429	St. Louis
		24	19	.558	
Total Postseason Games (43)		24	19	.558	

Continued

Manager	Year–Team	Games W	L	%	Opponent
Billy Martin					
World Series					
(1–1)	1976 New York AL	0	4	.000	Cincinnati
	1977 New York AL	<u>4</u>	<u>2</u>	<u>.667</u>	Los Angeles
		4	6	.400	
LCS	1969 Minnesota ALW	0	3	.000	Baltimore
(2–3)	1972 Detroit ALE	2	3	.400	Oakland
	1976 New York ALE	3	2	.600	Kansas City
	1977 New York ALE	3	2	.600	Kansas City
	1981 Oakland ALW	<u>0</u>	<u>3</u>	<u>.000</u>	New York
		8	13	.381	
Div. Playoff	1981 Oakland ALW	3	0	1.000	Kansas City
(1–0)					
Total Postseason Games (34)		15	19	.441	
Gene Mauch					
LCS	1982 California ALW	2	3	.400	Milwaukee
(0–2)	1986 California ALW	<u>3</u>	<u>4</u>	<u>.429</u>	Boston
		5	7	.417	
Total Postseason Games (12)		5	7	.417	
Joe McCarthy					
World Series	1929 Chicago NL	1	4	.200	Philadelphia
(7–2)	1932 New York AL	4	0	1.000	Chicago
	1936 New York AL	4	2	.667	New York
	1937 New York AL	4	1	.800	New York
	1938 New York AL	4	0	1.000	Chicago
	1939 New York AL	4	0	1.000	Cincinnati
	1941 New York AL	4	1	.800	Brooklyn
	1942 New York AL	1	4	.200	St. Louis
	1943 New York AL	<u>4</u>	<u>1</u>	<u>.800</u>	St. Louis
		30	13	.698	
Total Postseason Games (43)		30	13	.698	

Continued

Manager	Year–Team	Games			Opponent
		W	L	%	
John McGraw					
World Series	1905 New York NL	4	1	.800	Philadelphia
(3–6)	1911 New York NL	2	4	.333	Philadelphia
	1912 New York NL	3	4	.429	Boston
	1913 New York NL	1	4	.200	Philadelphia
	1917 New York NL	2	4	.333	Chicago
	1921 New York NL	5	3	.625	New York
	1922 New York NL	4	0	1.000	New York
	1923 New York NL	2	4	.333	New York
	1924 New York NL	<u>3</u>	<u>4</u>	<u>.429</u>	Washington
		26	28	.481	
Total Postseason Games (56)*		26	28	.481	

*Includes one tie game in 1912 World Series and one tie game in 1922 World Series

Manager	Year–Team	Games			Opponent
Bill McKechnie					
World Series	1925 Pittsburgh NL	4	3	.571	Washington
(2–2)	1928 St. Louis NL	0	4	.000	New York
	1939 Cincinnati NL	0	4	.000	New York
	1940 Cincinnati NL	<u>4</u>	<u>3</u>	<u>.571</u>	Detroit
		8	14	.364	
Total Postseason Games (22)		8	14	.364	

Manager	Year–Team	Games			Opponent
John McNamara					
World Series	1986 Boston AL	3	4	.429	New York
(0–1)					
LCS	1979 Cincinnati NLW	0	3	.000	Pittsburgh
(1–1)	1986 Boston ALE	<u>4</u>	<u>3</u>	<u>.571</u>	California
		4	6	.400	
Total Postseason Games (17)		7	10	.412	

Manager	Year–Team	Games			Opponent
Sam Mele					
World Series	1965 Minnesota AL	3	4	.429	Los Angeles
(0–1)					
Total Postseason Games (7)		3	4	.429	

Continued

Manager	Year–Team	Games W	L	%	Opponent
Fred Mitchell					
World Series	1918 Chicago NL	2	4	.333	Boston
(0–1)					
Total Postseason Games (6)		2	4	.333	
Pat Moran					
World Series	1915 Philadelphia NL	1	4	.200	Boston
(1–1)	1919 Cincinnati NL	5	3	.625	Chicago
		6	7	.462	
Total Postseason Games (13)		6	7	.462	
Joe Morgan					
LCS	1988 Boston ALE	0	4	.000	Oakland
(0–2)	1990 Boston ALE	0	4	.000	Oakland
		0	8	.000	
Total Postseason Games (8)		0	8	.000	
Danny Murtaugh					
World Series	1960 Pittsburgh NL	4	3	.571	New York
(2–0)	1971 Pittsburgh NL	4	3	.571	Baltimore
		8	6	.571	
LCS	1970 Pittsburgh NLE	0	3	.000	Cincinnati
(1–3)	1971 Pittsburgh NLE	3	1	.750	Cincinnati
	1974 Pittsburgh NLE	1	3	.250	Los Angeles
	1975 Pittsburgh NLE	0	3	.000	Cincinnati
		4	10	.286	
Total Postseason Games (28)		12	16	.429	
Johnny Oates					
LC 1st Round	1996 Texas ALW	1	3	.250	New York
(0–2)	1998 Texas ALW	0	3	.000	New York
		1	6	.143	
Total Postseason Games (7)		1	6	.143	

Continued

Manager	Year–Team	Games W	L	%	Opponent
Steve O'Neill					
World Series (1–0)	1945 Detroit AL	4	3	.571	Chicago
Total Postseason Games (7)		4	3	.571	
Paul Owens					
World Series (0–1)	1983 Philadelphia NL	1	4	.200	Baltimore
LCS (1–0)	1983 Philadelphia NLE	3	1	.750	Los Angeles
Total Postseason Games (9)		4	5	.444	
Danny Ozark					
LCS	1976 Philadelphia NLE	0	3	.000	Cincinnati
(0–3)	1977 Philadelphia NLE	1	3	.250	Los Angeles
	1978 Philadelphia NLE	1	3	.250	Los Angeles
		2	9	.182	
Total Postseason Games (11)		2	9	.182	
Lou Piniella					
World Series (1–0)	1990 Cincinnati NL	4	0	1.000	Oakland
LCS	1990 Cincinnati NLW	4	2	.667	Pittsburgh
(1–1)	1995 Seattle ALW	2	4	.333	Cleveland
		6	6	.500	
LC 1st Round	1995 Seattle ALW	3	2	.600	New York
(1–1)	1997 Seattle ALW	1	3	.250	Baltimore
		4	5	.444	
Total Postseason Games (25)		14	11	.560	
Jim Riggleman					
LCS 1st round (0–3)	1998 Chicago NLC	0	3	.000	Atlanta
Total Postseason Games (3)		0	3	.000	

Continued

Manager	Year–Team	Games W	L	%	Opponent
Bill Rigney					
LCS	1970 Minnesota ALW	0	3	.000	Baltimore
(0–1)					
Total Postseason Games (3)		0	3	.000	
Wilbert Robinson					
World Series	1916 Brooklyn NL	1	4	.200	Boston
(0–2)	1920 Brooklyn NL	2	5	.286	Cleveland
		3	9	.250	
Total Postseason Games (12)		3	9	.250	
Buck Rodgers					
Div. Playoff	1981 Milwaukee ALE	2	3	.400	New York
(0–1)					
Total Postseason Games (5)		2	3	.400	
Pants Rowland					
World Series	1917 Chicago AL	4	2	.667	New York
(1–0)					
Total Postseason Games (6)		4	2	.667	
Bill Russell					
LC 1st Round	1996 Los Angeles NLW	0	3	.000	Atlanta
(0–1)					
Total Postseason Games (3)		0	3	.000	
Eddie Sawyer					
World Series	1950 Philadelphia NL	0	4	.000	New York
(0–1)					
Total Postseason Games (4)		0	4	.000	

Continued

Manager	Year–Team	Games W	L	%	Opponent
Red Schoendienst					
World Series	1967 St. Louis NL	4	3	.571	Boston
(1–1)	1968 St. Louis NL	3	4	.429	Detroit
		7	7	.500	
Total Postseason Games (14)		7	7	.500	
Luke Sewell					
World Series	1944 St. Louis AL	2	4	.333	St. Louis
(0–1)					
Total Postseason Games (6)		2	4	.333	
Burt Shotton					
World Series	1947 Brooklyn NL	3	4	.429	New York
(0–2)	1949 Brooklyn NL	1	4	.200	New York
		4	8	.333	
Total Postseason Games (12)		4	8	.333	
Buck Showalter					
LC 1st Round	1995 New York ALE	2	3	.400	Seattle
(0–1)					
Total Postseason Games (5)		2	3	.400	
Mayo Smith					
World Series	1968 Detroit AL	4	3	.571	St. Louis
(1–0)					
Total Postseason Games (7)		4	3	.571	
Billy Southworth					
World Series	1942 St. Louis NL	4	1	.800	New York
(2–2)	1943 St. Louis NL	1	4	.200	New York
	1944 St. Louis NL	4	2	.667	St. Louis
	1948 Boston NL	2	4	.333	Cleveland
		11	11	.500	
Total Postseason Games (22)		11	11	.500	

Continued

Manager	Year–Team	Games W	L	%	Opponent
Tris Speaker					
World Series (1–0)	1920 Cleveland AL	5	2	.714	Brooklyn
Total Postseason Games (7)		5	2	.714	
Jake Stahl					
World Series (1–0)	1912 Boston AL	4	3	.571	New York
Total Postseason Games (8)*		4	3	.571	
*Includes one tie game in 1912 World Series					
George Stallings					
World Series (1–0)	1914 Boston NL	4	0	1.000	Philadelphia
Total Postseason Games (4)		4	0	1.000	
Casey Stengel					
World Series (7–3)	1949 New York AL	4	1	.800	Brooklyn
	1950 New York AL	4	0	1.000	Philadelphia
	1951 New York AL	4	2	.667	New York
	1952 New York AL	4	3	.571	Brooklyn
	1953 New York AL	4	2	.667	Brooklyn
	1955 New York AL	3	4	.429	Brooklyn
	1956 New York AL	4	3	.571	Brooklyn
	1957 New York AL	3	4	.429	Milwaukee
	1958 New York AL	4	3	.571	Milwaukee
	1960 New York AL	<u>3</u>	<u>4</u>	<u>.429</u>	Pittsburgh
		37	26	.587	
Total Postseason Games (63)		37	26	.587	
Gabby Street					
World Series (1–1)	1930 St. Louis NL	2	4	.333	Philadelphia
	1931 St. Louis NL	<u>4</u>	<u>3</u>	<u>.571</u>	Philadelphia
		6	7	.462	
Total Postseason Games (13)		6	7	.462	

Continued

Manager	Year–Team	Games W	L	%	Opponent
Chuck Tanner					
World Series (1–0)	1979 Pittsburgh NL	4	3	.571	Baltimore
LCS (1–0)	1979 Pittsburgh NLE	3	0	1.000	Cincinnati
Total Postseason Games (10)		7	3	.700	
Bill Terry					
World Series (1–2)	1933 New York NL	4	1	.800	Washington
	1936 New York NL	2	4	.333	New York
	1937 New York NL	1	4	.200	New York
		7	9	.438	
Total Postseason Games (16)		7	9	.438	
Joe Torre					
World Series (2–0)	1996 New York AL	4	2	.667	Atlanta
	1998 New York AL	4	0	1.000	San Diego
		8	2	.800	
LCS (2–1)	1982 Atlanta NLW	0	3	.000	St. Louis
	1996 New York ALE	4	1	.800	Baltimore
	1998 New York ALE	4	2	.667	Cleveland
		8	6	.571	
LC 1st Round (2–1)	1996 New York ALE	3	1	.750	Texas
	1997 New York ALE	2	3	.400	Cleveland
	1998 New York ALE	3	0	1.000	Texas
		8	4	.667	
Total Postseason Games (36)		24	12	.667	
Bill Virdon					
LCS (0–2)	1972 Pittsburgh NLE	2	3	.400	Cincinnati
	1980 Houston NLW	2	3	.400	Philadelphia
		4	6	.400	
Div. Playoff (0–1)	1981 Houston NLW	2	3	.400	Los Angeles
Total Postseason Games (15)		6	9	.400	

Continued

Manager	Year–Team	Games W	L	%	Opponent
Earl Weaver					
World Series	1969 Baltimore AL	1	4	.200	New York
(1–3)	1970 Baltimore AL	4	1	.800	Cincinnati
	1971 Baltimore AL	3	4	.429	Pittsburgh
	1979 Baltimore AL	3	4	.429	Pittsburgh
		11	13	.458	
LCS	1969 Baltimore ALE	3	0	1.000	Minnesota
(4–2)	1970 Baltimore ALE	3	0	1.000	Minnesota
	1971 Baltimore ALE	3	0	1.000	Oakland
	1973 Baltimore ALE	2	3	.400	Oakland
	1974 Baltimore ALE	1	3	.250	Oakland
	1979 Baltimore ALE	3	1	.750	California
		15	7	.682	
Total Postseason Games (46)		26	20	.565	
Dick Williams					
World Series	1967 Boston AL	3	4	.429	St. Louis
(2–2)	1972 Oakland AL	4	3	.571	Cincinnati
	1973 Oakland AL	4	3	.571	New York
	1984 San Diego NL	1	4	.200	Detroit
		12	14	.462	
LCS	1971 Oakland ALW	0	3	.000	Baltimore
(3–1)	1972 Oakland ALW	3	2	.600	Detroit
	1973 Oakland ALW	3	2	.600	Baltimore
	1984 San Diego NLW	3	2	.600	Chicago
		9	9	.500	
Total Postseason Games (44)		21	23	.477	
Jimmy Williams					
LCS 1st Round	1998 Boston ALE	1	3	.250	Cleveland
Total Postseason Games (4)		1	3	.250	
Don Zimmer					
LCS	1989 Chicago NLE	1	4	.200	San Francisco
(0–1)					
Total Postseason Games (5)		1	4	.200	

Whitey Herzog. A one-time Kansas City Royals manager, Herzog met up with his former team again when his 1985 Cardinals were nosed out in a memorable seven-game Series.

Bobby Cox. Between his two separate terms as Atlanta Braves dugout director, he managed the Toronto Blue Jays from 1982 through 1985. Later, his Braves were victims of Toronto in the six-game 1992 World Series.

All of these men, including Torre, are among the 43 managers who advanced teams to multiple league championships. Torre could yet pass some, as it is likely he will continue managing into the 21st century.

McGraw and Stengel with 10 titles each—achievements that may never be matched—are followed closely by Connie Mack and McCarthy with nine apiece. Mack managed the Philadelphia Athletics for *50 consecutive seasons.* It is a certainty that no one will ever again manage in the major leagues for that long. Of course, for most of those years—many in which he fielded dreary teams deep in the second division—Mack was the primary owner of the team. He elected not to fire himself! One of Mack's pennants, and one of McGraw's, were won in two early-century years in which no World Series was played. Later Mack took eight more pennant winners to the Series and won five times. McGraw, whose Giants were truly the toast of Manhattan for two decades before the Babe Ruth–led Yankees revolutionized the game with longball, fared poorly in his nine Series by winning only three. Of some consolation to McGraw were his two World Series conquests of the Yankees in 1921 and 1922, when Ruth was in his prime and when Stengel was outfielding for McGraw.

Joe McCarthy, whose career is described more fully elsewhere in this book where his .615 winning percentage is spotlighted, joins Stengel with the most Series championships—seven each. He was on the losing end of his first Series trip when Mack's Athletics downed McCarthy's Cubs in 1929. But after he took over the Yankees in 1931, his troops won seven of the eight Series in which they appeared. When his career wound down, McCarthy nearly won two more American League titles with Boston. His 1948 Red Sox lost a one-game playoff, and his 1949 club finished just one game behind the Yankees in Stengel's first year at New York.

Like fellow Hall of Famers McGraw, Mack, Huggins, Stengel, and Wilbert Robinson before him—and Tom Lasorda and Earl Weaver later—Walter Alston also won all of his league titles with the same team. Alston piloted the Dodgers—in both Brooklyn and Los Angeles—to seven pennants in his 23 years at their helm. The first of his four Series titles, in 1955, was the first World Championship in Dodgers history after losses to Boston (1916), Cleveland (1920), and the "despised" Yankees (1941, 1947, 1949, 1952, and 1953).

Huggins, whose Yankees' six World Series appearances came within a narrow space of eight seasons (1921–28) during Babe Ruth's prime, might have notched additional crowns for his distinguished career had not death claimed him at age 50 during the last fortnight of the 1929 season. What was thought to be merely a painful boil on Huggins's face developed into blood poisoning. Within a week he was dead. The Yankees, after 143 games when he left the team, were in second place, which is where they eventually finished the 1929 season. Just over a year after Huggins's early death, McCarthy was hired to direct the Yankees. Many observers close to the New York baseball scene believed that Huggins—at least for the next decade—would have enjoyed the same successes that McCarthy achieved with the "Bronx Bombers."

Before Torre joined this distinctive list of men who piloted World Series teams against their former employers, Whitey Herzog and Bobby Cox were the most recent additions. Herzog led Kansas City to three AL West titles but never advanced to the league crown. He left there after 1979 and soon became the Cardinals' general manager and field manager. Over a short span of six seasons Herzog's Cardinals won the National League East, then the National League Championship Series over Atlanta (1982), Los Angeles (1985) and San Francisco (1987). In each of his World Series Herzog's club went to a seventh game. St. Louis defeated Harvey Kuenn's 1982 Brewers, who won their only league title to date. But then in 1985 St. Louis lost to Kansas City after holding a three-games-to-one lead, as Royals manager Dick Howser completed his final season before his fatal illness was detected. In the 1987 Series Herzog's Cardinals were nosed out by Tom Kelly's first of two Minnesota World Champions.

Atlanta's Bobby Cox is clearly the most successful manager of the century's final decade and will merit strong consideration for Hall of Fame admittance after he eventually retires. His four pennants have all been won during the 1990s, and his team won its division title in all seven seasons in which races were decided between 1991 and 1998. (The 1994 campaign was discontinued by the player strike. No champion was crowned that year. When the schedule prematurely ended in mid-August, Felipe Alou's Montreal Expos were in first place.) Of Cox's seven Atlanta division winners, all except the 1993 Braves, who were defeated by Philadelphia, and 1997 and '98 LCS losers, advanced to the World Series, which Atlanta won in 1995 over Cleveland. Earlier, in four years as Toronto skipper, Cox won the AL East title in 1985. (Although Oakland won five AL West flags in a row [1971–75], two men— Dick Williams [1971–1973] and Alvin Dark [1974–1975]—skippered those Athletics.

THE PENNANT WINNERS

National League	Year	American League
Fred Clarke – Pittsburgh	1901	Clark Griffith – Chicago
Fred Clarke – Pittsburgh	1902	Connie Mack – Philadelphia
Fred Clarke – Pittsburgh	1903	*Jimmy Collins – Boston*
John McGraw – New York Giants	1904	Jimmy Collins – Boston
John McGraw – New York Giants	1905	Connie Mack – Philadelphia
Frank Chance – Chicago	1906	*Fielder Jones – Chicago*
Frank Chance – Chicago	1907	Hughie Jennings – Detroit
Frank Chance – Chicago	1908	Hughie Jennings – Detroit
Fred Clarke – Pittsburgh	1909	Hughie Jennings – Detroit
Frank Chance – Chicago	1910	*Connie Mack – Philadelphia*
John McGraw – New York Giants	1911	*Connie Mack – Philadelphia*
John McGraw – New York Giants	1912	*Jake Stahl – Boston*
John McGraw – New York Giants	1913	*Connie Mack – Philadelphia*
George Stallings – Boston	1914	Connie Mack – Philadelphia
Pat Moran – Philadelphia	1915	*Bill Carrigan – Boston*
Wilbert Robinson – Brooklyn	1916	*Bill Carrigan – Boston*
John McGraw – New York Giants	1917	*Pants Rowland – Chicago*
Fred Mitchell – Chicago	1918	*Ed Barrow – Boston*
Pat Moran – Cincinnati	1919	Kid Gleason – Chicago
Wilbert Robinson – Brooklyn	1920	*Tris Speaker – Cleveland*
John McGraw – New York Giants	1921	Miller Huggins – New York
John McGraw – New York Giants	1922	Miller Huggins – New York
John McGraw – New York Giants	1923	*Miller Huggins – New York*
John McGraw – New York Giants	1924	*Bucky Harris – Washington*
Bill McKechnie – Pittsburgh	1925	Bucky Harris – Washington
Rogers Hornsby – St. Louis	1926	Miller Huggins – New York
Donie Bush – Pittsburgh	1927	*Miller Huggins – New York*
Bill McKechnie – St. Louis	1928	*Miller Huggins – New York*
Joe McCarthy – Chicago	1929	*Connie Mack – Philadelphia*
Gabby Street – St. Louis	1930	*Connie Mack – Philadelphia*
Gabby Street – St. Louis	1931	Connie Mack – Philadelphia
Charlie Grimm – Chicago	1932	*Joe McCarthy – New York*
Bill Terry – New York Giants	1933	Joe Cronin – Washington
Frank Frisch – St. Louis	1934	Mickey Cochrane – Detroit
Charlie Grimm – Chicago	1935	*Mickey Cochrane – Detroit*
Bill Terry – New York Giants	1936	*Joe McCarthy – New York*
Bill Terry – New York Giants	1937	*Joe McCarthy – New York*
Gabby Hartnett – Chicago	1938	*Joe McCarthy – New York*
Bill McKechnie – Cincinnati	1939	*Joe McCarthy – New York*
Bill McKechnie – Cincinnati	1940	Del Baker – Detroit
Leo Durocher – Brooklyn	1941	*Joe McCarthy – New York*
Billy Southworth – St. Louis	1942	Joe McCarthy – New York

Continued

294

National League	Year	American League
Billy Southworth – St. Louis	1943	*Joe McCarthy – New York*
Billy Southworth – St. Louis	1944	Luke Sewell – St. Louis
Charlie Grimm – Chicago	1945	*Steve O'Neill – Detroit*
Eddie Dyer – St. Louis	1946	Joe Cronin – Boston
Burt Shotton – Brooklyn	1947	*Bucky Harris – New York*
Billy Southworth – Boston	1948	*Lou Boudreau – Cleveland*
Burt Shotton – Brooklyn	1949	*Casey Stengel – New York*
Eddie Sawyer – Philadelphia	1950	*Casey Stengel – New York*
Leo Durocher – New York Giants	1951	*Casey Stengel – New York*
Chuck Dressen – Brooklyn	1952	*Casey Stengel – New York*
Chuck Dressen – Brooklyn	1953	*Casey Stengel – New York*
Leo Durocher – New York Giants	1954	Al Lopez – Cleveland
Walter Alston – Brooklyn	1955	Casey Stengel – New York
Walter Alston – Brooklyn	1956	*Casey Stengel – New York*
Fred Haney – Milwaukee	1957	Casey Stengel – New York
Fred Haney – Milwaukee	1958	*Casey Stengel – New York*
Walter Alston – Los Angeles	1959	Al Lopez – Chicago
Danny Murtaugh – Pittsburgh	1960	Casey Stengel – New York
Fred Hutchinson – Cincinnati	1961	*Ralph Houk – New York*
Alvin Dark – San Francisco	1962	*Ralph Houk – New York*
Walter Alston – Los Angeles	1963	Ralph Houk – New York
Johnny Keane – St. Louis	1964	Yogi Berra – New York
Walter Alston – Los Angeles	1965	Sam Mele – Minnesota
Walter Alston – Los Angeles	1966	*Hank Bauer – Baltimore*
Red Schoendienst – St. Louis	1967	Dick Williams – Boston
Red Schoendienst – St. Louis	1968	*Mayo Smith – Detroit*
Gil Hodges – New York Mets	1969	Earl Weaver – Baltimore
Sparky Anderson – Cincinnati	1970	*Earl Weaver – Baltimore*
Danny Murtaugh – Pittsburgh	1971	Earl Weaver – Baltimore
Sparky Anderson – Cincinnati	1972	*Dick Williams – Oakland*
Yogi Berra – New York Mets	1973	*Dick Williams – Oakland*
Walter Alston – Los Angeles	1974	*Alvin Dark – Oakland*
Sparky Anderson – Cincinnati	1975	Darrell Johnson – Boston
Sparky Anderson – Cincinnati	1976	Billy Martin – New York
Tom Lasorda – Los Angeles	1977	*Billy Martin – New York*
Tom Lasorda – Los Angeles	1978	Bob Lemon – New York
Chuck Tanner – Pittsburgh	1979	Earl Weaver – Baltimore
Dallas Green – Philadelphia	1980	Jim Frey – Kansas City Royals
Tom Lasorda – Los Angeles	1981	Bob Lemon – New York
Whitey Herzog – St. Louis	1982	Harvey Kuenn – Milwaukee
Paul Owens – Philadelphia	1983	*Joe Altobelli – Baltimore*
Dick Williams – San Diego	1984	*Sparky Anderson – Detroit*

Continued

THE PENNANT WINNERS (Continued)

National League	Year	American League
Whitey Herzog – St. Louis	1985	*Dick Howser – Kansas City Royals*
Davey Johnson – New York Mets	1986	John McNamara – Boston
Whitey Herzog – St. Louis	1987	*Tom Kelly – Minnesota*
Tom Lasorda – Los Angeles	1988	Tony LaRussa – Oakland
Roger Craig – San Francisco	1989	*Tony LaRussa – Oakland*
Lou Piniella – Cincinnati	1990	Tony LaRussa – Oakland
Bobby Cox – Atlanta	1991	*Tom Kelly – Minnesota*
Bobby Cox – Atlanta	1992	*Cito Gaston – Toronto*
Jim Fregosi – Philadelphia	1993	*Cito Gaston – Toronto*
No Pennant; incomplete season	1994	No Pennant; incomplete season
Bobby Cox – Atlanta	1995	Mike Hargrove – Cleveland
Bobby Cox – Atlanta	1996	*Joe Torre – New York*
Jim Leyland – Florida	1997	Mike Hargrove – Cleveland
Bruce Bochy – San Diego	1998	*Joe Torre – New York*

Note: Names in italic denote World Series winners. (No World Series in 1901, 1902, 1904, and 1994).

Of only 14 men enshrined under the Hall of Fame's manager category, all except Ned Hanlon managed primarily in the 20th century, and all won league titles—more than once. (Names of all Hall of Fame managers appear in the Cooperstown Honors section elsewhere in this book.)

Some of the multiple flag winners are still active or recently retired. That group includes Cox, LaRussa, Torre, Anderson, Tom Lasorda, Mike Hargrove, and Tom Kelly. When one considers that the average career for full-time managers (excluding the short-term interim pilots) is about six years, and that 421 men have held field-managing jobs this century, it becomes apparent that those who have led their teams to pennants constitute an exclusive group. Especially when prominent and generally respected longtime managers such as Gene Mauch, Jimmie Dykes, Paul Richards, Herman Franks, Buck Rodgers, Bill Rigney, Birdie Tebbetts, and Bill Virdon have never made it to October's big dance.

	Manager	Teams/Years
10 Titles	John McGraw	New York Giants / 1904, '05, '11, '12, '13, '17, '21, '22, '23, '24
	Casey Stengel	New York Yankees / 1949, '50, '51, '52, '53, 55, '56, '57, '58, '60
9 Titles	Connie Mack	Philadelphia Athletics / 1902, '05, '10, '11, '13, '14, '29, '30, '31
	Joe McCarthy	Chicago Cubs / 1929
		New York Yankees / 1932, '36, '37, '38, '39, '41, '42, '43
7 Titles	Walter Alston	Brooklyn/Los Angeles Dodgers / 1955, '56, '59, '63, '65, '66, '74
6 Titles	Miller Huggins	New York Yankees / 1921, '22, '23, '26, '27, '28
5 Titles	Sparky Anderson	Cincinnati Reds / 1970, '72, '75, '76
		Detroit Tigers / 1984
4 Titles	Frank Chance	Chicago Cubs / 1906, '07, '08, '10
	Fred Clarke	Pittsburgh Pirates / 1901, '02, '03, '09
	Bobby Cox	Atlanta Braves / 1991, '92, '95, '96
	Tom Lasorda	Los Angeles Dodgers / 1977, '78, '81, '88
	Bill McKechnie	Pittsburgh Pirates / 1925
		St. Louis Cardinals / 1928
		Cincinnati Reds / 1939, '40
	Billy Southworth	St. Louis Cardinals / 1942, '43, '44
		Boston Braves / 1948
	Earl Weaver	Baltimore Orioles / 1969, '70, '71, '79
	Dick Williams	Boston Red Sox / 1967
		Oakland Athletics / 1972, '73
		San Diego Padres / 1984
3 Titles	Leo Durocher	Brooklyn Dodgers / 1941
		New York Giants / 1951, '54
	Charlie Grimm	Chicago Cubs / 1932, '35, '45
	Bucky Harris	Washington Senators / 1924, '25
		New York Yankees / 1947
	Whitey Herzog	St. Louis Cardinals / 1982, '85, '87
	Ralph Houk	New York Yankees / 1961, '62, '63
	Hughie Jennings	Detroit Tigers / 1907, '08, '09
	Tony LaRussa	Oakland Athletics / 1988, '89, '90
	Bill Terry	New York Giants / 1933, '36, '37
2 Titles	Yogi Berra	New York Yankees / 1964
		New York Mets / 1973
	Bill Carrigan	Boston Red Sox / 1915, '16
	Mickey Cochrane	Detroit Tigers / 1934, '35

WINNERS OF MULTIPLE FLAGS (Continued)

	Manager	Teams/Years
2 Titles	Jimmy Collins	Boston Red Sox / 1903, '04
	Joe Cronin	Washington Senators / 1933
		Boston Red Sox / 1946
	Alvin Dark	San Francisco Giants / 1962
		Oakland Athletics / 1974
	Chuck Dressen	Brooklyn Dodgers / 1952, '53
	Cito Gaston	Toronto Blue Jays / 1992, '93
	Fred Haney	Milwaukee Braves / 1957, '58
	Mike Hargrove	Cleveland Indians / 1995, '97
	Tom Kelly	Minnesota Twins / 1987, '91
	Bob Lemon	New York Yankees / 1978, '81
	Al Lopez	Cleveland Indians / 1954
		Chicago White Sox / 1959
	Billy Martin	New York Yankees / 1976, '77
	Pat Moran	Philadelphia Phillies / 1915
		Cincinnati Reds / 1919
	Danny Murtaugh	Pittsburgh Pirates / 1960, '71
	Wilbert Robinson	Brooklyn Dodgers / 1916, '20
	Red Schoendienst	St. Louis Cardinals / 1967 , '68
	Burt Shotton	Brooklyn Dodgers / 1947, '49
	Gabby Street	St. Louis Cardinals / 1930, '31
	Joe Torre	New York Yankees / 1996, '98

Managers of Pennant Winners in Both Leagues

Sparky Anderson	NL Cincinnati (4), AL Detroit (1)
Yogi Berra	AL New York (1), NL New York (1)
Alvin Dark	NL San Francisco (1), AL Oakland (1)
Joe McCarthy	NL Chicago (1), AL New York (8)
Dick Williams	AL Boston (1) & Oakland (2), NL San Diego (1)

Well-Deserved, Overdue Salutes

Some traditionalists among baseball's followers have offered the opinion that Sparky Anderson and Earl Weaver should be ranked right up there with Miller Huggins and the other five men who have managed teams to a half dozen or more titles. It's an interesting point. But not valid.

They base their stance on a solid mathematical fact: In certain years Anderson's and Weaver's teams won more regular season games than anyone else in their league. But what they don't mention is that when the playoffs were over, somebody else went on to the World Series.

Best records don't necessarily merit the top prize anymore.

Ardent baseball aficionados know all about the long-season strategies and the necessity to prepare, mold, and manipulate a 25-man squad for six months' worth of 150-plus games. In football (manager Billy Martin continually criticized Yankee owner George Steinbrenner for his "football mentality"), one victory or loss constitutes between 5 and 10 percent of a gridiron season; baseball's managers know that if roughly *only one of three* games is lost, the team is still likely to wind up in first place.

A generation ago Bill Veeck astutely stated that professional football people promoted their product far better than baseball does. They still do. "Football keeps saying that on any given Sunday anybody can beat anybody else. The fact is," continued Veeck, "that the last-place baseball team defeats the first-place club a much higher percentage of the time than it happens in football."

A baseball manager consciously tries to guide his team to victory every time out, but he recognizes the need to hold back an ace pitcher for a mightier opponent next series or to rest some of the regular players from time to time in an effort to keep his entire roster fresh for the stretch drive. With games scheduled nearly every day (or night) for six months, baseball players are prone to occasional slumps. Sometimes two or three key players slump simultaneously, and maybe a teammate or two are on the disabled list. The on-field result? Perhaps a three-game sweep by a mediocre second-divison opponent. In football, that would be a disaster. But in baseball's long seasons, the teams with the best and the healthiest players over 26 full weeks will ultimately contend—even if the last-place team whipped them a few times during the summer.

A short series, be it regular season, the LCS, or even the World Series, proves only this: The winning team was better for those three, four, five, six, or seven *days.* Not necessarily the cream at the top for that *season.* The often hapless St. Louis Browns used to beat the Yankees once in a while. The title-winning Cardinals of 1964 were subdued by the lowly New York Mets in the first two matches of a crucial season-ending weekend series before slugging out a victory in the final game to clinch the pennant en route to a World Series title. As recently as 1997 the Philadelphia Phillies, tying Chicago for the National League's worst record that year, opened September with three straight victories over the defending World Champion Yankees and ended the month with a 3–0 mark against 1997 World Series winner Florida.

Over a long baseball season the champion seldom wins 67 percent of its games; last-place teams rarely lose as many as two out of three. Most years the difference between best and worst is only about one win or one loss a week!

Until 1969, the team with the best record—a club with long-haul pacing and usually with the fewest key injuries—won the pennant. Seems logical, right? But then division play was introduced. Despite its many merits (more teams in contention longer, better gates at late-September games and, of course, greater broadcast revenues), it did not guarantee a World Series entry to the team with its league's most wins . Two teams, not just one season-long champ, would wind up in first place in both the American and National leagues. Now, since 1994, three divisons exist. And there's even a wild card thrown into the mix to help accommodate television. That might disgust purists, but it doesn't upset fans of the 1997 Florida Marlins, who eventually won the Series that year with baseball's fourth-best regular-season record. Those significant format alterations bring us back to the viewpoint expressed by the traditionalists who propose greater recognition of the Sparky Andersons, Tom Lasordas, Earl Weavers, Whitey Herzogs, and others for their first-place finishes.

The accompanying chart focuses on the teams and their managers that earned appearances in League Championship Series only to be defeated there and thus fail to advance to the World Series—even though they owned the league's best record. Discounting 1994, that incomplete season of labor disputes when no division or league champions were named, the team that lost the LCS had a better overall record than the league champ 24 times. Recent occasions are good examples. In 1996, the club with baseball's best record (Cleveland at 99–62) was defeated in the first play-off round by a wild-card team, Baltimore, which had won 11 fewer games than the Indians during the regular season. A year later Cleveland (86 wins) turned the tables on Baltimore (98 victories).

Sparky Anderson exemplifies a manager whose team posted the best record but missed out on the league title. Five times a director of World Series teams—Cincinnati in 1970, 1972, 1975, 1976 and Detroit in 1984—Anderson piloted three other division winners only to go down to defeat in the League Championship Series. Two of those clubs, his 1973 Reds and his 1987 Tigers, registered better regular-season records than the teams that subdued them in the LCS. Sparky's 1973 Cincinnati club outflanked the rest of the National League West with a solid 99–63 record. In the NL East, New York, with the league's worst-ever won-lost ratio for a league champ, was just 82–79. Yet the Mets won the pennant with their best-of-five play-off series victory and were borne by momentum to a seventh World Series game before falling to Oakland. Had no divisions existed, and discounting the unbalanced schedule in effect at the time, the Reds' 99 wins would easily have carried Anderson to another league championship. The same scenario held true in 1987 when Sparky's Tigers lost to the Twins in the postseason, yet had a 13-game edge on Minnesota during the regular year. Those 1987 Twins logged the lowest winning percentage ever of all 96 American League champs. So instead of five league championships to his credit, Sparky Anderson would be a seven-time winner under the format that prevailed from 1901 through 1968—the same number of league titles achieved by Walter Alston. The accompanying chart shows that Earl Weaver, according to this mythical accounting, would have won six American League pennants instead of four, and that Tom Lasorda would have been a five-flag winner.

Even though these observations are merely hypothetical gymnastics, managers Bill Virdon (1972, 1980), Danny Ozark (1977), and Don Zimmer (1989) can be excused for wondering what if divisions had never been formed. None

Text continues on page 304

AMERICAN LEAGUE

Year	Team/Manager	Record	Pennant Winner
1973	Orioles – Earl Weaver	97–65	Athletics – Dick Williams (90–72)
1974	Orioles – Earl Weaver	91–71	Athletics – Alvin Dark (90–72)
1975	Athletics – Alvin Dark	98–64	Red Sox – Darrell Johnson (95–65)
1977	Royals – Whitey Herzog	102–60	Yankees – Billy Martin (100–62)
1980	Yankees – Dick Howser	103–59	Royals – Jim Frey (97–65)
1983	White Sox – Tony LaRussa	99–63	Orioles – Joe Altobelli (98–64)
1985	Blue Jays – Bobby Cox	99–62	Royals – Dick Howser (91–71)
1987	Tigers – Sparky Anderson	98–64	Twins – Tom Kelly (85–77)
1992	Oakland (Tony LaRussa) and Toronto (Cito Gaston) each posted a 96–56 regular season record. Toronto won ALCS four games to two.		
1996	Indians – Mike Hargrove	99–62 *	Yankees – Joe Torre (92–69)
1997	Orioles – Davey Johnson	98–64	Indians – Mike Hargrove (86–75)

NATIONAL LEAGUE

Year	Team/Manager	Record	Pennant Winner
1972	Pirates – Bill Virdon	96–59	Reds – Sparky Anderson (95–59)
1973	Reds – Sparky Anderson	99–63	Mets – Yogi Berra (82–79)
1977	Phillies – Danny Ozark	101–61	Dodgers – Tom Lasorda (98–64)
1980	Astros – Bill Virdon	93–70	Phillies – Dallas Green (91–70)
1983	Dodgers – Tom Lasorda	91–71	Phillies – Paul Owens (90–72)
1984	Cubs – Jim Frey	96–65	Padres – Dick Williams (92–70)
1988	Mets – Davey Johnson	100–60	Dodgers – Tom Lasorda (94–67)
1989	Cubs – Don Zimmer	93–69	Giants – Roger Craig (92–90)
1990	Pirates – Jim Leyland	95–67	Reds – Lou Piniella (91–71)
1991	Pirates – Jim Leyland	98–64	Braves – Bobby Cox (94–68)
1993	Braves – Bobby Cox	104–58	Phillies – Jim Fregosi (97–65)
1997	Braves – Bobby Cox	101–61	Marlins – Jim Leyland (92–70)†
1998	Braves – Bobby Cox	106–56	Padres – Bruce Bochy (98–64)

*Cleveland lost LC 1st round series to wild-card Baltimore (88–74)

†Florida was wild-card entry with overall second best record in NL

AMERICAN LEAGUE

Year	East	West	Central
1969	Baltimore – Earl Weaver *	Minnesota – Billy Martin	
1970	Baltimore – Earl Weaver *	Minnesota – Bill Rigney	
1971	Baltimore – Earl Weaver *	Oakland – Dick Williams	

Continued

Year	East	West	Central
1972	Detroit – Billy Martin	Oakland – Dick Williams *	
1973	Baltimore – Earl Weaver	Oakland – Dick Williams *	
1974	Baltimore – Earl Weaver	Oakland – Alvin Dark *	
1975	Boston – Darrell Johnson *	Oakland – Alvin Dark	
1976	New York – Billy Martin *	Kan. City – Whitey Herzog	
1977	New York – Billy Martin *	Kan. City – Whitey Herzog	
1978	New York – Bob Lemon *	Kan. City – Whitey Herzog	
1979	Baltimore – Earl Weaver *	California – Jim Fregosi	
1980	New York – Dick Howser	Kan. City – Jim Frey *	
1981	New York – Bob Lemon *	Oakland – Billy Martin	
1982	Milwaukee – Harvey Kuenn *	California – Gene Mauch	
1983	Baltimore – Joe Altobelli *	Chicago – Tony LaRussa	
1984	Detroit – Sparky Anderson *	Kan. City – Dick Howser	
1985	Toronto – Bobby Cox	Kan. City – Dick Howser *	
1986	Boston – John McNamara *	California – Gene Mauch	
1987	Detroit – Sparky Anderson	Minnesota – Tom Kelly *	
1988	Boston – Joe Morgan	Oakland – Tony LaRussa*	
1989	Toronto – Cito Gaston	Oakland – Tony LaRussa *	
1990	Boston – Joe Morgan	Oakland – Tony LaRussa*	
1991	Toronto – Cito Gaston	Minnesota – Tom Kelly *	
1992	Toronto – Cito Gaston *	Oakland – Tony LaRussa	
1993	Toronto – Cito Gaston *	Chicago – Gene Lamont	
1994	Incomplete season	Incomplete season	
1995	Boston – Kevin Kennedy	Seattle – Lou Piniella	Cleveland – Mike Hargrove *
1996	New York – Joe Torre *	Texas – Johnny Oates	Cleveland – Mike Hargrove
1997	Baltimore – Davey Johnson	Seattle – Lou Piniella	Cleveland – Mike Hargrove *
1998	New York – Joe Torre*	Texas – Johnny Oates	Cleveland – Mike Hargrove

NATIONAL LEAGUE

Year	East	West	Central
1969	New York – Gil Hodges *	Atlanta – Lum Harris	
1970	Pittsburgh – Danny Murtaugh	Cincinnati – Sparky Anderson *	
1971	Pittsburgh – Danny Murtaugh *	San Francisco – Charlie Fox	
1972	Pittsburgh – Bill Virdon	Cincinnati – Sparky Anderson*	
1973	New York – Yogi Berra *	Cincinnati – Sparky Anderson	
1974	Pittsburgh – Danny Murtaugh	Los Angeles – Walter Alston *	
1975	Pittsburgh – Danny Murtaugh	Cincinnati – Sparky Anderson *	
1976	Philadelphia – Danny Ozark	Cincinnati – Sparky Anderson *	
1977	Philadelphia – Danny Ozark	Los Angeles – Tom Lasorda*	
1978	Philadelphia – Danny Ozark	Los Angeles – Tom Lasorda*	
1979	Pittsburgh – Chuck Tanner *	Cincinnati – John McNamara	

Continued

DIVISION WINNERS (continued)

Year	East	West	Central
1980	Philadelphia – Dallas Green *	Houston – Bill Virdon	
1981	Montreal – Jim Fanning	Los Angeles – Tom Lasorda *	
1982	St. Louis – Whitey Herzog *	Atlanta – Joe Torre	
1983	Philadelphia – Paul Owens *	Los Angeles – Tom Lasorda	
1984	Chicago – Jim Frey	San Diego – Dick Williams*	
1985	St. Louis – Whitey Herzog *	Los Angeles – Tom Lasorda	
1986	New York – Davey Johnson *	Houston – Hal Lanier	
1987	St. Louis – Whitey Herzog *	San Francisco – Roger Craig	
1988	New York – Davey Johnson	Los Angeles – Tom Lasorda *	
1989	Chicago – Don Zimmer	San Francisco – Roger Craig*	
1990	Pittsburgh – Jim Leyland	Cincinnati – Lou Piniella *	
1991	Pittsburgh – Jim Leyland	Atlanta – Bobby Cox*	
1992	Pittsburgh – Jim Leyland	Atlanta – Bobby Cox*	
1993	Philadelphia – Jim Fregosi *	Atlanta – Bobby Cox	
1994	Incomplete season	Incomplete season	
1995	Atlanta – Bobby Cox *	Los Angeles – Tom Lasorda	Cincinnati – Davey Johnson
1996	Atlanta – Bobby Cox *	San Diego – Bruce Bochy	St. Louis – Tony LaRussa
1997	Atlanta – Bobby Cox	San Francisco – Dusty Baker	Houston – Larry Dierker
	World Series won by wild-card Florida, Jim Leyland, manager *		
1998	Atlanta – Bobby Cox	San Diego – Bruce Bochy*	Houston – Larry Dierker

*League champion

of that trio ever managed a pennant winner. But their teams' records were the best in the league!

Some Overlooked Skippers

Elsewhere in this book are the names of every major league manager of this century in alphabetical form for quick reference, and in chronological order under the teams they managed. Perhaps many readers feel they know all they need to know about the Hall of Fame legends—the Macks, McCarthys, Lasordas, McGraws, Lopezes, Griffiths, Weavers, Stengels, McKechnies, and so on, and about Cooperstown hopefuls such as Tony LaRussa, Jim Leyland, Billy Martin, Bobby Cox, and Sparky Anderson.

The names of other notable managers do not always come quickly to mind, however. This chapter, on overlooked or too lightly regarded pilots, begins with a spotlight on nine men whose managing careers merit far more recognition than they usually receive.

Career Summaries

Steve O'Neill

Cleveland 1935–37, Detroit 1943–48, Boston AL 1950–51, Philadelphia NL 1952–54

When Chicago baseball writer Warren Brown was asked to forecast the outcome of the 1945 World Series between Detroit and the Chicago Cubs, he replied, "After watching the Tigers from time to time, and seeing the Cubs frequently during this wartime season, I carefully conclude that neither team can win this World Series!"

Well, if no one was expected to emerge victorious, as Brown facetiously suggested, then manager Steve O'Neill can be characterized as a magician. It wasn't easy, though, for his Tigers required seven games to nudge the Cubs for the world's title. Detroit heroes were two future Hall of Famers—slugger Hank Greenberg, recently returned from a four-year armed service assignment, and young southpaw Hal Newhouser. Chicago's finest World Series hour was Claude Passeau's one-hitter in Game 3.

Because the title was recorded in the final World War II summer, this championship posted by Steve O'Neill's 1945 club is considered by many baseball students to be a rather bland accomplishment. And while it was the only time he managed a pennant winner, O'Neill himself might well have considered it to be secondary to some of his other managing achievements that have been largely overlooked by the game's historians.

Aside from the Tigers, whom O'Neill managed for six years—four times ranking either first or second in the American League—he posted winning records in three seasons at Cleveland, two at Boston with the Red Sox, and three as Philadelphia Phillies skipper.

Never—not once—did an O'Neill team have a cumulative record below .500. Thrice, over full seasons, Steve's teams finished fifth (Cleveland 1936, Detroit 1943 and 1948) but still managed to win more games than they lost. Eleven times he was a first-division pilot.

As is hypothesized elsewhere in this book, one key measure of a manager's abilities is the record of his team immediately before and directly following his tenure. Steve O'Neill's success is a clear example of that. His first major league assignment was at Cleveland in mid-1935 when he replaced manager Walter Johnson, whose record was 46–48 at the time, and the team in fifth place. For the rest of 1935, under O'Neill, the Tribe went 36–23 and finished third. When legendary Joe McCarthy resigned as Red Sox pilot in early 1950, with a 31–28 log, O'Neill was tabbed as the replacement. With essentially the same players who ranked a lukewarm fourth under McCarthy, the Red Sox won 63 of their final 95 games—an astounding .663 pace—to finish just four games behind New York and one game beneath second-place Detroit.

Two years later, following his departure from Boston where he went 87–67, and another third-place ranking in 1951, Steve was again called on to rehabilitate a team. This would be his only venture in the National League. The Phillies were poking along with 28 wins and 35 losses at a sixth-place level when O'Neill came on board. For the season's final 91 games under him they accelerated to fourth place via .648 baseball (59–32). When the Phillies dismissed him at the halfway point of the 1954 season (apparently they noticed that 40 wins and 37 losses were short of Steve's norm), the team was in third place. At season's finish the Phils had dropped to fourth, winning only 35 of 77 games under the replacement manager, Terry Moore.

Steve O'Neill, like many successful managers, had been a catcher in his playing days. In 17 seasons behind the plate he totaled 1,586 games, a figure ranking high among all-time number of games caught. He was a spark plug for 13 seasons with Cleveland, and a key member of the Indians' 1920 World Championship team. He hit .321 that season, then followed with a .337 mark in a seven-game World Series against Brooklyn. O'Neill officially retired after 10 games with the 1928 St. Louis Browns, but he donned catcher's paraphernalia eight years later for one of the most heralded exhibition games of all time. Then the manager of the Indians, the old backstop, at age 45, activated himself for one July afternoon when the Tribe hosted St. Louis's Gas House Gang Cardinals in an exhibition at Cleveland's old League Park. A home team pitcher that day was Iowa teenager Bob Feller, then still a hot young prospect. Four weeks earlier he had just finished his junior year in high school. The baseball world had been told of the youngster's blazing speed and his great potential. Manager O'Neill wanted to see for himself. When he waved in Feller to start the fourth inning, O'Neill entered the game as his battery mate. He quickly learned that the high expectations were, indeed, legitimate. In the three innings he pitched, Feller struck out eight batters. It took less than an hour for O'Neill to be convinced that Feller was the genuine article.

O'Neill was one of the many Irish Americans who dominated baseball during the first three decades of the 20th century. He was part of a family of coal miners from northeastern Pennsylvania, the third in a line of four brothers who played major league baseball—Jack 1902–6, Mike 1901–7, then Steve 1911–28, and Jim 1920 and 1923.

With only one pennant to his credit for 14 managing seasons, Steve O'Neill has never been seriously considered for Hall of Fame nomination. It is reasonably certain that, by now, he never will be. Regardless, he should be far better recognized than he has been. Only one other manager of 14 seasons or longer (McCarthy) has ever matched O'Neill's record of never having posted a losing season. Only *14* managers (with 450 or more games managed) have a better overall winning percentage this century than Steve's .559. Seldom have managers consistently revived mediocre clubs at midseason as well as O'Neill did.

Steve O'Neill. A highly successful major league manager who is unfairly overlooked and was too quickly forgotten.

Billy Southworth
St. Louis NL 1929, 1940–45, Boston NL 1946–51

Billy Southworth is *not* in the Hall of Fame.

That might be the most startling fact in this book.

Joe McCarthy *is* in the Hall of Fame. His right to be there is not debatable. After all, McCarthy is the only manager in history—except for a handful of one- or two-game interim pilots—to complete his career with a winning percentage that exceeded .600. McCarthy's .615 is baseball's high-water mark. It may never be matched.

The next best this century? Billy Southworth's .597. While directing two different National League franchises to championships (St. Louis, three pennants; Boston, one), Southworth was in the driver's seat for 1,044 regular-season victories and only 704 losses. Two of his St. Louis winners posted World Series triumphs. The Cardinals upset the favored New York Yankees in 1942 and downed their St. Louis neighbors, the Browns, in the 1944 classic.

Technically, Southworth is Number 3 on the all-time percentage list of managers. The highly regarded Frank Selee was a point better at .598. Selee's achievements, however, were registered largely in the 1890s with Boston's National League entry, although he continued with Boston, and then with the Chicago Cubs, until 1905. Because this book concentrates on major league managers from 1901 forward, Southworth is this century's second best—right behind McCarthy.

The 1940s, in a sense, belonged to Billy Southworth. When he came on board at St. Louis in mid-May of 1940, the Cardinals had won only 15 of 44 games and ranked a drab seventh in the National League standings. Southworth advanced them to a final finish of third by going 69 and 40 for the remainder of the season. During the next five years the Cardinals never finished lower than second. His club *averaged* 101.6 victories during that five-season span. Their *poorest* record was 95–59 to finish in second place three games behind Chicago in 1945. Earlier, in 1941, the Redbirds' 97 wins came up short against Brooklyn's 101. Between Southworth's 97 victories in 1941 and his 95 four years later, he led St. Louis to 100-plus wins three years in a row. In the 98 years of managerial records since 1901 only *two other managers* can claim three such successive seasons. Both are in the Hall of Fame—Connie Mack with 100-plus wins for the Philadelphia Athletics in 1929, 1930, and 1931, and Earl Weaver of Baltimore in the 162-game seasons of 1969, 1970, and 1971. John McGraw never won 100 three straight times, nor did McCarthy, nor Al Lopez, nor Sparky Anderson, nor anyone else. Casey Stengel, in maneuvering those excellent Yankees of the 1950s to nearly annual pennants, led New York to 100 victories only once. That was in 1954—one of only two years under Stengel in which the Yanks did *not* take the American League flag. Lopez's Cleveland Indians set a league record with 111 wins that year.

Southworth's Cardinals needed nearly all of their 106 wins in 1942 to outlast Brooklyn, which posted 104 victories. The following two seasons St. Louis checked in with identical 105–49 logs. The string broke in 1945 with *only* those 95 wins in a year in which the Cubs won their most recent league title.

Some say that Southworth should have won pennants with the Cardinals of the Cooper brothers, Stan Musial, Johnny Hopp, Marty Marion, Terry Moore, Whitey Kurowski, and Enos Slaughter, among others. If so, then give him credit for getting the job done. It will never be known, of course, if any other manager would have been equally successful at St. Louis. What is quite clear, however, is Southworth's masterful performance in leading the Boston Braves to their first pennant in 34 years.

He had taken the Boston position in 1946 after the Cardinals' second-place finish of the preceding season had disappointed St. Louis's fickle owner, Sam Breadon. Boston, which had finished beneath the first division every year since Bill McKechnie brought the Braves home fourth in 1933 and 1934, was happy to land the widely respected Southworth. The manager was anxious to meet the challenge of guiding a relatively average team of big leaguers, who represented a significant contrast to the cast of All-Stars Billy had piloted in St. Louis. In that first season, 1946, Boston ascended to fourth place with a respectable 81–72 record. The following year the Braves were third, only eight games from the top, as their third baseman, Bob Elliott, was the league's MVP. Boston fortunes continued on the upswing in 1948 with the franchise's first pennant since the George Stallings "Miracle Braves" of 1914.

Baseball journalists and other wags still recall the team's rallying cry, "Spahn and Sain and pray for rain!" While those two standout pitchers indeed played vital roles in that championship season, Southworth was unquestionably the craftsman who molded a good squad—but a club not overly stocked with household baseball names—to outlast solid Brooklyn and St. Louis teams. Of course rain didn't fall every other day, so Southworth carefully platooned his catchers (Bill Salkeld and Phil Masi) and first basemen (Earl Torgeson and Frank McCormick), and when second baseman Eddie Stanky and outfielder Jeff Heath suffered late-season injuries, Billy added the right blend of replacements into his pennant-winning mix. Southworth was well aware that the Spahn-Sain slogan was fanciful, but unrealistic. So instead of "two days of rain," the manager employed the pitching services of Bill Voiselle, rookie Vern Bickford, Bob Hogue, Clyde Shoun, Red Barrett, Nelson Potter, and a few others to handle Boston's mound work. The result: a solid 39 combined victories by Sain (24) and Spahn (15), and—52 wins from the "rain."

The 1948 season was a last hurrah, though, for most of the pitchers except Spahn and Sain, and it foreshadowed the declining careers of several of the platooners and the regulars such as Tommy Holmes and Elliott. The 1949 Braves were mediocre throughout the summer, and manager Southworth, by his own choice, did not finish the season. His son, William Harrison Southworth Jr., had been killed in a plane crash after World War II, and his father became more and more despondent as time passed. That depression, combined with the Braves' lackluster follow-up to the flag-winning season led him to request a leave of absence after 111 games. Physically and emotionally stronger by the next season, Billy came back to guide Boston to fourth place again with an 83–71 record in 1950. A legitimate contender throughout most of the summer, the Braves ranked just eight games behind the pennant-winning Phillies at the season's end.

Before the 1951 season was completed, Billy Southworth's noteworthy managing career ended, too. At age 58 he had lost his enthusiasm and drive. With the team a little under .500 in fifth place by mid-June, Southworth was replaced by Tommy Holmes, who would be a player-manager for the remainder of the season and into early 1952. Just a year after that, the Boston Braves no longer existed. They had bolted to Milwaukee in what was big-league baseball's first franchise transfer in 50 years.

Billy Southworth lived long enough to see the Braves move yet again, this time to Atlanta in 1966. After nearly a quarter century there, the Braves finally constructed another ultrasuccessful run. Sadly, with the overabundance of forecasts and replays and background and trivia surrounding the Braves on national television at play-off and World Series time, Billy Southworth—the manager with the most major league victories in the 1940s, the most successful Boston Braves pilot this century, the three pennants in a row at St. Louis, the only manager surpassed by Joe McCarthy's .615 winning percentage this century—is carelessly overlooked. He shouldn't be.

Danny Murtaugh

Pittsburgh 1957–64, '67, 1970–71, 1973–76

Two pennants. Two World Series titles. Four division championships. Ten first-division finishes in 14 seasons.

Those are the bare statistics of this successful Pittsburgh manager whose creditable record for more than 2,000 games was .540—1,115 victories, only 950 losses. Beyond the numbers, however, was a gentle, charming Irishman who personified respect—respect from his players, his employers, his fellow managers, and the media, which found him to be accessible, forthright, patient, and often playfully humorous.

Daniel Edward Murtaugh was born and raised in Chester, Pennsylvania, an industrial community near the southwest edge of Philadelphia. At age 59 he died in Chester after suffering a heart attack. Danny Murtaugh had battled heart disease for nearly a decade before his death, and for most of those years he continued—off and on—to pilot the Pirates. It was off and on because, after each of three retirements, Pittsburgh officials asked Murtaugh to step back in to resurrect what they felt was a stagnating team. Most times the "smilin' Irishman" brought them back to life.

He had been a Pittsburgh coach under manager Bobby Bragan (a fellow infielder with the Phillies 15 years earlier) when he was elevated to the skipper's post in mid-1957. The team was in last place with a dreary 36–67 record. The Pirates were so deep in the basement at that point that their major turnaround to 26–25 baseball under Murtaugh wasn't enough to elevate them above a tie for seventh that season. But with a number of solid young players, including Dick Groat, Bob Friend, Vernon Law, Bill Virdon, Bob Skinner, and superstar Roberto Clemente as a nucleus, and with Murtaugh's leadership, Pittsburgh advanced to second place in 1958. It was the team's highest finish in 14 years, and the first time in a decade that it ranked in the first division. After finishing fourth the next year, Murtaugh's 1960 Pirates brought Pittsburgh its first National League championship since 1927, and topped off the pennant with a seventh-game World Series triumph over New York. Bill Mazeroski's game-winning home run ranks among the top half-dozen Series highlights this century.

Murtaugh managed Pittsburgh for four more seasons, during which his team usually finished in the middle of the National League pack. Following a sixth-place tie in 1964 he stepped down—for the first time. Manager Harry Walker was sacked halfway through the 1967 campaign, and Murtaugh, then scouting for the Bucs, was asked to be the on-field caretaker for the remainder of the season. He agreed but insisted that the assignment be temporary. Two years later team officials asked him again to step in as manager. The loyal veteran Pirate responded affirmatively and immediately led Pittsburgh to division titles in 1970 and 1971. The 1971 club won its second World Series under Murtaugh, overcoming a three-games-to-one deficit to outlast Baltimore. By employing six different starting pitchers in the Series' first six games—against a Baltimore staff headed by four 20-game winners—Murtaugh's orchestration of a rather ordinary pitching staff was a key factor in the come-from-behind win. So was the offensive leadership of Clemente, who hit safely in all seven games (as he had done 11 years earlier against the Yankees).

When the Series ended, Murtaugh announced his retirement. It was time, he said, to take it easy and to distance himself from the stress of managing. His successor, longtime associate Bill Virdon, led Pittsburgh to the East Division crown again in 1972, before Cincinnati won the League Championship Series. Murtaugh was among Virdon's strongest boosters. But when the team faltered early in 1973, there was Danny again, physically refreshed, being urged to return to the dugout. He accepted the team's plea, of course, and would enjoy the best consecutive three years of his managing career. The Pirates averaged nearly 91 victories under him over 1974, 1975, and 1976, won two division titles, and finished second the other time. Finally, after the 1976 campaign, Murtaugh retired for the final time, leaving successor Chuck Tanner with a solid roster that would be a strong contender (including a 1979 World Championship) for several more seasons.

Murtaugh's health was clearly deteriorating. Less than two months beyond his retirement Danny succumbed to the fatal heart attack.

During the era in which Murtaugh managed, his career was often overshadowed by such National League headliners as Leo Durocher, Sparky Anderson, Gene Mauch, and Walt Alston. History seems to have sidetracked him into hazy memory. The majority of the men who played for him, however, and his dugout counterparts from the late 1950s, enthusiastically give Danny high marks for his leadership, his strategic maneuvering, and his sportsmanship.

And longtime Pittsburgh fans rank Murtaugh high among their popular favorites. They seemed to enjoy having him quoted—most of the time! Asked once about judging baseball talent, Murtaugh remarked, "Certainly I'd like to have that fellow who hits a home run every time up, who strikes out every opposing batter when he's pitching, who throws strikes to any base or plate when he's playing the outfield, and who always thinks about two innings ahead just what he'll do to baffle the other team. Any manager would want a guy like that. The only trouble is getting him to put down his cup of beer and come out of the stands and do those things."

Ty Cobb

Detroit 1921–26

One of baseball's old chestnuts, generally intended as a denigration, states that the most accomplished players cannot be successful managers. Examples such as Rogers Hornsby, Ted Williams, and Ty Cobb are usually offered. The speaker—either deliberately or carelessly—neglects to mention Frank Frisch, Mickey Cochrane, Frank Chance, Joe Cronin, Clark Griffith, Bill Terry, Tris Speaker, and others whose managing careers belie his contention.

Hornsby, though, is one of the all-star-caliber players whose overall achievements as a manager do, indeed, rank poorly. And in the case of Ted Williams, little opportunity existed for him to disprove the theory, because he managed for only four years—all of them with an expansion team that had not yet grown into maturity. His first year, with the expansion Washington Senators (1969), was clearly his most successful as manager. Washington went 86–76 that year, a 20½-game improvement over its immediate predecessor. The next three seasons, however, were gloomy ones for his ball club, and, after its first year following the franchise transfer to Texas, Williams resigned and decided never to return to managing.

Seven decades have elapsed since Ty Cobb, as player-manager, directed the fortunes of the Detroit Tigers. His accomplishments are noteworthy, but they have been maligned over the years by the "great players can't manage" fallacy. It is a fair guess that Cobb's character—its belligerent, combative, unpleasant nature—has often been the basis of negative feeling about the man. Because detractors cannot legitimately deride his playing ability, they have often criticized his managing.

It is true that his charges never won a championship. It is also a fact that Cobb, because of his competitive intensity, was a hard-driving taskmaster. That, in itself, might well have been an important element in Detroit's position as a contender under most of Cobb's stewardship, which resulted in a second-place, two third-place, and a fourth-place ranking during his six seasons as manager from 1921 through 1926. If Cobb's forces did not want to play for him, their performance didn't reflect it.

Cobb is baseball's all-time batting-average leader with his .367 mark over 24 seasons. If his intensity sometimes provoked his players, his teaching skills and the example he set in the batter's box surely rubbed off. Four of his Detroit teams still rank in the top 21 of this century's American League team batting leaders.

In 1921, his first managing year after he reluctantly replaced longtime skipper Hughie Jennings, who had become disinterested and was battling the bottle, the Tigers hit .316, the highest team batting average ever for any American League season. Yet it was the only one of Cobb's six managing seasons that did not result in at least a .500 record. The following five summers Detroit was often in first-place competition with the Huggins-Ruth Yankees and high-quality Washington teams. An overview of Ty Cobb's Tigers:

1921	71–82, 6th place, .316 team batting average, best in AL history
1922	79–75, 3rd place, .305 average, 8th best in AL history
1923	83–71, 2nd place, .300 average, 21st best in AL history
1924	86–68, 3rd place, .298 average, best in league
1925	81–73, 4th place, .302 average, 16th best in AL history
1926	79–75, 6th place, .291 average

One might wonder why Detroit never won the pennant with that kind of hitting. Pitching, or lack of it, is the answer. It usually is. At no time during his managing tenure did Cobb's mound staff post a collective earned run average as low as four. Its sad ERA during those six years was 4.40, 4.27, 4.09, 4.19, 4.61, and 4.41. Three times the Detroit staff was sixth best; another year it was only the fifth-best American League pitching corps in terms of ERA.

Could Cobb have improved the pitchers to the extent that he helped his hitters? There is no way of knowing for certain, of course, but odds are strong that he could not have been much of a force in enhancing their performances. Many of his pitchers had short, nondescript major league careers. Among them were Red Oldham, Carl Holling, Jim Middleton, Bert Cole, Ray Francis, Sam Gibson, Ed Wells, Augie Johns, and Lil Stoner. Not exactly household names that come trippingly off the tongue of even the most ardent of baseball followers. Other Detroit pitchers were better known—Howard Ehmke, Hubert "Dutch" Leonard, Hooks Dauss, Syl Johnson, Herman Pillette, and Earl Whitehill. But not one of them is in the Hall of Fame either. Of this group, most of whose careers were much longer than the aforementioned list of journeymen, none showed any appreciable improvement when they played for other managers before or after hurling for Cobb. Leonard is one example. In three seasons under Cobb he posted a 25–17 record at the end of his 11-year career, a .595 percentage. His overall career mark: .554. Ehmke was 166–166 in 15 American League seasons; pitching for Cobb he won 30 games and lost 31. It was roughly the same scenario for Whitehill. He broke in with Detroit when Cobb was managing there and registered 45 victories against 33 losses (.577). He totalled 17 big-league seasons, spending time with the Senators, Indians, and Cubs in addition to Detroit, and finished with a .541 mark.

Cobb's leadership, it appears, neither hampered nor helped a pitching staff that was mediocre in Detroit and everywhere else its members played during their careers.

With an all-star-calibre hurler or two, and taking into account the Tigers' decent records despite pedestrian pitching figures, Detroit might well have earned championships under Cobb. Combine relatively strong pitching with the Detroit hitters, and more victories most likely would have resulted. Unlike the team's obscure hurlers, the majority of Tiger batsmen were headliners at one time or another: shortstop Donie Bush, outfielder Harry Heilmann, first baseman Lu Blue, catcher Johnny Bassler, outfielder Bobby Veach, outfielder Heinie Manush, utility players Fred Haney, Del Pratt, and Al Wingo. A fellow named Ty Cobb made some offensive contributions, too, *averaging* .365 during those six seasons of his managership. Tiger players won four batting championships during that six-year span. Ironically, none was achieved by Cobb (although his .401 was second to George Sisler's .420 in 1922). Heilmann was the league leader three times with .394 in 1921, .403 in 1923, and .393 in 1925. Manush was the top hitter in 1926 with a .378 mark.

Ty Cobb was a bitter, feisty, acerbic man. That is a certainty. But for a man who directed a team with generally inadequate pitching to continual improvement, to pennant contention frequently, and to five winning seasons in six years, Ty Cobb and his managing accomplishments have been obscured and degraded beyond reason. That, too, is certain.

Ralph Houk

New York AL 1961–63, 1966–73; Detroit 1974–78; Boston AL 1981–84

Twenty-season manager Ralph Houk enjoyed the widespread admiration and high regard of his peers. Yet his greatest successes in the American League standings have been overlooked by the casual fan because of an accident of timing.

Houk's three straight league titles (1961–63) immediately followed the enormous achievements of Casey Stengel, who, in the age of television, surpassed the notoriety of earlier Yankee Hall of Fame managers Miller Huggins and Joe McCarthy. Houk's celebrity, in fact, was later overshadowed by one of his famous but less successful successors, Billy Martin (two Yankee pennants, one World Series crown). And that was before popular Joe Torre, in 1996, led New York to its first World Championship in 18 years.

Of the 421 men who've directed major league teams this century, Ralph Houk ranks 11th on the all-time list of games managed. That, too, surprises the casual fan. Few men surpassed his 20 seasons as a big-league manager—11 years in two separate terms with the Yankees, five in Detroit, and four with the Boston Red Sox. Houk's teams won 1,619 regular-season games for a solid .514 winning percentage.

Only Houk and Detroit's Hughie Jennings won pennants in their initial three seasons of big-league managing. Houk's first two culminated in World Championships—1961 in a five-game Series win against Cincinnati, then an exciting seven-game triumph over the 1962 Giants. (Los Angeles swept New York in the 1963 World Series.)

When Stengel was "retired" by the Yankees in late 1960, Houk was elevated from his coaching post. A former U.S. Marine, he had attained the rank of major and would be known throughout his baseball career as "the Major," who'd been a Yankee catcher for eight seasons beginning in 1947. But as the second- or third-string receiver behind Yogi Berra most of that time, he appeared in a total of only 91 games (158 at bats, .272 average, 20 RBI, no home runs). Nearly half of that playing time was assigned by manager Bucky Harris in 1947 and 1948 when the young Berra was learning his skills under the direction of coach Bill Dickey.

For the next six seasons Houk spent most of his time as a bull-pen catcher. Working with New York's esteemed pitching coach Jim Turner, he absorbed the intricacies of major league pitching. In 1955, by then highly regarded by Yankee brass for his baseball acumen and the leadership abilities honed during his military career, Houk was assigned to manage Denver, New York's Triple-A farm team. Three years later he was back at Yankee Stadium as a coach under Stengel, who was nearing the end of his tenure there. It appeared that Yankee officials were grooming Houk to replace Stengel, and when the time came he was, indeed, ready to step in. With Mickey Mantle, Roger Maris, Berra, Bill Skowron, and Johnny Blanchard leading an offense that hit a then-record 240 home runs, and with a strong infield defense and Whitey Ford's 25–4 pitching record, Houk's initial Yankee team won 109 games. The next two pennants followed immediately. Then Houk was asked to take over the club's general managership. Berra was named field manager, and New York won again. But it took a late-season rally to lift the Yankees to the 1964 title, and when the team floundered early that summer, a front office decision was made to dismiss Berra—regardless of the outcome. (In one of baseball's weirdest sets of circumstances ever, Yogi was replaced by Johnny Keane, whose St. Louis Cardinals had just defeated New York in a seven-game World Series.)

Houk was not particularly comfortable behind an executive suite desk, and after the Yankees went into a tailspin, Houk returned to the dugout with less than a month gone in the 1966 season. CBS had recently taken over ownership of the Yankees, Keane seemed overwhelmed in the hot New York spotlight, the farm system was much less productive than before, and the immediate on-field future was dim. It took a few years for the Yankees to return to contention under Houk, and he was never again quite able to achieve another championship.

He remained in charge of the Yankees' dugout through 1973. Shortly after new owner George Steinbrenner took command, Houk recognized that philosophical differences would be a major distraction. So he resigned after three decades as a member of the Yankees family. He went directly to Detroit and built a solid base of young talent into perennial contenders before retiring after five seasons with the Tigers. Out of baseball for two summers, Houk was hired to manage the Red Sox in 1981. He stayed there for four seasons, and then, at age 65, decided to retire permanently from the dugout.

Houk was never considered a man who "overmanaged" in the Gene Mauch–Alvin Dark mold, and he did not platoon players to the extent his mentor Stengel had. He pretty much put a set lineup on the field and let his players play. With few exceptions, his troops applaud Houk for his one-on-one style, his attention to both their baseball abilities and their personal concerns, and his almost fanatical support when discussing his players with the media. Braves manager Bobby Cox played for only one big-league manager, Houk. When Cox is asked whom he patterns his own successful managing style after, he quickly answers, "Ralph Houk. He treated us like men."

Eddie Dyer

St. Louis NL 1946–50

In their storied history the St. Louis Cardinals have more pennant-winning managers than any other major league team. Of the nine men who led St. Louis to the World Series, the least remembered might be Eddie Dyer. Yet, after Billy Southworth, he recorded the team's next-best four-year run of consecutive winning seasons.

When Dyer, a longtime Cardinal farm system manager, was tapped to direct the organization's big-league club, he was expected to excel immediately. The Redbirds, under Southworth, had finished no lower than second for five years in a row before Dyer's 1946 arrival and had won three pennants and two World Series during that stretch. In the seasons in which they were runners-up, the Cardinals finished only 2½ games behind in 1941, and just three back in 1945, after which Southworth was dismissed.

With Stan Musial, Marty Marion, Whitey Kurowski, Enos Slaughter, Harry Brecheen, Howie Pollet, and Ted Wilkes among his players still in their prime, Dyer, with some trepidation, was well aware of the high expectations for him.

The relatively quiet, mild-mannered organization veteran did not disappoint. His very first season resulted in major success. St. Louis checked in with 96 regular-season victories, good enough for first place. But only for a top-spot deadlock. The major leagues' first postseason play-off in history—a best-of-three match—was required. Dyer's forces won the first two games from Brooklyn, then advanced to an exciting World Series that ended with St. Louis's four-games-to-three triumph over the Boston Red Sox. Dyer, a rather ordinary southpaw pitcher for the 1922–27 Cardinals (15–15 lifetime; two-thirds of his mound appearances as a relief pitcher), used his starters and relievers strategically and successfully throughout the season, and he was able to work Brecheen's World Series itinerary to the utmost. Harry "the Cat" earned three of his team's four World Series wins. Dyer frequently employed the controversial "Boudreau shift" against Ted Williams in this series, and Ted, in his only postseason appearance of a luminous career, hit just .200 (5-for-25, no extra base hits, one RBI) off Dyer's pitching staff.

St. Louis won no more pennants during Dyer's remaining four years there but ranked as a solid contender in all but the last of those seasons. In 1947, 1948, and 1949 they came in second, with the 1949 club registering 96 wins only to be nosed out by just one game by Brooklyn. When the 1950 Cardinals dropped to fifth place, albeit with a winning record of 78–75 and a roster of aging batsmen and pitchers, Dyer's contract was not renewed. At season's end he was still a few days shy of his 50th birthday, but he never managed again. Ironically, the Cardinals never won another pennant in his lifetime. Eddie Dyer succumbed to heart disease in the early days of the 1964 baseball season. Six months later his old team won its first pennant since he had led it to the 1946 championship. Despite Dyer's .578 winning percentage, which ranks among the top dozen this century, his St. Louis accomplishments remain overshadowed by such deservedly celebrated predecessors and successors as Southworth, Frankie Frisch, Red Schoendienst, and Whitey Herzog.

Bill Terry

New York NL, 1932–41

Following directly in the footsteps of a legend can be tricky. Dyer succeeded Southworth; Jimmie Dykes took over for Connie Mack; Wes Westrum followed Casey Stengel at the helm of the hapless but popular Mets; Joe Altobelli went in for Earl Weaver. Imagine the pressure that Bill Terry surely felt when he was personally elevated by his mentor and predecessor, John McGraw.

McGraw had been the toast of the town for a substantial portion of the three decades in which he managed and partially owned the New York Giants.

He had managed them to 10 league pennants, a record that was never exceeded and has been matched only once since—by Casey Stengel. When power baseball overshadowed the "inside baseball" that had been conducted so successfully by McGraw two and three decades earlier, and when poor health started to sap enthusiasm and energy from him, John J. McGraw walked into the Giants clubhouse one early July day in 1932 and abruptly turned the team over to his all-star-caliber first baseman, Bill Terry.

Interestingly, McGraw and Terry didn't much like each other. Terry thought his manager boorish and unpleasant. Terry was regarded much the same way by many of his National League contemporaries. Perhaps McGraw believed that Terry could not be a consistent success and, therefore, would be compared unfavorably with the old master. A few years earlier, when the Giants prepared to trade Frankie Frisch to St. Louis, many onlookers were surprised that McGraw did not name Frisch as his successor. Others, aware that those two similar personalities frequently tangled, felt McGraw expected Frisch to manage equally successfully and, if in a Giants uniform, to possibly overshadow his mentor.

Whether or not either of those scenarios was merited is academic. Frisch never got the chance to manage in New York; Terry did, effectively, for a decade. Three times his Giants won the pennant during a period in which they were often involved in exciting races with good Chicago, St. Louis, and Pittsburgh clubs.

When Terry stepped in for McGraw, the Giants were a lackluster 17–23 and in last place. By season's end they had advanced to sixth and were playing at nearly .500. The following season was the first of Terry's title winners. That 1933 campaign culminated in a World Series victory over Washington. Beaten out by the Gas House Gang Cardinals in 1934, then by the Cubs with their fantastic late-season winning streak the following year, New York was king of the National League again in 1936 and 1937. After both seasons, however, the Polo Grounders fell victim to the powerhouse Yankees of Lou Gehrig, young Joe DiMaggio, Red Ruffing, Tony Lazzeri, Lefty Gomez, Bill Dickey, and manager Joe McCarthy.

Terry would pilot the Giants for four more seasons (a third-place finish, then three years in the second division) before departing in favor of the team's popular Mel Ott who, like Terry, would be elected to the Hall of Fame. Bill Terry, especially in his active baseball life, was often sarcastic and elusive. His Hall of Fame credentials as a first-rate first baseman, however, are legitimate.

Pat Moran

Philadelphia NL 1915–18, Cincinnati 1919–23

It has been rare, but not unknown, for a manager to win a pennant in his first year at a team's helm, as have, for example, Yogi Berra, Ralph Houk, Dick Williams, Eddie Dyer, and Chuck Dressen. Bucky Harris was a winner in his managerial debut at Washington in 1924. Then, after leading several other teams, he won an American League pennant in his first year as Yankees pilot 23 years later.

Pat Moran managed only two teams. In both cases he was in the World Series in his initial year with them. To put his accomplishments in an even more pronounced perspective, he was manager for each of those team's first National League championships—Philadelphia Phillies 1915; Cincinnati Reds 1919.

A journeyman catcher with the Braves, Cubs, and Phillies beginning in 1901, Moran concluded his active career as a player-coach with the 1914 Phillies, who finished sixth that year. Management replaced longtime skipper Red Dooin with Moran. Led by Grover Alexander's pitching and outfielder Gavvy Cravath's slugging, the 1915 Phils under Moran improved by 16 games to win their only NL flag until 1950. Even though Boston was a four-games-to one World Series winner, the Phillies appeared to be headed to continued successful seasons. Indeed, they finished a solid second in each of the two subsequent years. But by 1918, financial problems caused the front office to sell several key players, including Alexander, and Philadelphia dropped to the second division, where it would remain for 15 years. Manager Moran, a visible vocal critic of ownership's actions, was dismissed following a well-publicized argument and after compiling a 323–257 record, one pennant, and two runner-up finishes in his four seasons at Baker Bowl.

Cincinnati was delighted Moran's services were available, and he was signed immediately for the 1919 campaign. That season culminated with the controversial "Black Sox World Series." As that infamous situation has been rechronicled and dramatized in recent years, virtually all focus is on Chicago's scandalous game-throwing actions. As often as the notorious Sox are revisited these many decades later, casual fans are sometimes hard-pressed to name the opposition. The Reds, winning their first modern pennant that season, clearly dominated the National League under Moran's guidance. They finished nine games over second-place New York. It was a scrappy, "inside baseball"–oriented unit with strong pitching (two 20-game winners and a staff ERA of 2.23). Collectively, the Reds hit only 20 home runs during the regular season, but they ranked second in runs scored.

Their World Series triumph is forever tainted. Under normal circumstances Moran's club—whether or not it would have beaten the White Sox on a level playing field—might have been treated more kindly by historians. In three of the four subsequent seasons Cincinnati was a strong contender, finishing second twice and third another time. As the team came off 1923's 91 victories, in second place and only three games behind the Giants, expectations were high as spring training began in 1924. Less than three weeks later Pat Moran was dead, a victim of Bright's disease, an affliction related to kidney problems. He had just turned 48 years old.

His managing career extended over only nine seasons. If healthy, it is likely he would have continued for several more. Moran was one of his era's most highly regarded managers. His .561 winning percentage is among the top 15 this century. Along the way he guided his Phillies and later the Reds to first or second place six times. Ironic, isn't it, that his winning achievements in 1919 were overshadowed forever by another team's scandal? Pat Moran and his Reds triumphed in the World Series, but their accomplishment is just another un-witting victim claimed by the "Black Sox."

Walter Johnson
Washington 1929–32, Cleveland 1933–35

Walter Johnson was nicknamed "The Big Train," was owner of the all-time strikeout record for a half century, was one of the best-hitting pitchers in base-ball history, and was one of five legendary standouts honored at the Baseball Hall of Fame's first induction in 1936.

Largely because of Walter Johnson's enormous achievements as a genuine headliner on the field throughout his 21-year career, entirely in the uniform of the Washington Senators, his respectable seven seasons as a manager are usually dismissed as less than ordinary. In that sense he is unfairly placed in the same category as his contemporary Ty Cobb. "They were great players," the de-tractors say, "but they failed as managers. No championships."

If Johnson had a failing as a manager it was his innate gentlemanly nature and his continuous personification of sportsmanship and fairness. In his four years piloting the Senators, and especially during three later seasons with Cleveland, his authority was often undermined and he was frequently ridiculed—usually by second-line players who felt they deserved more playing time but whose talents were probably appraised more accurately by Johnson than by themselves. At Cleveland, some of the malcontents were aided and abetted by a few members of the sporting press, who criticized Johnson for lack of control over this team.

Indeed, Johnson did not operate with a heavy hand on tight reins. The as-sessment of him as "too soft" is most likely quite accurate. He admitted, throughout his managing career and especially after it, that he did not enjoy managing very much. When his contract was terminated by the Indians in mid-season, 1935, he appeared to welcome his departure. He never managed again and had no inclination to return to it.

Walter Johnson, a perfectionist in matters of his own public and personal life, was not emotionally equipped to be a hard-driving boss. His managing career is not deserving of special plaudits, as he would readily admit. However, neither does it deserve to be maligned as simply another typical failure by a big-name player.

A record of 529 wins against 432 losses—a .550 winning percentage—does not constitute failure. In four of the five full seasons he managed, his teams finished in the first division. In 1933 when he took over at Cleveland as Roger Peckinpaugh's replacement 51 games into the season, the Indians ranked higher at the end of the year than they did when he arrived.

Senators owner Clark Griffith was Johnson's longtime employer and admirer. Following his favorite pitcher's 1927 retirement, Griffith arranged for Johnson to get a "feel" for managing with the Newark club of the International League. For the next season, 1929, Griffith (another pitcher who also had managed) prevailed on "the Big Train" to pilot the Senators, then officially still known as the Washington Nationals. His first year resulted in a disappointing 71–81 record and a fifth-place finish. But the next three years, battling Connie Mack's champion Athletics and the powerful Yankees, Johnson's team posted 94, 92, then 93 victories. No pennants, but always in solid contention. Interestingly, following 1932's strong third-place finish, Griffith asked Johnson to step down as manager. Still friendly with his one-time pitching ace, and still very fond of him, Griffith nonetheless felt four years was long enough for Johnson, and that his young shortstop (and eventually his son-in-law), Joe Cronin, would be an energetic spark plug as manager. We'll never know if Johnson-led Senators could have won the 1933 pennant, but it's a matter of record that Griffith pulled the right strings. Cronin led Washington to its third and last American League flag that year. By then Walter Johnson had resurfaced in Cleveland, where his record over parts of three seasons was a creditable 179-168.

By his own admission "the Big Train" had neither the aptitude nor the strong desire for managing. But compared to many career pilots with more elevated reputations, Walter Johnson had the better record.

Overlooked Oldtimers, Short Timers . . . and Still Timers

Surely other managers deserve to be remembered for their leadership of 20th-century baseball teams. But this kind of judgment can be largely subjective; thus, it automatically fosters debate (one of baseball's charms). Based primarily on their teams' accomplishments, my pick of generally overlooked managers fall into three categories: (1) oldtimers, men who managed with distinction mostly in the first half of the 20th century; (2) short timers, men whose successful managing careers were relatively brief; and (3) still timers, current and recent managers.

Oldtimers

The passage of time has dimmed memories about these long ago successful managers.

Fred Clarke. Pirates' player-manager 1901–15. Four-time National League pennant winner; won 1909 World Series; considered an effective instructor and motivator; 1,343–909 record in 15 years; also managed four years in NL before 1901; member of Hall of Fame as a player.

Frank Chance. Cubs 1905–12, Yankees 1913–14, Red Sox 1923. Baseball's most successful five consecutive years with 116, 107, 99, 104, and 104 wins for Cubs from 1906 through 1910, while serving as first baseman in famous Tinker, Evers, Chance (and Steinfeldt) infield. The 116 victories, a one-season major league record still standing, were accomplished in only 152 regular-season games. Only Cubs' pilot to win a World Series (1907–8); .593 winning percentage (946–648) is this century's third best behind McCarthy and Southworth; member of Hall of Fame in Player category.

Tris Speaker. Indians 1919–26. Led Tribe to its first pennant and world title (1920); in first division six of his eight years; a solid 617–520 record; player-manager, who as a center fielder, frequently exchanged signals with catcher Steve O'Neill for pitching strategy; relinquished manager's job at behest of Commissioner Landis, who ordered both Speaker and Cobb to step down following unsubstiantiated allegations of their involvement in a betting scandal many years earlier. Speaker and Cobb subsequently were teammates on the 1928 A's, the final active year for both.

Pants Rowland. White Sox 1915–18. An organization man and crony of owner Charles Comiskey, who was brought on initially as caretaker; team immediately jumped from sixth to third in his first year, then to second and, in 1917, to the pennant and a World Series win over Giants; many of the 1919 "Black Sox" players came into their own during Rowland's stewardship; posted four-year record of 339–247; became one of baseball's oldest ex-managers—was 90 at his 1969 death.

Jimmy Collins. 1901–06 Red Sox. Winner of history's first World Series, 1903, over Pittsburgh; Boston won AL title the next year, too, but John Brush, owner of the NL-winning Giants, refused to allow his team to participate; third baseman was player-manager; when American League was formed Collins was recruited across town from Boston's NL team, where he was a very popular infielder/future Hall of Fame player; six-year record of 455–376; first five years in first division.

Charlie Grimm. Cubs 1932–38, '44-'49, '60; Braves 1952–56. A more recent "oldtimer" whose managing successes have been dimmed through time by the Cubs' half century of futility; two pennants in his first Chicago tenure (1932 and 1935) and then won the team's most recent flag (1945); not a stern disciplinarian, more the "friendly uncle" style of managing; since Chance's time he owns the best winning record as Cubs pilot, 1,287 wins-1,067 defeats, .547 percentage; in 4 ½ years with Braves he went 341–285; was their last manager in Boston, their first in Milwaukee where young talent under Grimm finished second, third, and second.

Fielder Jones. White Sox 1904–8, Browns 1916–18. Outfielder/manager directed Sox to Chicago's first World Championship with 1906 victory over crosstown Cubs; in five years as pilot White Sox never lower than third with overall 426–293 record; not nearly as successful with Browns at end of managing career after two seasons in short-lived Federal League; played and managed at a time when many colorful and/or weird nicknames permeated baseball— Jones's given name, believe it or not: Fielder Allison Jones.

Hugh Jennings. Tigers 1907–20, Giants 1924. Old Baltimore Oriole infielder with Ned Hanlon's champion scrappers that included John McGraw and Wilbert Robinson; proponent of "inside baseball" who spurred Tigers to three straight AL flags (1907-9); Ty Cobb was a member of the Tigers during every one of Jennings's Detroit seasons; member of Hall of Fame as player, but posted good managing record of 1,163–984; last 32 of those wins as fill-in for McGraw for whom he was coaching in New York during 1924 season; had advanced Giants into first place for McGraw's return to dugout.

Short Timers

The men named in this section managed relatively few seasons, and although they attained success in their short terms, they are seldom automatic "givens" when baseball's top managers are listed. For some of them, short tenures were abruptly terminated by illness or injury.

Dick Howser. Yankees 1978, 1980; Royals 1981–86. A former American League shortstop, Howser managed four division winners and registered a pair of second-place finishes in the six full seasons in which he directed the Yankees and Royals. His 1985 Kansas City club won the World championship after coming from a three-games-to-one deficit against St. Louis in the World Series. A brain tumor forced his retirement midway through the following season, and he succumbed just a year later at age 51. A .544 winning percentage and just one losing season (79–83, second place AL West 1983) rank Howser among the leading pilots of his time. Ironically, his best year in terms of wins and losses was 1980, when he directed the Yankees to a 103–59 record. But after Kansas City swept New York in the ALCS, Howser resigned after an argument with owner George Steinbrenner, who had sacked Howser's third-base coach because of a base-running blunder.

Mickey Cochrane. Tigers 1934–38. Cochrane is a name familiar to even the most casual of baseball followers, but as a Hall of Fame catcher rather than as a manager. Yet, he was the toast of the town during the Depression years in Detroit when, as player-manager, he led the Tigers to a league title his first year there, 1934, and followed with a World Series victory the next season. Detroit had not won a pennant for a quarter century until Cochrane's arrival. Early in 1936, however, he suffered one of baseball's most critical beanings while batting against New York. Unconscious for several days, he ultimately survived the injury but was never again able to play regularly. Dizziness and headaches continued for years, and Cochrane was forced to relinquish the team's leadership for several dozen games in both 1936 and 1937. He was retired late in the 1938 campaign. Regarded as an intelligent, motivating leader, Cochrane had been expected to enjoy a long, successful managing career. The untimely injury, however, limited him to 625 games in the manager's chair. Two pennants in the only full seasons he managed, and a .579 winning percentage, place him among his era's finest.

Sam Mele. Twins 1961–67. During the Twins' first season in Minnesota after the franchise transferred from Washington, where it generally finished deep in the second division, Sam Mele, then a coach, replaced Cookie Lavagetto as manager. Under Mele the team turned in a pedestrian 47–54 record for the remainder of that initial Minneapolis–St. Paul season but rebounded to contend with 91 victories in each of the following two summers. After slipping to sixth place in 1964 Minnesota, under Mele, won 102 games in 1965 for the franchise's first American League pennant since Joe Cronin led Washington 32 years earlier. The 102 victories posted by Mele's 1965 Twins represent the only time during the franchise's 98-year history that the century mark in wins has been reached. Although only 44 when he was forced out in 1967, Mele never seriously considered managing again, even though he finished in the first division four times during his five full seasons, and produced a highly respectable .546 career percentage.

Yogi Berra. Yankees 1964, 1984–85; Mets 1972–75. As is the case with Mickey Cochrane, Berra is widely known as a baseball player. But as a manager he is probably best remembered for being fired following the 1964 season, after he led the Yankees to the pennant in a tight race before a loss in the seventh World Series game. His replacement at New York? Johnny Keane, the fellow who led St. Louis to the Series championship. As of Labor Day neither Berra's nor Keane's team had been given much chance to win the pennants they eventually captured, and both managers were considered lame ducks at that point. Berra, angered by his treatment from the front office, quickly moved across town to coach (and play very briefly) under Casey Stengel with the Mets. When manager Gil Hodges was felled by a heart attack during spring training of 1972, Berra was named Mets manager. He elevated the club to third place that year, then to the National League title in 1973. Again, his pennant winner was a seventh-game World Series victim (against Oakland). New York fell from contention the following season, but Yogi had the Mets in third place when he was fired in 1975. Often characterized—and caricatured—as a buffoon, Berra was generally considered to be a good strategist and the type of manager who built a solid rapport with his troops. A .523 winning percentage for six full seasons, and two pennants won under New York's critical microscope, place Yogi Berra among baseball's underrated short-term pilots.

Oscar Vitt. Indians 1938–40. His former players would likely deride Oscar Vitt's inclusion on our list of overlooked, or underrated, managers. It was he, after all, who was the target of this century's most notorious "mutiny" this side of the USS *Caine*. Vitt managed only three major league seasons following success in the high minors, most notably at Newark, New Jersey, in the Yankees' system. He was regarded as a hard-driving autocrat. Many felt Vitt reflected the style of his Tiger manager Hughie Jennings (a famous "old Oriole") and his longtime Detroit teammate, the acerbic Ty Cobb. Vitt had been a scrappy third baseman for 10 American League seasons, mostly with Detroit. When he finally earned a major league managership after guiding Newark, "the greatest minor league team of all time," to a 1937 flag, Vitt was continually accused of playing favorites and of undermining his players by sniping behind their backs. The "Crybaby Rebellion," chronicled elsewhere in this book, resulted. Although strong evidence points to Vitt's inability to build morale and to his overall lack of effective leadership, I include him among the overlooked short-termers for his creditable .570 percentage, a 262–198 record, and solid first-division finishes as Cleveland faced exceptionally strong competition from New York, Detroit, and Boston during his brief tenure as Indians manager.

Still Timers

Many current or recently retired managers who have produced notable results with their teams cannot be considered "overlooked." Yet. It is likely, in fact expected, that some eventually will be admitted to the Hall of Fame. Sparky Anderson is a shoo-in. Supporters will make strong Cooperstown cases for Whitey Herzog, Jim Leyland, Billy Martin, Dick Williams, Tony LaRussa, and Bobby Cox. For those in the list that follows, there is still time to add luster and notoriety to their already significant achievements.

Tom Kelly. Twins, 1986– . Whether it's because of the relative obscurity that comes with working in one of the smaller media regions, or his own laid-back nature, Tom Kelly is surely among the least known of baseball's best managers. Many self-professed students of the game are surprised to learn that Kelly began his 13th season as Twins pilot in 1998. Twins free agents come and go—mostly go—but Kelly's teams, often outmanned, are rarely outhustled. Add the fact that he already has two World Series titles to his credit, and an overall record of nearly .500, and one is mystified by the lack of recognition accorded this grossly underrated and overlooked manager.

Felipe Alou. Expos 1992– . Improved team's record in each of first three seasons. Advanced team from fourth to second during his 125 games of 1992, won a franchise second-best 94 games the next year, had a substantial first-place lead in 1994 at time of work stoppage, and, by 1996, had risen again to second. Despite loss of free agents, his Expos are invariably competitive. It has been suggested, when predicting finishes, to pick an Alou team—as one might a Jim Leyland club—one position higher than you would if he were not managing it. Because he was 56 when offered his first big-league assignment, Alou probably will not attain the managing longevity achieved by the more prominent all-timers.

Don Baylor. Rockies 1993–98. Perhaps too soon to forecast lengthy managing success, but Baylor directed Colorado into the postseason (1995 National League wild card) faster than any other expansion team to reach that level. After a 67–95 initial season the Rockies were on a pace to better that by several games when the 1994 campaign ended prematurely. Not deterred, Baylor led a power-hitting team, with little previous pitching success, to 77–67 and into the 1995 NL playoffs. Baylor is considered an excellent instructor and a confidence builder.

Jim Fregosi. Angels 1978–81, White Sox 1986–88, Phillies 1991–96. A two-time division winner (California 1979; Philadelphia 1993), Fregosi guided the

1993 Phillies into the World Series. Never blessed with an abundance of all-star-caliber players at any one time, his overall mediocre record of under .500 overshadows his effectiveness as a "veteran players' manager" who has earned respect from most of his troops in exchange for his understanding of their capabilities and limitations. A willing candidate if a job opening occurs again, Fregosi is now special assistant to the Giants' general manager.

Cito Gaston. Blue Jays 1989–97. A perfect example of a relatively small-market manager whose achievements far exceed the notoriety and visibility he receives. Yes, Toronto ownership and management developed a productive farm system, traded well, and excelled with free-agent signings, but it was Gaston who molded the personnel into a smooth, winning machine. Two World Championships, four times American League East champs, an overall 426–315 record before free-agent departures caused the Blue Jays to nose dive. A non-demonstrative yet decisive leader. Having seen how free agency can decimate a team and disappoint its manager, he might forgo any future managing opportunies that beckon.

Dusty Baker. Giants, 1993– . As a rookie pilot in 1993 he led San Francisco to 103 victories, the most since the club moved from New York 35 years earlier. (Alvin Dark's Giants also won 103, but that figure included two play-off victories in 1962.) In his fifth season at Candlestick Point, Dusty directed San Francisco to the NL West Division crown, its first in nearly a decade. Three times Baker has been saluted as Manager of the Year. He is considered to excel as both a motivator and a teacher and, as a dedicated student of the game in the LaRussa mold (and, yes, Stengel too), he is regarded as an astute strategist extremely accomplished in his knowledge of his players' strengths in specific game situations.

Mike Hargrove. Indians, 1991– . After several decades in the American League hinterlands, Cleveland has gained nationwide exposure in the 1990s under Hargrove's guidance. The Indians won their first pennant in more than four decades in 1995 after improving continually during his tenure and at a time when a new ballpark helped build local interest. Two years later they returned to the World Series. Several All-Stars adorn his roster, so Hargrove might best be judged in subsequent years if his talent base gets thinner. Still, credit him with outstanding leadership abilities, as he daily directed a clubhouse that has contained such divergent personalities as Orel Hershiser and Albert Belle!

Davey Johnson. Mets 1984–90, Reds 1993–95, Orioles 1996–97. As he ended his third managing tenure—at Baltimore, where he played second base for Earl Weaver's juggernauts in the late 1960s and early 1970s—Johnson owned *the* best winning percentage among active managers, .575, the 12th highest of all time. Yet in the minds of fans, he seems overshadowed by contemporaries such as Lasorda, LaRussa, Leyland, Cox, Herzog, and Anderson. His 11-year record through 1997: 985 wins, 727 losses, one World Series title, three division flags, and a postseason wild-card berth.

Other managers, as of Opening Day 1998, appeared to have bright futures, for time and relative youth are on their side if further opportunities to manage exist for them. This group included Buddy Bell, then at Detroit; Phil Garner, Milwaukee; Johnny Oates, Texas; Terry Collins, Anaheim; Jim Riggleman, Chicago Cubs; Terry Francona, Philadelphia; and Bruce Bochy, San Diego. Buck Showalter gained notable success during his four years piloting the contending New York Yankees, and returned in 1998 as the first manager of Arizona's expansion Diamondbacks.

As the 1999 campaign got underway, these other, often overlooked veteran managers hoped to enhance their previous accomplishments.

Art Howe. Athletics. Won nearly 400 games in five seasons at Houston, then led a young Athletics club to a better-than-predicted finish in 1996. But his laid-back style and sometimes a tendency to keep ineffective pitchers on the mound have been criticized when his teams aren't contending.

Lou Piniella. Mariners. Even though he won a World title at Cincinnati in 1990, his visibility level increased significantly as Seattle won its first-division crowns in 1995 and 1997, and he is likely to be a strong contender for years to come.

Joe Torre. Yankees. After 14 years of piloting experience with Mets, Braves, and Cardinals, including a NL West championship at Atlanta in 1982, he guided the New York Yankees to the 1996 and '98 World Series crowns and earned overdue national notoriety. His 1997 Yanks were wild-card participants.

Bobby Valentine. Mets. Owner of the Texas Rangers' longest managerial tenure (1985–92), and a 581–605 record there, he was called to New York for the final 31 games of 1996 and was expected to develop the young Mets into contenders just as he had done with youthful players at Texas. Despite an enormous number of pitching-staff injuries, he managed the Mets to a competitive 88–74 logs in 1997 and '98.

An Honor and a Privilege

The franchise known as the Minnesota Twins represented Washington, D.C., for 60 years, most of them during Clark Griffith's baseball administration. The Senators there won three pennants—two by Bucky Harris, the other under Joe Cronin. Over their first 37 years in the Minneapolis–St. Paul area, the transplanted Senators also have three American League flags to their credit. Just as in Washington, one manager has guided the team to two of its crowns: Tom Kelly.

As Al Lopez is our arbitrarily designated "dean" of the Hall of Fame's living members, Tom Kelly is the "dean" of current major league baseball managers.

At age 48, as the 1998 season concluded, Kelly held the distinction of heading his team continuously for a longer period of time than any other current manager or head coach connected with the four major professional spectator sports—major league baseball, National Football League, National Basketball Association, National Hockey League. Twenty-nine big-league ball clubs, 30 NFL teams, 29 NBA teams, and 26 NHL units had replaced their bench bosses, opened for business, or both, since Tom Kelly started to run the Twins' dugout. Literally hundreds of managers and head coaches later, only Tom Kelly has operated out of the same stand since 1986. By opening Day 1998 baseball alone had welcomed 108 new managers since Kelly took over in Minnesota.

Bucky Harris directed the franchise in 18 seasons when it was in Washington. But that was over a stretch of three different managing terms. Kelly's 13 years, and counting, is the franchise record for consecutive seasons managed and, in fact, ties New York's Miller Huggins and Casey Stengel for eighth longest in American League history after Connie Mack, Philadelphia (50); Sparky Anderson, Detroit (17); Joe McCarthy, New York (16); Earl Weaver, Baltimore (15); and Hughie Jennings, Detroit (14). Joe Cronin, Boston, and Jimmie Dykes, Chicago, like Kelly, had 13 seasons. That's heady company.

Tom Kelly's two World Championships (1987 and 1991) are more than were ever registered by Al Lopez, Whitey Herzog, Joe Cronin, Charlie Grimm, Gene Mauch, Bill Rigney, Jimmie Dykes, Frankie Frisch, Chuck Dressen, Wilbert Robinson, or Jim Leyland, among other notable and very able longtime managers. Yet Kelly, even with his distinctive longevity, is probably one of our lesser-known managers. That's partly due to his team's so-called small-market location at some distance from major media centers, and partially because of Kelly's own laid-back personality and his hesitancy to seek out spotlights and headlines.

When owner Carl Pohlad signed Kelly, then a Twins coach, as manager late in the 1986 season there was no special reason to expect managing brilliance. Tom had a good but not spectacular minor league career as an outfielder, was a reserve at Minnesota for about half of the 1975 season, then turned in respectable managing performances with Twins farm teams for awhile prior to his three years as a Minnesota coach under managers Billy Gardner and Ray

Miller. As his playing days were ending, the Twins offered Tom his first managing assignment at Tacoma.

"I figured I'd give it a year or two, see if I could help anybody," he recalls. "I had some good players in those early years in the minors, so that made it easier for me and encouraged me to continue managing for awhile." "Awhile" turned into baseball's equivalent of an eternity. Less than four years is a manager's average tenure with one club. Kelly has more than tripled that already.

His comments, recollections, evaluations of current conditions, and managing philosophy provide revealing insights into his humanity, maturity, sensitivity, and genuine love for baseball: "It's important to recognize that the game changes. Everything does. Economics force you to adjust your ball club—we all know that. It behooves you [a manager] to understand what the owner can do and can't do. I owe our owner, Carl Pohlad, a lot. He has an enormous responsibility to his people and the organization. You might not like the way economics dictate circumstances, but once you understand the owner's situation, then you can move forward. You live and work with what you have. And with the way things change and the way players move around, maybe next year your situation will change.

"Here with the Twins we try to get men who want to play in our system, and each day we tend to feel that this is the most important game we'll play."

Observe the Twins in action, and preferably during pregame drills too, and you can't miss the enthusiasm they exude. Don't use Opening Day as your gauge. Catch them some hot August afternoon when they might be out of realistic contention. They show up feeling, as Kelly said, that it's their most important game. Chuck Knoblauch, their peppery All-Star second baseman at the time, personified the Twins', and Kelly's, philosophy. Watch him in the on-deck circle as he examines the pitcher's every movement, and between pitches as he intensely practices his well-honed batting stroke.

"I appreciate it when people say how impressed they are with our team's hustle and spirit," said Knoblauch. "But that's the way big leaguers are supposed to be, isn't it? If you don't go all out all the time you're cheating everybody—the fans, your teammates, and yourself. I was brought up to put complete effort into the game. Unfortunately, not everybody takes advantage of the opportunity to be in the big leagues, and it really bugs me to see that."

Knoblauch's actions and words perfectly exemplify Kelly's approach to successful baseball. "We work to get our people to play the game as it's supposed to be played," repeats Kelly. "And that goes for everybody—the coaches, manager, clubhouse people, trainers. When they come to the ballpark they're ready to perform their jobs. Those coaches, by the way, have always worked hard for us. Nowadays more teaching has to be done than in years past. With free agency you lose people, and when you combine that with expansion now, all teams rush young players through the organization too fast. There's a big difference between Triple-A and the majors. When these youngsters get here they require a lot of teaching. So I thank our coaches for not only the teaching of mechanics, but for their enthusiastic attitude that carries over to these young players."

The majority of current managers, as we have seen, look upon much of their responsibility to the media as a necessary evil. Kelly astutely assesses that situation, too. "All I ask is that the press be fair. I understand the media's responsibilties, and we certainly owe information to them and their readers and listeners. As long as they handle their job professionally, fine. But don't try to dig up extraneous things just to create sensations. Rip us for things that don't go right on the field. Fine. But don't cause trouble. I've always told our players not to drop to the level of writers who appear to be troublemakers. That's bound to affect performance on the field, and cause distractions."

Kelly has been a World Series winner twice, has been a contending runner-up on other occasions, and has been there for some long dry spells, too. What's his summary of those first 13 years as the Twins' dugout director?

"So many things happen that are just plain fun. There are so many things that draw a baseball team together, and the public will never know about them. But that's okay, because being together for six months or more builds a kind of private togetherness. Nobody else is there on the airplane, or for a joke in the clubhouse. Outsiders aren't a part of those grand things that go on that create unity. The kinds of things that are so special about being part of a team."

Entering middle age now, Kelly has been around professional baseball teams for close to 5,000 games. He's not certain that pressures on a manager ever ease off, or if the euphoria of winning the big one can elude even the most hardened of veterans. He relates two incidents that closely followed the seven-game World Series triumph over Atlanta in 1991.

"First of all, there was a lot of excitement through the play-offs leading up to the Series. Then the Series itself was so pressure packed. Every game was a tight one. [Jack Morris's 10-inning complete-game victory in Game 7 is an all-time World Series highlight.] We had celebrations right afterward, and a trip to the White House to be greeted by the president. Then we flew back to Minneapolis where they had 18 inches of snow on the ground. They worked hard to get the runway open for us, though. A day or two later—after all the excitement, travel, shoveling snow, and what not—I woke up with a start. My first thought was Who's my pitcher tonight? Imagine that, the last game's been over for days, and my mind hasn't adjusted to the off-season. Your subconscious can really play tricks on you. I guess maybe being exhausted was a factor. Still . . .

"Let me wrap this up by using a World Series incident to try to explain the special feeling I still have about being part of baseball, and this team. And how winning a championship can affect you no matter how old you are or how long you've been around.

"Wayne Terwilliger—you might remember him as an infielder years ago with the Dodgers, Cubs, and Senators in the late 1940s and '50s—well 'Twig' was one of our coaches, and before that he'd been connected with the game as a player and coach for 40-some years. Now he's still living in Mounds, Minnesota, and helping out with the independent league St. Paul club. One of his many responsibilites with us during that 1991 season was to stay in charge of the baseballs—the ones for batting practice, infield drills, fungo hitting, and so forth. When that seventh game of the Series was over, and we'd beaten the Braves, and the celebration on the field was dying down and we're gathering in the clubhouse, there was Twig, still out there near the infield, just walking around with the ball bag on his arm. Kinda wandering aimlessly in a daze with a strange look of bewildered contentment on his face. Here was a man, nearly 70 years old, who had spent almost a half century in baseball and had never been on a championship team before. No winning team anywhere. Never, until that night. He couldn't let go of that feeling.

"It's just about impossible to describe the joy that baseball can bring you."

From Adair To Zimmer:
The 421 Big League Managers,
1901–1998

This alphabetical chart of managers describes regular season records only. Postseason accomplishments are spotlighted on pages 269–291. From 1901 through 1968 the Best Finish column refers to overall league standings. From 1969 through 1998 it designates rankings within the team's division and winners of the league pennant (see Sparky Anderson). Where a manager did not finish his team's season, the Best Finish figure (in parentheses) denotes the team's standing at the time of *his* final game, not the team's final standing for that season (see Joe Altobelli, Chicago).

Manager	Team	W	L	Best Finish
BILL ADAIR b. March 10, 1913, Mobile, AL Marion Danne Adair	Chicago AL 1970	4	6	(6th)
JOE ADCOCK b. Oct. 30, 1927, Coushatta, LA Joseph Wilbur Adcock	Cleveland 1967	75	87	8th
FELIPE ALOU b. May 12, 1935, Dominican Rep. Felipe Rojas y Alou	Montreal 1992–98	535	496	2nd
WALTER ALSTON b. Dec. 1, 1911, Venice, OH Walter Emmons Alston d. age 72	Brooklyn/Los Angeles NL 1954–76	2,040	1,613	7 pennants
JOE ALTOBELLI b. May 26, 1932, Detroit, MI Joseph Salvatore Altobelli	San Francisco 1977–79 Baltimore 1983–85 Chicago NL 1991	225 212 0 437	239 167 1 407	3rd 1 pennant (5th)

Continued

Manager	Team	W	L	Best Finish
JOEY AMALFITANO b. Jan. 23, 1934, San Pedro, CA John Joseph Amalfitano	Chicago NL 1979–81	66	116	5th
SPARKY ANDERSON b. Feb. 22, 1934, Bridgewater, SD George Lee Anderson	Cincinnati 1970–78 Detroit 1979–95	863 1,247 2,110	586 1,248 1,834	4 pennants 1 pennant
LUKE APPLING b. April 2, 1907, High Point, NC Lucius Benjamin Appling d. age 83	Kansas City A's 1967	10	30	10th
BILL ARMOUR b. Sept. 3, 1869, Homestead, PA William R. Armour d. age 53	Cleveland 1902–4 Detroit 1905–6	232 150 382	195 152 347	3rd 3rd
KEN ASPROMONTE b. Sept. 22, 1931, Brooklyn, NY Kenneth Joseph Aspromonte	Cleveland 1972–74	220	260	4th
JIMMY AUSTIN b. Dec. 8, 1879, Wales James Philip Austin d. age 85	St. Louis AL 1913, '18, '23	31	44	5th
DEL BAKER b. May 3, 1892, Sherwood, OR Delmar David Baker d. age 81	Detroit 1933, 1936–42 Boston AL 1960	410 2 412	352 5 357	1 pennant 8th
DUSTY BAKER b. June 15, 1949, Riverside, CA Johnnie B. Baker Jr.	San Francisco 1993–98	472	436	1st NL West
GEORGE BAMBERGER, b. Aug. 1, 1925, Staten Island, NY George Irvin Bamberger	Milwaukee AL 1978–80 New York NL 1982–83 Milwaukee AL 1985–86	235 81 142 458	180 127 171 478	2nd 6th 6th

Continued

Manager	Team	W	L	Best Finish
DAVE BANCROFT b. April 20, 1891, Sioux City, IA David James Bancroft d. age 81	Boston NL 1924–27	238	336	5th
FRANK BANCROFT b. May 9, 1846, Lancaster, MA Frank Carter Bancroft d. age 74 Also managed 8 years before 1901.	Cincinnati 1902	9	7	(5th)
ED BARROW b. May 10, 1868, Springfield, IL Edward Grant Barrow d. age 85	Detroit 1903–4 Boston AL 1918–20	97 <u>213</u> 310	117 <u>203</u> 320	5th 1 pennant
JACK BARRY b. April 26, 1887, Meriden, CT John Joseph Barry d. age 73	Boston AL 1917	90	62	2nd
HANK BAUER b. July 31, 1922, E. St. Louis, IL Henry Albert Bauer	Kansas City A's 1961–62 Baltimore 1964–68 Oakland 1969	107 407 <u>80</u> 594	157 318 <u>69</u> 544	9th 1 pennant 2nd
DON BAYLOR b. June 28, 1949, Austin, TX Don Edward Baylor	Colorado 1993–98	440	469	2nd
BUDDY BELL b. Aug. 27, 1951, Pittsburgh, PA David Gus Bell	Detroit 1996–98	184	277	3rd
VERN BENSON b. Sept. 19, 1924, Granite Quarry, NC Vernon Adair Benson	Atlanta 1977	1	0	(6th)

Continued

335

Manager	Team	W	L	Best Finish
YOGI BERRA				
b. May 12, 1925, St. Louis, MO	New York AL 1964	99	63	1 pennant
Lawrence Peter Berra	New York NL 1972–75	292	296	1 pennant
	New York AL 1984–85	93	85	3rd
		484	444	
TERRY BEVINGTON				
b. July 27, 1956, Akron, OH	Chicago AL 1995–97	222	214	2nd
Terry Paul Bevington				
HUGO BEZDEK				
b. April 1, 1883, Austria-Hungary	Pittsburgh 1917–19	166	187	4th
Hugo Francis Bezdek				
d. age 69				
JOE BIRMINGHAM				
b. Aug. 6, 1884, Elmira, NY	Cleveland 1912–15	170	191	3rd
Joseph Leo Birmingham				
d. age 61				
DEL BISSONETTE				
b. Sept. 6, 1899, Winthrop, ME	Boston NL 1945	25	34	6th
Delphia Louis Bissonette				
d. age 72				
LENA BLACKBURNE				
b. Oct. 23, 1886, Clifton Hgts., PA	Chicago AL 1928–29	99	133	5th
Russell Aubrey Blackburne				
d. age 81				
RAY BLADES				
b. Aug. 6, 1896, Mt. Vernon, IL	St. Louis NL 1939–40	106	85	2nd
Francis Raymond Blades	Brooklyn 1948	1	0	(5th)
d. age 82		107	85	
OSSIE BLUEGE				
b. Oct. 24, 1900, Chicago, IL	Washington 1943–47	375	394	2nd
Oswald Louis Bluege				
d. age 84				

Continued

Manager	Team	W	L	Best Finish
BRUCE BOCHY b. April 16, 1955, France Bruce Douglas Bochy	San Diego 1995–98	335	295	1 pennant
JOHN BOLES b. Aug. 19, 1948, Chicago, IL John Egan Boles	Florida 1996	40	35	3rd
BOB BOONE b. Nov. 19, 1947, San Diego, CA Robert Raymond Boone	Kansas City Royals 1995–97	181	206	2nd
STEVE BOROS b. Sept. 3, 1936, Flint, MI Stephen Boros	Oakland 1983–84 San Diego 1986	94 <u>74</u> 168	112 <u>88</u> 200	4th 4th
JIM BOTTOMLEY b. April 23, 1900, Oglesby, IL James LeRoy Bottomley d. age 59	St. Louis AL 1937	21	56	8th
LOU BOUDREAU b. July 17, 1917, Harvey, IL Louis Boudreau	Cleveland 1942–50 Boston AL 1952–54 Kansas City A's 1955–57 Chicago NL 1960	728 229 151 <u>54</u> 1,162	649 232 260 <u>83</u> 1,224	1 pennant 4th 6th 7th
LARRY BOWA b. Dec. 6, 1945, Sacramento, CA Lawrence Robert Bowa	San Diego 1987–88	81	127	5th
FRANK BOWERMAN b. Dec. 5, 1868, Romeo, MI Frank Eugene Bowerman d. age 79	Boston NL 1909	22	54	8th

Continued

Manager	Team	W	L	Best Finish
KEN BOYER b. May 20, 1931, Liberty, MO Kenton Lloyd Boyer d. age 51	St. Louis NL 1978–80	166	190	3rd
BILL BRADLEY b. Feb. 13, 1878, Cleveland, OH William Joseph Bradley d. age 76	Cleveland 1905	20	21	(2nd)
BOBBY BRAGAN b. Oct. 30, 1917, Birmingham, AL Robert Randall Bragan	Pittsburgh 1956–57 Cleveland 1958 Milwaukee NL/Atlanta 1963–66	102 31 310 443	155 36 287 478	7th (5th) 5th
ROGER BRESNAHAN b. June 11, 1879, Toledo, OH Roger Philip Bresnahan d. age 65	St. Louis NL 1909–12 Chicago NL 1915	255 73 328	352 80 432	5th 4th
DAVE BRISTOL b. June 23, 1933, Macon, GA James David Bristol	Cincinnati 1966–69 Milwaukee AL 1970–72 Atlanta 1976–77 San Francisco 1979–80	298 144 130 85 657	265 209 192 98 764	3rd 5th 6th 4th
EARLE BRUCKER b. May 6, 1901, Albany, NY Earle Francis Brucker d. age 80	Cincinnati 1952	3	2	(7th)
AL BUCKENBERGER b. Jan. 31, 1861, Detroit, MI Albert C. Buckenberger d. age 56 Also managed 7 years before 1901.	Boston NL 1902–4	186	242	3rd
JIMMY BURKE b. Oct. 12, 1874, St. Louis, MO James Timothy Burke d. age 67	St. Louis NL 1905 St. Louis AL 1918–20	34 172 206	56 180 236	(6th) 4th

Continued

Manager	Team	W	L	Best Finish
BILL BURWELL b. March 27, 1895, Jarbalo, KS William Edwin Burwell d. age 78	Pittsburgh 1947	1	0	7th
DONIE BUSH b. Oct. 8, 1887, Indianapolis, IN Owen Joseph Bush d. age 84	Washington 1923 Pittsburgh 1927–29 Chicago AL 1930–31 Cincinnati 1933	75 246 118 <u>58</u> 497	78 178 189 <u>94</u> 539	4th 1 pennant 7th 8th
NIXEY CALLAHAN b. March 18, 1874, Fitchburg, MA James Joseph Callahan d. age 60	Chicago AL 1903–04, 1912–14 Pittsburgh 1916–17	309 <u>85</u> 394	329 <u>129</u> 458	4th 6th
JOE CANTILLON b. Aug. 19, 1861, Janesville, WI Joseph D. Cantillon d. age 68	Washington 1907–9	158	297	7th
MAX CAREY b. Jan. 11, 1890, Terre Haute, IN Maximilian Carnarius d. age 86	Brooklyn 1932–33	146	161	3rd
BILL CARRIGAN b. Oct. 22, 1883, Lewiston, ME William Francis Carrigan d. age 85	Boston AL 1913–16, 1927–29	489	500	2 pennants
PHIL CAVARRETTA b. July 19, 1916, Chicago, IL Philip Joseph Cavarretta	Chicago NL 1951–53	169	213	5th
FRANK CHANCE b. Sept. 9, 1877, Fresno, CA Frank Leroy Chance d. age 47	Chicago NL 1905–12 New York AL 1913–14 Boston AL 1923	768 117 <u>61</u> 946	389 168 <u>91</u> 648	4 pennants 7th 8th

Continued

Manager	Team	W	L	Best Finish
BEN CHAPMAN b. Dec. 25, 1908, Nashville, TN William Benjamin Chapman d. age 88	Philadelphia NL 1945–48	196	276	5th
HAL CHASE b. Feb. 13, 1883, Los Gatos, CA Harold Homer Chase d. age 64	New York AL 1910–11	86	80	2nd
FRED CLARKE b. Oct. 3, 1872, Winterset, IA Fred Clifford Clarke d. age 77 Also managed 4 years before 1901.	Pittsburgh 1901–15	1,343	909	4 pennants
TY COBB b. Dec. 18, 1886, Narrows, GA Tyrus Raymond Cobb d. age 74	Detroit 1921–26	479	444	2nd
MICKEY COCHRANE b. April 6, 1903, Bridgewater, MA Gordon Stanley Cochrane d. age 59	Detroit 1934–38	361	262	2 pennants
ANDY COHEN b. Oct. 25, 1904, Baltimore, MD Andrew Howard Cohen d. age 84	Philadelphia NL 1960	1	0	(4th)
BOB COLEMAN b. Sept. 26, 1890, Huntingburg, IN Robert Hunter Coleman d. age 68	Boston NL 1943–45	128	165	(6th)
JERRY COLEMAN b. Sept. 14, 1924, San Jose, CA Gerald Francis Coleman	San Diego 1980	73	89	6th

Continued

Manager	Team	W	L	Best Finish
EDDIE COLLINS b. May 2, 1887, Millerton, NY Edward Trowbridge Collins d. age 63	Chicago AL 1924–26	174	160	5th
JIMMY COLLINS b. Jan. 16, 1870, Buffalo, NY James Joseph Collins d. age 73	Boston AL 1901–6	455	376	2 pennants
SHANO COLLINS b. Dec. 4, 1885, Charlestown, MA John Francis Collins d. age 69	Boston AL 1931–32	73	143	6th
TERRY COLLINS b. May 27, 1949, Midland, MI Terry Lee Collins	Houston 1994–96 Anaheim 1997–98	224 <u>169</u> 393	197 <u>155</u> 352	2nd 2nd
DUSTY COOKE b. June 23, 1907, Swepsonville, NC Allen Lindsey Cooke d. age 80	Philadelphia NL 1948	6	6	(6th)
JACK COOMBS b. Nov. 18, 1882, LeGrand, IA John Wesley Coombs d. age 74	Philadelphia NL 1919	18	44	(8th)
JOHNNY COONEY b. March 18, 1901, Cranston, RI John Walter Cooney d. age 85	Boston NL 1949	20	25	4th
PAT CORRALES b. March 20, 1941, Los Angeles, CA Patrick Corrales *Dismissed at mid-season with team in first place.	Texas 1978–80 Philadelphia NL 1982–83 Cleveland 1983–87	160 132 <u>280</u> 572	164 115 <u>355</u> 634	2nd 1st* 5th

Continued

Manager	Team	W	L	Best Finish
RED CORRIDEN b. Sept. 4, 1887, Logansport, IN John Michael Corriden d. age 72	Chicago AL 1950	52	72	6th
CHUCK COTTIER b. Jan. 8, 1936, Delta, CO Charles Keith Cottier	Seattle Mariners 1984–86	98	119	6th
BOBBY COX b. May 21, 1941, Tulsa, OK Robert Joe Cox	Atlanta 1978–81 Toronto 1982–85 Atlanta 1990–98	266 355 797 1,418	323 292 523 1,138	4th 1st AL East 4 pennants
HARRY CRAFT b. April 19, 1915, Ellisville, MS Harry Francis Craft d. age 80	Kansas City A's 1957–59 Chicago NL 1961 Houston 1962–64	162 7 191 360	196 9 280 485	7th 7th 8th
ROGER CRAIG b. Feb. 17, 1930, Durham, NC Roger Lee Craig	San Diego 1978–79 San Francisco 1985–92	152 586 738	171 566 737	4th 1 pennant
DEL CRANDALL b. March 5, 1930, Ontario, CA Delmar Wesley Crandall	Milwaukee AL 1972–75 Seattle 1983–84	271 93 364	338 131 469	5th 7th
GAVVY CRAVATH b. March 23, 1881, Escondido, CA Clifford Carlton Cravath d. age 82	Philadelphia NL 1919–20	91	137	8th
JOE CRONIN b. Oct. 12, 1906, San Francisco, CA Joseph Edward Cronin d. age 77	Washington 1933–34 Boston AL 1935–47	165 1,071 1,236	139 916 1,055	1 pennant 1 pennant

Continued

Manager	Team	W	L	Best Finish
MIKE CUBBAGE b. July 21, 1950, Charlottesville, VA Michael Lee Cubbage	New York NL 1991	3	4	5th
BILL DAHLEN b. Jan. 5, 1870, Nelliston, NY William Frederick Dahlen d. age 80	Brooklyn 1910–13	251	355	6th
ALVIN DARK b. Jan. 27, 1922, Comanche, OK Alvin Ralph Dark	San Francisco 1961–64 Kansas City A's 1966–67 Cleveland 1968–71 Oakland 1974–75 San Diego 1977	366 126 266 188 48 994	346 155 321 136 65 954	1 pennant 7th 3rd 1 pennant 5th
JIM DAVENPORT b. Aug. 17, 1933, Siluria, AL James Houston Davenport	San Francisco 1985	56	88	(6th)
GEORGE DAVIS b. Aug. 23, 1870, Cohoes, NY George Stacey Davis d. age 70 Also managed 2 years before 1901.	New York Giants NL 1901	52	85	7th
HARRY DAVIS b. July 19, 1873, Philadelphia, PA Harry H. Davis d. age 74	Cleveland 1912	54	71	(6th)
SPUD DAVIS b. Dec. 20, 1904, Birmingham, AL Virgil Lawrence Davis d. age 79	Pittsburgh 1946	1	2	7th
BUCKY DENT b. Nov. 25, 1951, Savannah, GA Russell Earl Dent	New York AL 1989–90	36	53	5th

Continued

Manager	Team	W	L	Best Finish
BILL DICKEY b. June 6, 1907, Bastrop, LA William Malcolm Dickey d. age 83	New York AL 1946	57	48	(3rd)
LARRY DIERKER b. Sept. 22, 1946, Hollywood, CA Lawrence Edward Dierker	Houston 1997–98	186	138	1st NL Central
LARRY DOBY b. Dec. 13, 1924, Camden, SC Lawrence Eugene Doby	Chicago AL 1978	37	50	5th
PATSY DONOVAN b. March 16, 1865, Ireland Patrick Joseph Donovan d. age 88 Also managed 2 years before 1901.	St. Louis NL 1901–03 Washington 1904 Brooklyn 1906–08 Boston AL 1910–11	175 37 184 159 555	236 97 270 147 750	4th 8th 3rd 4th
(WILD) BILL DONOVAN b. Oct. 13, 1876, Lawrence, MA William Edward Donovan d. age 47	New York AL 1915–17 Philadelphia NL 1921	220 25 245	239 62 301	4th 8th
RED DOOIN b. June 12, 1879, Cincinnati, OH Charles Sebastian Dooin d. age 72	Philadelphia NL 1910–14	392	370	2nd
CHUCK DRESSEN b. Sept. 20, 1898, Decatur, IL Charles Walter Dressen d. age 67	Cincinnati 1934–37 Brooklyn 1951–53 Washington 1955–57 Milwaukee NL 1960–61 Detroit 1963–66	214 298 116 159 221 1,008	282 166 212 124 189 973	5th 2 pennants 7th 2nd 3rd
HUGH DUFFY b. Nov. 26, 1866, Cranston, RI Hugh Duffy d. age 87	Milwaukee AL 1901 Philadelphia NL 1904–6 Chicago AL 1910–11 Boston AL 1921–22	48 206 145 136 535	89 251 159 172 671	8th 4th 4th 5th

Continued

Manager	Team	W	L	Best Finish
LEO DUROCHER b. July 27, 1905, W. Springfield, MA Leo Ernest Durocher d. age 86	Brooklyn 1939–46, '48 New York Giants NL 1948–55 Chicago NL 1966–72 Houston 1972–73	738 637 535 <u>98</u> 2,008	565 485 526 <u>95</u> 1,709	1 pennant 2 pennants 2nd 2nd
FRANK DWYER b. March 25, 1868, Lee, MA John Francis Dwyer d. age 74	Detroit 1902	52	83	7th
EDDIE DYER b. Oct. 11, 1900, Morgan City, LA Edwin Hawley Dyer d. age 63	St. Louis NL 1946–50	446	325	1 pennant
JIMMIE DYKES b. Nov. 10, 1896, Philadelphia, PA James Joseph Dykes d. age 79	Chicago AL 1934–46 Philadelphia AL 1951–53 Baltimore 1954 Cincinnati 1958 Detroit 1959–60 Cleveland 1960–61	899 208 54 24 118 <u>103</u> 1,406	940 254 100 17 115 <u>115</u> 1,541	3rd 4th 7th 4th 4th 4th
DOC EDWARDS b. Dec. 10, 1936, Red Jacket, WV Howard Rodney Edwards	Cleveland 1987–89	173	207	6th
KID ELBERFELD b. April 13, 1875, Pomeroy, OH Norman Arthur Elberfeld d. age 68	New York AL 1908	27	71	8th
LEE ELIA b. July 16, 1937, Philadelphia, PA Lee Constantine Elia	Chicago NL 1982–83 Philadelphia NL 1987–88	127 <u>111</u> 238	158 <u>142</u> 300	5th 4th

Continued

Manager	Team	W	L	Best Finish
BOB ELLIOTT b. Nov. 26, 1916, San Francisco, CA Robert Irving Elliott d. age 49	Kansas City Royals 1960	58	96	8th
JEWEL ENS b. Aug. 24, 1889, St. Louis, MO Jewel Winklemeyer Ens d. age 60	Pittsburgh 1929–31	176	167	2nd
CAL ERMER Nov. 10, 1923, Baltimore, MD Calvin Coolidge Ermer	Minnesota 1967–68	145	129	2nd
JIM ESSIAN b. Jan. 2, 1951, Detroit, MI James Sarkis Essian	Chicago NL 1991	59	63	4th
JOHNNY EVERS b. July 21, 1881, Troy, NY John Joseph Evers d. age 65	Chicago NL 1913, '21 Chicago AL 1924	129 51 180	120 72 192	3rd 8th
BIBB FALK b. Jan. 27, 1899, Austin, TX Bibb August Falk d. age 90	Cleveland 1933	1	1	(5th)
JIM FANNING b. Sept. 14, 1927, Chicago, IL William James Fanning	Montreal 1981–82, '84	116	103	1st NL East
KERBY FARRELL b. Sept. 3, 1913, Leapwood, TN Major Kerby Farrell d. age 62	Cleveland 1957	76	77	6th
JOHN FELSKE b. May 30, 1942, Chicago, IL John Frederick Felske	Philadelphia NL 1985–87	190	194	2nd

Continued

Manager	Team	W	L	Best Finish
MIKE FERRARO				
b. Aug. 14, 1944, Kingston, NY	Cleveland 1983	40	60	(7th)
Michael Dennis Ferraro	Kansas City Royals 1986	36	38	3rd
		76	98	
FREDDIE FITZSIMMONS				
b. July 26, 1901, Mishawaka, IN	Philadelphia NL 1943–45	105	181	7th
Frederick Landis Fitzsimmons				
d. age 78				
ART FLETCHER				
b. Jan. 5, 1885, Collinsville, IL	Philadelphia NL 1923–26	231	378	6th
Arthur Fletcher	New York AL 1929	6	5	2nd
d. age 65		237	383	
HORACE FOGEL				
b. March 2, 1861, Macungie, PA	New York Giants NL 1902	18	23	(4th)
Horace S. Fogel				
d. age 67				
Also managed 1 year before 1901.				
LEE FOHL				
b. Nov. 28, 1870, Pittsburgh, PA	Cleveland 1915–19	327	310	2nd
Leo Alexander Fohl	St. Louis AL 1921–23	221	183	2nd
d. age 94	Boston AL 1924–26	93	212	7th
		713	792	
LEW FONSECA				
b. Jan. 21, 1899, Oakland, CA	Chicago AL 1932–34	120	196	6th
Lewis Albert Fonseca				
d. age 90				
CHARLIE FOX				
b. Oct. 7, 1921, New York, NY	San Francisco 1970–74	348	327	1st NL West
Charles Francis Fox	Montreal 1976	12	22	6th
	Chicago NL 1983	17	22	5th
		377	371	
TERRY FRANCONA				
b. April 22, 1959, Aberdeen, SD	Philadelphia NL 1997–98	143	181	3rd
Terry Jon Francona				

Continued

Manager	Team	W	L	Best Finish
HERMAN FRANKS				
b. Jan. 4, 1914, Price, UT	San Francisco 1965–68	367	280	2nd
Herman Louis Franks	Chicago NL 1977–79	238	241	3rd
		605	521	
JOE FRAZIER				
b. Oct. 6, 1922, Liberty, NC	New York Mets NL 1976–77	101	106	3rd
Joseph Filmore Frazier				
JIM FREGOSI				
b. April 4, 1942, San Francisco, CA	California 1978–81	237	249	1st AL West
James Louis Fregosi	Chicago AL 1986–88	193	226	5th
	Philadelphia NL 1991–96	431	463	1 pennant
		861	938	
JIM FREY				
b. May 26, 1931, Cleveland, OH	Kansas City Royals AL 1980–81	127	105	1 pennant
James Gottfried Frey	Chicago NL 1984–86	196	182	1st NL East
		323	287	
FRANKIE FRISCH				
b. Sept. 9, 1898, Bronx, NY	St. Louis NL 1933–38	458	354	1 pennant
Frank Francis Frisch	Pittsburgh 1940–46	539	528	2nd
d. age 74	Chicago NL 1949–51	141	196	7th
		1,138	1,078	
JUDGE FUCHS				
b. April 17, 1878, Germany	Boston NL 1929	56	98	8th
Emil Edwin Fuchs				
d. age 83				
JOHN GANZEL				
b. April 7, 1874, Kalamazoo, MI	Cincinnati 1908	73	81	5th
John Henry Ganzel				
d. age 84				
DAVE GARCIA				
b. Sept. 15, 1920, E. St. Louis, IL	California 1977–78	60	66	3rd
David Garcia	Cleveland 1979–82	247	244	5th
		307	310	

Continued

Manager	Team	W	L	Best Finish
BILLY GARDNER				
b. July 19, 1927, Waterford, CT	Minnesota 1981–85	268	353	2nd
William Frederick Gardner	Kansas City Royals 1987	62	64	(4th)
		330	417	
PHIL GARNER				
b. April 30, 1949, Jefferson City, TN	Milwaukee AL/NL 1992–98	511	557	2nd
Philip Mason Garner				
CITO GASTON				
b. March 17, 1944, San Antonio, TX	Toronto 1989–97	683	636	2 pennants
Clarence Edwin Gaston				
GEORGE GIBSON				
July 22, 1880, Canada	Pittsburgh 1920–22, '32–34	201	171	2nd
George C. Gibson	Chicago NL 1925	12	14	8th
d. age 86	Pittsburgh 1932–34	200	159	2nd
		413	344	
KID GLEASON				
b. Oct. 26, 1866, Camden, NJ	Chicago AL 1919–23	392	364	1 pennant
William J. Gleason				
d. age 66				
PRESTON GOMEZ				
b. April 20, 1923, Cuba	San Diego 1969–72	180	316	4th
Pedro Gomez y Martinez	Houston 1974–75	128	161	4th
	Chicago NL 1980	38	52	(6th)
		346	529	
MIKE GONZALEZ				
b. Sept. 24, 1890, Cuba	St. Louis NL 1938, '40	9	13	6th
Miguel Angel Gonzalez y Cordero				
d. age 86				
JOE GORDON				
b. Feb. 18, 1915, Los Angeles, CA	Cleveland 1958–60	184	151	2nd
Joseph Lowell Gordon	Detroit 1960	26	31	6th
d. age 63	Kansas City A's 1961	26	33	(8th)
	Kansas City Royals 1969	69	93	4th
		305	308	

Continued

Manager	Team	W	L	Best Finish
JOHN GORYL b. Oct. 21, 1933, Cumberland, RI John Albert Goryl	Minnesota 1980–81	34	38	3rd
HANK GOWDY b. Aug. 24, 1889, Columbus, OH Henry Morgan Gowdy d. age 76	Cincinnati 1946	3	1	6th
ALEX GRAMMAS b. April 3, 1926, Birmingham, AL Alexander Peter Grammas	Pittsburgh 1969 Milwaukee AL 1976–77	4 133 137	1 190 191	3rd 6th
DALLAS GREEN b. Aug. 4, 1934, Newport, DE George Dallas Green	Philadelphia NL 1979–81 New York AL 1989 New York Mets NL 1993–96	169 56 229 454	130 65 283 478	1 pennant (6th) 2nd
CLARK GRIFFITH b. Nov. 20, 1869, Clear Creek, MO Clark Calvin Griffith d. age 85	Chicago AL 1901–02 New York AL 1903–08 Cincinnati 1909–11 Washington 1912–20	157 419 222 693 1,491	113 308 238 646 1,367	1 pennant 2nd 4th 2nd
BURLEIGH GRIMES b. Aug. 18, 1893, Emerald, WI Burleigh Arland Grimes d. age 92	Brooklyn 1937–38	131	171	6th
CHARLIE GRIMM b. Aug. 28, 1898, St. Louis, MO Charles John Grimm d. age 85	Chicago NL 1932–38, 1944–49 Boston/Milwaukee NL 1952–56 Chicago NL 1960	940 341 6 1,287	771 285 11 1,067	3 pennants 2nd (8th)
HEINIE GROH b. Sept. 18, 1889, Rochester, NY Henry Knight Groh d. age 78	Cincinnati 1918	7	3	3rd

Continued

Manager	Team	W	L	Best Finish
DON GUTTERIDGE June 19, 1912, Pittsburgh, KS Donald Joseph Gutteridge	Chicago AL 1969–70	109	172	5th
EDDIE HAAS b. May 26, 1935, Paducah, KY George Edwin Haas	Atlanta 1985	50	71	(5th)
STAN HACK b. Dec. 6, 1909, Sacramento, CA Stanley Camfield Hack d. age 70	Chicago NL 1954–56 St. Louis NL 1958	196 <u>3</u> 199	265 <u>7</u> 272	6th 5th
FRED HANEY b. April 25, 1898, Albuquerque, NM Fred Girard Haney d. age 79	St. Louis AL 1939–41 Pittsburgh 1953–55 Milwaukee NL 1956–59	125 163 <u>341</u> 629	227 299 <u>231</u> 757	6th 8th 2 pennants
NED HANLON b. Aug. 22, 1857, Montville, CT Edward Hugh Hanlon d. age 79 Also managed 12 years before 1901.	Brooklyn 1901–5 Cincinnati 1906–7	328 <u>130</u> 458	387 <u>174</u> 561	2nd 6th
MEL HARDER b. Oct. 15, 1909, Beemer, NE Melvin LeRoy Harder	Cleveland 1961,'62	3	0	5th
MIKE HARGROVE b. Oct. 26, 1949, Perryton, TX Dudley Michael Hargrove	Cleveland 1991–98	624	526	2 pennants
TOBY HARRAH b. Oct. 26, 1948, Sissonville, WV Colbert Dale Harrah	Texas 1992	32	44	4th
BUD HARRELSON b. June 6, 1944, Niles, CA Derrel McKinley Harrelson	New York Mets NL 1990–91	145	129	2nd

Continued

Manager	Team	W	L	Best Finish
BUCKY HARRIS				
b. Nov. 8, 1896, Port Jervis, NY	Washington 1924–28	429	334	2 pennants
Stanley Raymond Harris	Detroit 1929–33	355	410	5th
d. age 81	Boston AL 1934	76	76	4th
	Washington 1935–42	558	663	4th
	Philadelphia NL 1943	38	52	(5th)
	New York AL 1947–48	191	127	1 pennant
	Washington 1950–54	349	419	5th
	Detroit 1955–56	161	147	5th
		2,157	2,218	
LUM HARRIS				
b. Jan. 17, 1915, New Castle, AL	Baltimore 1961	17	10	3rd
Chalmer Luman Harris	Houston 1964–65	70	105	9th
d. age 81	Atlanta 1968–72	379	373	1st NL West
		466	488	
JOHN HART				
b. July 21, 1948, Tampa, FL	Cleveland 1989	8	11	6th
John Henry Reen				
GABBY HARTNETT				
b. Dec. 20, 1900, Woonsocket, RI	Chicago NL 1938–40	203	176	1 pennant
Charles Leo Hartnett				
d. age 72				
ROY HARTSFIELD				
b. Oct. 25, 1925, Chattahoochee, GA	Toronto 1977–79	166	318	7th
Roy Thomas Hartsfield				
GRADY HATTON				
b. Oct. 7, 1922, Beaumont, TX	Houston 1966–68	164	221	8th
Grady Edgebert Hatton				
DON HEFFNER				
b. Feb. 8, 1911, Rouzerville, PA	Cincinnati 1966	37	46	(8th)
Donald Henry Heffner				
d. age 78				
TOMMY HELMS				
b. May 5, 1941, Charlotte, NC	Cincinnati 1988–89	28	36	(4th)
Tommy Vann Helms				

Continued

Manager	Team	W	L	Best Finish
SOLLY HEMUS b. April 17, 1923, Phoenix, AZ Solomon Joseph Hemus	St. Louis NL 1959–61	190	192	3rd
JACK HENDRICKS b. April 9, 1875, Joliet, IL John Charles Hendricks d. age 68	St. Louis NL 1918 Cincinnati 1924–29	51 469 520	78 450 528	8th 2nd
BILLY HERMAN b. July 7, 1909, New Albany, IN William Jennings Bryan Herman d. age 83	Pittsburgh 1947 Boston AL 1964–66	61 128 189	92 182 274	(8th) 8th
BUCK HERZOG b. July 9, 1885, Baltimore, MD Charles Lincoln Herzog d. age 68	Cincinnati 1914–16	165	226	7th
WHITEY HERZOG b. Nov. 9, 1931, New Athens, IL Dorrel Norman Elvert Herzog	Texas 1973 California 1974 Kansas City Royals 1975–79 St. Louis NL 1980–90	47 2 410 822 1,281	91 2 304 728 1,125	6th (6th) 1st AL West 3 pennants
MIKE (PINKY) HIGGINS b. May 27, 1909, Red Oak, TX Michael Franklin Higgins d. age 59	Boston AL 1955–59, 1960–62	560	556	3rd
VEDIE HIMSL b. April 2, 1917, Plevna, MT Avitus Bernard Himsl	Chicago NL 1961	10	21	6th
BILLY HITCHCOCK b. July 31, 1916, Inverness, AL William Clyde Hitchcock	Detroit 1960 Baltimore 1962–63 Atlanta 1966–67	1 163 110 274	0 161 100 261	(6th) 4th 5th

Continued

Manager	Team	W	L	Best Finish
BUTCH HOBSON b. Aug. 17, 1951, Tuscaloosa, AL Clell Lavern Hobson Jr.	Boston AL 1992–94	207	232	5th
GIL HODGES b. April 4, 1924, Princeton, IN Gilbert Ray Hodges d. age 47	Washington 1963–67 New York Mets NL 1968–71	321 <u>339</u> 660	444 <u>309</u> 753	6th 1 pennant
GLENN HOFFMAN b. July 7, 1958, Orange, CA Glenn Edward Hoffman	Los Angeles NL 1998	47	41	3rd
TOMMY HOLMES b. March 29, 1917, Brooklyn, NY Thomas Francis Holmes	Boston NL 1951–52	61	69	4th
ROGERS HORNSBY b. April 27, 1896, Winters, TX Rogers Hornsby d. age 66	St. Louis NL 1925–26 New York Giants NL 1927 Boston NL 1928 Chicago NL 1930–32 St. Louis AL 1933–37, '52 Cincinnati 1952–53	153 22 39 141 255 <u>91</u> 701	116 10 83 116 381 <u>106</u> 812	1 pennant 3rd 7th 2nd 6th 6th
RALPH HOUK b. Aug. 9, 1919, Lawrence, KS Ralph George Houk	New York AL 1961–63, 1966–73 Detroit 1974–78 Boston AL 1981–84	944 363 <u>312</u> 1,619	806 443 <u>282</u> 1,531	3 pennants 4th 2nd
FRANK HOWARD b. Aug. 8, 1936, Columbus, OH Frank Oliver Howard	San Diego 1981 New York Mets NL 1983	41 <u>52</u> 93	69 <u>64</u> 133	6th 6th
ART HOWE b. Dec. 15, 1946, Pittsburgh, PA Arthur Henry Howe Jr.	Houston 1989–93 Oakland 1996–98	392 <u>217</u> 609	418 <u>269</u> 687	3rd 3rd

Continued

Manager	Team	W	L	Best Finish
DAN HOWLEY				
b. Oct. 16, 1885, Weymouth, MA	St. Louis AL 1927–29	220	239	3rd
Daniel Philip Howley	Cincinnati 1930–32	177	285	7th
d. age 58		397	524	
DICK HOWSER				
b. May 14, 1936, Miami, FL	New York AL 1978, '80	103	60	1st AL East
Richard Dalton Howser	Kansas City Royals 1981–86	404	365	1 pennant
d. age 51		507	425	
GEORGE HUFF				
b. June 11, 1872, Champaign, IL	Boston AL 1907	2	6	6th
George A. Huff				
d. age 64				
MILLER HUGGINS				
b. March 27, 1879, Cincinnati, OH	St. Louis NL 1913–17	346	415	3rd
Miller James Huggins	New York AL 1918–29	1,067	719	6 pennants
d. age 50		1,413	1,134	
BILLY HUNTER				
b. June 4, 1928, Punxsutawney, PA	Texas 1977–78	146	108	2nd
Gordon William Hunter				
FRED HUTCHINSON				
b. Aug. 12, 1919, Seattle, WA	Detroit 1952–54	155	235	5th
Frederick Charles Hutchinson	St. Louis NL 1956–58	232	220	2nd
d. age 45	Cincinnati 1959–64	443	372	1 pennant
		830	827	
HUGHIE JENNINGS				
b. April 2, 1869, Pittston, PA	Detroit 1907–20	1,131	972	3 pennants
Hugh Ambrose Jennings	New York Giants NL 1924	32	12	(1st)*
d. age 58		1,163	984	
*Served as interim during illness of John McGraw				
who began and finished season as Giants manager.				
DARRELL JOHNSON				
b. Aug. 25, 1928, Horace, NE	Boston AL 1974–76	220	188	1 pennant
Darrell Dean Johnson	Seattle Mariners 1977–80	226	362	6th
Texas 1982		26	40	6th
		472	590	

Continued

Manager	Team	W	L	Best Finish
DAVEY JOHNSON				
b. Jan. 30, 1943, Orlando, FL	New York Mets NL 1984–90	595	417	1 pennant
David Allen Johnson	Cincinnati 1993–95	204	172	1st NL Central
	Baltimore 1996–97	186	138	1st AL East
		985	727	
ROY JOHNSON				
b. Oct. 1, 1895, Madill, OK	Chicago NL 1944	0	1	(8th)
Roy J. Johnson				
d. age 90				
TIM JOHNSON				
b. July 22, 1949, Grand Forks, ND	Toronto 1998	88	94	3rd
Timothy Evald Johnson				
WALTER JOHNSON				
b. Nov. 6, 1887, Humboldt, KS	Washington 1929–32	350	264	2nd
Walter Perry Johnson	Cleveland 1933–35	179	168	3rd
d. age 59		529	432	
FIELDER JONES				
b. Aug. 13, 1871, Shinglehouse, PA	Chicago AL 1904–8	426	293	1 pennant
Fielder Allison Jones	St. Louis AL 1916–18	158	196	5th
d. age 62		584	489	
EDDIE JOOST				
b. June 5, 1916, San Francisco, CA	Philadelphia AL 1954	51	103	8th
Edwin David Joost				
MIKE JORGENSEN				
b. Aug. 16, 1948, Passaic, NJ	St. Louis NL 1995	42	54	4th
Michael Jorgensen				
BILLY JURGES				
b. May 9, 1908, Bronx, NY	Boston AL 1959–60	59	63	5th
William Frederick Jurges				
d. age 88				
EDDIE KASKO				
b. June 27, 1932, Linden, NJ	Boston AL 1970–73	345	295	2nd
Edward Michael Kasko				

Continued

Manager	Team	W	L	Best Finish
JOHNNY KEANE				
b. Nov. 3, 1911, St. Louis, MO	St. Louis NL 1961–64	317	249	1 pennant
John Joseph Keane	New York AL 1965–66	81	101	6th
d. age 55		398	350	
JOE KELLEY				
b. Dec. 9, 1871, Cambridge, MA	Cincinnati 1902–5	275	230	3rd
Joseph James Kelley	Boston NL 1908	63	91	6th
d. age 71		338	321	
TOM KELLY				
b. Aug. 15, 1950, Graceville, MN	Minnesota 1986–98	923	977	2 pennants
Jay Thomas Kelly				
BOB KENNEDY				
b. Aug. 18, 1920, Chicago, IL	Chicago NL 1963–65	182	198	7th
Robert Daniel Kennedy	Oakland 1968	82	80	6th
		264	278	
KEVIN KENNEDY				
b. May 26, 1954, CA	Texas 1993–94	138	138	2nd
Kevin Curtis Kennedy	Boston AL 1995–96	171	135	1st AL East
		309	273	
DON KESSINGER				
b. July 17, 1942, Forrest City, AR	Chicago AL 1979	46	60	(5th)
Donald Eulon Kessinger				
BILL KILLEFER				
b. Oct. 10, 1887, Bloomingdale, MI	Chicago NL 1921–25	300	293	4th
William Lavier Killefer	St. Louis AL 1930–33	224	329	5th
d. age 72		542	622	
CLYDE KING				
b. May 23, 1925, Goldsboro, NC	San Francisco 1969–70	109	95	2nd
Clyde Edward King	Atlanta 1974–75	96	101	3rd
	New York AL 1982	29	33	5th
		234	229	

Continued

Manager	Team	W	L	Best Finish
MAL KITTREDGE b. Oct. 12, 1869, Clinton, MA Malachi Jedidiah Kittredge d. age 58	Washington 1904	1	16	(8th)
LOU KLEIN b. Oct. 22, 1918, New Orleans, LA Louis Frank Klein d. age 57	Chicago NL 1961, '62, '65	65	82	7th
JOHNNY KLING b. Feb. 25, 1875, Kansas City, MO John Kling d. age 71	Boston NL 1912	52	101	8th
RAY KNIGHT b. Dec. 28, 1952, Albany, GA Charles Ray Knight	Cincinnati 1996–97	124	137	3rd
BOBBY KNOOP Oct. 18, 1938, Sioux City, IA Robert Frank Knoop	California 1994	1	1	Incomplete Season
JACK KROL b. July 5, 1936, Chicago, IL John Thomas Krol d. age 57	St. Louis NL 1978, '80	1	2	(6th)
KARL KUEHL b. Sept. 5, 1937, Monterey Park, CA Karl Otto Kuehl	Montreal 1976	43	85	(6th)
HARVEY KUENN b. Dec. 4, 1930, W. Allis, WI Harvey Edward Kuenn d. age 57	Milwaukee AL 1975, 1982–83	160	118	1 pennant
JOE KUHEL b. June 25, 1906, Cleveland, OH Joseph Anthony Kuhel d. age 77	Washington 1948–49	106	201	7th

Continued

Manager	Team	W	L	Best Finish
MARCEL LACHEMANN b. June 13, 1941, Los Angeles, CA Marcel Ernest Lachemann	California 1994–96	160	170	2nd
RENE LACHEMANN b. May 4, 1945, Los Angeles, CA Rene George Lachemann	Seattle Mariners AL 1981–83 Milwaukee AL 1984 Florida 1993–96	140 67 221 428	180 94 285 559	4th 7th 4th
NAP LAJOIE b. Sept. 5, 1874, Woonsocket, RI Napoleon Lajoie d. age 84 *Dismissed with team in first place in 1905. Returned to manage in mid-season of 1906.	Cleveland 1905–9	377	309	1st*
FRED LAKE b. Oct. 16, 1886, Canada Frederick Lovett Lake d. age 65	Boston AL 1908–9 Boston NL 1910	110 53 163	80 100 180	3rd 8th
GENE LAMONT b. Dec. 25, 1946, Rockford, IL Gene William Lamont	Chicago AL 1992–95 Pittsburgh 1997–98	258 148 406	210 176 386	1st AL West 2nd
HAL LANIER b. July 4, 1942, Denton, NC Harold Clifton Lanier	Houston 1986–88	254	232	1st NL West
TONY LaRUSSA b. Oct. 4, 1944, Tampa, FL Anthony LaRussa	Chicago AL 1979–86 Oakland 1986–95 St. Louis NL 1996–98	522 798 244 1,564	510 673 242 1,425	1st AL West 3 pennants 1st NL Central
TOM LASORDA b. Sept. 22, 1927, Norristown, PA Thomas Charles Lasorda	Los Angeles NL 1976–96	1,599	1,439	4 pennants

Continued

Manager	Team	W	L	Best Finish
COOKIE LAVAGETTO b. Dec. 1, 1912, Oakland, CA Harry Arthur Lavagetto d. age 77	Washington/Minnesota 1957–61	271	384	5th
JIM LEFEBVRE b. Jan. 7, 1942, Inglewood, CA James Kenneth Lefebvre	Seattle Mariners 1989–91 Chicago NL 1992–93	233 162 395	253 162 415	5th 4th
BOB LEMON b. Sept. 22, 1920, San Bernardino, CA Robert Granville Lemon	Kansas City Royals 1970–72 Chicago AL 1977–78 New York AL 1978–79, 1981–82	207 124 99 430	218 112 73 403	2nd 3rd 2 pennants
JIM LEMON b. March 23, 1928, Covington, VA James Robert Lemon	Washington 1968	65	96	10th
JIM LEYLAND b. Dec. 15, 1944, Toledo, OH James Richard Leyland	Pittsburgh 1986–96 Florida 1997–98	851 146 997	863 178 1,041	1st NL East 1 pennant
NICK LEYVA b. Aug. 16, 1953, Ontario, CA Nicholas Tomas Leyva	Philadelphia NL 1989–91	148	189	4th
BOB LILLIS b. June 2, 1930, Altadena, CA Robert Perry Lillis	Houston 1982–85	276	261	2nd
JOHNNY LIPON b. Nov. 10, 1922, Martin's Ferry, OH John Joseph Lipon	Cleveland 1971	18	41	6th
HANS LOBERT b. Oct. 18, 1881, Wilmington, DE John Bernard Lobert d. age 86	Philadelphia NL 1938, '42	42	111	8th

Continued

Manager	Team	W	L	Best Finish
WHITEY LOCKMAN b. July 25, 1926, Lowell, NC Carroll Walter Lockman	Chicago NL 1972–74	157	162	2nd
TOM LOFTUS b. Nov. 15, 1856, St. Louis, MO Thomas Joseph Loftus d. age 53 Also managed 6 years before 1901.	Chicago NL 1901 Washington 1902–3	53 <u>104</u> 157	86 <u>169</u> 255	6th 6th
ED LOPAT b. June 21, 1918, New York, NY Edmund Walter Lopatynski d. age 73	Kansas City A's 1963–64	90	124	8th
AL LOPEZ b. Aug. 20, 1908, Tampa, FL Alfonso Raymond Lopez	Cleveland 1951–56 Chicago AL 1957–65, 1968–69	570 <u>840</u> 1,410	354 <u>650</u> 1,004	1 pennant 1 pennant
BOBBY LOWE b. July 10, 1868, Pittsburgh, PA Robert Lincoln Lowe d. age 83	Detroit 1904	30	44	7th
FRANK LUCCHESI b. April 24, 1927, San Francisco, CA Frank Joseph Lucchesi	Philadelphia NL 1970–72 Texas 1975–77 Chicago NL 1987	166 142 <u>8</u> 316	233 149 <u>17</u> 399	5th 3rd 6th
HARRY LUMLEY b. Sept. 29, 1880, Forest City, PA Harry G. Lumley d. age 57	Brooklyn 1909	55	98	6th
TED LYONS b. Dec. 28, 1900, Lake Charles, LA Theodore Amar Lyons d. age 85	Chicago AL 1946–48	185	245	5th

Continued

Manager	Team	W	L	Best Finish
CONNIE MACK b. Dec. 22, 1862, E. Brookfield, MA Cornelius Alexander McGillicuddy d. age 93 Also managed 3 years before 1901.	Philadelphia AL 1901–50	3,582	3,814	9 pennants
EARLE MACK b. Feb. 1, 1890, Spencer, MA Earle Thaddeus Mack d. age 77 *Served as interim manager to complete 1937 and 1939 seasons. His father, Connie Mack, resumed fulltime managing at the beginning of the following seasons.	Philadelphia AL 1937, '39*	45	77	7th
JIMMY MANNING b. Jan. 31, 1862, Fall River, MA James H. Manning d. age 67	Washington 1901	61	73	6th
JERRY MANUEL b. Dec. 23, 1953, Hahira, GA Jerry Manuel	Chicago AL 1998	80	82	2nd
RABBIT MARANVILLE b. Nov. 11, 1891, Springfield, MA Walter James Vincent Maranville d. age 62	Chicago NL 1925	23	30	(8th)
MARTY MARION b. Dec. 1, 1917, Richburg, SC Martin Whitford Marion	St. Louis NL 1951 St. Louis AL 1952–53 Chicago AL 1954–56	81 96 <u>179</u> 356	73 161 <u>138</u> 372	3rd 7th 3rd
JIM MARSHALL b. May 25, 1931, Danville, IL Rufus James Marshall	Chicago NL 1974–76 Oakland 1979	175 <u>54</u> 229	218 <u>108</u> 326	4th 7th

Continued

Manager	Team	W	L	Best Finish
BILLY MARTIN b. May 16, 1928, Berkeley, CA Alfred Manuel Martin d. age 61	Minnesota 1970	97	65	1st AL West
	Detroit 1971–73	248	204	1st AL East
	Texas 1973–75	137	141	2nd
	New York AL 1975–78, '79	334	320	2 pennants
	Oakland 1980–82	215	218	1st AL West
	New York AL 1983, '85, '88	222	153	2nd
		1,253	1,013	
MARTY MARTINEZ b. Aug. 23, 1941, Cuba Orlando Martinez y Oliva	Seattle Mariners 1986	0	1	(6th)
EDDIE MATHEWS b. Oct. 13, 1931, Texarkana, TX Edwin Lee Mathews	Atlanta 1972–74	149	161	4th
CHRISTY MATHEWSON b. Aug. 12, 1880, Factoryville, PA Christopher Mathewson d. age 45	Cincinnati 1916–18	164	176	4th
BOBBY MATTICK b. Dec. 5, 1915, Sioux City, IA Robert James Mattick	Toronto 1980–81	104	164	7th
GENE MAUCH b. Nov. 18, 1925, Salina, KS Gene William Mauch	Philadelphia NL 1960–68	646	684	2nd
	Montreal 1969–75	499	627	4th
	Minnesota 1976–80	378	394	3rd
	California 1981–82, 1985–87	379	332	1st AL West
		1,902	2,037	
JIMMY McALEER b. July 10, 1864, Youngstown, OH James Robert McAleer d. age 66	Cleveland 1901	55	82	7th
	St. Louis AL 1902–9	551	632	2nd
	Washington 1910–11	130	175	7th
		736	889	

Continued

Manager	Team	W	L	Best Finish
GEORGE McBRIDE b. Nov. 20, 1880, Milwaukee, WI George Florian McBride d. age 92	Washington 1921	80	73	4th
JACK McCALLISTER b. Jan. 19, 1879, Marietta, OH John McCallister d. age 67	Cleveland 1927	66	87	6th
JOE McCARTHY b. April 21, 1887, Philadelphia, PA Joseph Vincent McCarthy d. age 90	Chicago NL 1926–30 New York AL 1931–46 Boston AL 1948–50	442 1,460 _223_ 2,125	321 867 _145_ 1,333	1 pennant 8 pennants 2nd
JOHN McCLOSKEY b. April 4, 1862, Louisville, KY John James McCloskey d. age 78 Also managed 2 years before 1901.	St. Louis NL 1906–8	153	304	7th
MEL McGAHA b. Sept. 26, 1926, Bastrop, LA Fred Melvin McGaha	Cleveland 1962 Kansas City A's 1964–65	78 _41_ 123	82 _91_ 173	6th 10th
JOHN McGRAW b. April 7, 1973, Truxton, NY John Joseph McGraw d. age 60 Also managed 1 year before 1901.	Baltimore 1901–2 New York Giants NL 1902–32	94 _2,604_ 2,698	96 _1,801_ 1,897	5th 10 pennants
DEACON McGUIRE b. Nov. 18, 1863, Youngstown, OH James Thomas McGuire d. age 72 Also managed 1 year before 1901.	Boston AL 1907–8 Cleveland 1909–11	98 _91_ 189	123 _117_ 240	6th 5th
STUFFY McINNIS b. Sept. 19, 1890, Gloucester, MA John Phalen McInnis d. age 69	Philadelphia NL 1927	51	103	8th

Continued

Manager	Team	W	L	Best Finish
BILL McKECHNIE b. Aug. 7, 1886, Wilkinsburg, PA William Boyd McKechnie d. age 79	Pittsburgh 1922–26	409	293	1 pennant
	St. Louis NL 1928,'29	129	88	1 pennant
	Boston NL 1930–37	560	666	4th
	Cincinnati 1938–46	798	676	2 pennants
		1,842	1,678	
JACK McKEON b. Nov. 23, 1930, S. Amboy, NJ John Aloysius McKeon	Kansas City Royals 1973–75	215	205	2nd
	Oakland 1977, '78	71	105	6th
	San Diego 1988–90	193	164	2nd
	Cincinnati 1997–98	110	115	3rd
		589	589	
MARTY McMANUS b. March 14, 1900, Chicago, IL Martin Joseph McManus d. age 65	Boston AL 1932–33	248	95	7th
ROY McMILLAN b. July 17, 1930, Bonham, TX Roy David McMillan d. age 67	Milwaukee AL 1972	1	1	(6th)
	New York Mets NL 1975	26	27	3rd
		27	28	
JOHN McNAMARA b. June 4, 1932, Sacramento, CA John Francis McNamara	Oakland 1969–70	97	78	2nd
	San Diego 1974–77	224	310	4th
	Cincinnati 1979–82	279	244	1st NL West
	California 1983–84	151	173	2nd
	Boston AL 1985–88	297	273	1 pennant
	Cleveland 1990–91	102	137	4th
	California 1996	18	32	4th
		1,168	1,247	
BID McPHEE b. Nov. 1, 1859, Massena, NY John Alexander McPhee d. age 83	Cincinnati 1901–2	79	124	(7th)
HAL McRAE b. July 10, 1945, Avon Park, FL Harold Abraham McRae	Kansas City Royals 1991–94	286	267	3rd

Continued

Manager	Team	W	L	Best Finish
SAM MELE b. Jan. 21, 1923, Astoria, NY Sabath Anthony Mele	Minnesota 1961–67	524	436	1 pennant
OSCAR MELILLO b. Aug. 4, 1899, Chicago, IL Oscar Donald Melillo d. age 64	St. Louis AL 1938	2	7	7th
STUMP MERRILL b. Feb. 25, 1944, Brunswick, ME Carl Harrison Merrill	New York AL 1990–91	120	155	5th
CHARLIE METRO b. April 28, 1919, Nanty Glo, PA Charles Moreskonich	Chicago NL 1962 Kansas City Royals 1970	43 19 62	69 33 102	9th (5th)
BILLY MEYER b. Jan. 14, 1892, Knoxville, TN William Adam Meyer d. age 65	Pittsburgh 1948–52	317	452	4th
GENE MICHAEL b. June 2, 1938, Kent, OH Eugene Richard Michael *1st under Michael in first half of split season of 1981; replaced by Bob Lemon during second half.	New York AL 1981,'82 Chicago NL 1986–87	92 114 206	76 124 200	(1st)* 5th
CLYDE MILAN b. March 24, 1887, Linden, TN Jesse Clyde Milan d. age 65	Washington 1922	69	85	6th
RAY MILLER b. April 30, 1945, Takoma Park, MD Raymond Roger Miller	Minnesota 1985–86 Baltimore 1998	109 79 188	130 83 213	4th 4th
BUSTER MILLS b. Sept. 16, 1908, Ranger, TX Colonel Buster Mills d. age 83	Cincinnati 1953	4	4	6th

Continued

Manager	Team	W	L	Best Finish
FRED MITCHELL				
b. June 5, 1878, Cambridge, MA	Chicago NL 1917–20	308	269	1 pennant
Frederick Francis Yapp	Boston NL 1921–23	186	274	4th
d. age 92		494	543	
JACKIE MOORE				
b. Feb. 19, 1939, Jay, FL	Oakland 1984–86	163	190	4th
Jackie Spencer Moore				
TERRY MOORE				
b. May 27, 1912, Vernon, AL	Philadelphia NL 1954	29	44	4th
Terry Buford Moore				
d. age 82				
PAT MORAN				
b. Feb. 7, 1876, Fitchburg, MA	Philadelphia NL 1915–18	323	257	1 pennant
Patrick Joseph Moran	Cincinnati 1919–23	425	329	1 pennant
d. age 48		748	586	
JOE MORGAN				
b. Nov. 19, 1930, Walpole, MA	Boston AL 1988–91	301	262	1st AL East
Joseph Michael Morgan				
GEORGE MORIARTY				
b. July 7, 1884, Chicago, IL	Detroit 1927–28	150	157	4th
George Joseph Moriarty				
d. age 79				
LES MOSS				
b. May 14, 1925, Tulsa, OK	Chicago AL 1968	12	24	(9th)
John Lester Moss	Detroit 1979	27	26	(5th)
		39	50	
BILL MURRAY				
b. April 13, 1864, Peabody, MA	Philadelphia NL 1907–9	240	214	3rd
William Jeremiah Murray				
d. age 72				
DANNY MURTAUGH				
b. Oct. 8, 1917, Chester, PA	Pittsburgh 1957–64, '67,	1,115	950	2 pennants
Daniel Edward Murtaugh	1970–71, 1973–76			
d. age 59				

Continued

Manager	Team	W	L	Best Finish
TONY MUSER b. Aug. 1, 1947, Van Nuys, CA Anthony Joseph Muser	Kansas City Royals 1997–98	103	137	3rd
GEORGE MYATT b. June 14, 1914, Denver, CO George Edward Myatt	Philadelphia NL 1968, '69	20	35	(5th)
JOHNNY NEUN b. Oct. 28, 1900, Baltimore, MD John Henry Neun d. age 89	New York AL 1946 Cincinnati 1947–48	8 <u>117</u> 125	6 <u>137</u> 143	3rd 5th
JEFF NEWMAN b. Sept. 11, 1948, Ft. Worth, TX Jeffrey Lynn Newman	Oakland 1986	2	8	(7th)
KID NICHOLS b. Sept. 14, 1869, Madison, WI Charles Augustus Nichols d. age 83	St. Louis NL 1904–5	80	88	5th
RUSS NIXON b. Feb. 19, 1935, Cleves, OH Russell Eugene Nixon	Cincinnati 1982–83 Atlanta 1988–90	101 <u>130</u> 231	131 <u>216</u> 347	6th 6th
BILL NORMAN b. July 16, 1910, St. Louis, MO Henry Willis Patrick Norman d. age 51	Detroit 1958–59	58	64	5th
JOHNNY OATES b. Jan. 21, 1946, Sylva, NC Johnny Lane Oates	Baltimore 1991–94 Texas 1995–98	291 <u>329</u> 620	270 <u>301</u> 571	3rd 1st AL West
JACK O'CONNOR b. June 2, 1869, St. Louis, MO John Joseph O'Connor d. age 68	St. Louis AL 1910	47	107	8th

Continued

Manager	Team	W	L	Best Finish
HANK O'DAY				
b. July 8, 1862, Chicago, IL	Cincinnati 1912	75	78	4th
Henry Francis O'Day	Chicago NL 1914	<u>78</u>	<u>76</u>	4th
d. age 72		153	154	
BOB O'FARRELL				
b. Oct. 19, 1896, Waukegan, IL	St. Louis NL 1927	92	61	2nd
Robert Arthur O'Farrell	Cincinnati 1934	<u>30</u>	<u>60</u>	(8th)
d. age 91		122	121	
STEVE O'NEILL				
b. July 6, 1891, Minooka, PA	Cleveland 1935–37	199	168	3rd
Stephen Francis O'Neill	Detroit 1943–48	509	414	1 pennant
d. age 70	Boston AL 1950–51	150	99	3rd
	Philadelphia NL 1952–54	<u>182</u>	<u>140</u>	3rd
		1,040	821	
JACK ONSLOW				
b. Oct. 13, 1888, Scottdale, PA	Chicago AL 1949–50	71	113	6th
John James Onslow				
d. age 72				
MEL OTT				
b. March 2, 1909, Gretna, LA	New York Giants NL 1942–48	464	530	3rd
Melvin Thomas Ott				
d. age 49				
PAUL OWENS				
b. Feb. 7, 1924, Salamanca, NY	Philadelphia NL 1972,1983–84	161	158	1 pennant
Paul Francis Owens				
DANNY OZARK				
b. Nov. 24, 1923, Buffalo, NY	Philadelphia NL 1973–79	594	510	1st NL East
Daniel Leonard Orzechowski	San Francisco 1984	<u>24</u>	<u>32</u>	6th
		618	542	
SALTY PARKER				
b. July 8, 1913, E. St. Louis, IL	New York Mets NL 1967	4	7	10th
Francis James Parker	Houston 1972	<u>1</u>	<u>0</u>	(2nd)
d. age 79		5	7	
LARRY PARRISH				
b. Nov. 10, 1953, Winter Haven, FL	Detroit 1998	13	2	5th
Larry Alton Parrish				

Continued

Manager	Team	W	L	Best Finish
ROGER PECKINPAUGH b. Feb. 5, 1891, Wooster, OH Roger Thorpe Peckinpaugh d. age 86	New York AL 1914 Cleveland 1929–33,'41	10 490 500	10 481 491	6th 3rd
TONY PEREZ May 14, 1942, Cuba Atanasio Perez y Rigal	Cincinnati 1993	20	24	(5th)
JOHNNY PESKY b. Sept. 27, 1919, Portland, OR John Michael Paveskovich	Boston AL 1963–64,'80	147	179	4th
LEFTY PHILLIPS b. May 16, 1919, Fullerton, CA Harold Ross Phillips d. age 53	California 1969–71	222	225	3rd
LOU PINIELLA b. Aug. 28, 1943, Tampa, FL Louis Victor Piniella	New York AL 1986–87, '88 Cincinnati 1990–92 Seattle Mariners 1993–98	224 255 461 940	193 231 442 866	2nd 1 pennant 1st AL West
BILL PLUMMER b. March 21, 1947, Oakland, CA William Francis Plummer	Seattle Mariners 1992	64	98	7th
EDDIE POPOWSKI b. Aug. 20, 1913, Sayerville, NJ Edward Joseph Popowski	Boston AL 1969,'73	6	4	2nd
DOC PROTHRO b. July 16, 1893, Memphis, TN James Thompson Prothro d. age 78	Philadelphia NL 1939–41	138	320	8th
FRANK QUILICI b. May 11, 1939, Chicago, IL Francis Ralph Quilici	Minnesota 1972–75	280	287	3rd

Continued

Manager	Team	W	L	Best Finish
MEL QUEEN				
b. March 26, 1942, Johnson City, NY	Toronto 1997	4	1	5th
Melvin Douglas Queen				
DOUG RADER				
b. July 30, 1944, Chicago, IL	Texas 1983–85	155	200	3rd
Douglas Lee Rader	Chicago AL 1986	1	1	(5th)
	California 1989–91	<u>232</u>	<u>216</u>	3rd
		388	417	
VERN RAPP				
b. May 11, 1928, St. Louis, MO	St. Louis NL 1977–78	89	90	3rd
Vernon Fred Rapp	Cincinnati 1984	<u>51</u>	<u>70</u>	(5th)
		140	160	
DEL RICE				
b. Oct. 27, 1922, Portsmouth, OH	California 1972	75	80	5th
Delbert W. Rice				
d. age 60				
PAUL RICHARDS				
b. Nov. 21, 1908, Waxahachie, TX	Chicago AL 1951–54	342	265	3rd
Paul Rapier Richards	Baltimore 1955–61	517	539	2nd
d. age 77	Chicago AL 1976	<u>64</u>	<u>97</u>	6th
		923	901	
BRANCH RICKEY				
b. Dec. 20, 1881, Stockdale, OH	St. Louis AL 1913–15	139	179	5th
Wesley Branch Rickey	St. Louis NL 1919–25	<u>458</u>	<u>485</u>	3rd
d. age 83		597	664	
GREG RIDDOCH				
b. July 15, 1945, Greeley, CO	San Diego 1990–92	200	194	3rd
Gregory Lee Riddoch				
JIM RIGGLEMAN				
b. Nov. 9, 1952, Ft. Dix, NJ	San Diego 1992–94	112	179	3rd
James David Riggleman	Chicago NL 1995–98	<u>307</u>	<u>324</u>	3rd
		419	503	

Continued

Manager	Team	W	L	Best Finish
BILL RIGNEY				
b. Jan. 29, 1918, Alameda, CA	New York NL/San Francisco 1956–60	406	430	2nd
William Joseph Rigney	Los Angeles AL/California 1961–69	625	707	3rd
	Minnesota 1970–72	208	184	1st AL West
	San Francisco 1976	74	88	4th
		1,239	1,321	
CAL RIPKEN, Sr.				
b. Dec. 17, 1935, Aberdeen, MD	Baltimore 1985, 1987–88	68	101	4th
Calvin Edwin Ripken				
FRANK ROBINSON				
b. Aug. 31, 1935, Beaumont, TX	Cleveland 1975–77	186	189	4th
Frank Robinson	San Francisco 1981–84	264	277	3rd
	Baltimore 1988–91	230	285	2nd
		680	751	
WILBERT ROBINSON				
b. June 29, 1863, Bolton, MA	Baltimore 1902	24	57	8th
Wilbert Robinson	Brooklyn 1914–31	1,375	1,341	2 pennants
d. age 71		1,399	1,398	
MATT ROBISON				
b. March 30, 1859, Pittsburgh, PA	St. Louis NL 1905	19	31	6th
Matthew Stanley Robison				
d. age 51				
BUCK RODGERS				
b. Aug. 16, 1938, Delaware, OH	Milwaukee AL 1980–82	124	102	1st
Robert Leroy Rodgers	Montreal 1985–91	529	499	3rd
	California 1991–94	140	172	5th
		793	773	
COOKIE ROJAS				
b. March 6, 1939, Cuba	California 1988	75	79	(4th)
Octavio Victor Rojas y Rivas	Florida 1996	1	0	(4th)
		76	79	

Continued

Manager	Team	W	L	Best Finish
RED ROLFE b. Oct. 17, 1908, Penacook, NH Robert Abial Rolfe d. age 60	Detroit 1949–52	278	256	2nd
PETE ROSE b. April 14, 1941, Cincinnati, OH Peter Edward Rose	Cincinnati 1984–89	412	373	2nd
LARRY ROTHSCHILD b. March 12, 1954, Chicago, IL Lawrence Lee Rothschild	Tampa Bay 1998	63	98	5th
PANTS ROWLAND b. Feb. 12, 1879, Platteville, WI Clarence Henry Rowland d. age 90	Chicago AL 1915–18	339	247	1 pennant
DICK RUDOLPH b. Aug. 25, 1887, New York, NY Richard Rudolph d. age 62	Boston NL 1924	11	27	8th
MUDDY RUEL b. Feb. 20, 1896, St. Louis, MO Herold Dominic Ruel d. age 67	St. Louis AL 1947	59	95	8th
TOM RUNNELLS b. April 17, 1955, Greeley, CO Thomas William Runnells	Montreal 1991–92	68	81	(4th)
PETE RUNNELS b. Jan. 28, 1928, Lufkin, TX James Edward Runnels d. age 63	Boston AL 1966	8	8	9th
BILL RUSSELL b. Oct. 21, 1948, Pittsburg, KS William Ellis Russell	Los Angeles 1996–98	173	149	2nd

Continued

Manager	Team	W	L	Best Finish
CONNIE RYAN b. Feb. 27, 1920, New Orleans, LA Cornelius Joseph Ryan d. age 75	Atlanta 1975 Texas 1977	9 <u>2</u> 11	18 <u>4</u> 22	5th (4th)
EDDIE SAWYER b. Sept. 10, 1910, Westerly, RI Edwin Milby Sawyer d. age 87	Philadelphia NL 1948–52, 1958–60	390	423	1 pennant
BOB SCHAEFER b. May 22, 1944, Putnam, CT Robert Walden Schaefer	Kansas City Royals 1991	1	0	(7th)
RAY SCHALK b. Aug. 12, 1892, Harvey, IL Raymond William Schalk d. age 77	Chicago AL 1927–28	102	125	5th
BOB SCHEFFING b. Aug. 11, 1913, Overland, MO Robert Boden Scheffing d. age 72	Chicago NL 1957–59 Detroit 1961–63	208 <u>210</u> 418	254 <u>173</u> 427	5th 2nd
RED SCHOENDIENST b. Feb. 2, 1923, Germantown, IL Albert Fred Schoendienst	St. Louis NL 1965–76, '80, '90	1,041	955	2 pennants
JOE SCHULTZ b. Aug. 29, 1918, Chicago, IL Joseph Charles Schultz Jr. d. age 77	Seattle Pilots 1969 Detroit 1973	64 <u>14</u> 78	98 <u>14</u> 112	6th 3rd
FRANK SELEE b. Oct. 26. 1859, Amherst, NH Frank Gibson Selee d. age 49 Also managed 12 years before 1901.	Boston NL 1901 Chicago NL 1902–5	69 <u>280</u> 349	69 <u>213</u> 282	5th 2nd
LUKE SEWELL b. Jan. 5, 1901, Titus, AL James Luther Sewell d. age 86	St. Louis AL 1941–46 Cincinnati 1949–52	432 <u>174</u> 606	410 <u>234</u> 644	1 pennant 6th

Continued

Manager	Team	W	L	Best Finish
BOB SHAWKEY b. Dec. 4, 1890, Sigel, PA James Robert Shawkey d. age 90	New York AL 1930	86	68	3rd
TOM SHEEHAN b. March 31, 1894, Grand Ridge, IL Thomas Clancy Sheehan d. age 88	San Francisco 1960	46	50	5th
LARRY SHEPARD b. April 3, 1919, Lakewood, OH Lawrence William Shepard	Pittsburgh 1968–69	164	155	3rd
NORM SHERRY b. July 16, 1931, New York, NY Norman Burt Sherry	California 1976–77	76	71	4th
BILL SHETTSLINE b. Oct. 25, 1863, Philadelphia, PA William Joseph Shettsline d. age 69 Also managed 3 years before 1901.	Philadelphia NL 1901–2	139	138	2nd
BURT SHOTTON b. Oct. 18, 1884, Brownhelm, OH Burton Edwin Shotton d. age 77	Philadelphia NL 1928–33 Cincinnati 1934 Brooklyn 1947, 1948–50	370 1 <u>326</u> 697	549 0 <u>215</u> 764	4th (8th) 2 pennants
BUCK SHOWALTER b. May 23, 1956, DeFuniak, FL William Nathaniel Showalter III	New York AL 1992–95 Arizona 1998	313 <u>65</u> 378	268 <u>97</u> 365	2nd 5th
KEN SILVESTRI b. May 3, 1916, Chicago, IL Kenneth Joseph Silvestri d. age 75	Atlanta 1967	0	3	7th
DICK SISLER b. Nov. 2, 1920, St. Louis, MO Richard Allan Sisler d. age 78	Cincinnati 1964–65	121	94	2nd

Continued

Manager	Team	W	L	Best Finish
GEORGE SISLER b. March 24, 1893, Manchester, OH George Harold Sisler d. age 80	St. Louis AL 1924–26	218	241	3rd
FRANK SKAFF b. Sept. 30, 1913, LaCrosse, WI Francis Michael Skaff d. age 74	Detroit 1966	40	39	3rd
BOB SKINNER b. Oct. 3, 1931, La Jolla, CA Robert Ralph Skinner	Philadelphia NL 1968–69 San Diego 1977	92 <u>1</u> 93	123 <u>0</u> 123	5th (5th)
JACK SLATTERY b. Jan. 6, 1878, S. Boston, MA John Terrence Slattery d. age 71	Boston NL 1928	11	20	(7th)
HARRY SMITH b. Oct. 31, 1874, England Harry Thomas Smith d. age 68	Boston NL 1909	23	54	(8th)
HEINIE SMITH b. Oct. 24, 1871, Pittsburgh, PA George Henry Smith d. age 77	New York Giants NL 1902	5	27	(8th)
MAYO SMITH b. Jan. 17, 1915, New London, MO Edward Mayo Smith d. age 62	Philadelphia NL 1955–58 Cincinnati 1959 Detroit 1967–70	264 35 <u>363</u> 662	282 45 <u>285</u> 612	4th (7th) 1 pennant
JIMMY SNYDER b. Aug. 15, 1932, Dearborn, MI James Robert Snyder	Seattle Mariners 1988	45	60	7th

Continued

Manager	Team	W	L	Best Finish
ALLEN SOTHORON b. April 27, 1893, Bradford, OH Allen Sutton Sothoron d. age 46	St. Louis AL 1933	2	6	(8th)
BILLY SOUTHWORTH b. March 9, 1893, Harvard, NE William Harrison Southworth d. age 76	St. Louis NL 1929, 1940–45 Boston NL 1946–49, 1950–51	620 424 1,044	346 358 704	3 pennants 1 pennant
TRIS SPEAKER b. April 4, 1888, Hubbard, TX Tristram E. Speaker d. age 70	Cleveland 1919–26	617	520	1 pennant
CHICK STAHL b. Jan. 10, 1873, Avila, IN Charles Sylvester Stahl d. age 34	Boston AL 1906	14	26	8th
JAKE STAHL b. April 13, 1879, Elkhart, IL Garland Stahl d. age 43	Washington 1905–6 Boston AL 1912–13	119 144 263	182 88 270	7th 1 pennant
GEORGE STALLINGS b. Nov. 17, 1867, Augusta, GA George Tweedy Stallings d. age 61 Also managed 2 years before 1901.	Detroit 1901 New York AL 1909–10 Boston NL 1913–20	74 152 579 805	61 136 597 794	3rd 3rd 1 pennant
EDDIE STANKY b. Sept. 3, 1916, Philadelphia, PA Edward Raymond Stanky	St. Louis NL 1952–55 Chicago AL 1966–68 Texas 1977	260 206 1 467	238 197 0 435	3rd 4th (2nd)

Continued

Manager	Team	W	L	Best Finish
CASEY STENGEL				
b. July 30, 1890, Kansas City, MO	Brooklyn 1934–36	208	251	5th
Charles Dillon Stengel	Boston NL 1938–42, '43	373	491	5th
d. age 85	New York AL 1949–60	1,149	696	10 pennants
	New York Mets NL 1962–65	<u>175</u>	<u>404</u>	10th
		1,905	1,842	
GEORGE STOVALL				
b. Nov. 23, 1878, Independence, MO	Cleveland 1911	74	62	3rd
George Thomas Stovall	St. Louis AL 1912–13	<u>91</u>	<u>158</u>	7th
d. age 72		165	220	
GABBY STREET				
b. Sept. 30, 1882, Huntsville, AL	St. Louis NL 1929, 1930–33	312	242	2 pennants
Charles Evard Street	St. Louis AL 1938	<u>53</u>	<u>90</u>	(7th)
d. age 68		365	332	
GEORGE STRICKLAND				
b. Jan. 10, 1926, New Orleans, LA	Cleveland 1964, '66	48	63	5th
George Bevan Strickland				
LARRY STUBING				
b. March 31, 1938, Bronx, NY	California 1988	0	8	4th
Lawrence George Stubing				
CLYDE SUKEFORTH				
b. Nov. 30, 1901, Washington, ME	Brooklyn 1947	2	0	(1st)*
Clyde LeRoy Sukeforth				
*Interim manager first two games				
of season prior to hiring of Burt				
Shotton.				
BILLY SULLIVAN				
b. Feb. 1, 1875, Oakland, WI	Chicago AL 1909	78	74	4th
William Joseph Sullivan				
d. age 89				
HAYWOOD SULLIVAN				
b. Dec. 15, 1930, Donalsonville, GA	Kansas City A's 1965	54	82	10th
Haywood Cooper Sullivan				

Continued

Manager	Team	W	L	Best Finish
BOB SWIFT b. March 6, 1915, Salina, KS Robert Virgil Swift d. age 51	Detroit 1965, '66	56	43	(3rd)
CHUCK TANNER b. July 4, 1929, New Castle, PA Charles William Tanner	Chicago AL 1970–75 Oakland 1976 Pittsburgh 1977–85 Atlanta 1986–88	401 87 711 <u>153</u> 1,352	414 74 685 <u>208</u> 1,381	2nd 2nd 1 pennant 5th
EL TAPPE b. May 21, 1927, Quincy, IL Elvin Walter Tappe	Chicago NL 1961–62	46	70	7th
ZACK TAYLOR b. July 27, 1898, Yulee, FL James Wren Taylor d. age 76	St. Louis AL 1946, 1948–51	235	410	6th
BIRDIE TEBBETTS b. Nov. 10, 1912, Burlington, VT George Robert Tebbetts	Cincinnati 1954–58 Milwaukee NL 1961–62 Cleveland 1963, 1964–66	372 98 <u>278</u> 748	357 89 <u>259</u> 705	3rd 4th 5th
GENE TENACE b. Oct. 10, 1946, Russellton, PA Fiore Gino Tennaci *Interim manager during mid- season absence of Cito Gaston, who began and finished season as Blue Jays manager.	Toronto 1991	19	14	(1st)*
FRED TENNEY b. Nov. 26, 1871, Georgetown, MA Frederick Tenney d. age 80	Boston NL 1905–7, '11	202	402	7th

Continued

Manager	Team	W	L	Best Finish
BILL TERRY b. Oct. 30, 1896, Atlanta, GA William Harold Terry d. age 92	New York Giants NL 1932–41	823	661	3 pennants
JACK TIGHE b. Aug. 9, 1913, Kearny, NJ John Thomas Tighe	Detroit 1957–58	99	104	4th
JOE TINKER b. July 27, 1880, Muscotah, KS Joseph Bert Tinker d. age 68	Cincinnati 1913 Chicago NL 1916	64 67 131	89 86 175	7th 5th
JEFF TORBORG b. Nov. 26, 1941, Plainfield, NJ Jeffrey Allen Torborg	Cleveland 1977–79 Chicago AL 1989–91 New York Mets NL 1992–93	157 250 85 492	201 235 115 551	5th 2nd 5th
JOE TORRE b. July 18, 1940, Brooklyn, NY Joseph Paul Torre	New York Mets NL 1977–81 Atlanta 1982–84 St. Louis NL 1990–95 New York AL 1996–98	286 257 351 302 1,196	420 229 354 183 1,186	4th 1st NL West 2nd 2 pennants
DICK TRACEWSKI b. Feb. 3, 1935, Eynon, PA Richard Joseph Tracewski	Detroit 1979	2	0	(5th)
PIE TRAYNOR b. Nov. 11, 1899, Framingham, MA Harold Joseph Traynor d. age 72	Pittsburgh 1934–39	457	406	2nd
TOM TREBELHORN b. Jan. 27, 1948, Portland, OR Thomas Lynn Trebelhorn	Milwaukee AL 1986–91 Chicago NL 1994	422 49 471	397 64 461	3rd Incomplete season

Continued

Manager	Team	W	L	Best Finish
TED TURNER b. Nov. 19, 1938, Cincinnati, OH Robert Edward Turner	Atlanta 1977	0	1	(6th)
BOB UNGLAUB b. July 31, 1881, Baltimore, MD Robert Alexander Unglaub d. age 35	Boston AL 1907	9	20	(8th)
BOBBY VALENTINE b. May 13, 1950, Stamford, CT Robert John Valentine	Texas 1985–92 New York Mets NL 1996–98	581 <u>188</u> 769	605 <u>167</u> 772	2nd 2nd
MICKEY VERNON b. April 22, 1918, Marcus Hook, PA James Barton Vernon	Washington 1961–63	135	227	9th
BILL VIRDON b. June 9, 1931, Hazel Park, MI William Charles Virdon	Pittsburgh 1972–73 New York AL 1974–75 Houston 1975–82 Montreal 1983–84	163 142 544 <u>146</u> 995	128 124 522 <u>147</u> 921	1st NL East 2nd 1st NL West 3rd
OSCAR VITT b. Jan. 4, 1890, San Francisco, CA Oscar Joseph Vitt d. age 73	Cleveland 1938–40	262	198	2nd
JOHN VUKOVICH b. July 31, 1947, Sacramento, CA John Christopher Vukovich	Chicago NL 1986 Philadelphia NL 1988	1 <u>5</u> 6	1 <u>4</u> 5	(5th) 6th
HEINIE WAGNER b. Sept. 23, 1880, New York, NY Charles F. Wagner d. age 62	Boston AL 1930	52	102	8th

Continued

Manager	Team	W	L	Best Finish
HONUS WAGNER b. Feb. 24, 1874, Mansfield, PA John Peter Wagner d. age 81	Pittsburgh 1917	1	4	(8th)
HARRY WALKER b. Oct. 22, 1916, Pascagoula, MS Harry William Walker	St. Louis NL 1955 Pittsburgh 1965–67 Houston 1968–72	51 224 <u>355</u> 630	67 184 <u>353</u> 604	7th 3rd 3rd
BOBBY (RHODY) WALLACE b. Nov. 4, 1873, Pittsburgh, PA Rhoderick John Wallace d. age 86	St. Louis AL 1911–12 Cincinnati 1937	57 <u>5</u> 62	134 <u>20</u> 154	8th 8th
ED WALSH b. May 14, 1881, Pittsburgh, PA Edward Augustine Walsh d. age 78	Chicago AL 1924	1	2	6th
BUCKY WALTERS b. April 19, 1909, Philadelphia, PA William Henry Walters d. age 82	Cincinnati 1948–49	81	123	7th
JOHN WATHAN b. Oct. 4, 1949, Cedar Rapids, IA John David Wathan	Kansas City Royals 1987–91 California 1992	287 <u>39</u> 326	270 <u>50</u> 320	2nd (5th)
EARL WEAVER b. Aug. 14, 1930, St. Louis, MO Earl Sidney Weaver	Baltimore 1968–82, 1985–86	1,480	1,060	4 pennants
WES WESTRUM b. Nov. 28, 1922, Clearbrook, MN Wesley Noreen Westrum	New York Mets NL 1965–67 San Francisco 1974–75	142 <u>118</u> 260	237 <u>129</u> 366	9th 3rd

Continued

Manager	Team	W	L	Best Finish
JO-JO WHITE b. June 1, 1909, Red Oak, GA Joyner Clifford White d. age 77	Cleveland 1960	1	0	(4th)
DEL WILBER b. Feb. 24, 1919, Lincoln Park, MI Delbert Quentin Wilber	Texas 1973	1	0	(6th)
KAISER WILHELM b. Jan. 26, 1874, Wooster, OH Irvin Key Wilhelm d. age 62	Philadelphia NL 1921–22	83	137	7th
DICK WILLIAMS b. May 7, 1928, St. Louis, MO Richard Hirschfeld Williams	Boston AL 1967–69 Oakland 1971–73 California 1974–76 Montreal 1977–81 San Diego 1982–85 Seattle Mariners 1986–88	260 288 147 380 337 159 1,571	217 190 194 347 311 192 1,451	1 pennant 2 pennants 4th 2nd 1 pennant 4th
JIMY WILLIAMS b. Oct. 4, 1943, Santa Maria, CA James Francis Williams	Toronto 1986–89 Boston AL 1997–98	281 170 451	241 154 395	2nd 2nd
TED WILLIAMS b. Aug. 30, 1918, San Diego, CA Theodore Samuel Williams	Washington/Texas 1969–72	273	364	4th
MAURY WILLS b. Oct. 2, 1932, Washington, DC Maurice Morning Wills	Seattle Mariners 1980–81	26	56	7th
JIMMIE WILSON b. July 23, 1900, Philadelphia, PA James Wilson d. age 46	Philadelphia NL 1934–38 Chicago NL 1941–44	280 213 493	478 257 735	7th 5th

Continued

Manager	Team	W	L	Best Finish
BOBBY WINE b. Sept. 17, 1938, New York, NY Robert Paul Wine	Atlanta 1985	16	25	5th
IVY WINGO b. July 8, 1890, Gainesville, GA Ivey Brown Wingo d. age 50	Cincinnati 1916	1	1	(8th)
BOBBY WINKLES b. March 11, 1930, Tuckerman, AR Bobby Brooks Winkles	California 1973–74 Oakland 1977–78	109 61 170	127 86 213	4th 6th
HARRY WOLVERTON b. Dec. 6, 1873, Mt. Vernon, OH Harry Sterling Wolverton d. age 63	New York AL 1912	50	102	8th
RUDY YORK b. Aug. 17, 1913, Ragland, AL Rudolph Preston York d. age 56	Boston AL 1959	0	1	(8th)
EDDIE YOST b. Oct. 13, 1926, Brooklyn, NY Edward Frederick Yost	Washington 1963	0	1	(10th)
CY YOUNG b. March 29, 1867, Gilmore, OH Denton True Young d. age 88	Boston AL 1907	3	3	(4th)
CHIEF ZIMMER b. Nov. 23, 1860, Marietta, OH Charles Louis Zimmer d. age 88	Philadelphia NL 1903	49	86	7th
DON ZIMMER b. Jan. 17, 1931, Cincinnati, OH Donald William Zimmer	San Diego 1972–73 Boston AL 1976–80 Texas 1981–82 Chicago NL 1988–91	114 411 95 265 885	190 304 106 258 858	6th 2nd 2nd 1st NL East

Index

Page numbers are shown for names in text only. Names in tables are not included. A page number in italics indicates a photograph.